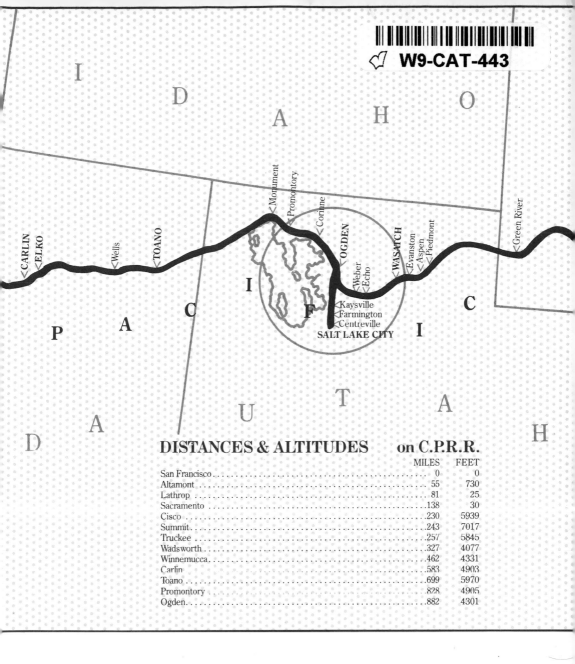

IDAHO

UTAH

NEVADA

PACIFIC

CARLIN
ELKO
Wells
TOANO
Monument
Promontory
Corinne
OGDEN
WASATCH
Evanston
Aspen
Piedmont
Green River
Weber
Echo
Kaysville
Farmington
Centreville
SALT LAKE CITY

DISTANCES & ALTITUDES on C.P.R.R.

	MILES	FEET
San Francisco	0	0
Altamont	55	730
Lathrop	81	25
Sacramento	138	30
Cisco	230	5939
Summit	243	7017
Truckee	257	5845
Wadsworth	327	4077
Winnemucca	462	4331
Carlin	583	4903
Toano	699	5970
Promontory	828	4905
Ogden	882	4301

PACIFIC RAILROAD

CONNECTIONS

A GREAT & SHINING ROAD

JOHN HOYT WILLIAMS

A GREAT & SHINING ROAD

THE EPIC STORY
OF THE
TRANSCONTINENTAL RAILROAD

𝕿𝖎𝖒𝖊𝖘 BOOKS

Library of Congress Cataloging-in-Publication Data

Williams, John Hoyt.
A great and shining road.
Bibliography: p.
Includes index.
1. Pacific railroads—History. 2. Railroads—West
(U.S.)—History. I. Title.
HE2763 1988 385'.0979 87-40199
ISBN 0-8129-1668-9

Book design by Jennifer Dossin
Manufactured in the United States of America
9 8 7 6 5 4 3 2
First Edition

FOR MARTHA

ACKNOWLEDGMENTS

I OWE a great deal to a great many people for their help in the preparation of this book, people cast geographically from Concord, New Hampshire, to San Francisco Bay, from San Marino, California, to New York City. They are, in fact, too many to name. The staffs of the Huntington Library in San Marino, the Bancroft Library at the University of California, Berkeley, the Nebraska State Historical Society at Lincoln, the Union Pacific Railroad Museum at Omaha, the Lilly Library at Indiana University, Bloomington, and the patient ladies of the Inter-Library Loan Department of my own Indiana State University: all were exceedingly helpful and professional. One can at times find one without the other. Individuals such as Steve Cox and Robert Gottlieb also played important, albeit different, parts, which I greatly appreciate. My family, Elisabeth, Owen, and especially my wife, Martha, had to live with my dream and with my railroad eccentricities. They did so, and with style, grace, and wit. I thank them.

CONTENTS

A GREAT & SHINING ROAD

INTRODUCTION

THE diminutive, dust-covered figures worked without speaking in the uneven glow of the guttering torches. The clash and clang of pickaxes, shovels, and prying bars created an ungodly din in the narrow confines of the tunnel. Those continual noises were punctuated from time to time by the shuddering, basso-profundo "crump" of explosive charges that shattered granite at the tunnel's facings. When the charges went off, a numbing concussive wave swept through the tunnel, sometimes bowling over the slender workers, followed by a dense, roiling wall of fine granite dust that coated the men.

On they toiled in shifts every hour of the day and night, as many men as could be used effectively in the cramped tunnel facings. There were four crews at work at all times, for this, Summit Tunnel, had four distinct facings. The east and west bores were supplemented by a vertical shaft sunk in the middle of the long tunnel line. Into that vertical shaft, seventy-eight feet deep, crews were lowered to work in both directions toward the men laboring in the east and west bores. The dangerous, backbreaking work had been under way for almost two years, since mid-August 1865 through two hellish winters, the last of which had dropped forty feet of snow on the Sierra Nevadas and killed scores of workers with slashing winds and avalanches.

And so the dust-clad Chinese and their Caucasian crew bosses and engineers had burrowed into the unforgiving California mountains. Daily, men were carried from the facings, dead, injured, or felled by exhaustion. Healthy men in their prime simply keeled over where they worked. Temporarily replaced at their positions by standby workers, they were swiftly dragged to the entrance of their bore and given time to recover in the sharp, fresh mountain air.

The four sets of crews worked round the clock with a grim, almost manic determination, for Summit Tunnel was nature's most brazen challenge and greatest obstacle between Sacramento and distant Omaha.

Then, at one in the morning on May 3, 1867, a great, noisy crumbling took place at the east facing, and light from torches in the west could be seen flickering through the dust. No longer silent, the men from Shanghai, Canton, and Macao, and their American bosses, almost stunned, rent the icy caverns with a new din: a wave of bellowing cheers. The Summit had been pierced. The Sierras had been bested.

There was awesome work yet to be done, months of wearing toil before the first track could be laid within the tunnel, but in that one ecstatic moment in 1867, the "Pacific Railroad" had become a reality. America would be bound, east to west, by iron. The transcontinental nation was a reality.

With a visible, palpable nervousness, young Lewis Clement, the engineer in charge of Summit Tunnel, strode into the now widened bore a week after the breakthrough, surveyor's instruments in hand. With torchbearers stationed every few yards in the 1,659-foot bore, Clement began his first series of observations in the damp and eerie tunnel. During the preceding two years' work he and his assistants had been measuring under conditions never taught about in engineering schools. They had made their calculations under poor visibility on a wildly uneven tunnel floor, plotting a bore not only divided into four distinct parts, but one that had to gradually rise, descend, and curve as it penetrated from west to east. Not that their work consisted in mere guesswork, but the expected margin of error was large, and if the various bores were seriously misaligned, many months of expensive remedial work would have to be done, delaying the Central Pacific Railroad's progress east. For two years Summit Tunnel had been a tough bone to be chewed by the Central Pacific, whose leaders knew only too well that the Union Pacific Railroad was racing across the flat Great Plains, its crews laying rails in the obstacle-free Platte Valley at world-record speed.

As Clement finished his measurements and worked out the geometric statistics at a rude desk near the tunnel mouth, he found his most fervent prayers answered. Summit Tunnel's four bores fitted together almost perfectly, with a total error in true line of less than two inches. The seemingly impossible had been achieved. The longest tunnel anyone had cut through natural granite, cut at a daunting altitude in an abominable climate, had been bored by a small army of Chinese thousands of miles from their ancestral home. The Sierras were truly breached and now only the parched, table-flat Nevada desert confronted the Central Pacific. The great race across the continent was on.

The dream that began more than thirty years before, the dream of a railroad across America, was about to enter its final stage.

1

AMERICA, THE MACHINE, AND THE IDEA WHOSE TIME HAD COME

THE NATION

O N JULY 2, 1862, as General John Pope prepared to march his army south to a disaster known as the Second Battle of Bull Run, a much harried President Lincoln signed the Pacific Railroad Act, mandating the greatest engineering feat ever attempted, a feat that would fundamentally change Mr. Lincoln's nation.

Signing that act, which obligated private interests to risk more than $100 million, was the culmination of some thirty years of growing pressure. If Manifest Destiny had earlier impelled American expansion to the Pacific Ocean, it also demanded the bridging of the Great American Desert, whose emptiness bifurcated the nation into Atlantic and Pacific coastal communities. And Manifest Destiny would perhaps not halt at the coasts. In 1857, messianic Theodore Dehone Judah, a man fueled by dreams of *the* railroad, wrote of the wider world it would open:

> And be it remembered that it is not the through lines to California alone upon which the road is to rely for through travel. There is Utah, Oregon, Washington, the Russian possessions, the Sandwich Islands [Hawaii], China and the Far East Indies—all of which are brought, more or less within the influence of this road.[1]

America was ready in 1862, despite its internecine bloodbath. Constantly fortified with the new blood of immigrants who saw America as a place where anything was possible, the nation had adopted an ethos that elevated problem solving to the status of religion. In large part this was due to the uniquely American free public educational system, under which schoolhouses were erected in even the most out-of-the-way hamlets. There was also, in the decades before the Civil War, a proliferation of specialized academies, engineering schools, and polytechnical institutes that put problem solving on a scientific base. In fact, for more than a generation, West Point, America's only "national" college, had been conceived of as an engineering school rather than a military academy. With a modern and rewarding national patent system at their service, engineers in their growing numbers, self-taught and school-certified, turned their energies to proving that *any* problem could be rationally solved, that no barriers were immutable. There is a harmony in the fact that the same year President Lincoln signed the Pacific Railroad Act, Congress passed the Homestead Act, which not only provided virtually free federal lands for settlers of the frontier, but also provided for a system of state agricultural and mechanical colleges in even the most remote territories. That same year, almost symbolically, thinker-essayist-abolitionist Henry David Thoreau died, while in France, Léon Foucault measured and recorded the "unmeasurable" speed of light.

Problems could be solved. Of that, America was itself proof, and additional proofs could be found throughout the vast land. Between 1820 and 1860, despite national growing pains, engineers and tinkerers had dotted the landscape with an amazing pattern of canals and turnpikes, while steamboats plied hundreds of rivers and lakes. This frenzied "transportation revolution" knit together communities, states, and even regions, but fell short, largely because of geographical obstacles, of binding together the nation. Americans traveling from one coastal community to the other avoided the hostile Great American Desert and felt forced to take a circuitous sea route.[2]

IN 1851, the newspaper *Panama Star* opined clairvoyantly that "the future of Panama centres in the union of the Atlantic and Pacific, by the completion of the railroad."[3] Finished in 1855, ironically with the muscle of Irish "bogtrotters" and Chinese coolies,* the Panama Railroad, for fourteen years, boosted the fortunes of that backward Colombian province.

A glance at Panama conveys the magnitude of the traffic between America's two communities and reveals the desperate need for a railroad across the Great American Desert. From Mexico's 1848 cession of California and the modern-day Southwest by the Treaty of Guadalupe Hidalgo, to the May 1869 completion of the first transcontinental railroad, more than 375,000 people transited Panama on their way to San Francisco, while some 225,000 crossed the steaming isthmus

*Unlike the Chinese who later helped build the Central Pacific, those brought to Panama were poor workers. Given to "fatal melancholy," and prone to disease, most were soon "sent to Jamaica in exchange for Negroes."[4]

in the other direction. So did a staggering $700 million in gold and silver from scores of Western mines.[5] In fact, shipments of $185 million in California gold in the first three years of the Civil War kept the government of Abraham Lincoln solvent enough to preserve the Union.[6]

The risk of traveling across Panama, a trek far shorter than the seventeen-thousand-mile-long voyage around Cape Horn, was nevertheless one barely worth taking. Before 1855, the California-bound traveler would disembark at a village on the fetid Caribbean coast, wait for a week or so for a small vessel to take him up the torturous Chagres River to head of navigation, and then continue by coach, wagon, or horseback along a jungle-choked trail to filthy, festering Panama City. There he might have to wait a month or more for passage to San Francisco. Ubiquitous "Panama Fever" struck untold thousands, many fatally, as did malaria, yellow fever, and a veritable encyclopedia of other tropical diseases, while with grim monotony cholera stalked the isthmus. In 1852 the passenger steamer *Philadelphia,* bound for New York City from Panama, lost one third of those aboard to cholera. The victims, many of them prominent citizens, were unceremoniously heaved overboard in a hapless effort to halt the spread of the plague.[7]

Vessels plying the Panama route, unlike those clearing for Cape Horn, were mostly steamers, and over the years dozens exploded, foundered, or simply disappeared, adding thousands of deaths to those resulting from disease. A seafaring people, Americans were nonetheless shocked in 1853 when the steamer *Central America* broke up in a hurricane off the Carolinas, taking with it to the bottom 423 souls and more than $8 million in California gold.[8] A new port, Aspinwall, built by New York merchant William Henry Aspinwall on Panama's Caribbean shore, and the Panama railroad after 1855 improved the situation somewhat, but the isthmus route remained difficult, expensive, and hazardous, claiming hundreds, sometimes thousands of lives annually—among them that of quiet young engineer Theodore D. Judah, in 1863.[9]

Other alternatives to the Cape Horn route were eagerly explored, for a hundred and more continuous days at sea, some of it in the treacherous South Atlantic, made even experienced Nantucket whalers blanch. One such alternative was a trans-Nicaragua coach and wagon service developed by the legendary Cornelius Vanderbilt and the unlegendary but equally wealthy Edward Mills. This route appeared to be a viable competitor to the isthmus, but eccentric soldier of fortune William Walker ruined it by conquering and briefly misruling Nicaragua before he was executed. Nicaragua gave itself over to political chaos and a rather nasty strain of anti-*Yanqui* xenophobia.[10] Some use was briefly made of Mexico's narrow Isthmus of Tehuantepec (use of which was guaranteed by the Gadsden Purchase Treaty), but traversing it was even more difficult, time-consuming, and hazardous than the others.[11]

So by the time President Lincoln signed the Pacific Railroad Act, about half of all California-bound passengers sailed the relatively healthy Cape Horn route, along with almost all of the freight, for the interests that monopolized the Panama "highway" levied freight charges higher than the market could normally bear. In time of national emergency—and the Civil War must rank as America's only true emergency—could the United States rely upon such tenuous links between its two communities? This is the question answered by President Lincoln on July 2, 1862.

THE United States had perhaps grown too swiftly during the first half of the nineteenth century. The slender coastal republic of 1800 with its 5 million or so inhabitants had exploded west and south, signing treaties with a congeries of Indian tribes, and negotiating such brilliant and timely agreements as the Louisiana and Gadsden purchases. The immense geographical booty of the Mexican War, together with Anglo-American settlement of the vexing and complicated Oregon Territory boundary question, rounded out the continental United States.

One of the largest nations on earth by 1853, when the ink dried on the Gadsden Purchase Treaty, the United States had a population of some 24 million, burgeoning through tremendous natural increase and massive drafts of European and African immigration. An impressive 400,000 European immigrants were added to the American genetic pool in 1850 alone. This growing population—energetic, brawling, and often visionary—was still, however, closely tied to the coastal plains, seemingly forever halted by the ice-tipped crags of the Sierra Nevadas in the West and the turgid Mississippi River in the East: a nation severed by topography.

Between those imposing physical and psychological barriers lay a void, labeled frankly on most maps the Great American Desert. Henry Varnum Poor, railroad engineer and editor and compiler of the annual *Poor's Manual of Railroads of the United States,* wrote in 1854 that the oft-discussed transcontinental, or Pacific, railroad would have to pass some two thousand miles

> through an uninhabited, and, for the greater part, we may say an uninhabitable country, nearly destitute of wood, extensive districts of it destitute of water; over mountain ranges whose summits are white with eternal snows; over deserts parched beneath an unclouded sky, and over yawning chasms which the process of disintegration since the volcanic fires were put out, has not yet filled up.[12]

This grim void, continued the editor, "seems not to have been disturbed since the warring forces of Nature laid down their arms," and it remained in 1854 an awesome "record of a great crisis in the earth's history."[13] Poor, railroad fanatic that he was—and later, briefly, secretary of the Union Pacific Railroad—was skeptical of the success of such a mammoth construction effort.

The sprawling reaches of the void, and the lack of even a veneer of civilization within it, were acutely described by the anonymous "Old Block," who had traversed them in 1849 in search of California gold:

> The only places on the Plains, in the wide stretch of two thousand miles, where the crude elements of Civilization could be seen, were at Forts Kearny, Laramie and Bridger, with Salt Lake City on one route and Fort Hall on the more Northern road, and at none of these places could food or the comforts of life be obtained to supply our wants.[14]

Nowhere could one find a civilization-nurturing river; the fertile soil was covered for the most part with thick, plow-blunting sod; and harsh Canadian winds, undeterred by the treeless plains, razored their way south to create winters that made those of New England appear positively benign. Lieutenant Theodore Talbot, who accompanied peripatetic John Charles Frémont on two expeditions across the Plains, found "the country sublimely desolate."[15] Then, west of the Plains, came the mountains, in ranges like rows of shark's teeth. Farther west, the Black Hills and the Wasatch Range of the Rockies loomed, while snowdrifts in the Sierra Nevadas could reach a hundred feet in depth, often lingering into May and June.[16]

If the California Sierras offered cheerless prospects for railroaders (and their all-important would-be investors), so did the Platte River Valley, which began in Nebraska and was one of the most logical avenues leading west. Described by Josiah Copley as late as 1867, the region was depressing: "It tires the eye to look at . . . the Valley is a miserable waste, and I fear ever must be."[17] Since any railroad, once constructed, would have to create paying *local* traffic to prosper, Copley's estimate was a bleak one indeed, and his dismissal of the stark Nevada desert—"The Indians live on it, but how no one knows"—was unlikely to spur the sale of any Pacific Railroad stocks.[18] Nor was Horace Greeley's assessment in his 1860 best seller, *An Overland Journey, from New York to San Francisco, in the Summer of 1859:* "I thought I had seen barrenness before. . . . Here on the Humboldt, famine sits enthroned, and waves his sceptre over a dominion expressly made for him."[19] The future presidential candidate's description was read by hundreds of thousands of Americans, confirming their prejudices concerning the possibility, or advisability, of building railroads in the void.

In addition to the apparent sterility and unrelieved harshness of the land, one could factor in the unrelieved hostility of the mounted Plains Indians: the Sioux in all their subtribes, Arapaho, Cheyenne, Paiute, Pawnee, Kiowa, Comanche, and more. Heroically cast warrior cultures, these tribes were often described by experienced army officers as the finest light cavalry in the world. They were certain to resist the railroad and, indeed, white encroachment in general. It has been calculated that from the late 1830s to 1862, Indian conflicts (there were few genuine "wars") had cost the United States government an astonishing daily average of $144,000*[20] and caused tremendous financial loss to farmers and businessmen like "Stagecoach King" Ben Holladay.[22] Only the Mormons managed in part to escape the fury of the tribes after their hegira to Utah in the 1840s, building with incredible nonchalance their isolated state of Deseret in the heart of Indian country. A Union Pacific engineer who knew the Saints well recorded somewhat sarcastically that "the Mormons felt that if they had an Endowment garment on they were safe anywhere."[23] For the most part it appears that they were, but gentile freighting firms that serviced Salt Lake City were hardly as lucky.[24]

Compounding these difficulties were the buffalo in their uncounted millions. The length of one herd of the unkempt creatures was measured at twenty-five miles.[25] Even a few dozen of them could damage track, and, later, thousands of telegraph poles would go crashing to the ground as the heavy beasts of the treeless plains discovered they made marvelous scratching posts.[26] Clearly, the buffalo would have to go, and this in turn would doom the bison-centric Plains Indians. Then there were the insects. The Great American Desert was their petri dish. Lewis and Clark wrote at length on the continual torment inflicted upon them by "green heads," or huge horseflies, in the early years of the century, and forty years later John C. Frémont unhappily concurred.[27] Grasshoppers in the billions swept periodically across the Plains, scything them clean and panicking livestock.†

The Great American Desert, then, apparently useless and hostile, was a void not to be filled, but merely crossed.

THE MACHINE

B EFORE the void could be effectively crossed, a vehicle capable of doing so had to be developed. Born in the first stirrings of the first industrial revolution in history, this vehicle saw its infancy in England. It was in the new American republic, however, that it rapidly grew to maturity.

In 1775, as the thirteen colonies of British America were goaded into open

---

*This oft-repeated figure is apocryphal, for at more than $52 million a year, it approaches Civil War costs. For example, *army* expenditures in 1850 represented some 23.7 percent of the federal budget (averaging $25,753 a day). By 1855, the figure had grown to $40,395 a day; a considerable sum indeed, but hardly the figure normally bandied about.[21]

†This writer in 1985 encountered a major grasshopper storm at Promontory Point that forced him into his car and restricted his driving speed to a bare ten miles an hour.

rebellion, James Watt and a colleague were building a functioning steam engine. Within a score or so of years this odd contraption found limited employment on vessels and provided power to looms in some prototypical factories.[28] It took somewhat longer for engineers, scientists, and innovators to learn how to harness the power of boiling water to the wheels of a vehicle.

Finally, however, they did, and in 1825 the short Stockton & Darlington Railroad was built in northeastern England; however, more often than not its freight cars sported sails and were pulled by teams of horses rather than by an undependable locomotive. Railroads had actually been in use for centuries in Britain's mining pits, where specially designed ore cars were pulled along rickety wooden rails by mule, horse, oxen, or even man, but it was only with steam power that the railroad era could commence.[29] By a queer coincidence, the year the first railroad began to function haltingly in England, Colonel John Stevens built a small, one-cylinder steam locomotive and used it as a plaything on a diminutive circular track he had installed on his Hoboken, New Jersey, estate.[30]

The Stockton & Darlington experiment touched off railroad fever in England, and soon a score of short, often competing, lines were chartered by Parliament and under construction. In view of later scandals in the United States, it is worth noting that during the early British railroad boom, more than a hundred railroad company directors (to say nothing of stockholders) were serving as members of Parliament.[31]

In 1828 American engineer Horatio Allen paid a visit to England to study the new railroad phenomenon. Impressed by what he saw and learned, he promptly purchased four locomotives and had them shipped across the Atlantic. The first to arrive, named the *Stourbridge Lion,* was unloaded in May 1829 on a New York City wharf, where it was regarded by a crowd of onlookers as a possibly dangerous curiosity.

By then, however, events had moved so swiftly that two railroads were already under construction in the United States. Work began on the Baltimore & Ohio (B&O) on July 4, 1828, the first shovel of earth turned by Charles Carroll, sole surviving signer of the Declaration of Independence.* He is said to have remarked that he felt this groundbreaking "among the most important acts of my life, second only to that of signing the Declaration of Independence, even if second to that."[32] The other line, the Charleston & Savannah (later, Charleston & Hamburg), commenced construction a few months later. By January 1, 1830, the latter was operating 6 miles of track (and, in 1833, with more than 130 miles, was briefly the world's longest linc)[33] and by May, utilizing horsepower, the B&O was providing service on 13 miles of somewhat uneven rail.[34]

---

*To put the issue into perspective, when work commenced on America's first railroad, perhaps one third of the nation's population had been alive during George Washington's lifetime.

Engineer Allen not only helped plan and build the South Carolina road, but he also designed and constructed its first locomotive, christening it wordily the *Best Friend of Charleston*. It entered service only a few months after the B&O fired the boilers of the first American-made locomotive, Peter Cooper's minuscule and aptly named *Tom Thumb*, which jerkily lurched down the tracks for the first time on August 28, 1830. But the new gadget was an unpredictable one. In June 1831, with South Carolina threatening secession from the Union during the nullification crisis, the *Best Friend of Charleston*'s boiler exploded, killing the fireman and spraying chunks of hot boiler plate like shrapnel. Rebuilt within weeks and understandably renamed *Phoenix*, it remained a company workhorse for more than a decade.[35]

If England had experienced a railroad boom, the United States was to undergo a veritable explosion, both in number of chartered railroads and miles of track and in rapid technological change.

At the end of 1830 there were 23 miles of working track in the United States (actually, in the Western Hemisphere), the rails of hardwood covered with a thick strip of iron. In 1840 trackage reached a total of 2,818 miles—for the most part, of iron rails. Over a hundred distinct railroads were incorporated in the 1830s in New York State alone, although many were "paper" railroads, legally incorporated but never built.[36] In 1850 there were 9,021 miles of functioning track, and in the next ten years an imposing 30,626.[37] An average of 2,160 miles of new track was laid every year of the 1850s. In that last decade before the Civil War more miles of track were laid in the United States than in all the rest of the world, and just under half of the world's railroad tracks were in the various states of the Union. The brand-new rail network was then carrying some 60 percent of all domestic freight.[38] Cities sprang up where only nature had reigned. One new town, where several lines came together, was Terminus, Georgia, soon to be renamed Atlanta. In 1864 the tracks that had created it would make that city General Sherman's principal target.[39]

While the first American railroads utilized wooden tracks, converted stage-coaches as cars, and small, weak, unreliable, and dangerous engines, change—stimulated by the generous national patent system—was almost immediate. In 1831 a Philadelphia jeweler and part-time bookbinder, Matthias W. Baldwin, began building locomotives. He, Thomas Rogers of the same city, and the Norris brothers of Paterson, New Jersey, each manufactured a thousand or more locomotives before Fort Sumter was fired upon. These competing firms oversaw a steady evolution in design, safety, power, and speed as they subjected their bulky machines to something like mass production.[40] While Baldwin and his rivals were innovating, so were other railroaders, including the brilliant engineer Robert L. Stevens, Colonel John Stevens's son. In rapid succession Stevens invented the T-shaped rail (a shape that distributes weight evenly, holds a vehicle's wheel flanges securely, and wears well), the fishplate, to bind rail ends to one another, and also the hook-headed spike. Others contributed the wooden crosstie, which replaced expensive, heavy stone blocks, and dozens of other gadgets and techniques.[41]

At an increasing tempo, American-made locomotives grew in size and power, from about thirteen tons with thirteen-by-eighteen-inch cylinders and 80 pounds maximum steam pressure, to some twenty-five tons, sixteen-by-twenty-two-inch cylinders, and 110 pounds of pressure.[42] Further, while the country was at first dependent upon imported British rails, George W. Scranton and his brother Joseph opened a rail factory in 1847, in the town they had founded seven years earlier, and soon Pennsylvania, blessed with enormous deposits of both coal and iron, could claim more rail manufactories than all of England. Foreign rails, however, were cheaper (through lower labor costs) and continued to hold a large share of the American market.[43]

Other currents of change were keeping the tinkerers occupied. One of the most important, the swiveling truck, was the brainchild of John Jervis, chief engineer of the Mohawk & Hudson. A pair of four-wheel swiveling trucks, one under each end of each car, greatly enhanced stability on rough roads (which most were) and curves, permitting much higher speeds. Also, as a result of this breakthrough, American railroads could be built with much sharper curves than was the rule elsewhere, hence lessening construction costs. Even mountain ridges could now be negotiated by means of zigzag switchbacks.[44] Concurrently, rails grew in length from a standardized fifteen feet to thirty, and in weight (and hence strength) from some thirty pounds per yard to a much more durable average of fifty-five to sixty.[45]

In the America of the 1850s more powerful locomotives and more stable cars permitted engineering feats that would have seemed laughable a decade earlier. While switchbacks and tighter curves helped in scaling heights, it was also the brute power of the new generation of locomotives that enabled the expanding B&O to create a portion of its line with grades so steep as to create vertigo in its passengers.[46] A decade later Congress was to mandate a *maximum* grade of 116 feet per mile for the Pacific Railroad, a grade one third as steep as that on parts of the B&O and some other lines.

Complementing these innovations was the invention in America of the truss bridge and the cantilever railroad bridge, both of which were relatively easy to prefabricate in sections, haul to the site, and erect, and they could support unusually great weights.[47] Truly, as one observer succinctly noted, "The key to the evolution of the American railway is the contempt for authority displayed by our engineers."[48] No problem was insurmountable, and nowhere was their contempt to be so lavishly displayed than on the lines of the Central and Union Pacific railroads in the 1860s.

Rail types, sizes, and weights were becoming rigidly standardized by the 1850s, but rail gauges remained wildly and uneconomically individualistic. Although Britain had adopted a standard gauge of four feet, eight and a half inches early in that decade, in America, individual states—even some companies—determined their own gauges, and in 1860 six distinct gauges were in use. These ranged from the increasingly popular British standard, used exclusively in eight states and common in nine others, to a less common six-foot broad gauge. This helter-skelter approach to gauges led to delays and costly transfers of passengers and freight.[49]

Despite the innumerable improvements and the rapid evolution of the modern railroad, rail travel was not a conspicuously safe mode of transportation. According to the statistics-addicted *American Railroad Journal* (also edited by Henry V. Poor), there were 903 railroad accidents in the last seven years of the 1850s, some of them spectacular. In these wrecks 1,109 people (mostly employees) were killed and another 3,611 injured. However, bragged the *Journal,* in those same years, 2,304 people were killed in a recorded 203 steamboat accidents.[50]

As one might guess, the growing presence of the American railroad fostered the faltering and decay of other means of transportation, most notably the network of turnpikes (toll roads), the patchwork of canals, and even the steamboat. Canals, for example, were confined by clear topographical constraints that did not affect the much more flexible railroad. They were also expensive to build ($20,000 to $30,000 per mile), frequently needed repair or dredging, and were closed down by flood, drought, or winter ice. They were also slow. Much the same could be said for steamboats. And while roads were certainly flexible, they were often filled with axle-breaking ruts or covered with glutinous, impassable mud. Speed on a turnpike was limited to the pace of a wagon and team, and toll charges were onerous in the best of times. Masked, often vicious bandits made the toll roads their preying fields. The railroad would consign most other forms of transportation to the unremunerative shadows.[51]

Of course, not everyone was looking to the future. As a letter to the editor of the *Vincennes* (Indiana) *Western Sun*[52] put it:

Upon the whole sirs, this railroad is a pestilential, topsyturvy, harum scarum, whirligig scheme. Give me the old, solemn, straightforward, regular Dutch canal . . . it is more primitive and scriptural and suits a moral and religious people better. . . . [The railroad] will upset all the gravity of the nation. . . . A set of bailiffs, mounted on bombshells, would not overtake an absconding debtor!

THE IDEA

L ONG before technology even hinted at the feasibility of a transcontinental railroad, some visionaries voiced the idea, despite the fact that most Americans viewed the concept as sheer fantasy if not outright lunacy. However, America's palpable sense of geographic destiny in this era was soon to converge with an almost messianic faith in technology. The problem *could* be solved.

While there are various claims concerning the first person to seriously fantasize about the Pacific Railroad, it is known that fully eleven years before the first track was laid in this hemisphere one Robert Mills of New York was openly suggesting a railroad from the headwaters of the Mississippi to the Oregon Territory. His idea was dismissed with hearty guffaws.[53] In 1832, with less than 140 miles of track operating in the United States, a Dr. Hartwell Carver, of Rochester, New York, actually proposed to Congress that the federal government build a railroad from New York to San Francisco. That San Francisco, then known as Yerba Buena, was then a Mexican city apparently did not faze Carver, but the august body sitting in Washington declined to discuss the wild idea.[54] The doctor, however, did not lose heart and published a series of articles in the *New York Courier and Enquirer* over the next several years, sending copies, along with complicated memorials, to members of both houses of Congress. In 1839 he was urging that body to grant him personally a charter to construct a rail line—upon a foundation of solid stone—to the coast, and grant him large amounts of public land along the right-of-way. By selling that land to eager immigrants and emigrants, Carver expected to generate the cash needed for actual construction.[55] Meanwhile, Dr. Samuel B. Barlow, of Granville, Massachusetts, was writing a series of articles for the *Westfield Intelligencer,* claiming that the Pacific Railroad, three thousand miles long, was not only feasible, but that it would be inexpensive. He argued that its cost would average but $10,000 per mile.[56] Barlow was a trifle weak on both geography and finance. Congress continued to demur, but by the late 1830s Carver and Barlow were but two of a growing number of Pacific Railroad advocates, some of whom had considerable clout.

Welsh-born civil engineer John Plumbe, living in the frontier state of Iowa, on the edge of the Great American Desert, was one of the first and most tenacious to follow in the doctors' footsteps. He wrote an influential pamphlet on the subject of a transcontinental railroad in 1836, and in the succeeding two years sent memorials to Congress, spoke to interested groups in a dozen states, and called the first Pacific Railroad Convention in the United States.

Meeting in tiny Dubuque, Iowa, on March 31, 1838, several score of both the believers and the scoffers heard Plumbe explain in rather technical—but convincing—terms the solvable nature of the problem. Unlike previous proponents, the young engineer fully grasped the true magnitude of the undertaking, claiming that nothing less than a company capitalized at $100 million could transform dream to reality. His listeners recoiled in horror at the mention of such a sum: after all, this was a year when the entire federal budget was $33,865,000.*[57] Successful as propagator of an idea, Plumbe proselytized for many more years, but concrete achievements eluded him, and in deep despair he took his own life.[58]

Still, 1838 was a banner year. For in addition to the Dubuque conclave, the Reverend Samuel Parker published his *Tour Beyond the Rocky Mountains.* This influential paean to the Oregon Territory not only mentioned and advocated a Pacific Railroad, but claimed that it could be swiftly, easily, and inexpensively constructed.[59] A mere month or so later, while readers were thumbing the *Tour*'s pages, additional support came from an article in the June issue of New York City's *Knickerbocker Magazine,* written by Willis Gaylord Clark. He dwelt at great length upon the Pacific Railroad and emphasized the role it could, would, and should play in the development of the vast West—a sort of economic corollary to Manifest Destiny.[60]

It was in the forties, however, that the transcontinental movement attracted influence as well as attention. That was, after all, the decade that saw American acquisition of half of Mexico (if one includes Texas), the first streams of cross-country emigrants, the Mormon trek to Utah, the discovery of California's gold, and a growing North-South sectional split.

Among the significant railroad futurists of the 1840s was Lillburn W. Boggs, a former governor of Missouri, who wrote, gave speeches and lectures, and hounded Congress with increasingly complete plans and cost estimates.[61] Boggs's ideas found a growing audience, but the man who truly caught the imagination of the public was a wealthy Connecticut-born New York City merchant, Asa Whitney. A convert to railroads from the time he studied them in England in the 1830s, Whitney was the first to stress the use of the Pacific Railroad in diverting the rich trade of the Orient, so long controlled by Europeans. He had been in China in 1843 when the emperor opened the first five ports to free trade.† That this was followed a decade later by Commodore Perry's "opening" of Japan was pure serendipity.[62] One of the merchant's most enthusiastic and well-known converts, explorer John C. Frémont, later put Whitney's vision eloquently:

---

*The only reason it was that high was the costly Second Seminole War. By 1845, the budget was $22,937,000.

†Here was born America's enduring myth of the vast "China market," a myth reborn in the 1980s by China's economic reforms and drive for modernization.

America will be between Asia and Europe—the golden vein which runs through the history of the world will follow the track to San Francisco, and the Asiatic trade will finally fall into its last and permanent road.[63]

Similarly, ignorant of the possibility of the long-studied Suez Canal, the *Railroad Record* noted rhapsodically that "the old ocean route must be abandoned . . . all Europe will be obliged to make New York its branch office, if it expects to keep up any permanent or profitable relations with the East."[64]

Whitney's original plan, devised after a long personal reconnaissance of the proposed route in 1845, was for a railroad to link Milwaukee with Puget Sound. In his first memorial to Congress late that year, drawing upon both personal observation and his recognized business acumen, he estimated that a railroad along that relatively short route could be constructed—by him—for about $50 million.[65]

Unfortunately for the merchant, Southern congressmen were in no mood to hear of a Northern route to the Pacific, especially one so far north. They were even less willing to listen the following year, when war with Mexico promised huge land acquisitions in the South. Such powerful "border state" men as Missouri senator Thomas Hart Benton also rejected Whitney's scheme out of hand. Benton, an avid supporter of the Pacific Railroad, saw St. Louis as its "natural" eastern terminus, and, like today's "pork barrelers," he fervently argued his case while obstructing those of others.

The stubborn Whitney modified and publicized his plan, traveling throughout the Northern states to spread his gospel and spinning off more memorials to Congress. Some of these prompted intense debate and some were even drafted into bills, but, alas, sectionalism, increasing in virulence, made any agreement impossible. In 1848, with American troops garrisoning Chapultepec Castle in Mexico, Whitney unveiled another plan. He personally would drum up enough investment capital to begin building the road in the immediate future if Congress would grant him a strip of public lands thirty miles wide on either side of the track along the entire route.[66] On a line fifteen hundred miles long, this would total a nation-sized ninety thousand square miles. Whitney planned to sell to settlers parcels of the now useless but, he hoped, potentially valuable land, reinvesting the proceeds in further construction. In return for the land, he promised to carry the government's mail, troops, and war matériel without charge for twenty years and regular passengers at only half the normal price for that same period. This appealed to Washington's concerns over national defense, but once again, congressmen favoring their own routes, and others who wanted the government itself to build the line, doomed the proposal in vitriolic debate. A frustrated Whitney nonetheless continued to hold meetings and speak at railroad conventions, and by 1850 eighteen state legislatures had endorsed his plan and recommended it officially to Congress.[67]

A dozen other plans thumped onto congressmen's desks in this epoch; some, like P.P.F. DeGrand's, were extremely detailed. DeGrand advocated in 1849 that Congress charter a private company with a capitalization of $100 million to build a double-track road and adjacent telegraph along one of several routes being considered. When the company had subscribed 2 percent of its stock to the public, Congress would permit it to borrow 6-percent-interest government bonds to a maximum (if needed) of $98 million, with which the actual construction would be financed. The bonds would be repaid with interest after a fifty-year grace period. The company would also be given a ten-mile-wide strip of land along the north side of the right-of-way. DeGrand claimed that within two years of the road's completion, the government—and the American people—would be saving vast amounts of money on transportation, and that "by a single act of legislation, $100,000,000 worth of American labor to be realized within a few years, and to be paid for in good money," would tremendously benefit the working class.[68] Powerful logic this, but Congress was not convinced, not even by DeGrand's trump card: "Let this road be constructed, and there will be no North and no South, no East and no West, but our country will be everywhere!"[69] Even in 1849, the United States were too disunited to accept the promoter's farsighted plan.

Other plans were proposed. Bostonian Josiah Perham proposed a "People's Pacific Railroad," in which a million citizens were to purchase hundred-dollar railroad stocks, while Perham himself would benefit from large grants of government aid.[70] Senator Thomas Hart Benton officially proposed his St. Louis route, following a line surveyed by his army engineer son-in-law, John C. Frémont, but it never reached a vote. The same fate befell a bill sponsored by Sam Houston for a Texas to California line. So were others given short—if any—shrift by the two fractious houses. As the cynical "Old Block" observed of this phenomenon, "The people called for it—the politicians made it their hobby."[71]

Even as disillusioned Asa Whitney sailed to England in a vain attempt to interest Parliament in a trans-Canada railroad, deepening sectionalism in the United States raised artificial barriers to supplement those of nature, and no proposal submitted to Congress was seriously considered by both North and South. The best the divided Congress could do was appropriate money in 1849 to fund an official government survey of potential transcontinental routes. Unfortunately, congressmen could not agree on precisely how to use those funds, and the money remained unspent.[72]

While at the first meeting of Union Pacific incorporators in 1862, S. De Witt Bloodgood would speak of "the poetry of the idea" of the Pacific Railroad, Congress before the Civil War was decidedly unpoetic, and it would be events, not words, that would prove the necessity of the transcontinental.[73]

2

UNDERSTANDING THE VOID

INTO THE GREAT AMERICAN DESERT

THE much misunderstood Great American Desert, although virtually unpopulated save for nomadic tribes and, after the 1840s, sedentary pockets
of Mormons, was not totally *terra incognita* before the Pacific Railroad Act
was signed. Far from it. White men had been roaming, and writing descrip-
tions of, large parts of it since the early-sixteenth-century peregrinations of
Cabeza de Vaca, Coronado, and other conquistadores.

Britons had covered California and Oregon since the voyages of Sir Francis
Drake and Thomas Cavendish, but those "sea dogs" were content with pillaging
and looting farther south on the Spanish Main. Officially and permanently settled
only in 1769, California's villages and presidios were at the end of a long chain
of settlements stretching from Mexico's central Anáhuac Valley across northern
Mexico's deserts and the future American Southwest. Russians sporadically
retraced the paths of Vitus Bering and Alexei Cherikov across the Pacific Northwest after 1741, and Spanish expeditions had straggled into the Platte Valley by
the 1720s, one disappearing without a trace. French and Canadians, cleric and
lay, had been prowling the Great American Desert since Pierre Esprit Radisson
crossed the Mississippi in the 1660s, and eighty years later Canadian merchants
were routinely cutting across the continent to trade in adobe-built Santa Fe.[1] It
is a testament to the region's perceived lack of charm and resources that for
nearly three hundred years no one and no nation truly claimed it or tried to do

anything with it. Further, those of various nationalities who traversed the Great American Desert rarely had anything good to say about it.

American experience with the void in the nation's center began with the Lewis and Clark expedition of 1804–1805, although the War Department had attempted to explore the Upper Missouri River area as early as 1790. Lewis and Clark and their party spanned the continent, and their reports on the northern segment of the newly acquired Louisiana Territory excited the imagination of President Jefferson and much of the American public.

In the decades following Lewis and Clark's trek, a number of army officers conducted reconnaissances for the government, including the celebrated Zebulon Pike and Major Stephen Long, whose written reports were encyclopedic.[2] Often preceding the army's expeditions into the West, scores, if not hundreds of Mountain Men—hunters and trappers such as Jedediah Smith, Manuel Lisa, and Robert Stuart—explored, lived in, and made money from the Great American Desert.[3] Others made it more hostile. Trader Joseph Walker and his party in the 1830s wantonly massacred peaceful Indians in Utah and Nevada, bequeathing war whoop and arrow to Americans of a later age.[4] In 1841 the first party of emigrants reached Mexican California through the Sierras' ice-flecked passes, albeit "with incredible suffering."[5]

It was only in 1842, however, that a true spotlight was turned on the shadowy interior, a spotlight emanating from the eyes of that bundle of kinetic energy, John C. Frémont, then a lieutenant in the Corps of Topographical Engineers of the United States Army.

At the urging of his father-in-law, Senator Thomas Hart Benton, young Frémont was assigned by the corps to explore the Platte Valley and beyond. There is little doubt that Benton's motive was to gather hard scientific data to bolster his hopes of getting congressional approval for a railroad connecting St. Louis to the Pacific. Linking up with veteran Mountain Man Kit Carson, already an American legend, whom he hired as scout, Frémont galloped through the low valley to Laramie, and then northwest toward the Oregon Territory.[6]

While this expedition gathered a good deal of scientific-engineering data, Frémont's second official exploration, and the reports springing from it, truly inspired American public opinion. Ostensibly sent to reconnoiter a passable wagon route to California, in 1843 and 1844 the lieutenant, again in company with Kit Carson, endured a thrilling epic of exploration and survival, all of which was put to paper by the erudite officer upon his return. When he wrote of his first view of the Great Salt Lake from a ridgetop, he expounded, "I am doubtful if the followers of Balboa felt more enthusiasm" when they first gazed down at the Pacific Ocean."[7] His enthusiasm was at fever pitch throughout the expedition, although when approaching the majestic Sierra Nevadas he was somewhat chagrined, for he found that instead of charting virgin territory there, "we found here a broad and plainly marked trail, on which there were tracks of horses, and we appeared to have regained one of the thoroughfares" that had long been used by Indians and emigrants heading west.[8]

Discovering magnificent Lake Tahoe, the bullheaded engineer decided to cross the Sierras in midwinter, despite Carson's wise and vociferous objections. Soon reduced to eating "pea soup, mule and dog,"[9] Frémont and his men nearly died amidst gigantic snowdrifts, the engineer laconically recording on several occasions that, despite a day's exhausting exertions, "the night had been too cold to sleep."[10] Admitting that "the times were severe when stout men lost their minds from extremity of suffering," and when "even the Indians had sung their death songs," the lieutenant irrepressibly floundered onward through the snow and ice, taking copious notes on everything visible, including the few Indians encountered.[11] No Indian lover, he said of the Snake Indians: "these may be considered, among human beings, the nearest approach to the mere animal" found on earth.[12]

Frémont explored, took barometric readings to establish elevation, wandered, wondered, filled notebooks with scientific oddities, and thoroughly enjoyed himself on three official and two private expeditions. Moreover, he communicated his enthusiasm to the reading public well before California was in American hands. He, more than anyone, made the West come alive. After his third expedition, in 1845–46, he wrote for public consumption: "I had returned inspired with California. Its delightful climate and the uncommon beauty of surface; the great strength of its vegetation and its grand commercial position took possession of my mind."[13] And, through his facile pen, the minds of many of his countrymen. In fact, according to one observer, "By 1845, magazines and newspapers had become imbued with and convinced of the need of a Pacific Railroad." John C. Frémont provided the media with heady, thrilling copy.[14]

His third expedition produced what has often been called "the most important map of the decade," drawn by Prussian cartographer Charles Preuss from the engineer's scientific data and superb memory. Exquisitely detailed, the map was printed by the government and sold cheaply to the public. Many used it as their trail guide as they headed west. Senator Benton effectively disseminated in Congress what his son-in-law provided and helped shape a coherent policy of national development.[15]

THE Treaty of Guadalupe Hidalgo in 1848 had awarded the United States—in return for a token payment—338 million acres of largely unexplored terrain, in addition to recognizing Texas as a state in the Union. Two years later the frantic scramble known as the California gold rush was well under way, mushrooming that territory's population so swiftly that it became a state in 1850, and a rich one at that. The 1846 agreement with Great Britain setting the definitive western Canadian and American borders added Oregon and Washington territories to the American patrimony, and they were even then attracting scores of overland emigrants each week, many putting their faith unwisely in the wildly inaccurate 1845 best seller by Lansford Hastings, the *Emigrant's Guide to Oregon and California*. This "guide" has often been blamed for the 1846 Donner party disaster in the Sierras, and it certainly misled many another group of settlers.[16]

Army posts and forts were soon spread thinly from Fort Kearny, Nebraska, to Fort Laramie and beyond, and each one needed provisioning, which by wagon was horrendously expensive. The freight-hauling firm of Russell and Waddell alone was earning $3 million to $4 million a year in the 1850s for carting army matériel from the Missouri River to the various Plains forts. With irrefutable logic, Pacific Railroad proponents argued that once a railroad was constructed through the Plains, there would be no need for forts there at all. Troops and munitions could be shifted at will to any crisis points.[17] Perhaps equally compelling was that the Mormon settlements in Utah were growing and prospering. Under Brigham Young's leadership, Deseret was fast becoming a state within a state.

In spite of the fact that the modest sum allocated by Congress in 1849 to fund a Pacific Railroad survey was never spent, the army's engineers were almost constantly in the field. The most prolific explorers in uniform were members of the small Corps of Topographical Engineers, headed by dynamic Colonel John Abert. Founded in 1828 as distinct from the Army Corps of Engineers (with which it was merged in 1863), Abert's organization served the executive branch of government exclusively and enjoyed great prestige. Colonel Abert had sent an expedition under his son, John, Jr., to explore and chart Colorado Territory in 1845, and the following year dispatched Lieutenant William H. Emory to explore and gather information from Texas to San Diego. A number of engineering teams went into the field in 1849 and 1850 to determine the precise boundary between the United States and Mexico. Information from their charts and maps led to the Gadsden Purchase of 1853. James Gadsden, who negotiated the treaty, was then American minister to Mexico. He was also a well-known Southern advocate of a Southern Pacific Railroad.[18]

Abert, himself much in favor of a Pacific Railroad built along a Southern route, nonetheless in 1850 sent out an engineering team under Captain Howard Stansbury to reconnoiter a more central route, one that might pass through or near Salt Lake City. Stansbury, who reported seeing emigrants everywhere, was the first to survey the western shores of the saline lake. Lauding the general lay of the central route as more than viable, Stansbury's report was printed by the government in 1851 and was soon in such demand that Lippincott published it commercially the following year. It promptly appeared in Europe, where it was snapped up by prospective immigrants and large numbers of converted Mormons, who used it as a guide to the land of the Saints. The captain had estimated that at least three hundred emigrants were daily crossing the Sierras into California, that several (difficult) wagon roads or trails had been discovered, and that the central route, long worn smooth by the buffalo, was the natural one for the Pacific Railroad.[19] Most of the route surveyed by Stansbury was soon in use by the Overland Stage Company and several freighting firms, then by the short-lived Pony Express, and finally by the Union Pacific Railroad.

The excitement generated by such reports as Stansbury's was reinforced by aggressive sectional interests. Pressure groups, both local and regional, sprang up to champion Chicago, Council Bluffs, the Omaha area, St. Louis, Memphis, New Orleans, Fort Smith, and several towns in Texas as the logical eastern terminus of the Pacific Railroad. There was no question about it: Pacific Railroad fever, if not the railroad itself, was building.

In part to mollify these contending forces and still their raucous voices, Secretary of War Jefferson Davis, a strong transcontinental booster himself, asked Congress for sufficient funds to make a thorough railroad survey of the most potentially feasible routes west. While it has been assumed that his true purpose was simply to prove to the nation that the Southern route was clearly superior, he did decide to send large survey parties to examine all promising avenues.[20]

In March 1853 senators Salmon P. Chase of Ohio and William Gwin of California introduced an amendment to the annual Army Appropriations Act, allotting $150,000 for the survey. The Corps of Topographical Engineers was assigned to undertake the work and complete it in a highly unrealistic ten months.[21] Before the reports appeared, two years would be consumed and three times the money initially appropriated. Ironically, instead of defusing local and sectional rivalries, the survey reports were destined to only confuse the issue.[22]

As five major surveying teams took to the field with considerable fanfare, Theodore Dehone Judah quietly began constructing California's first railroad, the Sacramento Valley line. In equal obscurity, Grenville Dodge, another young engineer, was completing the first trans-Iowa survey to Council Bluffs.[23]

At the recommendation of the Smithsonian Institution, some of the finest civilian scientists of the day accompanied the survey teams. They included botanists, geologists, cartographers, artists, and other specialists from the United States, Germany, Britain, France, and Switzerland. This was to be a major effort indeed.

The basic routes to be surveyed were:

1. The Northern route, from St. Paul to Seattle. The leader of this team was Governor Isaac Stevens, who had just resigned from the Corps of Topographical Engineers to administer the new Washington Territory; he was determined to prove this route the best. The Northern Pacific Railroad later traversed much of the route he charted.

2. The Council Bluffs to San Francisco route, explored by a small team led by the unusually observant Lieutenant E. G. Beckwith. Much of the path he surveyed was tracked by the Union Pacific Railroad.

3. The Central route, between the 38th and 39th parallels, from the Arkansas River to San Francisco. Lieutenant John W. Gunnison led this party until it was massacred by Utah Indians. Though part of this line was later surveyed by Beckwith, data was less complete for it than for the others.

4. The route from Fort Smith on the Arkansas River to Los Angeles via Albuquerque (the 35th parallel route) was covered by Lieutenant Amiel Weeks Whipple's expedition. Some of the ground Whipple inspected later supported tracks of the Atchison, Topeka & Santa Fe line.

5. The Southern, or 32d parallel path, from Fulton on the Red River to San Diego, explored by Captain John Pope and Lieutenant John G. Parke. The land they examined was later used by both the Southern Pacific and Texas Pacific.[24]

Several smaller teams set out from California on limited east-bound explorations.

After collecting and collating the resultant mass of data, a preliminary edition of the *Pacific Railroad Survey* was printed by the government in 1855, in three octavo volumes, with a separate folio of maps. In 1857 appeared the first of thirteen large, expensive quarto volumes of the definitive second edition, the last volume of which was published in 1860. Each lavishly illustrated tome had superb maps, and there was a total of 147 magnificent lithographs.* They have together been hailed as an American publishing triumph, filled with notes on flora, fauna, natural history, ethnography, and "hard" scientific data: "An American encyclopedia of Western experience."[25]

Unfortunately, they did not represent what they claimed to be: a railroad survey. Not a single qualified railroad engineer had gone into the field with the various parties, and many questions fundamental to railroad construction had not even been addressed. Experienced railroad engineers such as Judah dismissed the survey teams as "mere barometric reconnaissances," whose findings were of use only for fixing elevations.[26]

Cost estimates—based on the flimsiest information—ranged from about $68 million (for the Southern route) to a high of some $169 million (for the 35th parallel avenue), with the Council Bluffs line estimated at $116,095,000. The reports discussed the relative merits and drawbacks of each projected path, and, while some were more difficult than others, none was judged impossible. In fact, the survey's prime value—to the consternation of many partisans—was to indicate that a Pacific Railroad could be constructed almost anywhere. Few at

---

*"Lavish" is an apt description. The volumes cost the government hundreds of thousands of dollars to publish.

the time noted that not a single pass through the Sierra Nevadas north of the 35th parallel had even been sought out, let alone explored.

The many potential avenues west tended to heighten both local boosterism and sectionalism rather than ameliorate them, and made compromise and concert even more difficult on Capitol Hill. Yet deep in the Great American Desert, even before the survey reports were printed in Washington, silver and gold were discovered in bleak Nevada. And soon the legendary Comstock Lode was literally stumbled upon by "a toss-pot and tavern valiant named James Finney" and three other "boozy and disreputable scoundrels." Nearby Virginia City was instantly awash in "20,000 wildly irresponsible inhabitants," and emigrants "came by the roaring thousands, on mule back and foot," in search of fabulous riches.[27]

THE NATION AT RISK

I N 1854 railroad savant Henry V. Poor evaluated the survey teams' documents before they were published and aired his views in a paper presented before the American Geographical Society of New York, which he had helped found. He strongly endorsed the Northern route, seeing it as the only possible one, "a highway, already provided . . . and the best possible one for commercial purposes." The others he dismissed because of excessive elevations, impossible snowfalls, or horrendously sterile terrain. He was especially harsh toward Jefferson Davis's supposedly inexpensive Southern route, for "the territory upon its line is the most barren of all."[28] Kit Carson once dryly remarked of the same terrain that "a wolf could not make his living on it."[29] An eternal optimist, Davis had the War Department import a hundred dromedaries for use in further exploration of his preferred highway west. One of these was run into by a Central Pacific locomotive, utterly astounding the engineer, ten years later and hundreds of miles removed.[30]

The survey did help spur a veritable barrage of new railroad bills in Congress, but each ground to a halt in committee, if it made it that far. Sectionalism was winning its last barren victories, and few were as yet aware that trouble was brewing in the deepest interior.

The blight of sectionalism, fueled by the issue of slavery, had by now turned violent. If increasingly harsh words were hurled about in Congress, blood flowed freely in "Bleeding Kansas" by 1855, as pro- and anti-slavery forces battled for control. The new Republican party, itself basically Northern in 1856, turned to none other than John C. Frémont for its first presidential candidate. Virulently anti-slavery, his candidacy did little to heal the sectional rift that was threatening the nation, and even the "railroad plank" in his platform awakened suspicions in the South. That he had been a Pacific Railroad advocate for a decade was hardly a secret, but his party officially called for a transcontinental to be constructed as soon as possible along "the most central and practicable route." Frémont would not countenance a Southern route.[31] One of the most common (if ineuphonious) Republican campaign slogans in 1856 was "Freedom, Frémont, and the Railroad!"[32]

Frémont and his infant party met a crashing defeat in the election, in part because of the blatant sectionalism they displayed and elicited.* New president James Buchanan seemed less strident to the voters and more national in his thinking. While faithful to the Democrats' advocacy of the Pacific Railroad, Buchanan had far more than railroads to occupy his energies: his nation was coming apart. Dealing from the first days of his administration with sectional crises and rebellion in the West, Buchanan could not even spare the time to read a pamphlet published in January 1857 and sent to him by its author, Theodore Dehone Judah. Entitled *A Practical Plan for Building the Pacific Railroad,* the pamphlet—and its author—would soon have more impact than the hundreds of memorials and petitions presented to Congress over the years.[33]

Ironically, President Buchanan's first real crisis (his last would be the act of secession) would not have occurred had there been a Pacific Railroad in place in 1857. The "Mormon Problem," festering ever since Brigham Young had led the Saints to isolated Utah, exploded in open defiance of the laws of the United States. Deseret all but seceded from the Union; "the Mormon War was the first open wound in the American body politic," and a harbinger of conflict to come.[34]

Buchanan found himself faced with having to use force against some eighty thousand armed religious zealots in a desert fifteen hundred miles from the nearest Eastern railhead. With only one small army garrison, Fort Bridger, anywhere in proximity to the Mormons, the president was forced to wage a long-distance campaign.† Under orders from the White House, Colonel Albert Sidney Johnston hurriedly collected a few regiments. But there were horrendous delays, for wagons had to be bought or leased, teamsters had to be hired in their hundreds, and all the food, supplies, and other impedimenta of a military campaign had to be hauled from the East to the edge of the Great American Desert before the first step could be taken for Utah.[36]

Once actually moving out of his Fort Leavenworth base, Johnston, with his command, took an agonizing three months to straggle into Mormon territory and awe the Saints—with surprisingly little bloodshed—into passivity, if not love for

---

*The new Republican party, however, did gain a respectable 33 percent of the popular vote, as against Buchanan's 45 percent.

†The Mormons *were* heavily armed, for Indian hostility had grown in proportion to the number of Saints. In 1857 a party of 120 men, women, and children were massacred in Utah.[35]

the Union. Worse yet, the "Mormon War" and subsequent pacification and garrisoning cost the government about $30 million. By far the greatest proportion of that vast sum was spent on wagons, teamsters, and commercial freight charges. Less than half the money would have sufficed had the Union Pacific Railroad been built by 1857. This cogent argument for speedy construction of a Pacific Railroad was immediately grasped by the American taxpayer and many of his representatives in Washington.[37]

In an 1858 speech to his colleagues, California senator William Gwin clearly stressed the national defense aspect of the Pacific Railroad when he addressed the War Department:

> You have already expended upwards of $500,000,000 since the government was founded, and are increasing your expenditures upon them [the military] every year, although they consume, instead of increase your wealth and products. But this railway, whilst it would secure you against war . . . would augment your means and resources every year.*[38]

As late as 1862, with the Civil War raging and the Sioux devastating manpower-short Minnesota, another "Mormon rebellion was feared," with the Saints perhaps even joining the states'-rights-conscious Confederacy. Farfetched as it might have been, this fear drove the government to increase its garrisons, and hence increase transportation expenses, in Utah.[40]

As the 1850s came to a close, American eyes were fixed on the spectre of secession. The hanging of John Brown in 1859 (for attempting to incite a slave uprising) and two nervous financial panics in 1854 and 1857 also took attention away from the railroad issue. Although a few pundits noted that iron rails were ties that could bind the mineral-rich West (and the Mormons) to the Union, little was done to bring this about. Meanwhile, Abraham Lincoln, who had defended railroad companies in court, and who knew that a transcontinental was in the wind, had quietly bought up building lots in Council Bluffs, a likely terminus.

---

*It has been estimated that it cost some $2.5 million (mostly in transport fees) to keep each regiment in the field out west. There were five to six regiments there in pretranscontinental years.[39]

3

"CRAZY" JUDAH, THE BIG FOUR, AND THE PACIFIC RAILROAD ACT

"CRAZY" JUDAH

THEODORE Dehone Judah stood on the ridgetop in the raging wind, his long hair trailing behind him as he gazed eastward at jewellike Donner Lake, shimmering bluish green below. "Crazy" Judah, as he was known by 1860, knew his Sierras as few men did, and he knew railroad engineering even more intimately. Born in Bridgeport, Connecticut, in 1826, when he was a young boy he moved with his father, an Episcopal minister, to Troy, New York, a small, prosperous community with which an astounding number of leaders of the Union and Central Pacific railroads were connected. After public school he graduated from the Troy School of Technology, showing an unusual, intuitive grasp of the principles of engineering. His first employment was as an assistant engineer on the Troy & Schenectady Railroad, and he gave himself over to it entirely, his only other true passion being playing the organ.[1] In the next decade his career skyrocketed as others recognized his brilliance and initiative. Here was a young man to whom problems were merely interesting exercises, not obstacles. Following an unexciting stint as resident engineer of the Erie Canal, Judah married Anna Pierce, a wealthy, artistic girl from Massachusetts. They were, until he died, unusually close, and their letters indicate a deep, romantic love.

At age twenty-five, Judah was named chief engineer for construction of the Buffalo & New York Railroad, earning high praise for his guidance of the work. After the road was completed, he was chosen to survey, lay out, and direct construction of the "impossible" Niagara Gorge Railroad. The successful completion of that daunting task ahead of schedule made him one of the nation's most celebrated railroad engineers. Here indeed was a problem solver.[2]

The Niagara Gorge coup brought him many new offers of employment. Among these was a bid from Colonel C. L. Wilson, president of the newly incorporated but as yet unbuilt Sacramento Valley Railroad, destined to be California's first. Wilson had come east in 1854 in search of the finest engineering talent his money could buy, and he was advised to contact Judah. Would the young man be interested in constructing the Pacific Coast's first railroad? In the flush of his excitement Judah enthusiastically told his wife, "Anna, I am going to California to be the pioneer railroad engineer of the Pacific Coast!" More important, Anna later recalled, "Everything he did from the time he went to California to the day of his death, was for the great Continental Pacific Railway." While he worked on Colonel Wilson's rather pedestrian railroad, Judah's mind was on far greater things: the Sierra Nevadas. Now, that was a problem to be solved![3]

Passing overland to California via Nicaragua (Judah was one of the first to note that country's potential for an interoceanic canal), he arrived with Anna, sketch pad in hand, at the rude tent city of Sacramento. Because of the nearby gold mines, the population of California's capital, founded near Captain John Sutter's legendary fort in 1849, had grown from 110 to almost 10,000 within twelve months. Five years later, the town was still swelling with people at a rate that construction could not keep up with. Newcomers essentially had to "camp out."[4] In this sprawling, brawling community, Judah plunged immediately into his work. Although his initial estimate of $30,000 a mile was barely half of what it would ultimately cost to build the line, he turned his boundless energies loose and the Sacramento Valley Railroad was in operation far ahead of schedule. After the last spike was hammered home, he agreed to remain with Wilson's railroad as chief engineer, a rather unchallenging post he assumed in 1856 chiefly because it kept him in California.[5]

Even while he was frenetically pushing the Sacramento Valley work, Judah fell under the spell of the towering Sierras, visibly impressive from his construction site. He found himself spending more and more of his free time roaming the Sierras on foot and on muleback, often with Anna sketching the beautiful mountain scenes. Soon he was doing preliminary surveys of the best railroad routes across the Sierras and he also surveyed and plotted a wagon-road route from Sacramento through the mountains to the distant Nevada mines. The only previous—and very preliminary—survey work that had been done in this part of the Sierra Nevadas had been carried out in 1849 by callow Lieutenant William Tecumseh Sherman, who, a general years later, would influence his brother John, a senator, to support the Pacific Railroad.[6]

As his postconstruction tasks were hardly onerous or exciting (although they did provide a steady and decent income), Judah found himself spending much of his time in the Sierras, a fortress that he was willing himself to breach. In 1857, with a number of his surveys completed, Judah published, at his own expense, his *Practical Plan for Building the Pacific Railroad,* sending copies to President Buchanan and every member of Congress. This was the first genuinely "practical" plan of its nature, based upon data far more scientific than had been gathered by any of the 1853–55 survey teams, and in fact, covering a portion of the Sierras totally ignored by Jefferson Davis's engineers.[7]

In addition to roaming through the mountains with Anna—who was now painting full-blown Sierra landscapes of great beauty—Judah was also buttonholing everyone who would listen to his dreams of a Pacific Railroad.[8] Colonel Wilson, he sadly learned, was not a visionary, but Judah's frequent letters to the editor of the *Sacramento Union* did attract a great deal of local attention. Editor Lauren Upson became converted to Judah's vision, and soon the engineer was using the newspaper as a vehicle for "Pacific Railroadism," filling its pages with more letters, editorials, and articles.[9]

To "Crazy" Judah, his vision had indeed become an *-ism,* and in large part because of his facile preaching, the state legislature called a convention to meet at San Francisco in September 1859, to consider a transcontinental railroad. Oregon, Washington, and Nevada were also invited to send delegates.[10]

More than a hundred influential men gathered at the convention and heard Sacramento delegate Judah speak almost mystically of the wonders to be experienced by all Californians through the medium of the iron rail. He also explained, in layman's terms, just how the railroad could be built. He was not, however, perfectly candid, for he had yet to locate a viable pass through the highest points of his projected route. Nonetheless, the engineer was so persuasive that a memorial written by him was officially adopted by the convention and he was personally selected by that body to deliver it to Congress.[11]

Leaving San Francisco on October 20, Judah and his wife reached Washington at a tense moment, for John Brown's trial was under way, further exacerbating sectional bitterness. Perhaps realizing that the trial and the events behind it made preservation of the Union yet more germane, Judah played upon the "nationalizing" effects of the Pacific Railroad. He told those who would listen that "his" railroad would not only populate the Great American Desert but would swiftly add many new anti-slavery states to the nation. In the same vein, he stressed that the Pacific Railroad would assure California's allegiance and adherence to the Union. This was no small concern, given that state's gold- and silver-mining output. Also, there were many in Washington that winter who worried about California's loyalty, for the state was a land of emigrants, and many Californians had strong family and business ties with the South and might favor secession. The 1860 presidential election was to prove that there was indeed discord in the state. In that three-way race (John Bell, a fourth candidate, was not on the California ballot), Lincoln barely carried the state and did not receive a majority with his 38,699 votes. Moderate Democrat Stephen Douglas drew an almost equal 37,957, while Southern extremist John C. Breckinridge attracted 33,969. Clearly, the state *was* dangerously divided, a point hardly lost on President-elect Abraham Lincoln.[12]

Also, asked the intense engineer, had not Iowa risen with unparalleled speed from frontier to statehood, and had not Chicago risen from village to Western metropolis because of the railroad?[13] The recent silver strikes in California and Nevada, and Colorado's newly discovered, isolated gold fields reinforced Judah's argument, and he managed to get an invitation to the White House. After an interview by "faltering President Buchanan," the engineer was loaned an old vice-president's office in the Capitol building. There he soon set up what he called his "Pacific Railroad Museum," a popular display of Anna's drawings and paintings, his maps and data, and geological exhibits he had collected in the Sierras. While the curious streamed through the museum, Judah roamed the halls in search of congressmen and influential visitors, distributed hundreds more copies of his pamphlet, and visited New York and Philadelphia to sound out bankers and potential investors. In all these endeavors he had the unflinching support of California's congressmen as well as such luminaries as Senator Salmon P. Chase of Ohio, soon to become Lincoln's secretary of the treasury and later chief justice of the United States. However, despite many kind words and encouragements, Congress, in the throes of disunion, declined to act on his recommendations.[14]

Frustrated and angry, Judah was at least somewhat buoyed to learn that a second California railroad convention, meeting at Sacramento in February 1860, had accepted a revised version of his Pacific Railroad Plan. It was soon officially endorsed by the state legislature. That body instructed Judah to officially introduce the plan to Congress.

Key elements of this plan called for: (*a*) the government to guarantee payment of 5 percent interest on the projected railroad company's bonds for a three-year period; (*b*) the government to guarantee those first-mortgage bonds to a maximum of $50 million for the duration of the construction phase; (*c*) the work to be completed within a period of ten years; (*d*) the company to be given a four-hundred-foot right-of-way and appropriate acreage for depots and other necessary buildings; (*e*) the government to give to the company alternate sections (square miles, or 640 acres) of public land on either side of the right-of-way for a depth of twenty miles so that the company could raise operating capital; (*f*) the company to carry the United States mails at prices not to exceed $600 per mile each year.

With the aid of the California delegation to Congress, Judah managed to get the plan introduced in both houses, but it was almost instantly tabled and never made it to a vote in either.[15] Dejected as never before, the Judahs headed west in July 1860. There was clearly more work to be done.

Never one to wallow in self-pity, "Crazy" Judah was soon once more on muleback in the Sierras. This time he had been summoned there by the druggist of the small mining town of Dutch Flat, some fifty-five miles northeast of the state capital. "Dr." Daniel W. Strong, who was also an amateur surveyor, had met Judah in the mountains a few years before and had been impressed by his zeal for the Pacific Railroad and his firm belief that the Sierras could be bested. This passion to burst the bonds of geology evinced by Judah impelled Strong himself to reconnoiter the surrounding passes more carefully. The druggist, who had nothing against making money for himself, was also keen to boost the prosperity of his isolated village. He knew the mountains well, but he was no engineer. In September he contacted Judah, informing him that he thought he had located a "door" through the Sierras, and the engineer was in the saddle immediately. In early October, Strong led Judah into the High Sierras, and the engineer's practiced eye, professional instruments, and previously collected data all confirmed the druggist's conviction.[16]

Strong led Judah through the Donner Pass region and showed him a broad ridge, or saddle, between two deep river valleys (the north fork of the American River and the south forks of the Yuba and Bear) that managed to avoid one of the Sierras' two spines. The ridge was just broad enough for railroad construction. The engineer was thrilled, for the route was far superior to any he himself had encountered in his previous twenty-three forays into the mountains. The railroad would be difficult to build, to be sure, with steep grades at points and many tunnels, but it was demonstrably possible. With the druggist in tow, Judah prowled every inch of the pass, jotting down elevations, mapping bridge and tunnel sites, and carefully examining the geological structure. Problems there were aplenty, but that merely stimulated Judah, and the fact that the Pony Express (which had charged a whopping five dollars per half-ounce letter) had just collapsed gave him yet another argument to use on legislatures and prospective investors.[17]

Back at the Doctor's rude drugstore Judah began writing his first genuine railroad "profile" and cost estimates. To have these published he had to use his last cash reserves, for by then he had been fired from the Sacramento Valley line for absenteeism and conflict of interest. Not a worrier, Judah was certain that the small investment would be a wise one, for he could not fail, he thought, to generate capital on the basis of this prospectus.[18] At the same time he drew up a document creating the Central Pacific Railroad Company of California, and he and Dr. Strong immediately began soliciting stock orders in Dutch Flat and neighboring mining towns. Under the laws of the state, a railroad company could not legally incorporate until at least $1,000 per projected mile of track had been subscribed in company stock, with at least 10 percent of the face value of that stock paid in.

Judah's pamphlet, its title simply the new company's name, was published in

San Francisco—where the state's millionaires resided—on November 1, 1860. It was a marvelous proposition to "organize a company" to take advantage of a railroad bill sponsored by Senator Samuel R. Curtis of Iowa, which appeared likely to pass Congress in 1861.* The route Judah had charted, 115 miles long, to the Nevada border, necessitated raising subscriptions of $115,000 (with at least $11,500 paid in) before he could file for incorporation. There were men in San Francisco who lost more than that each month in the city's gambling halls, and he doubted not a bit that such a piddling sum could be raised within a week or so. He informed his readers that the initial capital raised would be used to make a final and thorough survey of grades, cuttings, fillings, tunnels, and the like, which could be used for actual construction. He also announced that already a "bona fida [*sic*] subscription of $46,500" had been collected in the small upland mining communities, leaving only some $70,000 "to be made up in the cities of San Francisco and Sacramento." It is clear that he was optimistic enough to believe that he would not even have to canvass the latter city to complete the initial, required subscription.

He assured his readers that Congress would pass the Curtis Bill (which mandated two railroads) in 1861, and stressed that if his Central Pacific Railroad Company was already incorporated at the time of the bill's passage, with full survey data and profile maps, it and not some other company would be permitted to build at least the western portion of the transcontinental. The pamphlet then went on to pose and answer what Judah thought were the most relevant questions prospective investors might have, from angles of grade, to cost of locomotive fuel, availability of rails, the virtually assured city, county, and state aid and subsidies, and future earnings: "Its profitableness will exceed that of any known road in the world," wrote the normally sober engineer. Cagily, he estimated that even if the road was to halt at the state line, local traffic—and, above all, transportation of gold and silver—would guarantee large and steady profits.

Appended to the report was a letter dated November 4 from the San Francisco firm of Ogden and Wilson, testifying to the feasibility and moneymaking potential of the road, which "would make [California] the richest and most prosperous state in the Union." The cost estimate of per-mile construction—depending upon the nature of the terrain—ranged from $50,000 to a shocking $150,000, or an average of $88,428—high indeed, but not the highest of the epoch.[20]

Copies of *The Central Pacific Railroad of California* were distributed immediately, and Judah, armed with scores of extras, sallied forth to confront San

---

*Actually, there were a number of railroad bills before Congress, calling for one, two, or three transcontinentals. Senate and House differences over the number to be authorized and aided led to the tabling of most of them. Senator (soon Secretary of State) William Seward remarked to his colleagues on January 5, 1861, "I vote for two railroads [one in the South], instead of one as I would have preferred," as a gesture to preserve the Union; but within a week Mississippi, Florida, and Alabama joined South Carolina in secession.[19]

Francisco's capitalists. He might just as well have attempted to claw through the Sierra granite with his fingernails.

Despite the ostentatious wealth of San Francisco and the large and varied investments of its denizens, as future investor Mark Hopkins remembered, only one sale of two hundred-dollar shares "was ever subscribed in San Francisco and $20 all that was paid in—although the company had an office there." An itinerant Frenchman bought the two shares, but he wandered off in search of his destiny, never paid the balance, and his shares were later forfeited to the company.[21] In a city brimful of buccaneer businessmen, Judah's stock certificates failed dismally, and he was deeply shaken. He had not reckoned on conservatism from such financial sharks as Darius Ogden Mills, a Croesus-rich banker soon to create the mammoth Bank of California and buy virtual control of the huge Comstock Lode. The skepticism of the business community was as nothing, however, compared with the outright hostility of the various interests that stood to lose from a successful Pacific Railroad. Shipping companies—Wells, Fargo and other stage and freight companies, and rival railroaders—all fought the Central Pacific from its inception. While one observer has correctly noted that "the project was thoroughly saturated and fairly dripping with the elements of adventure and romance," these were not attractive elements to West Coast financiers.[22] Although somewhat naïvely Judah did not anticipate genuine opposition, he perhaps should have realized that it was a fact of West Coast economic life that the best local investments, with high and immediate returns (of up to 2 percent a month) were in mining, an industry that was still expanding dizzily.[23] Still, the fact that not a single San Francisco businessman took his (admittedly long-range) plan seriously all but destroyed him.

As he set out for Sacramento in December, he learned that only one share had so far been sold in Nevada (a territory that would so obviously benefit from the project), and only 155 more throughout northern California, mostly to recent immigrants who would forfeit for nonpayment of the balance. As he entered Sacramento that dismal morning, he bitterly calculated that he could count on a mere $6,230 (on subscriptions of $62,300) for a work that even he must have known would require tens of millions.[24] And this merely weeks after Abraham Lincoln had been elected president on a platform strongly stressing that "a railroad to the Pacific Ocean is imperatively demanded by the interests of the whole country . . . the Federal Government ought to render immediate and efficient aid in its construction."[25]

On December 20, ironically, just two days after the Curtis Bill—which called for a Northern *and* a Southern transcontinental—passed in the House, South Carolina, by a unanimous vote of a special convention, seceded from the Union. The bill passed in the Senate as well, but in a much amended form, and it died rather noisily in a committee of the House. Debate on the bill in both chambers, however, had made it clear that a one-railroad bill would soon take its place, calling for a Pacific Railroad through the *loyal* states and territories.[26] Senator Gwin, railing angrily from his seat, provided the Curtis Bill with a fitting epitaph: "We are having exhibited now what I have seen for ten years; that the Pacific Railroad is always destroyed by its friends, and not by its enemies."[27] Truly, most congressmen agreed that a transcontinental was necessary and wise, but disagreed heartily on where it should be located and what the government should do to aid it.

One evening in early January, Judah gave a well-publicized, impassioned address before a large gathering at the St. Charles Hotel, on Sacramento's prestigious K Street.* After his lengthy presentation there were some handshakes, some polite questions, but not a single stock changed hands. However, an overweight, florid businessman approached the engineer as he was dejectedly leaving and introduced himself. He was Collis Potter Huntington, and he and his partner, Mark Hopkins, owned a thriving hardware business just down the street. Huntington, as pragmatic as Judah was visionary, was not a man easily swayed by oratory, but he did ask Judah to drop by his office some evening to talk at length. The businessman was not at all a gambler—he once characteristically remarked that "you can't follow me through life by the quarters I've dropped"—but he certainly did not think Judah crazy.[29]

THE BIG FOUR

A FTER an encouraging meeting a few days later with Huntington, who arranged another get-together at his brother-in-law's house, the engineer once more made his pitch. In addition to Huntington and his in-law, Mark Hopkins was there, and a W. H. Stoddard. Judah was highly persuasive, for it was apparently at this meeting that Huntington made up his mind, albeit without committing himself directly. He requested one more meeting with Judah, promising to have present some associates who might well be willing to invest. Scenting success at last, although from an unexpected quarter, the engineer agreed and returned to his hotel to share the news with anxious Anna.

At this last, climactic meeting, held above the hardware store owned by Huntington and Hopkins, Judah for the first time faced the "Big Four"—Huntington, Hopkins, Charles Crocker, and Leland Stanford—men who, unlike him, "were not dreamers, visionaries, idealists; they were shopkeepers."[30]

---

*He had apparently delivered his pitch there before, in November or December, and Collis Huntington and Charles Crocker had been in the audience.[28]

Collis Huntington was thirty-nine years old in 1861, a hardworking, ultra-respectable businessman, with, according to one who knew him, an "abnormal retentiveness of his memory."[31] Born in Harwinton, Connecticut, into a large family in which "industry was the motto of the household," Collis moved to Oneonta, New York, and by his teens was a moderately successful businessman, with "the physique of a young Hercules."[32] He sold butter in New York City, clocks throughout the South, and, one of the original 'Forty-niners, the nonsmoking teetotaler even found a way to make money in Nicaragua on his way west.[33] "I hardly remember the time I was not doing something," he later wrote, and "I have always had a good time" keeping busy.[34] In California he made a small fortune by monopolizing the supply of Ames brothers Old Colony shovels, buying twelve hundred dozen at a time. In business in a state whose economy was predicated on mining, he noted, "I had all the shovels in California in 1850."[35] A few years later he made another windfall profit by cornering the market on potatoes. "I have always been plotting," he later admitted, and while he "never had any chums," he did form a partnership in 1854 with Mark Hopkins, and their business was soon the largest single retail operation in the state.[36] He was a large figure physically (he weighed 250 pounds)* and figuratively, in California's nascent Republican party, which he had helped form and through which he made and kept many contacts. As a stalwart Republican and prominent Californian, he was worried about the strong vein of Southern sympathy he saw all around him, later writing, "About the time of the war . . . there was a question where California would land."[38] The Pacific Railroad, he felt, would secure the allegiance of almost all Californians to the Union. Fellow pioneer Republicans, including most of his future railroad partners, agreed with him.

Mark Hopkins, at forty-seven the oldest of the Big Four, was yin to the big man's yang. Of medium height and so slender ("He had no flesh at all"[39]) that he appeared tubercular, "Uncle Mark" spoke with a pronounced lisp when he spoke at all, and was the "balance wheel" of the hardware business and later the Central Pacific.[40] A natural bookkeeper and naturally dour and uncharismatic, Hopkins was born in Henderson, Massachusetts, son of a Methodist minister and ardent abolitionist who was used as a model by novelist Harriet Beecher Stowe when writing *Uncle Tom's Cabin.*[41] He became a clerk in Niagara, New York, where he studied law and was admitted to the bar. For some reason he chose not to use his legal training, and instead sold farm implements and learned bookkeeping.

Hopkins, recalled an acquaintance, "possessed in a remarkable degree the gift of silence," and was, like his partner, an original 'Forty-niner and a founder of the state's Republican party.[42] On the West Coast he operated a grocery store

---

*He later bragged, "My son weighs 275 pounds; my son is sixteen."[37]

with E. H. Miller, Jr., in Hangtown—later, Placerville—and speculated in real estate and construction before going into the hardware business with Huntington, and it was his attention to detail that made that undertaking profitable.[43] So quietly dependable was Uncle Mark that he was routinely trusted for long periods of time with power of attorney and proxy voting rights by his future Central Pacific colleagues, making crucial legal and financial decisions in their names. He also handled the entire bookkeeping system for the huge Central Pacific operation. His partners never complained about the results.[44] While abhoring risks, Hopkins was the quintessential businessman, and Huntington frankly admitted, "I never thought anything finished until Hopkins looked at it."[45]

Leland Stanford, like Huntington, a man of imposing physical stature and also an early California Republican, was *not* by nature a businessman. He was, at age thirty-six, a politician at heart. Born just outside Troy, New York, where his father ran the Bull's Head Tavern, Stanford studied philosophy at a seminary and then law in Albany, and in 1848 moved to Port Washington, Wisconsin, to hang out his shingle and (unsuccessfully) debut in politics. The scent of California gold drew him west in 1852 (as it did all five of his brothers) via Nicaragua, and he went into the retail trade in El Dorado and later Placer counties, dabbling as well in mining claims and serving several years as justice of the peace.[46] In 1855 luck smiled upon him and he made an estimated $400,000 on the Lincoln Mine in Amador County, following which he moved to Sacramento, opened a large wholesale grocery store, and dove headlong into politics, promptly emerging as a major leader of the new Republican party.[47] While described as having "the ambition of an emperor and the spite of a peanut vendor,"[48] he was extremely active in civic affairs, and was one of eighteen men to donate $100 to help found the local library association. Coincidentally, the other seventeen included Huntington, Crocker, Hopkins, and E. H. Miller, Jr.[49]

In 1857 Stanford ran unsuccessfully for state treasurer with the infant party, and two years later was badly mauled in a bid for the governorship, receiving a bare 10 percent of the vote. A delegate to the 1860 Republican convention in Chicago, in 1861 he would win the governorship and do so running far ahead of his party.[50] Stanford, who had watched his father labor on one of America's first railroads (the Mohawk & Hudson), and who had sold horseradish in Schenectady and chestnuts in Albany when a youth, later purchased half a million acres of California's finest land—including the world's largest vineyard. The founder of Stanford University, he was long held up as a role model in Gilded Age America. An attractive man and a thoroughly political animal, Stanford was in 1861 probably the wealthiest of the Big Four.[51]

Different from his future partners in most ways was Charles Crocker, a bull of a man in size (260 pounds) and temperament. Thirty-nine years old, Crocker had also been born at Troy, and was later raised in rural Marshall County,

Indiana, where, as he recalled, "I had no nursery days,"[52] because of the need to help support his family. With the slimmest of educations but the stoutest of backs and an infinite cache of energy, he sold newspapers, split rails, worked as a sawyer, and ran a small iron forge.[53] He arrived in California after trudging cross-country in 1850 with a party that included his brothers Henry and Clark. After working briefly in the mines, he became a teamster and partner in a general store at Negro Hill in the mining region. Like Stanford, he bought and sold claims on the side. In 1852 he opened his own store in Sacramento, but it burned down the following year (so did much of the city) while he was in Indiana seeking a bride. He rebuilt the store and within a few years was prospering, later acknowledging, "I was always apt at trade."[54] A workaholic, Crocker habitually rose at four in the morning and worked until bedtime.[55] Both he and Mark Hopkins were elected city aldermen in 1855, and in 1860 Crocker became one of the few Republicans elected to the state legislature. "Utterly tactless,"[56] Charlie Crocker was a man of fierce stamina, strength, and stubbornness—the perfect man to have in the field, and one who would not trouble himself with the larger issues.[57]

In addition to the Big Four that critical evening, in attendance were future senator Cornelius Cole; grocer Lucius A. Booth; James W. Bailey, a Sacramento jeweler and friend of Huntington; Charles Marsh, a Nevada City mineowner; and a James Peel. Wealthy if not exceedingly rich, most of these men had met Horace Greeley in 1859 when he had traveled west to preach the Pacific Railroad gospel.[58] With Huntington in the lead, the group bombarded Judah with pointed questions, but the young engineer, radiating confidence, had the right answers for everyone. Perhaps the crucial point he made that evening was his insistence that at the very least, a railroad as far as the mining region, with feeder wagon roads, would be a certain money-maker. The project, according to Judah, simply could not lose, for any railroad reaching east more than seventy miles—to the mining towns—would make money.[59]

With Cole and Bailey initially abstaining, the Big Four, Booth, and Marsh agreed to divide equally among themselves the cost of Judah's full-scale Sierra survey and buy enough stock in the company to permit incorporation. Each of them, including Judah, would cover one seventh of the cost, the engineer's portion would be his labor on the actual survey, which he would make without salary. Each also apparently agreed to fund one seventh of the construction costs for the first thirty-one miles of track, to Newcastle. Judah estimated that his survey would cost about $35,000, and claimed that the railroad could be built to Newcastle for under $3 million.[60] Peel, who purchased some stock, soon got cold feet and was bought out by the Big Four.[61]

Elated, Judah pumped each of his backers' hands. Oddly, very little on this occasion and others was ever committed to paper by the Central Pacific leadership; most agreements were simply verbal. The engineer rushed back to his hotel to shock Anna with the long-awaited news, and within days began his dreamed-of work at the Sacramento levee within sight of his adoring wife, who gazed down from their hotel window.[62] Charlie Crocker, asked how his company would drive a railroad line through the massive mountains, shrugged and remarked bluntly that "luck has a hell of a lot to do with it."[63] And so it did.

THE FAIT ACCOMPLI

THINGS moved swiftly following the handshakes above the hardware store. The men involved added stock selling to their other vocations. Stanford announced that he would run again for the governorship, Judah disappeared into the Sierras with his theodolites, Huntington boned up on railroad technology, Crocker surveyed the labor market, Hopkins worried, and legal documents were discussed, debated, and drawn up by Crocker's brother E. (Edwin) B., a practicing lawyer.

By mid-April 1861, when General Pierre Gustave Toutant Beauregard ordered his batteries to fire upon Fort Sumter in Charleston harbor, more than enough stock had been subscribed to meet the legal requirements. By the time the board of directors was formed, some 1,250 shares had been sold of the 85,000 of its authorized capitalization. Of these, the Big Four, Judah, and Bailey each held 150, Marsh and Dr. Strong 50 apiece—a comfortable and controlling 1,000 shares among them. Booth and a John Williams of Nevada each had 10 shares, and a scattering of minor investors owned the remaining certificates, beautifully decorated with Anna Judah's mountain scenes.[64] While there was hardly a stampede to buy Central Pacific stock, others did soon come on board. Samuel Brannan,* a San Francisco businessman and railroad pioneer, finally saw the light and purchased 200 shares, Orville and Charles A. Lambard, Boston business tycoons, bought 320 shares between them (the largest block save that of the collective founders),† the firm of Glidden and Williams‡ bought 125, E. B. Crocker 10, and a handful of others subscribed perhaps a hundred more shares.[65] These men, however, had little to say in company policy or direction, and were essentially frozen (and many later bought) out of the action.

In June some Central Pacific stockholders were present for the election of the company's first official officers. The tenor of the meeting is not known, but

---

*Brannan, unimportant during the construction years, as a stockholder later sued the Big Four for fraud.
†They too sued the Big Four after the line was built.
‡William T. Glidden and John M. S. Williams, East Coast *and* California shippers, were later major investors in both the Union Pacific and the Crédit Mobilier.

Stanford emerged as president, Huntington vice-president, Hopkins treasurer, Bailey secretary, and Judah chief engineer. Crocker remained a member of the board of directors. This done, the legal articles of association were drawn up and signed on June 27, and legal incorporation was accomplished the following day.[66] Just eighteen days earlier, Leland Stanford had won the Republican nomination for the governorship.

Throughout the summer everyone connected with the Central Pacific bought and sold its stock, gave speeches extolling its potential, politicked, or surveyed. While stock sales to outsiders were appallingly slow, the survey progressed smoothly, with Huntington, Crocker, and Stanford visiting Judah in the field from time to time and roughing it in the Sierras, appraising the terrain with their own, unpracticed eyes. Also with Judah on several occasions was A. A. Sargent, newly elected to the House of Representatives, and the man who would introduce a new railroad bill to that chamber. The September 4 election of Stanford to the governor's mansion augured well for the new company.[67]

The survey was at last finished in early August, although it was not until October 1 that Judah submitted his formal report. On August 7, "Crazy" Judah presented a synopsis to the inner circle of rather anxious stockholders. He stood by his estimate of just over $13 million to the Nevada border, or an average of some $88,000 per mile, and this must have brought a sigh of relief from his backers. However, he now calculated eighteen tunnels through the Sierra's granite (three were later eliminated), totaling 17,410 feet of bore. The longest of these would be, according to his optimistic estimate, 1,370 feet long and, at the summit, at an elevation of 7,200 feet. He grossly underestimated the cost and time required for that tunneling, and even more naïvely figured the average depth of a season's snowfall in the Sierras at a moderate 6 feet.* Judah foresaw no problems of grade, with most inclines between 36 and 53 feet per mile. Only 2.84 miles would be at a steep 116-foot slope. In fact, he felt certain that he could reduce that figure to 105 feet.[68] Also, he could now state that curvature would represent no problem at all, for on the line he had plotted there were simply no sharp angles. He had scouted several other possible routes but had found that the one through Dutch Flat, Donner Pass, and Emigrant Gap to the Truckee River was clearly superior. He urged a wagon road from the Washoe mines to Dutch Flat, since in engineering terms it would be impossible to drive the railroad closer to the mines than that little town. The wagon road would also generate considerable earnings, which could be used to help finance construction of the Central Pacific. With unusual prescience, Judah also pressed the stockholders to fund a proper survey all the way across Nevada and into Utah, to Salt Lake City, estimating that a railroad from the California border to that center

---

*The average, measured over one eighty-winter span, was 31 feet, 1 inch at Donner Pass, with a record of 65 feet in the winter of 1879–80.

could be built for perhaps $40 million.[69] Finally, he informed his audience that a rail line from Sacramento across the mountains and Great American Desert to the Missouri River—some 1,858 miles by his calculation—could be put in place for just under $100 million.[70]

The very concept must have seemed staggering in the summer of 1861, for as late as June 1863, only 7,115 shares of Central Pacific stock had been sold—and no federal aid received—with a puny $210,930 paid in.[71] And most of the stock in circulation had been subscribed by the Big Four themselves. With Charlie Crocker still muttering about the role of luck, the founders of the Central Pacific set grimly to work to minimize precisely that feature of their operation. "They were shopkeepers," and they faced a financial and engineering problem unique in their nation's history.

THE ACT

O N OCTOBER 9, at a board meeting above the hardware store, Judah was asked to return to Washington to influence a new, bipartisan railroad bill that would be coming out of both houses of Congress the following spring. He was provided with $100,000 in company stock, to "distribute as need warranted" among congressmen.[72] In November, Nevada's first territorial legislature was to convene, and on the agenda was a proposal to grant aid to the first railroad to cross the territory's border. Horrified that this plum might attract frantic building by some other company, Stanford, Crocker, Huntington, and Dr. Strong descended on Carson City like the Four Horsemen. When the legislature came in session, the Californians successfully influenced the relevant legislation (Governor Stanford carried great prestige), and for good measure received legal incorporation for a Nevada Railroad Company, with preferential—and assignable—rights to build across the territory. The Big Four, Judah, and Bailey were each given $10,000 worth of stock in the paper company.[73]

As if this legerdemain were not enough, and perhaps with the Nevada charter acting as a stimulant, the Central Pacific leadership on November 27, with trail dust still clinging to their clothes, managed to legally incorporate the Dutch Flat and Donner Lake Wagon Road Company in California, despite flagrant hostility from other toll-road companies. It certainly helped to have the governor on the board. With a projected sixty-seven-mile length, the road would impose three rather high tolls, and was capitalized at $100,000 initially. The toll road's directors and stockholders were—of course—the Big Four (with Crocker as president), Strong, and one E. L. Bradley.[74]

In late November, a weary Judah and his wife stumbled off their ship at New York City. En route, he had jotted down in his notebook a list of the supplies an experienced traveler kept in his stateroom, and it is a tosspot's fantasy. Judah traveled with, among other things, Mumm's champagne, ale, "raw brandy," Scotch whiskey, Port wine, laudanum, Worcestershire sauce, and anchovy paste, and, he wrote, "in truth, my room looks like a small grocery store."[75]

Judah had been asked by California senator Jason A. McDougall "to arrive at Washington at least a week before the meeting of Congress to assist him in preparing a Bill," and also to work with fellow Californian A. A. Sargent to do the same in the House.[76] Pausing only long enough in New York to have a thousand copies of a propagandistic pamphlet printed, Judah hurried to the capital in the first days of December, abstaining from serious politicking until he had reassembled his Railroad Museum in the Capitol, where his old office was awaiting him.

One thing was certain that winter: this time there would be no lack of support for a Pacific Railroad, and a great deal less bickering about specifics. In fact, there was not even much in the way of criticism. The House soon created a subcommittee to study the old Curtis Bill and amend or drop it, naming as chairman Congressman Sargent, and Judah himself as clerk. The House also named a Select Committee on the Pacific Railroad, again with Judah as clerk. Even more incredible was the engineer's selection as clerk of the *Senate* Committee on Pacific Railroads as well.[77] Perhaps "Crazy" Judah was better at distributing company stock than he has been given credit for.

This was astonishingly good news to pass on to Huntington, who sailed into New York on Christmas Eve and appeared in Washington a few days later. Huntington, called by one biographer the "Great Persuader,"[78] must have enjoyed watching Judah work. The beauty of Judah's position was the simple fact that he knew far more about railroads than did any member of the three committees (or Congress), and they all knew it. They, in fact, deferred to him. He also—uniquely—had detailed specifics for the western portion of the Pacific Railroad as well as a legally organized company behind him. There were gaggles of other railroad lobbyists in the capital at the moment, but only Judah had the official (if conflicting) positions as clerk. Once serving the committees, it would be unnecessary for him to buy further support with company stock, for stock buys influence, and that he already had as clerk. The remainder of the company certificates were probably handed to Huntington to use as collateral when negotiating with industrialists for rails and equipment.

The engineer worked intensely with committee members, providing relevant information, rendering technical judgments, making suggestions, and even drafting official reports. It would not be entirely unfair to state that he—most certainly more than any other man—wrote the Pacific Railroad Act of 1862.[79]

Early in their deliberations, perhaps because of Judah's suggestion, the House committees decided, with some debate, to limit their bill to a single transcontinental. After considerably more debate, the St. Louis route was discarded, for it was too near the theater of military operations, and, even though still within the Union, Missouri was a slave state with a strong, pro-South underground. Instead, the House (and Senate) narrowed their focus to the Missouri River terminus, in the vicinity of Council Bluffs, Iowa, and Omaha, across the river in Nebraska. The only drawback was the lack of rail connection between either city and the East. Omaha, founded only in 1854, was on the more logical western, side of the river, but as the 1860 census revealed, it was a torpid little community of only 1,861 whites, 20 free Negroes, and 2 Indians.[80] Council Bluffs, on the other hand, was a thriving town three times the size of Omaha, but was on the wrong side of the river, and there were no bridges in the area. Congress, confused, refused to choose between the cities and was content to leave the ultimate decision to the president.

Slowly, in both houses, with the "crazy" engineer peering intently over their shoulders, congressmen drafted compatible bills, which were then submitted to debate. Few in Congress challenged the notion or the need for a transcontinental, but there were some who disagreed with one aspect or another of the bills, especially the role and scope of government aid. Although Washington was never expected to contribute actual cash to the Pacific Railroad, some members of Congress were upset that the projected value of bond loans and land grants approached the awesome figure of $100 million.

Not that there was anything new about federal and state land grants. As early as 1802 Congress had donated public lands to the state of Ohio to help finance the building of roads.[81] In 1850 this was done for the first time to stimulate railroad construction, with a whopping grant of 2,595,053 acres to the nascent Illinois Central Railroad, followed by another million or so acres to spur construction of the Mobile & Ohio line.[82] These lands were commonly given in alternate sections along either side of the right-of-way to a depth of six miles. More such grants were disbursed in 1851 and 1852, and in 1856 alone thirty-four land grants to railroads were approved and many millions of acres given up.[83] President Pierce signed railroad land-grant bills involving almost 15 million acres, and in all, seventy-nine railroads had received federal lands by 1861, to the tune of more than 150 million acres.[84] And, as Congressman Sargent told his chamber in an April debate, there were currently seven railroad companies engaged in construction in India "under the guarantee of the Government" for some $200 million.[85]

There was, it turned out, little serious resistance, for in the midst of war, the Pacific Railroad was an idea whose time had irrevocably come. Many besides Judah played up the geopolitical importance of the project. The Californian Sargent stated bluntly in Congress that "England desires California," and then rhetorically asked his colleagues, "Shall we idly doze in security until we lose our rich Pacific possessions?"[86] Four years before, Senator Seward had urged a crash transcontinental program for internal security, to "guarantee the loyalty of the Pacific states," as had Senator Gwin,[87] and influential navy commodore Matthew F. Maury a year later.[88] In 1860 the Republican platform committee had couched its Pacific Railroad plank in similar terms.

Lincoln was vocal in his advocacy of the Pacific Railroad, and Pennsylvania's Congressman Thaddeus Stevens—who later profited from his own amendment to the bill—renewed the economic argument, telling the Senate, "The Western soil is but a platform on which to lay the rails to transport the wealth of the furthest Indies to Philadelphia, Boston and Portland."[89]

On June 20, 1862, the amended bill passed in the Senate with ease, by a vote of 25 to 5. Four days later it was endorsed by the House, 104 to 21. A week later, President Lincoln signed it into law. Salmon P. Chase, now secretary of the treasury (and designing a ten-thousand-dollar bill featuring his own likeness), was to write that while during the war Congress had enacted some farsighted legislation, "Among these great acts the Pacific Railroad Bill will remain as one of the most illustrious monuments of the wisdom and courage of its members."[90]

The act, whose full title is "An Act to Aid in the Construction of a Railroad and Telegraph Line from the Missouri River to the Pacific Ocean, and to Secure to the Government the Use of the Same for Postal, Military, and other Purposes," is an exceedingly curious document, even by government standards. It created the Union Pacific Railroad Company by naming 158 prominent men as the company's directors, to work with five government commissioners who would represent Washington and national interests. Among the commissioners—who would serve only until the company was legally incorporated—were Cornelius Bushnell of Connecticut, Jesse L. Williams of Indiana, the venerable railroad booster Samuel R. Curtis of Iowa, Huntington, Judah, Bailey, Marsh, and Darius Ogden Mills (all of California), rail maker Joseph Scranton of Pennsylvania, and Ben Holladay of New York. Henry V. Poor was, briefly, one of the government commissioners.[91]

These exalted gentlemen, mandated to meet first in Chicago on September 2, 1862, were to set Union Pacific policy, see to the raising of investment capital, and, in general, usher the company into existence. The Union Pacific was to be capitalized at a full $100 million, with 100,000 shares of thousand-dollar stock, and a limit of 200 shares to be held by any one person. As soon as 2,000 shares had been subscribed, with 10 percent ($200,000) paid in, stockholders were to convene and elect a board of at least fifteen directors (an additional two were to be appointed by the president of the United States, again to represent both the government and the people), and begin the great labor. The Central Pacific was specifically named as the western arm of the Pacific Railroad, but, as an existing private company, it was not to be as closely regulated as the eastern arm. It would, however, be monitored by appointed government commissioners.

The California company was, on the other hand, to build only from its point of origin to the state line, and there await the rails of the Union Pacific. Since the object of the western arm of the Pacific Railroad was to link the great port of San Francisco to the East, the Central Pacific *could* build from Sacramento to the Bay area, with that mileage eligible for aid under the act. One of the great enigmas of this period concerns this Sacramento to San Francisco route. For some reason, probably because of a shortage of operating capital, shortly after the act was signed by the president Judah sold the Central Pacific's rights to this vital stretch of railroad to the owners of the San Francisco & San Jose. The Big Four later bought it back.[92]

By way of aid, the federal government was to issue to the companies United States 6 percent bonds (to be repaid, interest and all, beginning thirty years after completion of the railroad), at rates of $16,000, $32,000, and $48,000 per mile, depending on the nature of the terrain.* These would only be issued after government inspectors had certified, in forty-mile stretches of track, that the road was of "first quality" and in working order. The companies expected to sell these bonds on the open market to produce construction capital, and, said the act, the bonds were to be considered first-mortgage liens upon the railroads. Fifteen to 25 percent of all bonds due were to be withheld by the government until the Pacific Railroad was completed—as if the railroads were posting a bond *with* bonds. With the Civil War engulfing the country, however, the government's bonds inspired little market confidence, and they never sold at par. Hence, from the beginning, the aid was depreciated, or discounted. Those bonds sold particularly poorly, far below par, in California, where the legal tender was gold, rather than greenbacks. During the war, greenbacks commanded only between 57.97 cents and 81.88 cents in gold.[93] The companies could issue their own bonds in addition to stocks, but these would have to be market-defying second-mortgage notes, and would prove to be all but unsellable.

The government also awarded the companies a right-of-way extending two hundred feet on either side of the tracks, and five alternate sections (square miles) of public lands on either side of the line, or 6,400 acres per mile. This land, like the bonds, was to be given only upon certification of each forty-mile portion of continuous, working track. Land that had not been sold or otherwise used by the companies within three years after the completion of the railroad would revert to the public domain. Exempted by the government were lands known to be rich in minerals of any sort, although timberland was permitted in aid. It was quite clear to everyone, including the delighted Department of the Interior, that the alternate sections retained by the government would increase enormously in value as the railroads progressed and finally joined.

---

*Sixteen thousand dollars for gentle terrain such as the Platte Valley, $32,000 for desert wastes, and $48,000 for mountains.

Both companies were to give priority to the transportation of government mails, troops, and supplies, and payments due them for these services were to be withheld and used to help guarantee the government bonds and the interest thereon. Also, 5 percent of the companies' net earnings, as soon as such should be generated, was to be automatically turned over to the government each year to be applied to their "debt" to Washington.

Basically, then, while certainly an "Aid in the Construction of a Railroad and Telegraph Line," the act cost the government nothing. In granting bonds Washington was loaning its *credit,* not its money, and the companies had to pay back to Washington the bonds and interest. Even if both companies collapsed, the government, through its bonds, held the first mortgage and would hence own any extant trackage as well as property built or acquired. Washington further hedged its riskless bet by withholding 5 percent of the net profit, a proportion of its own bonds, and payment for official traffic. In addition, while reserving to the government all mineral lands, Congress could sit back and watch the alternate sections of the public domain (and land miles beyond) rise from worthless to valuable, a quantum increase in potential national wealth.* In fact, it is difficult to see today just how the government could have lost, especially as it also set minimum mileage to be constructed in specified periods: the Union Pacific was obligated to build a hundred miles in two years and another hundred miles each succeeding year, while the Central Pacific, due to mountainous terrain, was to build half that much. The act also specified that both companies were to be confiscated if the Pacific Railroad was not completed by July 1, 1874.

An amendment tacked onto the act by rail maker Senator Thaddeus Stevens and supported by other industrialists, specified that only American iron could be used in construction of the Pacific Railroad. This was a rude blow on two counts: During the war, the army had an insatiable (and priority) need for iron and iron products. Hence the companies would have to compete against their own government for enormous allotments of iron. The amendment was destined not only to cause delays but much higher than normal prices. Even in peacetime and even with a protective tariff, foreign (mostly British) rails were cheaper than the American product. During the war, American rails often sold at two to three times the price of the easily obtainable foreign product.

The act boosted construction expenses in other ways as well, chiefly through technical restrictions. No grade in excess of 116 feet per mile was to be permitted (even in the mountains), despite the fact that grades in excess of 200 feet were common in the Appalachians and New England. This meant that expensive cuts, fills, and tunneling would have to be relied upon. Also, a limitation on curves to less than 14 percent (a 400-foot radius) virtually eliminated the use of switch-

---

*This situation was somewhat similar to the fate of the United States gold reserve in the 1960s and 1970s, which increased in value by more than 1,000 percent because of events occurring elsewhere.

backs and forced the companies to resort in some cases to far more expensive tunneling.

The act placed an additional burden on the Union Pacific by requiring that two men be appointed by the president of the United States to sit on its board of directors. These men, who supposedly had no financial stake in the company, could—and often did—meddle and confuse the direction of the work. The same company suffered under yet another condition of the act, for that legislation stated that the *first* railroad to build westward to the 100th meridian (247 miles west of Omaha) would have the congressional mandate to be the Pacific Railroad. As an entity, then, the Union Pacific was guaranteed nothing, and at least one potential rival (the Leavenworth, Pawnee & Western, later the Union Pacific, Eastern Division, or UPED), chartered earlier, might well reach the 100th meridian first: it was already attracting capital.[94]

THE FIRST, FAINT STIRRINGS

FROM Washington, Theodore Dehone Judah, no longer to be called "crazy," ebulliently wired the Central Pacific's Sacramento headquarters: "We have drawn the elephant. Now let us see if we can harness him up."*[1]

On July 10, in a San Francisco that had done so little to help the Central Pacific, "there was a grand torchlight procession by the firemen, and a general illumination of the city," whose common citizens, at least, had grasped that the railroad was a vehicle created to burst the state forth from its isolation. Jury-rigged floats wobbled down the main thoroughfares bearing such legends as "Little Indian Boy, Step Out of the Way for the Big Engine," "The Pacific Railroad—Uncle Sam's Waistband," "Fresh No. 4 Mackerel, Six Days from Belfast," and "Married—in July, 1862, by the High Priest of North America, Mr. Atlantic to Miss Pacific."[2]

But could the elephant be harnessed by either company?

THE MEN BEHIND THE UNION PACIFIC

THE Central Pacific Railroad Company *was* a company (albeit an underfinanced one) when President Lincoln signed the Pacific Railroad Act. The Union Pacific was not, even on paper.

The Union Pacific directors who met, as mandated, in Chicago in Sep-

---

*The quote is sometimes attributed to Huntington, but he had earlier left Washington for New York.

tember were in a foul mood. They faced enormous problems and they knew it, and they also fully realized that at least some of those problems could only be solved by a new or amended Pacific Railroad Act. Hence, from the beginning, they were determined to change the very act the American people were raucously celebrating.[3]

On the first day of the three-day meeting, William B. Ogden was named president of the conclave, with Henry V. Poor elected provisional secretary of the railroad. Indicative of the doubts sown by the Pacific Railroad Act, only 67 of the 158 appointed directors bothered to show up, and they unanimously echoed Samuel Curtis's belief that "notwithstanding the grant is liberal, it may still be insufficient" to get the railroad built.[4] The crux of the issue, it was recognized, was the first-mortgage nature of the government bonds. This would seriously impede the sale of the company's own bonds. It was swiftly agreed that this situation would have to be changed.

There was remarkably little debate in Chicago, and most of that concerned the best geographical starting point, which in any case the act had left to President Lincoln. It was decided that the line should be constructed through Denver, no matter the engineering difficulties, and that Utah's Mormons, despite their odd "social habits," would have to be mobilized to work for the railroad. When Colorado governor John Evans rose and told the assemblage that "most of you are railroad men, and I can tell you you can build that road almost all the way without the use of a spade," nervous laughter could be heard.[5] On the third and final day it was resolved to petition Congress to amend the act immediately to permit issuance of a million hundred-dollar shares—to encourage small investors—with a limit of two thousand shares per person. The flashy entrepreneur George Francis Train, speaking at the company's groundbreaking a year later, urged the same change, claiming that only when it had been made would the Union Pacific become a "people's railway."[6]

It was then specified that company subscription books were to be opened at noon, the first Wednesday of November, in thirty-five cities from Portland, Maine, through Denver. One unsung hero, James T. Ryan, later moved "that it would be best to strike out the clause requiring the books to be closed at the end of two weeks." Had he not done so, insult would have been heaped upon injury, for in the first four dismal months of stock sales, a pathetic total of thirty-one shares were purchased by eleven brave men.[7] Brigham Young was the biggest buyer, and he alone paid in full for his five shares. This made the Mormon leader the Union Pacific's first—and, for a long time, only— stockholder "in good standing."[8]

In fact, it would take a full year to meet the minimum subscription of two thousand shares, and then that accomplishment would not be what it seemed. Even the ebullient George Francis Train failed to interest or bamboozle acquaintances in New York, Baltimore, or Philadelphia, selling not a single share despite his efforts and admitting that, for a while, "matters looked a little dark."[9] When things appeared "dark" to this eternal optimist, mere mortals must have been as blind.

The directors who left the Chicago meeting less than optimistic were further depressed by a wave of bad publicity for the company that soon swept the nation's media. Many newspapers hinted at the potential for corruption in so vast and complicated an endeavor, one openly warning the public that "a few intriguers of Wall Street should now reap the benefit" of congressional largess. It was widely feared that those who first advanced the required $200,000 (as the 10 percent down on $2 million worth of stock) would then elect shady officers to the board and would have "the control, the manipulation of these [government] bonds," which would probably result in more speculation than construction.[10] Such critics must have known of Thomas C. Durant.

A cast of characters, literal and figurative, was beginning to gather to help form, influence, dominate, and control the Union Pacific Railroad Company. For the most part they were already familiar with one another; many of them had been born or educated, or had worked in the Troy-Albany area.[11] It was about the only similarity they shared with the leadership of the Central Pacific.

Henry Farnam was a self-taught engineer born in Scipio, New York. Age fifty-nine in 1862, he had worked on the Erie Canal and a number of other New York and New England waterways. In the 1840s, appraising railroads as the wave of the future, he began constructing them in Connecticut and Massachusetts, building a splendid reputation as well.

Moving west in the late 1840s, he helped build the Michigan Southern line, which connected Chicago with the East, and in 1852, with Thomas C. Durant and others, he incorporated the Missouri & Mississippi, beneficiary of a huge government land grant. He and Durant also formed a construction company and made that railroad a reality. Further, in 1853 he chartered the Railroad Bridge Company, which built the first bridge across the Mississippi, at Davenport, Iowa. Rival steamboat operators attempted to sabotage this competition, and when they brought suit, claiming that the bridge was an "obstruction" to river travel, Farnam hired the young lawyer Abraham Lincoln to defend his company. The railroader and the future president became friends, and Farnam would mightily influence the 1860 Republican convention in favor of Lincoln, and the party platform railroad plank. In 1857 he had a serious falling-out with his sometime partner Durant over the latter's questionable financial practices. A rigidly honest man, Farnam became incensed by Durant's bleeding the construction company's treasury to pay unrealistically high dividends to stockholders (chief among whom was Durant), and by his speculation in railroad bonds acquired with stockholders' funds. The panic of 1857 very nearly bankrupted Farnam's various companies thanks to Durant's speculations, and years later, Peter Dey resigned as chief engineer of the Union Pacific because he could not "willingly see them repeat the history of the M&M."[12] Farnam was a major force in the early Union Pacific, but once again Durant's peculations outraged him, and he severed relations with the transcontinental in disgust.[13]

The man he twice broke with, Thomas C. Durant, was an openly, joyously flamboyant promoter, "a bird of striking plumage."[14] Born in 1820 at Lee, Massachusetts, he studied medicine at Albany College, and upon graduation became assistant professor of medicine there before turning briefly to private practice. He then dropped medicine altogether to become director of a New York City branch of a substantial family grain-exporting firm.[15] A man described in the *Railroad Record* as one who "sees no obstacles, fears no difficulties [and] laughs at impossibilities,"[16] the Doctor soon found railroad promotion and construction more rewarding, both financially and psychologically. In the early 1850s he became involved with Farnam's Chicago & Rock Island and Missouri & Mississippi lines, and in those operations he became closely acquainted with Chief Engineer Peter Anthony Dey, Construction Engineer Samuel Benedict Reed, and Junior Engineer Grenville Mellen Dodge, future builders of the Union Pacific.[17]

Unfortunately, Durant's modus operandi was to squeeze as much profit as he could from the construction phase: he was a slave to immediate pecuniary gratification. Farnam, who dissolved their relationship in acid, had a love of railroads that extended to their actual operation.[18] Not as influential as Farnam with politicians, nonetheless Durant is credited with guiding President Lincoln to select Omaha as the railroad's eastern terminus. Later, with his infamous "suspense account," Durant would become *the* symbol of business corruption.

Perhaps the only man in the hemisphere whose flamboyant "plumage" in both dress and life-style outshone that of the Doctor was George Francis Train, born in Boston in 1829. Orphaned in an epidemic when but a toddler, Train by his own terse account "supported self since babyhood."[19] A world-traveling human dynamo—Jules Verne's *Around the World in Eighty Days,* according to him, "made fiction of my fact"[20]—Train made and lost fortunes with the regularity of the tides.

Referred to by the late 1850s as the "Clipper Ship King" for the fleet he operated in the Pacific, he built street railroads in England, ran exporting firms from New York, Liverpool, and Australia, and drove a brisk trade through Canton. Described with a certain awe by the *Louisville Courier Journal* as "a human novel without a hero . . . a sermon that is all text . . . a noonday mystery, a solved conundrum . . . a practical joke in earnest . . . with the brains of twenty men in his head all pulling in different ways,"[21] he was more simply limned by the *Omaha Weekly Herald*: "Train reads lessons to the world at large."[22]

Train was a man who scrambled image and reality. He was, in fact, "the perfect front man,"[23] who later claimed that one day he simply decided he would "build a railway across the Rocky Mountains and the Great American Desert."[24]

To do this seemed relatively easy to him, for his greater scheme was to use the iron rails as tools to create "a chain of great towns across the continent, connecting Boston with San Francisco by a magnificent highway of cities."[25] He actually tried to do it. He expected to make one of his projected towns, Columbus, Nebraska, the new capital of the United States because of its location at the "precise" geographic center of the country. The fact that he owned seven hundred choice acres there might have influenced him.[26]

Wise men, however, while amused by his antics, did not dismiss George Francis Train. After all, he did help create the Union Pacific, and he literally made from whole cloth the scandalous Crédit Mobilier construction company (and owned the associated Crédit Foncier, a real-estate development company), remarking proudly in later years that while others had been disgraced or bankrupted by it, he had "three generations living off Crédit Mobilier" profits.[27] Further, he had unobtrusively bought up a large proportion of preboom Omaha's best building lots, which, as future African explorer Henry Morton Stanley reported in 1867, became a suburb known as Train Town, "filled with numerous cottages" built, to Train's great profit, by his own Crédit Foncier.[28]

As different as possible from the drum-beating Train, and appalled by him, was John A. Dix, destined to become the Union Pacific's first president. Age sixty-five in 1863, Dix had run away from his Boscawen, New Hampshire, farm at the age of fourteen to fight in the War of 1812, thus beginning a sporadic career with the army, from which he resigned a highly decorated major. A well-educated, scholarly man, Dix for a while published a highly regarded Albany scientific and literary journal, the *Northern Light,* and over the years wrote a number of books of essays and travel accounts.

An extremely influential man reputed to be of puritanical rectitude, Dix was secretary of state of New York, several times a United States senator, President Pierce's blocked choice for secretary of state, and briefly, in 1861, secretary of the treasury. This French-speaking, College of Montreal–educated soldier-scholar-politician had become, at Durant's suggestion, president of the Missouri & Mississippi in the 1850s. That railroad benefited from his prominence and respectability without suffering from his scrutiny while Durant benefited from his malleability and frequent absences.[29] A dedicated Pacific Railroader, he had remarked in 1854 to Dey, Dodge, and others, after a tour of the Chicago & Rock Island tracks, "Gentlemen, we may as well come to the point at once—we are on our way to the Pacific, and we intend to get there."[30] Lacking the energy and acquisitiveness of men like Durant and Train, Dix had the political and military connections they so desperately needed. Commissioned major general by President Lincoln when the war erupted, Dix by 1863 was commanding officer of the Department of the East, conveniently headquartered in New York City a few blocks from Union Pacific offices.

Not at all lacking in acquisitiveness was Sidney Dillon, a man with railroads in his blood. He was born into a dirt-poor family in rural Montgomery County, New York (very near Albany), in 1812. He worked from the age of seven, and in his twenties labored on the Mohawk & Hudson, New York's first railroad.[31] He then worked on various New England railroads and was construction boss for part of the Boston & Albany in 1839. Later, with his own company, he built other railroads in the New England area. His habit of taking part of his earnings in stock certificates paid off and he was, by 1862, an extremely wealthy financier. He became a Union Pacific director (and major stockholder in that company and the Crédit Mobilier) in 1864, and remained one for twenty-eight years, serving as president of the company for twelve.[32]

Also in the vanguard of the Pacific Railroad dream was Henry Varnum Poor, age forty-two. Born in a Maine hamlet, Poor trained as a lawyer, but was soon smitten by railroading. In 1849 he founded and edited the respected *American Railroad Journal* in New York City, and soon created the annual *Poor's Manual of Railroads of the United States,* a heroic compendium of raw data and financial commentary. Poor, also an accomplished cartographer, was paying attention to men like Judah when most railroaders were laughing at them.[33]

A firm supporter of the 1853 survey, Poor originally favored a government-built Pacific Railroad along a Northern route. He was appointed one of the government's five Union Pacific commissioners in 1862, and the year after his election as the company's provisional secretary (a potential conflict of interest), he became secretary, quitting in disgust a few months later after clashing with Durant. As the first, and for a time the only, full-time officer of the Union Pacific, Poor handled virtually all its routine business, and strained himself to the limit using his many contacts to stimulate investment capital.[34]

Born at tiny Romulus, New York, in 1825, Peter Anthony Dey received a classical education at Geneva College and then studied law. In 1846 he went to work at the New York City offices of the New York & Erie Railroad and caught the railroading virus, retraining himself as an engineer. In that capacity he found work on the Erie and other canals, and by the early 1850s was building railroads in Indiana, and, with young Grenville Dodge, the Chicago & Rock Island and Missouri & Mississippi lines. At Farnam's request Dey surveyed the entire Platte Valley and beyond, and while in the field became a convert to the Pacific Railroad concept.[35] Described by Dodge as "a man of great ability, probity and integrity,"[36] Dey was preordained to clash with Durant (with whom he had worked in Illinois) when he became chief engineer of the Union Pacific in 1863.

Dey's early assistant, Grenville Dodge, was born at Danvers, Massachusetts, in 1831, and trained at Vermont's Partridge's School and Norwich University, graduating as a civil and military engineer. When only twenty-two, he began specializing in railroad survey work, and Dey recognized his keen eye, hiring him for surveying and construction in Illinois, Iowa, and Nebraska. An early spokesman for the Pacific Railroad, Dodge was perhaps the first to openly champion the Platte Valley route. He had been sent as far west as the Rockies by Farnam, who was convinced that the Illinois and Iowa lines were but the first stages of a transcontinental.[37]

As a colonel, and later general in the Civil War, Dodge made a name for himself both on the battlefield (he was gravely wounded leading a charge at Pea Ridge, and shot in the head two years later at Atlanta) and as railroad repair and construction chief for Ulysses S. Grant, and later, Sherman. His connections with these men—and General Philip Sheridan, a friend since 1861—were of inestimable value to the Union Pacific, and went far to explain why it was Dodge who was chosen to succeed Peter Dey as chief engineer. His almost simultaneous election to Congress from his Iowa district (a job he all but ignored), while an inconvenience to him, was clearly a plus for the railroad.[38]

Many of these men, then, had the common bond of the Illinois and Iowa experience. They had built railroads on the very edge of the Great American Desert and had surveyed deep into the void. They had seen the railroads they built gush settlers onto new lands whose value was owed to the iron rails. Iowa's population had tripled in a decade because of the railroads, reaching 674,913 by 1860.[39]

Some of these men—notably Dodge, who made his home for a while west of Omaha, and Dey—had surveyed most or all of the six-hundred-mile-long Platte Valley. In the late summer of 1859, Abraham Lincoln visited Council Bluffs (where he had twelve building lots) and encountered Dodge, who had just returned from his third reconnaissance of the valley. It is known that the gangly lawyer talked at length with the engineer about the Pacific Railroad, and at one point the future president apparently asked, "Dodge, what's the best route for a Pacific Railroad to the West?" Dodge's retort was automatic: "From this town out the Platte Valley."[40]

This was no lightning bolt of inspiration on Dodge's part, for the buffalo, perhaps nature's most intuitive of engineers, had used the valley for millennia. Being lazy beasts, buffalo always found and followed the path of least resistance and exertion in their meanderings. It was not the shortest, but the *easiest* route between two points that appealed to the buffalo, and the broad, flat Platte Valley, like all major Western conduits, "had been worn deep long before the first human foot was planted on the North American Continent."[41] The Mormons had been transiting the valley since the 1840s, Judah had anticipated its use as a route from the scantiest data before the Central Pacific was created, and Ben Holladay's stagecoaches utilized it as a highway to link Salt Lake City and Denver to the East.[42] George L. Colegrove, a California railroad man who trekked through it before a rail was in place, recalled that "there was a regular beaten road all the way across the Plains."[43] The Platte Valley, then, was a natural, its only drawbacks being a dearth of good timber and a wealth of hostile Indians.

Hence, some in concert, others as individuals, the men who would create and build the Union Pacific determined its eastern terminus—within a twenty-mile radius—and the first third or more of the route to the Pacific. So perfect was the terrain, so mild the grade, so few the bridges, curves, and obstacles, that the respected *Railroad Record* [44] estimated that the first 600 miles or so past the Missouri River could be constructed for a paltry $5,000 per mile—more cheaply, in fact, than any comparable stretch of railroad in the world. [45] Durant, reading this, must have winced. Henry V. Poor, a man who certainly knew his railroads— especially this one—wrote in 1863 with only slightly less optimism that "the road could be built cheaper than any ever constructed in the States. As it is, $20,000 per mile will be *ample* for the first 600 miles." [46] Not at all what Dr. Durant wanted to hear. Similarly, Union Pacific engineer Jason A. Evans, after surveying the valley in 1864, wrote that "a region more favorable for railroad purposes does not exist in this or any other country," lauding the terrain for its "extreme uniformity." [47]

THE "SHOPKEEPERS" HARNESS
THE ELEPHANT

A S SOON as he had wound up his business—which included filing an official "location map" with the secretary of the interior on June 30, 1862— Judah and an assistant, Colonel George Trumble Moore Davis (George Francis Train's father-in-law), left Washington for New York. With Huntington already there, they sought to begin purchasing the initial hardware for the Central Pacific, "upon the best terms [Huntington] could get, before further advances [in price] took place." [48]

Huntington, the quintessential businessman, had spent weeks trying desperately to sell stocks, obtain credit, and talk with manufacturers. Virtually everything would have to be purchased in and shipped from the war-torn East: all iron products, from locomotives, handcars, and rails to spikes, fishplates, and telegraph insulators; blasting powder, fuses, and percussion caps; shovels, picks, and even nails. The list was endless, for California, blessed as it was by nature, could provide a railroad with only lumber, earth, stone, and perhaps labor. Huntington's list was as expensive as it was long, for what his railroad most urgently needed was precisely what generals McClellan, Halleck, Grant, and a score of other Union generals were demanding: iron products, locomotives, and explosives. Prices rose dizzyingly and, as a second-priority customer, the Californian had to accustom himself to long delays between order and shipment. Rails that had sold for $55 a ton or less in 1860 now fetched $115, with Huntington forced to pay as much as $250 for some batches. There were months when rails were simply unavailable at any price.[49] Each ton of rails, moreover, cost another $17.50 in shipping charges to San Francisco, and during the war insurance premiums soared. Also, the prewar price of common spikes—2.5 cents a pound—had become 6.5 cents, and blasting powder rose from $2.50 to as high as $15 a keg.[50] Everything was in short supply, and certain items, such as explosives, required special presidential license.

Shipping charges had risen dramatically, and shipping per se was scarce in wartime America, for the merchant marine was kept busy hauling government consignments to and (mostly) from Europe for the war effort. The first small locomotive Huntington shipped west, via Cape Horn, cost the company $13,688 (Judah had earlier estimated $8,000), an additional $2,282 in freight charges, and a huge insurance premium.[51] The shorter Panama route had become prohibitively expensive, and only true emergencies could justify its use.* Confederate commerce raiders such as the *Alabama* and *Florida* caused insurance rates on the Cape Horn route to inflate by some 700 percent, and had introduced the factor of risk; the Southern warship *Shenandoah* cruised off California in 1864, proving that the threat also existed there. While no vessel carrying Central Pacific equipment was ever taken by Confederate raiders, the mere existence of rebel warships severely complicated the company's logistics and kept Mark Hopkins awake nights.[53]

How on earth were four "shopkeepers" and an impecunious engineer going to buy and ship what was needed for the first thirty-one, or fifty, miles of road, miles that Judah had (under)estimated would cost some $3 million just to build? They were not rich, the Big Four; they were comfortable. Leland Stanford was probably twice as wealthy as Huntington, but Hopkins and Crocker were probably less so. Huntington later admitted to having been "worth" $200,000 in 1862, but most of that amount was in property rather than hard cash.† His reputation as a scrupulously honest businessman had, however, earned him a million-dollar credit line. But that credit line had been established for the hardware business, something he was an expert at, not for railroading. Whatever credit he had in the East he soon milked dry.[55]

In New York, Huntington could never rely upon his company's treasury, for stock sales long remained abysmal. Marcus Boruck, official Central Pacific stock agent in high-rolling San Francisco, advertised and all but waylaid passersby that fall, but closed down his office after twenty-two days, having sold a total of fifteen shares to three subscribers, whose 10 percent down (if the stocks were sold at

---

*In 1865, in an emergency, the company paid out $8,100 to get a single locomotive across the narrow isthmus.[52]

†David Lavender suggests convincingly that none of the Big Four was as wealthy as they later claimed (in the face of investigations of railroad profits), and he notes that of the four, only Hopkins ever paid in full for his early Central Pacific stock shares.[54]

par) would have produced only $150.[56] And few shares were sold at par. So little faith was put in company stock that some shares would sell in 1865 for nineteen cents on the dollar, and the company was ecstatic to get its hands on even that little dribble of cash.[57] With only a few thousand in the coffers and little hope of more to come from investors, the Big Four *as* the Big Four, rather than as the Central Pacific Railroad Company, would have to raise the requisite money on the strength of their own reputations as merchants, a phenomenon, on this scale, unique in American business history.

When Collis Huntington had sojourned east that summer, his pockets hardly bulged with his state's fabled gold. Instead, he brought with him a sheaf of letters of introduction and recommendation from some of the Pacific Coast's leading businessmen. One of these was written by San Francisco banking buccaneer Darius Ogden Mills, who at the time was a director of the Union Pacific, and who had several times declined the honor of buying Central Pacific stock. One of the richest men on the Coast, Mills had often done business with Huntington and Hopkins, and while too shrewd an operator to invest in any but a sure thing, he did give Huntington, as Crocker later recounted, "a paper testifying to our responsibility and our honor, as men and merchants and [saying] that whatever we agreed to he believed we would faithfully adhere to."[58] Another door-opening letter had been written by company investor and shipping tycoon Orville Lambard, who with his brother Charles had large-scale interests in California, as well as Boston and Newport.[59]

Such "papers" were destined to work miracles. Helped mightily by Huntington's arrogantly serene confidence, they smoothly unlocked the office doors of the nation's largest railroad manufacturers. With Judah and Colonel Davis inspecting and selecting the gear, Huntington visited boardrooms, factories, and foundries in New York, New Jersey, Pennsylvania, and Massachusetts, driving the best deals that could be had in a wartime economy by someone without cash.[60]

He also continued to try to hawk stock—at which he failed miserably—and procure loans as well as credit. From Massachusetts shovel maker (and future linchpin of the Union Pacific and Crédit Mobilier) Oliver Ames, who had shipped tens of thousands of his famous spades to Huntington and Hopkins, came a two-hundred-thousand-dollar loan and more letters of introduction to other bankers and manufacturers.[61] Ames desperately wanted the Pacific Railroad to get under way. After all, he did manufacture shovels. From him and anyone else who would chance it, the Californian borrowed every loose penny. Armed with written power of attorney for Crocker, Hopkins, Stanford, and Judah, he pledged all of their names, their honor, and their property to obtain the resources they needed, and he barely succeeded at that.[62] New York banker William E. Dodge risked a significant sum, and would optimistically continue to reach for his wallet, at one point holding personal (not company) notes from the Big Four totaling an incredible $3,250,000.[63] Very few Easterners were so quixotic.

In July, Judah embarked for California in another well-stocked cabin, leaving Colonel Davis to assist Huntington, who "borrowed, hocked and huckstered in the East" for years, only occasionally returning to Sacramento.[64] Huntington was a fine huckster, and, remembered Charlie Crocker, since "we could not borrow a dollar of money on the faith of the Company, we bought the first 50 miles of iron on our own personal obligations" through Huntington, who often divided his week to spend three days in New York, two in Boston, and two in the capital.[65] Over six thousand tons of rails, half a dozen locomotives, railroad cars, and the lesser paraphernalia of construction (worth $721,000) were soon ordered and earmarked for shipping. Most of this was "paid for" with heavily discounted company bonds whose interest was personally guaranteed by the Big Four.[66] In later years Huntington would proudly reflect that he never took a commission or fee on his myriad deals: "I handled $300,000,000, and never took a cent."[67] "We carried an immense load," he conceded. They carried it well.[68]

Judah arrived at Sacramento in mid-August, eager to join the survey parties he had ordered into the mountains, but he first informed the company directors that it was high time to send other survey teams deep into Nevada, no matter the restrictions of the railroad act. Both he and Huntington unflinchingly believed that Nevada would be theirs to track. The engineer was cheered to learn by telegraph that the secretary of the interior had accepted his location map on August 2, and had accordingly withdrawn from sale, preemption, or private entry the promised land-grant acreage along the route.[69] Also boosting his morale was news that the city of Sacramento had given the Central Pacific as a gift thirty valuable acres along its levee (thirteen hundred feet of riverfront) for the company's headquarters, depots, shops, and roundhouse.[70]

The engineer's elation soon withered in the harsh business climate of California. While Huntington was busily running up mammoth debts in their names in the East, and conferring with his old friend Richard Franchot, now a congressman and strategically placed on the House Select Committee on the Pacific Railroad,* Central Pacific stock, so lovingly embellished with Anna's artwork, could hardly be sold on either coast or in between. Also, the first spadeful of earth had yet to be turned on the railroad, yet somehow the Dutch Flat and Donner Lake Wagon Road was progressing with brio. This oddity prompted skeptics, rivals, and enemies to talk and write about the supposed "Dutch Flat Swindle," which put another ball and chain on company stock. So well organized were the "swindle" mongers that in 1864 they published an anonymous 128-page pamphlet, *Great Dutch Flat Swindle! The City of San Francisco Demands*

---

*He would soon resign, personally raise a New York Volunteer regiment, and rise to the rank of general.

Justice! Also, the prestigious San Francisco newspaper *Alta California* consistently raised the issue, and slandered the Central Pacific and its leadership in other ways as well.[71] The many who for their various reasons opposed the Central Pacific spread rumors that the railroad was never meant to be part of a transcontinental, and that its officers secretly planned only to drive it to Dutch Flat to tap the lucrative freight to and from the mines along their own wagon road.[72] The rumor scared off potential investors, and was partly the cause of Dr. Strong's resignation from the board. Exiting, he sold his stock in both the Central Pacific and the wagon road to the Big Four.[73] Partly to counteract all the rumors, Judah took out an advertisement in the *Sacramento Union* (August 22), almost begging anyone who knew of a better route through the Sierras to come forward with the facts and data by October 1. No one did.[74]

There were also contretemps among the company's founders, and a growing friction. One problem was the relatively minor issue of the Central Pacific's office. Judah had been insisting that a handsome office building be erected on one of Sacramento's main thoroughfares, increasing the company's visibility. He personally designed an impressive brick, confidence-inspiring edifice that he claimed could be built for about $12,000. He was peremptorily voted down at a board meeting, however, and on Huntington's distant (telegraphed) orders, an unpainted shack was raised in one working day at a cost of $150. That depressing little building stood forlornly on I Street until 1908, but in any event, almost all company business was transacted, as before, in an office over Stanford's grocery store on K Street.[75]

On October 22, the chief engineer issued his annual report, which in this case was a blatant prospectus to goad investment. Glossing over problems and stressing profits, Judah assured his credulous readers that the timber alone on the company's future 960,000 acres of California land grants would yield at least $162 an acre, or an astronomical (and utterly fanciful) $81 million in all. Henry V. Poor, back in New York, surely read Judah's report, and he must have chuckled, for a few years earlier he had written disparagingly of land-grant acreage. Most of it, he felt, was of such poor quality that its sale price "would hardly equal the expenses of a preliminary survey" of it.[76]

Judah also claimed enthusiastically and naïvely that the government would use the Central Pacific for so much official business "as to repay them before the bonds come due." That was nonsense, and he must have known it. The company's own bonds, he declared, "will probably command a premium in the market," and were destined to sell well in Europe. In reality, Central Pacific stocks and bonds were shunned like lepers in Europe.[77] In this report and even in his own personal notebooks, Judah continued to horrendously underestimate costs, citing tunneling at fifty dollars a foot (a thousand dollars was closer to the truth), rails at forty-eight dollars a ton, and locomotives at eight thousand dollars, including transportation costs. He displayed a singular naïveté for an engineering genius, and a strong tendency to be less than honest with the investing public.[78]

In November, after filing the company's official acceptance of the terms of the railroad act with the secretary of the interior, the Big Four, Judah, James Bailey, and Lucius A. Booth agreed to purchase additional large amounts of stock, both to provide day-to-day operating capital and to demonstrate their personal confidence in the company.[79] In Charlie Crocker's words, they "resolved that we would go in and subscribe enough stock to organize the company *and control it.*"[80] Each of the Big Four bought a further 345 shares, with the others subscribing for lesser amounts. A prime additional motivation might well have been to keep Brannan, the Lambards, and others distinctly minority stockholders and themselves clearly dominant on the board.

That same month, plans for actual construction were discussed and debated. Crocker, who had bossed a small iron foundry in Indiana for a while, felt himself a capable construction boss. This Judah openly doubted, but, supported by the rest of the Big Four, Crocker drew up a contract for constructing the first eighteen miles, from the foot of K Street to the village of Junction (now Roseville), to connect there with Sam Brannan's California Central line. Over Judah's and Bailey's protests, the Charles Crocker Contracting Company was awarded the first stretch of road two days after Christmas, and two days after Crocker had resigned from the board (keeping his stock, of course), to avoid charges of conflict of interest. His place on the board was taken by a new investor, his brother, E.B., who had recently been appointed the company's attorney. He had also—hardly coincidentally—just been named interim chief justice of the California Supreme Court, by the company's president, Governor Leland Stanford. Clearly, not all the huckstering was taking place back east.[81]

The contract, soon subcontracted, called for Crocker's company to receive for its labors $350,000 in cash, $50,000 in discounted company stock, and $10,000 in discounted company bonds. The stock and bond figures were par values, but Crocker received them at 50 percent of par for the former and 30 percent for the latter.[82] With the contract signed, Crocker began liquidating his retail business in order to fund his new venture. So little faith was there at this time in Central Pacific stock that Huntington, still in New York, had to write his own brother, Solon, urging him not to sell his shares. He told Solon to hold on to the certificates, for within a few years, he promised, Central Pacific stock earnings "will not be less than 24%" annually.[83]

To Judah, who constantly thought in terms of "my railroad," something was dramatically remiss. Suspecting (correctly) that *all* of the Big Four were involved with the construction company and might well bankrupt the railroad to profit from its building, Judah fumed, fretted, and began to plot. He must also have wondered why, when the Central Pacific treasury was habitually bare, there was no apparent lack of cash to continue what was to him the distinctly secondary wagon road.[84]

PLOT AND COUNTERPLOT IN CALIFORNIA

A S BOTH midpoint and turning point of the American Civil War, 1863 was a year suitably complex worldwide. Henry Ford was born and so were Norwegian painter Edvard Munch and Frenchman Lucien Pissarro, while Ferdinand Victor Eugène Delacroix died and James Whistler painted some of his finest works. John Stuart Mill wrote on utilitarianism, John Hanning Speke sought the White Nile, the London Underground was begun, roller skating was introduced into the United States, and a French army captured Mexico City. West Virginia became a state, Lincoln proclaimed the first Thanksgiving Day and supervised the capping of the Capitol dome, Cambodia became a French protectorate, and Perrier water was first marketed. Meanwhile, the Ruby Valley Treaty with several tribes gave railroads the right to traverse their lands in Nevada, Bethlehem Steel was founded to make rails, the first Bessemer-process steel plant opened its doors in Michigan, and the first railroad in New Zealand linked Christchurch to Ferrymead. More sand was excavated at Suez, and Sacramento witnessed a groundbreaking ceremony.

Sacramento's streets lay covered with an almost primeval mud that unseasonably warm January 8 when the Central Pacific Railroad Company ceremonially broke ground. Several days of torrential rain had, as always, turned the thirteen-year-old city into something resembling a populated swamp. It was not, perhaps, as calamitous as the day in 1862 when Leland Stanford had to go to his inauguration in a rowboat, but it was a mess. Even the bales of hay thoughtfully scattered along K Street for spectator seats were distinctly settling into the goo.[85] Those who used the bales actually stood on them, but most people preferred wagon beds or horseback for perches to view the ceremony. Stanford was there, and so was Crocker, but Hopkins, depressed by the enormity of their risk (he was, after all, the bookkeeper), had declined the honor. Huntington was still huckstering in the East, and Judah, as usual, was in the Sierras.[86]

After the typical and boring round of speeches (including one by Stanford that was a blatant plug for company stock), orchestrated by master of ceremonies Charlie Crocker, the governor used a borrowed, silver-bladed shovel to throw a few pounds of damp earth from a flag-draped cart onto the levee. The great labor had officially commenced. Crocker, perspiring profusely, also deposited a spadeful, and then barked out a rousing speech that ended with the promise "All that I have—all of my own strength, intellect and energy—are devoted to the building of this section which I have undertaken."[87] A reasonably charismatic man if not a spellbinding orator, Crocker drew a round of applause, which temporarily drowned out the rhythmic "thud, thud," of the company's steam pile driver, at work on the banks of the American River.*

As the redwood piles were being hammered into the riverbank, the Central Pacific suffered a hard and totally unexpected blow. President Lincoln had earlier agreed with Huntington that a five-foot gauge (California standard) should be adopted for the Pacific Railroad. In January, he had committed his decision to paper, but a storm of protest arose in Congress—in part inspired by the Union Pacific—and from the secretary of the interior. Under duress, the president signed an act mandating what was to become the American (it was already the British) standard gauge; four feet, eight and a half inches.[88] The Big Four were horrified, for Huntington had ordered locomotives and cars in the California gauge. He had to scramble madly to change all existing orders, and this caused delays and yet higher prices. Worse, it ultimately meant that on the first thirty miles or so of Central Pacific line, *three* rails would have to be laid, to accommodate the local feeder lines with their five-foot spans.[89]

All this while the governor had been using his position to lobby the legislature for additional aid to the railroad. With incredible openness, he bludgeoned legislators into passing various helpful bills, including one that authorized San Francisco, Sacramento, and Placer counties to purchase specified amounts of Central Pacific stock, at par. He also wangled in April a bill in which the legislature donated $15 million in state bonds, to be disbursed at a rate of $10,000 a mile upon completion of twenty-mile segments. The company in return was to transport state personnel and freight for free.[90] However, in the case of every aid bill that passed the legislature, suits were brought by the company's many enemies, and litigation gravely delayed the actual aid. That most suits were eventually won by the Central Pacific was due to Stanford's clout as governor and, later, former governor, and E.B.'s power both on and off the state supreme court bench.[91]

A typical example of this legal harassment came when San Francisco County voted 6,329 to 3,118 in May to purchase the authorized $600,000 of company stock (Placer County could and did subscribe to $250,000, and Sacramento to $300,000).[92] Almost immediately, "a drayman named French," who was hired by some local businessmen, brought suit on grounds of unconstitutionality. The aid was tied up for an agonizing year before the state supreme court ruled in the company's favor. Even then, another six months' delay ensued and the court had to issue a writ of mandamus to get county officials to act, and, when at last they did, instead of buying the Central Pacific stock—which would have been a vote of confidence in the company—they simply (almost humiliatingly) *gave* the railroad $400,000 in 7 percent, gold-bearing San Francisco city bonds, as if

---

*This machine was one of the few concessions to modern technology the company made prior to Promontory Point.

to demonstrate their total lack of faith.[93] Further distressing, as Hopkins soon found out, was the fact that city and county bonds, if sold at all by the company, had to be discounted an average of 30 percent; so San Francisco's tepid aid package actually generated only about $280,000 in fresh capital. Such things did not go unnoticed in the marketplace, and Central Pacific paper remained depressed.[94]

There was also a major delay on a legislative gift of $500,000 to the company (the fifteen-million-dollar bond scheme had been sidetracked), and that aid, eventually forthcoming, arrived in widely separated installments. Finally, in pecuniary agony, the Central Pacific begged the legislature to guarantee the interest on $1.5 million in company bonds, in return for "a valuable granite quarry, with free transportation of stone for public buildings, and of all state troops, criminals and lunatics." After much deliberation, and some litigation, in 1864 the state agreed, and those particular bonds became marketable with only a minor discount.[95]

All of the proposed aid arrived late—if at all—and, by mid-1863, as Lee and Meade clashed at Gettysburg, the Central Pacific and, in consequence, the Crocker Contracting Company, were almost penniless, with most of the former's anemic capital apparently siphoned off into the wagon road. With poverty, but not necessarily because of it, came disunion within the company,* with the Big Four normally in agreement among themselves, but with Judah and Bailey often dissenting outsiders. Even the chief engineer at this point was beginning to think that there just might be something to the "Dutch Flat Swindle" rumors. So did Darius Ogden Mills, who opened a virulent propaganda campaign against the "swindlers," claiming that his bank would "never invest a nickel" in the Central Pacific. Movement of company stock, always slow, became glacial.[97]

Judah's suspicions deepened when Hopkins—who had Huntington's power of attorney and proxy voting rights—demanded that all subscribers pay for their stock in full, ostensibly to pump some cash into the treasury. No longer the naïf, Judah must have immediately realized that this was an unsubtle ploy to drive the smaller stockholders out. Indeed, drawing money from some obscure source, the Big Four *were* beginning to buy the others out—and cheaply. Even Bailey, disenchanted, was to sell out of the Central Pacific in September, and was replaced on the board by Hopkins's old partner E. H. Miller, Jr. Charles Marsh, an enigmatic figure throughout, remained a stockholder.[98]

Judah, watching the growing power of the Big Four, was destined to be buffeted again, for sometime in the fall he was asked to pay at least 10 percent on the stock he had been given in lieu of salary. That amounted in his eyes to

---

*Stanford was also agitated because he had withdrawn from the 1863 gubernatorial race after savage political infighting. No more could the company rely on major political favors, though Stanford did retain a certain political influence.[96]

a tax on money already paid him. He had precious little in the way of financial resources, and the Big Four knew it, but somehow he did meet the challenge. The engineer was not about to back out of the project he had himself initiated.[99]

Increasingly, the chief engineer was treated as a mere employee by the Big Four, and, while he attended monthly board meetings when he could, he was not privy to dozens of Big Four conclaves held above the grocery or hardware store. He was, in short, being frozen out of his own railroad. As he worked, he fumed, spending most of his time in the Sierras, where he was happiest. With his new assistant, Samuel Skerry Montague, whom he had hired away from the Sacramento Valley road, he did the final geological tests and grading estimates. The thirty-three-year-old Montague was learning a portion of his trade from a master, and the next six years would reveal that he learned it superbly. So was another newcomer, Assistant Engineer Lewis M. Clement, a quiet Canadian canal engineer hired by Judah simply because there was a shortage of railroad engineers on the Coast. The chief engineer trained Clement as a location engineer, and succeeding years would find the Canadian excelling in areas of engineering he knew nothing about at all in 1863. He would do specialized tunnel engineering (as the engineer in charge of the exceedingly difficult Summit Tunnel), build dozens of bridges, and design the original snowsheds that protected the mountain line from avalanches.[100] Together that summer these men and their crews solved most of the engineering problems of railroading in the Sierras. They had the answers, but did the Big Four have the money?

Down on the flatlands, construction moved choppily ahead. Crocker contracted most of the work out and his contractors in their turn subcontracted. Most had labor problems, some were grossly incompetent, and none finished his allotted segment of line. Only work on the American River Bridge proceeded as planned. Crocker, himself a not too efficient novice at this type of work (albeit a good learner), eventually had to take the entire eighteen miles in hand personally, and by late April he could proudly—if belatedly—announce that the first seven miles were properly graded and ready for track.[101] But the wait until October for the arrival of the first rails was so long that some of the grading washed out and had to be redone. In any case, Charlie Crocker, stalking the line in his shirt sleeves, very nearly went broke, and that over the easiest eighteen miles of work the Central Pacific would see. He had naïvely expected to unload the portion of his pay in company stocks and bonds on the market at or near par (he must have read Judah's prospectus). He could barely get rid of them at all.[102]

Briefly in Sacramento in May for a directors' meeting, Judah found himself pressed by another scheme hatched by the Big Four. They now wanted every director to bear equally the costs of building the road. The Big Four themselves *might* have been able to bear that burden for a while, and Bailey could have (had he decided to), but Judah simply could not. Were they scheming to force him out? He returned to his mountains determined to turn the tables on the "shop-keepers."[103]

In an official July 1 report, the chief engineer, on the basis of his latest surveys, estimated the cost of the first fifty miles of construction at just over $3 million, exclusive of rolling stock and buildings. He noted that the first two bridges alone had consumed almost 300,000 board feet of very thick lumber, as well as hundreds of massive redwood piles. He admitted that more brick culverts had had to be built than he had anticipated, and that he had chosen to use sturdy and relatively expensive eight-foot-long redwood crossties; over sixty-eight thousand were then on order. The report also noted that rails were soon expected to arrive at a rate of five hundred tons a month, and that they could be laid as fast as they came in.[104]

About the time the report was going to press, Huntington returned to Sacramento with a fascinating idea that Judah alone found offensive. The federal government would grant bonds of $48,000 per mile for work in the mountains, but only $16,000 for the flatland approaches to them. Just where, Judah was asked, did the Sierras *legally* begin? It was clear to the engineer, as an engineer, that they began twenty-two miles from the start of track, where the first major granite outcroppings could be seen. Huntington disagreed: he wanted them closer to Sacramento. It was time for him to huckster in the West.

Although Judah insisted on mile 22 and refused to abuse his reputation by claiming otherwise, and despite the fact that the California Supreme Court had years before, in a mining case, ruled mile 31, Huntington and Crocker asked for and received a different judgment. This came from State Geologist Josiah D. Whitney, State Surveyor General J. F. Houghton, and Edward F. Beale, United States surveyor general for California. Crocker personally took Whitney into the field one day, and, he recalled (one can almost picture him winking), "did not ask him to do anything except that I wished him to decide where true justice would place the Western base of the Sierra Nevadas."[105] Whitney and Huntington's two other expert witnesses were soon in agreement. The base of the Sierras was found at Arcade Creek, where red and black soil met—a mere seven miles from the Sacramento levee.

In concrete terms this meant $480,000 more in government bonds than Judah would have awarded his own company and $768,000 more than the state supreme court would have permitted. Helping to pay for the first stretch of construction, these bonds were of crucial importance to the cash-poor company, and Huntington in September sent a report with affidavits from Whitney, Houghton, and Beale (but *not* Judah) to Washington, requesting approval of the "early" Sierras by the president and Department of the Interior.[106] The following January, President Lincoln formally assented to mile 7, and the company—destined to wait a long time for those bonds—hoped it would now be a bit easier to attract

Eastern capital.[107] Faith, the Big Four had demonstrated, can indeed move mountains.

An unusually moral man, Judah saw in this maneuver pressure brought to bear on public servants, outright cheating, and misuse of both the public trust and moneys. To him it was but one more sign of the Big Four's cynical greed. In league with Bailey, he determined that if the Central Pacific was to become a reality, the Big Four would have to go. Bailey, who had wide commercial contacts, knew that San Francisco banker Charles McLaughlin was both able and willing to buy a controlling interest in the company. It would have been a natural, for McLaughlin already owned the Western Pacific Railroad, full of potential but still on the drawing board, with a land grant of some of the state's finest acreage.[108] However, while McLaughlin was clearly interested, negotiations ended abruptly when he was told that Huntington was willing to sell out his interest. The banker sent Bailey a terse telegram that is a lasting tribute to Huntington's business reputation: "If old Huntington is going to sell out, I am not going in."[109] Bailey accepted the verdict and himself sold out, leaving Judah to stand alone.

The engineer had been in touch with Eastern financiers, and was optimistic that he would not have to stand alone. He was certain that he could attract powerful investors such as Vanderbilt in New York and Boston. Hence in a shouting-match, showdown meeting with the Big Four, he won their almost snide agreement that they would each sell out for $100,000 if any one of the directors could raise the money.[110] Things must have appeared bleak indeed if this was the case, for they would have been selling at a heavy loss. Or, perhaps more likely, they simply did not believe that the engineer could come up with the money.

Almost as if to mollify the chief engineer, the board of directors, which now included the governor's brother Asa P. ("Phil") Stanford, voted to pay him $25,000 in stock for his services. Judah was by this point enjoying a rather large salary, but apparently welcomed the stock. He must have been utterly nonplussed when, just three days later, the board voted him another $66,000 in company paper. No matter the market discounts, this was a hefty recompense indeed. For what?[111] What is all the more striking is that just a month earlier, the company's own books showed a total of only 7,115 shares subscribed and a paltry $210,930 paid in.[112] What *was* going on? One thing is clear. Judah did not refuse the stock.

Far from being bought off, the engineer made plans to leave for the East to talk with potential investors, some of whom he had been in correspondence with. In September he sold his Nevada Railroad stock to Crocker to provide cash for the trip. To this day there is controversy concerning whether or not Judah actually sold out of the Central Pacific as well, getting rid of his new stock. Some[113] claim that the Big Four bought him out for $100,000, but no record of this sale exists,[114] and it would hardly have made sense if he hoped to attract Eastern capital to buy the others out. The Big Four, by prior agreement, were not obligated to sell to anyone but a company director. Further, it is known that to his last day Judah drew his annual ten-thousand-dollar salary as chief engineer.[115]

On a gusty October 3, Anna and her husband boarded the steamer *St. Louis* at San Francisco, with no one on the pier to see them off. Ironically (and without knowing it), a few days later they passed the decrepit *Herald of the Morning,* beating up the wind to San Francisco out of New York. Aboard were the first hundred tons of rails, the first locomotive, and assorted hardware ordered by Huntington for the Central Pacific. Three more of the company's cargoes were not far behind.[116] On October 7, the locomotive, christened the *Governor Stanford,* was wrestled onto the Sacramento levee in knocked-down form. It was soon joined by the *Pacific,* the *C. P. Huntington,* and the *T. D. Judah,* each weighing some twenty-two tons.[117] A name on an undistinguished locomotive was the only honor Judah was to gain.

Judah would never see those first rails in place, nor the engine that bore his name. Transiting Panama he contracted a fever, probably yellow fever; his wife later wrote that "he was an overworked man, and just such men fall victim" to tropical disease.[118] Aboard ship in the Caribbean, Judah, with shaking hand, wrote a note to his old friend Dr. Strong. He told the druggist that if he was successful in the East, the company would "pass into the hands of men of experience and capital," unlike the corrupt and probably incompetent men then at the helm. If he failed, his old associates would "rue the day they ever embarked in [*sic*] the Pacific Railroad."[119]

He arrived at New York City on October 26, the same day Charlie Crocker watched the spiking of the first company rails. Weak and palsied, he was rushed by Anna to a hotel and doctors were sent for. All the medical men could do, however, was watch Judah die, and he expired in his wife's loving embrace on November 2. A few weeks later, as if in relief, the board of directors of the Central Pacific passed a brief, dry resolution of sympathy for the widow.[120]

Had he lived, he might have taken the Central Pacific away from the shopkeepers. His attorney, A. P. Catlin, who knew (but never divulged) Judah's final plans, later wrote: "that he would have succeeded if he had lived is a moral certainty."[121] The railroad, however, would have been built neither more swiftly nor better, no matter who Judah's shadowy backers may have been.

5

SCHEMING IN THE WILD EAST

MR. DURANT AND HIS ORGANIZATION

THE Central Pacific, as it prepared to lay its first rails in the fall of 1863, faced serious problems indeed, but the Union Pacific's future seemed utterly bleak. Aside from the odd fact that President Lincoln was apparently in no hurry to fulfill his mandate to specify the Pacific Railroad's eastern terminus, the Union Pacific Railroad Company almost literally could not give its stock away. Only a handful of the most bold, or most naïve, subscribed in those dreary initial months, and, for a while, it seemed that the Union Pacific would never become incorporated.

While financiers in the East yawned at Union Pacific prospectuses, a real threat to the company was developing in the West. In the summer of 1863, about the time that the Union Pacific got around to filing with the government its acceptance of the terms of the 1862 act, John C. Frémont, his pockets heavy with California gold profits, began buying what would become a controlling interest in the Leavenworth, Pawnee & Western Railroad. The 1862 act specified that this company was eligible to become *the* Pacific Railroad if it could reach the 100th meridian ahead of the others, and Frémont had both gold and appeal to investors. Pointedly renaming the line the Union Pacific Railroad, Eastern Division (commonly abbreviated UPED), Frémont and his partners John Perry and Sam Hallet announced rather grandiose plans for imminent and swift construction westward.[1] Moreover, Sam Hallett actually broke ground personally at Leavenworth in the fall. Only his murder by disgruntled, striking workers slowed that line down, for there was no one of Hallett's stature to fill his post, and the confidence of investors was buried with him. The trouble-plagued UPED did reach Denver by 1870, linking up with a Union Pacific branch line from Cheyenne. In later years it was known as the Kansas Pacific.[2]

It was clearly time to move, thought Thomas C. Durant, who was urged by George Francis Train to either get the railroad organized and its workers in the field or get out of the business entirely.

Future Union Pacific vice-president Durant already owned fifty shares of stock in the company, as did his friend Cornelius Bushnell, Connecticut politician, railroader, and manufacturer, and Colonel G.T.M. Davis, who had helped Judah and Huntington select railroad equipment the year before. Colonel Davis, an enigmatic figure, was the father of "Willie" (Wilhelmina) Wilkinson Davis, who had recently married George Francis Train. Davis was also a Union Pacific director and and acting as an agent for his son-in-law, who wished his own profile with the railroad to be as low as possible. Partially fronting for Train, Davis would become for a while the largest single investor in the Crédit Mobilier.[3] Train himself held a few shares of Union Pacific stock in his own name. An investor and gambler par excellence, Train had a cerebral dowsing stick that had already picked Omaha over Council Bluffs as the railroad's starting point, and he was now paying $175 or less per acre for land there. Eventually, he would own at least five hundred acres, much of which he subdivided into tiny building lots, upon which his Crédit Foncier would erect minuscule cottages.[4]

Other investors were enticed or cajoled into entering their names on the rolls, including Tiffany and Company and Massachusetts congressman John B. Alley, but the pace of investment was dreadfully slow. Never sluggish himself, Durant hit upon the first of his many financing plans. Liquidating his various business interests and calling upon every conceivable line of credit, he began pressuring friends and acquaintances. To those he could not convince to buy a few shares of stock—many were reluctant to hazard any money on a concern touted by such men as Durant and Train[5]—he offered a startling deal. He himself would front the initial 10 percent subscription payment, and he guaranteed to take back or buy back (if the investor subsequently put in any of his own money) the shares at any time. There was, he blithely explained, no risk to those who cooperated. Durant needed only their names on the stock certificates, and as swiftly as possible, in order to get the company incorporated before rivals began serious construction.[6] Doubtless he also realized that he would personally control a great block of voting stock if his plan succeeded, and "win" far more stock than the legal maximum (two hundred shares) established by the 1862 act. This, of course, was precisely what some outside observers had feared from the start. His ploy worked; his "persuasion campaign" was a sweet success.

By early October, some 2,117 shares had been subscribed, Durant accounting for perhaps 1,000 by putting up between 70 and 100 percent of the initial payments for scores of investors. A stockholders' meeting was frantically called in New York, and most of the putative 123 subscribers attended on October 29 and 30. The Doctor held proxies for most of those who did not show up.[7]

Predictably (and, predictably *sub rosa*), Durant dominated the meeting by sheer weight of votes as well as considerable charisma and an almost frightening energy. Soon the company was officially voted into existence and the chief officers were elected, with very little debate. The president would be—on the Doctor's nomination—General John A. Dix, commanding general of the Department of the East. Dix, Durant knew, would be a pliable, largely absentee president who already had a full-time (if basically ceremonial) job "guarding" New York.* Moreover, his name and placid visage conferred a respectability that the Union Pacific desperately needed to attract domestic and foreign capital.[8]

The Doctor garnered for himself the vice-presidency, and, as well, the amorphous but powerful position of general manager.[9] Henry V. Poor, like Dix a man of credibility and probity, was persuaded to serve as permanent secretary, although within a few months he would become so incensed with Durant's casual usurpation of power that he would resign in high dudgeon.[10] For treasurer they chose a man of undoubted financial acumen, experience, *and* conflict of interest—New York banker John J. Cisco. A figure of great influence in banking circles and in the capital, Cisco happened to be assistant secretary of the treasury at the moment. This blatant conflict of interest went unchallenged by a Congress preoccupied with the war.[11] Thirty directors were also named, including Cornelius Bushnell, Colonel Davis, John I. Blair, Charles A. Lambard, Henry McComb, William B. Ogden, Joseph H. Scranton, and Brigham Young.[12] The principal actors were now in place.

The Doctor had truly pulled off a coup. He controlled by far the largest block of company stock (which few realized), and hence votes, and held two distinct positions of power on the board. Further, the Union Pacific's president was busy with other matters and would reign rather than rule, which suited Dix fine and the energetic Durant even better. The treasurer would be out of the way in Washington most of the time, attempting to influence the government in the railroad's favor while keeping the national accounts. After Poor resigned, there would be no one at company headquarters to challenge the Doctor.

It was now imperative to begin construction toward the 100th meridian, even though company coffers were almost bare. Durant sent engineer Peter Dey into the field again to finish surveying the Platte Valley and to prepare a preliminary survey all the way to Salt Lake City, over terrain Dey had previously reconnoitered. Dey's resulting survey map to the 100th meridian was subsequently accepted by the secretary of the interior on November 2, 1864. The Doctor,

---

*Had he been appointed commanding general a week earlier, he would have *had* to guard it, for the July Draft Riot was the bloodiest mob action in United States history, and regiments had to be rushed in from Washington to help crush it.

through a mutual friend, Hubert M. Hoxie, made contact with Grenville Dodge, a colonel of Iowa Volunteers doing railroad engineering and construction with Grant in the Western theater of the war. He wanted Dodge's services enough to offer him the handsome sum of $5,000 a year, plus some stock, and he strongly hinted that he wanted to release Dey—a man of strong moral fiber—and make Dodge chief engineer, if only he could lure him out of uniform.[13] The Doctor knew that Dodge was a superb engineer, he knew that Lincoln had great faith in him, and he guessed that the colonel would be more flexible than the stalwart Dey. Dodge was flattered by the attention but asked for six months or so to think the offer over. Before he came to a decision he was almost mortally wounded in the Battle of Atlanta in 1864. Despite renewed offers during his convalescence in Iowa, he returned to uniform to finish the war, keeping a close eye on Union Pacific developments from afar.[14]

On November 17, President Lincoln, with an unexplained reluctance, officially designated the *area* of Omaha as the eastern terminus of the Pacific Railroad, to George Francis Train's titanic relief. Oddly, the recuperating Dodge, who had recently met with the president, had written his brother the previous month: "I had information that the President would fix the terminal of the road as recommended by me in Council Bluffs."[15] As soon as the news reached him, Durant in New York cabled Dey to prepare for formal groundbreaking ceremonies the instant that labor and equipment were in place.

Those groundbreaking ceremonies took place on December 2, 1863, and a gaggle of Union Pacific officials mingled with a thousand or so locals, employees, and drifters on the Nebraska flatlands. A herd of politicos was also present, shivering under a glowering prairie sky. As in Sacramento that January, there was a flurry of unmemorable speeches, by clergymen, the territorial governor, the mayors of Omaha and Council Bluffs, and Union Pacific directors, and much reading of congratulatory telegrams from absent luminaries.[16] Secretary of State William Seward, long committed to the Pacific Railroad, wrote of the impending labor: "When this shall have been done disunion will be rendered forever after impossible. There will be no fulcrum for the lever of treason to rest upon."[17]

Then it was time for the master of ceremonies: George Francis Train, aptly described as "visionary to the verge of insanity," and now Omaha's largest landowner.[18] The "Clipper Ship King" mounted a rude stage, "dressed in the only suit of white clothes that had ever been seen west of the Missouri River," and still white despite the mud and filth of the street.[19]

Since he happened to be "lying around loose in this part of the country," began the dapper Train, he thought he might just inform his audience of the importance of this special endeavor, destined to become "the people's railroad" if only Congress would permit hundred-dollar stock denominations. With crowd-thrashing hyperbole, he told the gaping throng that "America possesses the biggest head and the finest quantity of brain in the phrenology of nations. . . . Humanity, a puking babe in Asia, a lazy school boy in Europe, came here to America to air its magnificent manhood." America, he told his rapt listeners, "possesses one-half the common sense, three-fourths the enterprise, and seven-eighths the beauty of the world," and its people were destined to easily conquer the continent. The only thing that America lacked that the mature nations of Europe had was a substantial national debt, but he, on his Omaha platform, rose to that challenge, warning the Europeans "that one of these days we would roll up a national debt that would make them ashamed of themselves," and, no matter its size, we were a nation rich enough to retire it at will.[20] The promoter might have been spouting nonsense, but those listening loved it. Surely, as John Galloway has written, here was "a man who might have built the pyramids."[21] Wild applause followed Train from the platform, and the omnipresent Willie, and her omnipresent French maid, beamed with pride.

Following the simultaneous groundbreaking by Train, Dix, and an unusually subdued Durant, a reception was held, with free potables for all. Few of the ardent imbibers on that windswept plain realized that the mild celebration, recalled Sidney Dillon, quite literally cost the Union Pacific every penny then in its vaults.[22]

Nor was construction truly under way. Not a rail or a locomotive had yet been purchased—and precious little matériel had even been reserved. Dey's surveys were far from complete, and only small gangs of workers had been recruited. Typical of these was a gang of a "Mr. Carmichael, having 100 men, including fifteen able-bodied squaws." The Indians were paid a niggardly fifteen cents a day for their back-wrenching grading work.[23] Engineer Dey added to the gloom with his end-of-year report, in which he claimed that rich Denver, with its satellite mines, would probably have to be bypassed because a tunnel three and a half miles long through solid granite fourteen hundred feet beneath the summit of one pass would be needed for the main line to reach the city. *Perhaps* a branch line—narrow-gauge—could later be built. This news was held back from the public, for the Doctor knew it would be yet another deterrent to investors.[24] Small wonder that General Sherman, as firm a Pacific Railroad supporter as one could find, found cause to remark, "A railroad to the Pacific? I would hate to buy a ticket on it for my grandchildren."[25] Durant must have gloomily reflected that Dey's surveys, which had just removed Denver from the main line, and hinted at excising Salt Lake City as well, had cost a shocking $100,000. So much money spent to learn that the only two genuine communities in the Great American Desert would have to be bypassed.[26]

Work had begun, albeit haltingly, on the Central Pacific, Durant knew, but because of lack of funds real work could not yet be commenced at Omaha. In a wartime nation, funds would not be easy to gather. Nor, as the Big Four had so dishearteningly learned, could labor or equipment be obtained at acceptable prices. Yet the Union Pacific had to reach the 100th meridian—a full 247 miles—

and do so before any other line. Counting his few observable blessings, the Doctor knew that at least his company did not face the Californians' staggering shipping and insurance problems, nor the precipitous Sierras. All the requisite gear was manufactured in the East, and even shipping it from New York to New Orleans and then by river or rail to Omaha, or from Chicago by rail and river, was hardly an insoluble problem.

However, while, unlike California, Omaha was relatively accessible to manufacturers, the Union Pacific's route was through territory almost utterly devoid of timber (save for unsatisfactory cottonwood) for ties, trestles, and bridges, nor was there granite or other rock for culverts and bridge abutments. Until the road reached the distant Black Hills, some six hundred miles west, ties of good quality would have to be shipped in from the hardwood forests of Michigan and Wisconsin, or even distant western New York. Building stone would have to come from Indiana, and bridging materials from Chicago or farther afield. Durant also realized only too well that the plains to be traversed were the ancestral home of a dozen already hostile tribes. The Great Sioux Uprising and massacres of 1862, and the army's total commitment to fighting the Confederates, gave the Union Pacific leaders and the investing public more than food for thought. When the Union Pacific finally moved out onto the prairie, it would have to do so as an army itself.

THE CAPITAL CONNECTION

S THE grim year of 1863 ground itself out, both railroad companies had two overwhelming priorities. They needed an amended (or new) railroad act of considerably more generosity, and they needed money, bales of it.

Work had begun in California despite an appalling lack of confidence and cash. Named acting chief engineer was Sam Montague,* an almost mute New Hampshireman who had failed at gold mining in Colorado, taught himself location engineering, and had been hired by Judah to perform that job for the Central Pacific. While he was surveying and making estimates in the Sierras, the first rails were laid at Sacramento. With surprisingly little hoopla, Crocker oversaw a small work crew down by the levee as it spiked its first rails home. With only the idle curious to watch, his workers put eight rods of rail in place that nippy October 26: exactly 132 feet of iron.[27]

---

*He was promoted to chief engineer only in March 1868, and celebrated by getting married.

That was to be the best day's work for quite a while. Still, to stir publicity and build confidence, Stanford, having finished his term as governor, decided to throw a party. On November 9 he hosted a mobile champagne soirée aboard his namesake locomotive. He planned to entertain his carefully selected guests all the way from the company's head of track on I Street to end of track at Twenty-first Street, half a mile away. It would have been a fine outing indeed had the locomotive not malfunctioned. The engine was repaired, and the next day, unfazed and unapologetic, the "governor" plied his laughing guests with imported bubbly the full length of the line.[28]

Meanwhile, the work progressed erratically, matched by the slow progress of the litigation that tied up state and county aid. By year's end, just eleven miles of track had been laid, but by then the Central Pacific was four miles into the bond-lucrative Sierras.

In December, Huntington headed east to lobby for amendments to the railroad act, and Hopkins wrote—with Montague's help—the company's first actual annual report. Even with judicious wording the document did little to inspire confidence. To the end of the year $863,140 had been paid in on some $1,364,000 of subscribed stock. But of the money paid in, 64 percent had come from Placer and Sacramento counties. Most of the remainder had come from the pockets of the Big Four themselves. Hence two years and more after the founding of the company, only perhaps 10 percent of its subscription list was composed of true investors. The report also stated that the company had on hand six locomotives (cost: $67,995.59), six passenger and forty freight cars ($50,073.12), and a minuscule twelve-by-twelve-foot machine shop. In addition to the money spent on rolling stock there had been outlays of nearly a million dollars on what depressingly little grading and construction had been accomplished. There were, admitted Hopkins, no earnings whatsoever in 1863. It was hoped that 1864 would be a better year.

Throughout much of the globe 1864 was a year of chaos: the fourteen-year horror of the world's bloodiest conflict, China's T'ai P'ing Rebellion, ended, leaving the Celestial Kingdom in ruins, and the four-nation Paraguayan War, Latin America's most sanguinary conflict, began. The Indian head became the obverse motif on the new American penny as the Native American's way of life was crumbling about him, and Salmon P. Chase ordered the words *In God We Trust* printed on all United States money, even on the bill bearing his own likeness. Pasteur invented pasteurization, Tolstoi began writing *War and Peace,* Darius Ogden Mills founded the Bank of California, and Nevada became a state. The Kansas state legislature created the University of Kansas, the pope declared the doctrine of papal infallibility, and Yosemite was set aside by Congress as the first national scenic preserve. George M. Pullman and Ben Field patented a railroad sleeping car, while Jules Verne published his *Journey to the Center of the Earth* in France and a mammoth grasshopper plague sheared through the Plains. Meanwhile, in Milwaukee, Frederick Pabst began brewing beer.

Collis P. Huntington was not the only man heading for Washington with a glint in his eye. Durant was also on his way, pockets crammed with cash and stock certificates, and with him came a phalanx of other Union Pacific notables. Although the Pacific Railroad companies had friends and supporters in Congress, they would need more. There had already been a number of attempts by various congressmen to amend the 1862 railroad act—the first was introduced by California senator James McDougall in December 1862—but all had failed, perhaps more because of complacency than open opposition. The war was dominating Congress's attention. At any rate, the railroad men descending on Washington in early 1864 had no difficulty making new friends, for, as one observer has written of the scene, "The scent of boodle was in the air and reaching sensitive nostrils in Washington."[29] Boodle was something both Huntington and Durant understood.

On the first day of January 1864, General Dix initialed a note formally appointing Peter Dey the Union Pacific's chief engineer. This was done at Durant's request, for, with Dodge holding out, Dey, who knew the route thoroughly, was the only possible choice if work was to progress swiftly.[30] Colonel Silas Seymour, an undistinguished engineer who had been in charge of the old Washington aqueduct, was named consulting engineer, again at the Doctor's suggestion. Durant, whose own nostrils were extremely sensitive, was fully aware that the colonel's brother Horatio, governor of New York, was a leading Democratic presidential hopeful. It was best to have major allies in both parties, and it would certainly not hurt the Doctor to have his own man as eyes and ears in the engineering department, as a counter to Dey.[31] A New Yorker, Seymour was a crusty, overweight, eccentric, domineering dandy with little railroad experience (he was on record as having suggested that the entire transcontinental should be built on a granite foundation), but he was to be profitable putty in Durant's talented hands.[32]

Not that Durant was about to rush headlong into something as mundane as actual construction. He did not have the cash to do so. He had recently been rebuffed by several major contractors when he offered to pay them largely in company stock, even when he offered heavy discounts from par. So, although, according to one authority, "the Doctor was not a man to bribe when bribery was unnecessary," he traveled to Washington prepared to spend every cent in the company's already depleted treasury to win a new railroad act. Once the money was gone, he would have to come up with a new scheme for construction that would generate its own capital, some of it, of course, to wend its way in his direction.[33] He had probably heard how the Californians, through Charlie Crocker, were handling their construction, and perhaps there was the germ of an idea.

For his part, Huntington seemed to be at a disadvantage. The Central Pacific, buying almost everything it needed on credit, had an almost bone-dry treasury. He had very little cash to spread around and the Big Four were exceedingly reluctant to part with company stock, which they all but monopolized. Not that he would have hesitated to display his generosity in Washington. He later bragged, "I never bought a vote in Congress,"[34] but he also admitted offhandedly and rather obscurely, "If a man has the power to do evil and won't do right unless he is bribed to do it I think the time spent will be gained when it is a man's duty to go up and bribe the judge."[35] Pretty convoluted, but the message is clear, and Huntington was considerably more to the point when he referred to his interest in the Railroad Act Amendment of 1866: "I will be frank with you and tell you I brought over half a million dollars to use, every dollar of it if necessary to pass this bill."[36] To do him justice, it seems that he was approached far more often than he approached others. The Californian, then, was obviously willing to bribe to keep officials from doing what he considered "evil." He was, after all (at least in his own well-ordered mind), an honest man. Durant was another case, and he never vented pious justifications for his actions.

Durant and Huntington—and other players—met and talked frequently that winter and spring. They may well have compared notes, for their interests were almost entirely complementary (why should both bribe the same senator?). The arch-finagler no doubt was impressed to hear from his California counterpart that Huntington "boarded in the same house with the Secretary of the Interior, J. P. Usher, and sat at the table with him," discussing railroad problems.[37] Usher, from upper New York State, moved in 1840 to Terre Haute, Indiana, where he practiced law and became state attorney general. He had met and befriended Abraham Lincoln while in Indiana, and was called by the president in 1862 to become assistant secretary of the interior; he was elevated to the office of secretary the following year. He was very close to the president and known to influence Lincoln's judgment on railroad matters. Usher left the cabinet after Lincoln's assassination to spend the remainder of his life as attorney and general counsel for the Union Pacific.[38] Huntington was off to a good start.

Except for brief excursions to New York City, Boston, or Philadelphia to place or check upon orders and negotiate credit, the two prototypical lobbyists spent their time in the capital, politicking. If Huntington was fruitfully cultivating the secretary of the interior and several times meeting with President Lincoln, Durant was making himself a Washington legend, throwing parties, money, and stock at any congressman venal enough to catch them. Although it was, and is, assumed that the Doctor pocketed as much as half of the $435,000 he brought to the nation's capital (at Willard's Hotel alone he spent over $18,000 entertaining) he created among certain congressmen what amounted to an addiction to Union Pacific stock certificates.[39] Given the venality of the time, it might not have been necessary.

All was not politicking that spring. The Central Pacific, with eighteen miles of track down by February, was in desperate need of blasting powder, for it was approaching the true foothills of the Sierras, and some major cuts would have to be gouged from the broken country and successive ridgelines. Contracting for explosives, however, required presidential mandate for each shipment, acquired through the secretary of war. That gentleman, Edwin M. Stanton, despite Lincoln's approval of a large shipment out of Boston, dragged his feet for crucial weeks, refusing to sign a release for the powder. Enraged, Huntington went to see the president once more, and Lincoln wrote a terse note to his secretary of war; "You will please give him a permit." While Stanton finally did so a few days later, a still fuming Huntington, perhaps alluding to corruption, wrote of his relations with the president, "I made a mistake in not telling him his Secretary was a hog."[40] It was shortly after this incident that the Californian chanced to meet and befriend the eminent George Gray, chief engineer of the New York Central and one of the nation's most respected railroad builders. Gray would soon be on the Central Pacific payroll, and would perform a critical role.

By watching Durant wheedle, Huntington, always a fast learner, was acquiring new skills. Not that he had been a babe in the woods. As David Lavender has observed, "Corruption oozed everywhere" in Washington during the war, but "anyone who had spent the decade of the 1850's in Sacramento was no stranger to political malfeasance."[41]

In March 1864, Senator John Sherman, the general's brother, introduced a bill to amend the 1862 railroad act. One of its features was to authorize the Central Pacific to build up to 150 miles past the California border into Nevada, provided that the line was continuous and could be finished before the Union Pacific reached that point. The bill easily passed in the Senate in May (by a vote of twenty-three to five), by which time the House was debating sweeping new amendments of its own. There was a bit more resistance to change in the lower chamber. Indiana's William S. Holimen argued that the changes would cost American taxpayers an additional $99,088,000, a figure he never broke down, while Maine congressman Frederick Pike simply shrieked, "There is no travel to the Pacific Coast to justify it,"[42] entirely missing the point. Iowa's Senator Hiram Price later explained the important positive argument for greater liberality; "I do not believe that there is one man in five hundred who will invest his money, and engage in the building of this road, as the law now stands."[43] Central and Union Pacific stock sales neatly validated his point. Investment moneys were needed. Greater government generosity could attract them. Ultimately, on July 1, the House approved what amounted to a new railroad act, by a vote of eighty to thirteen. Lincoln signed it into law the next day. Except for the 150-mile Nevada clause—Huntington wanted no limit whatsoever, while Durant wanted the Central Pacific to remain within California—the new act gave the companies most of what they wanted and what they wanted most.

Federal bonds were now to be considered *second* liens, with the companies permitted to sell their own bonds (in the same amounts per mile) as first-mortgage paper, vastly improving their sales potential. Moreover, government bonds could be collected, and company bonds issued, for each twenty-, rather than forty-mile segment, with none withheld by the government. And, in the mountains, two thirds of the bonds could be collected and issued before trackage was formally certified by government inspectors. This was simple recognition of the difficulty and expense of building certain portions of the lines, especially in the Sierra Nevadas. In addition, land-grant acreage was doubled to twelve thousand acres per mile (from alternate sections within twelve miles on either side of the right-of-way). Iron and coal were no longer defined as "minerals" and deposits of either could be owned and exploited by the companies. The government would pay the standard rate for official use of the railroads and the attached telegraph services, with half the amount due the companies in cash, the other half credited against the bonds and their interest. Also, the president would appoint three commissioners for each company to inspect the lines and the companies' books, and would name five, rather than two, men to serve on the Union Pacific board of directors.* Every "important" committee of that board was to have at least one government member. The Union Pacific was also permitted to change its capital stock to 1 million hundred-dollar certificates (it did so immediately), with a maximum of two thousand to be held by any one person. And, finally, the Union Pacific was given a year's extension to reach the 100th meridian, while the Central Pacific was to be allowed a further four years to reach the Nevada-California line.[44]

In short, Congress did what it could (short of spending money) to keep both companies alive and get them working. It was clear that the 1862 railroad act had not sufficed to do either. The Central Pacific had but a handful of miles in place and was just now approaching the formidable (and expensive) mountains, while no hammer had yet connected with a Union Pacific spike. The 1864 act, though still hardly a giveaway, was designed through its greater liberality to make company securities marketable. Unfortunately, the greenback—and government bonds based on it as well—fell dramatically, for just a week after signing the act, President Lincoln was watching the battle flags of Jubal Early's Confederate army and hearing the ominous "crump" of rebel artillery in Washington's not-so-distant suburbs. The Confederates were soon in retreat, but it was obvious to all that the national trauma, after three blood-steeped years and hundreds

---

*One of these was another of the Sherman progeny, Charles T., who served until 1867. Another was the honest—if acerbic—Jesse L. Williams, who later blew the whistle on the company. He served until 1869.

of thousands of dead, was far from over.[45] Late in the year, however, with public confidence on the rise, Central Pacific bonds were selling at about 75 percent of par, ten to twenty points higher than the government's second-mortgage paper.[46]

How, even with a new and more generous act, was the Union Pacific to raise capital, slough off its leaden lethargy, and build westward? George Francis Train, sent earlier by Durant to forage for funds, soon had the answer.

Having failed to push Union Pacific stock on his friends and associates (a failure unusual for Train), "an idea occurred to me that cleared the sky," recalled the promoter, and he was soon sharing his cloudless vista with the enthusiastic and receptive doctor. The latter, recognizing brilliance when he saw it, immediately offered Train $50,000 to realize his vision and organize his scheme.[47]

Train's idea sprang from his previous experience in France, where he had observed the brothers Emile and Isaac Perrere, "shrewd and ingenious men," create credit systems capable of handling massive construction jobs. They had formed the Crédit Mobilier and the Crédit Foncier to manage such projects as the remodeling of Paris and the construction of several major rail lines, becoming very rich in the process. "I determined," remembered Train, "upon introducing this new style of finance into the country."[48]

But he would need an existing and broad business charter, one with a "limited liability" clause to sooth investors.* Snooping around, Train found his charter in Pennsylvania, granted by the state in 1859 to the Pennsylvania Fiscal Agency, organized by Duff Green, an eclectic writer, politician, businessman, and diplomat, and Charles M. Hall, a Philadelphia businessman. The agency was specifically chartered "to become an agency for the purchase and sale of railroad bonds and other securities," and it was finally incorporated in June 1863, when stock subscriptions reached the legal minimum. Hall and businessman-engineer Oliver Barnes together at that time owned over 90 percent of the agency's 5,329 shares.[49] The exceedingly flexible charter permitted the agency "to borrow and loan money without limit, upon the resources or without the resources of the company"; there was to be "no end to the avenues open to the Agency for operation"; and, best of all, the charter was a "perpetual grant" from the state.[50]

No doubt salivating, Train bought the charter from the agency's organizers for $5,000 in cash and $15,000 in "full paid stock" in the company itself; Hall and Barnes agreed "to assist in getting the name changed at the expense of Train," with the "present directors to resign upon the reorganization of the company."[51]

On March 22, Barnes wrote Train that "the bill changing the name passed the

---

*"Limited liability" means that investors can lose only the capital they invest and will not be liable for company debts.

Senate last evening . . . authorize me to draw on you for the expenses and tax on the bill say ($500) five hundred dollars—it cost rather more than we expected."[52] Ever the skeptic, Train held on to his $500 until a telegram from Hall arrived on March 28; "Govr has signed the bill." In fact, Train did not pay up until two months later.[53]

The name that emerged was the Crédit Mobilier of America (with a subsidiary, the Crédit Foncier of America, essentially a real-estate company owned by Train), and at the price it was a classic of economy. But when Train learned later that he could have gotten the name changed for a mere $50, for the paperwork presented to the legislature, he cynically remarked, "I did not know as much of the ways of legislation in Pennsylvania then as I did later."[54] Although he had made a tidy profit on the charter business, George Francis Train was not often taken, even for a measly $450.

Almost immediately, Train sold the Crédit Mobilier charter to Durant and headed for Boston to drum up investors, for the new company was capitalized at $5 million (with hundred-dollar certificates). As soon as five thousand shares were subscribed, with 10 percent paid in, the company could elect officers and function legally. Once Train explained the limited-liability safeguard and ultimate purpose of the Crédit Mobilier, he had little problem selling stock to financiers who would have recoiled in horror from Union Pacific paper, even though the two companies were to have a symbiotic relationship. After all, profits from construction would be realized relatively quickly, even if the railroad itself was to fail. Union Pacific profits—should there be any—were far down the road.

"My own subscription of $150,000 [actually made in the name of Colonel Davis] was the pint of water that started the great wheel of the machinery," Train unabashedly recalled, and he began taking large—there were no small—orders from a handful of capitalists, including the ever-watchful Ben Holladay.[55] The "Stagecoach King," an early Union Pacific investor and director, intuitively knew that the snorting iron monster would soon replace his blowing, wheezing freight teams, and, "sensationally successful financier" that he was, Holladay was busily diversifying, buying $100,000 of Crédit Mobilier paper. Famous for a money belt that often threatened to burst with $40,000 or more in cash, a garish emerald stickpin, and a gold watch and chain that weighed a full five pounds, the savvy Holladay would soon leave freighting and stagecoaching entirely.[56]

Charles Lambard came aboard with $100,000 in stock, while Cornelius Bushnell (increasingly an intimate of Durant) invested twice that amount, as did one H. W. Gray. Durant himself eventually *might* have taken as much as $600,000 (various lists of subscribers differ markedly), while G. G. Gray, Henry S. McComb, and Colonel Davis took lesser, but still substantial amounts.[57] Yet others, including Oakes Ames and his brother Oliver, the Massachusetts "Kings of Spades," were expressing sincere interest.[58] By early June some five thousand shares were spoken for, and within another eight months that number was to triple. Crédit Mobilier stockholders, always small in number, were large in terms of both dollars and influence.[59]

While Train was peddling his "idea" and rechartering the Crédit Foncier in Nebraska, the site of his first major real-estate forays, he was projecting well into the future. At this time he was scheming to have his Crédit Foncier develop and construct a chain of new communities in the empty Great American Desert, from his favorite, Columbus, Nebraska, to Laramie Springs, Wyoming, and beyond. Meanwhile, Dr. Durant, a visionary in his own right, was hard at work—the work he did best.

In early August, Durant met at a secluded Saratoga resort with a number of key Union Pacific backers, most of whom already figured significantly in the new Crédit Mobilier as well. Among the select few present were Bushnell, McComb, Charles Lambard, and a few other major stockholders. They already had a front organization; now they needed a front man. The good doctor had someone in mind.

Hubert M. Hoxie, a minor Iowa politician, neophyte in railroad construction, lower-echelon Union Pacific employee, and friend of Grenville Dodge, was offered—and immediately accepted—a construction contract for the first hundred miles of the Union Pacific. He signed the contract on August 8—promised by Durant $10,000 in cash for his cooperation—and he offered (at Durant's prompting) to subscribe, "or cause to be subscribed," at least $500,000 in Union Pacific stock if his contract was extended to the 100th meridian, an additional 147 miles. Having already decided to use him as a temporary front man, the Union Pacific directors primly waited until October to accept Hoxie's generous offer.[60]

A paper hoax, the famous "Hoxie contract" specified that Hoxie would build and equip the line, including side tracks, for a flat $50,000 per mile. He was not required to spend more than $85,000 on any one bridge nor exceed $5,000 per mile for buildings, water tanks, and other necessary infrastructure. If the company wanted its crossties Burnettized (specially treated) it would pay another sixteen cents per tie, and if the price of iron rose above $130 a ton, the company was to pay the difference.[61]

The contract appeared especially ludicrous to Chief Engineer Peter Dey, whose own professional and exceedingly detailed estimates specified, according to some authorities, a cost per mile of $27,000 to $30,000 for this portion of the road (and far beyond). Actually, Dey's personal field notebook contains figures for the early portion of the line that project a total cost of $20,396.99 per mile, including all bridges and a 10 percent contingency fund.[62] It should be noted that at this time Dey was seriously underestimating certain necessary expenses, assuming that good crossties could be had for sixty cents, and that excavation work would run no more than forty cents a cubic yard.[63] The Union Pacific's government directors also had grave misgivings about Hoxie's cost per mile.[64]* Dey, depressed mightily by the death of his young son on July 4, was already upset with the Doctor, whom he clearly saw as the man behind this "swindle." Dodge, while on campaign, received a letter from Dey in January 1865, complaining that "the Doctor needs common sense more than anything else and I have been so completely disgusted with his various wild ideas that I have been disposed repeatedly to abandon the whole thing." He bitterly continued, denouncing Durant's avarice and constant scheming:

> If the geography was a little larger, I think he would order a survey round by the moon and get a few of the fixed stars, to see if he could not get some more depot grounds or wild lands or something else that he doesn't want and he does not know what to do with when he gets it.[65]

The inflated Hoxie contract infuriated Dey, and he very well knew that Hoxie, who had never had more than about $2,000 to his name and precious little credit, was not, nor was he ever intended to be, the man to build $5 million worth of the great Pacific Railroad—or $12,350,000 to the 100th meridian. The whole idea smelled of the corruption that the chief engineer suspected was wafting from beneath the doors of the opulent company headquarters at 22 Nassau Street in Manhattan. Nor was Dey entirely enamored of the meddling, sycophantic consulting engineer Durant had foisted upon him. According to rumor, Colonel Seymour was already selling second-rate equipment to the railroad at first-rate prices. As pliable as Durant had hoped, Seymour did not question the per-mile figures of the Hoxie contract, even though he himself had gone on record earlier with an estimate of $34,141 per mile.[66] Public criticism by Seymour of Dey's location surveys also rankled the chief engineer and further estranged him from the Colonel.[67] Dey had several times written President Dix to apprise him of the lack of moral stature of both Durant and Seymour, but the general failed, as was his habit in such circumstances, to respond. Like Judah before him, Dey felt increasingly alone, a sardine among hungry sharks.

Perhaps not to Dey's surprise, on October 6, just three days after the board extended Hoxie's contract to the 100th meridian, the putative contractor signed over his 247-mile contract to a cabal of five financiers: McComb, Bushnell, Lambard, H. W. Gray, and Thomas C. Durant. These men, four of whom were Union Pacific directors and all of whom were major stockholders in both the railroad and the Crédit Mobilier, had managed (they said) to raise $1.6 million in capital among them.† About one quarter of those funds, of which the Doctor claimed a three eighths share, was immediately available in cash.[69]

With contract in hand, the Gang of Five took their $400,000 in cash and

---

*Dey was at this time calculating in *dollars,* while the Hoxie contract figures were in part based on bonds sold at prices far below par. Even so, these figures allowed for a wide profit margin.

†Bushnell alone, in one September transaction, invested $10,000 as his initial 10 percent payment.[68]

immediately used it, *not* to buy such mundane items as rails and locomotives, but Crédit Mobilier stock. Then, with consummate brazenness, the Crédit Mobilier—from its new headquarters adjoining those of the Union Pacific on Nassau Street—used those same dollars to begin buying back outstanding Union Pacific stock from the small "ten percenters" and other nervous investors.[70] It was clear to all but the dullest that Durant himself had been quietly buying back stock from the small investors for whom he had fronted, many of whom were visibly relieved to jettison the paper.[71] A few, instead of selling their stock, merely exchanged it for Crédit Mobilier certificates of equal value. Clearly, the goal was to have control of both the railroad and construction companies in the same few hands. The Crédit Mobilier, proudly referred to by its creator Train as "the first so-called 'Trust' organized in this country,"[72] was all but monopolizing the stock of the railroad it was expected to build, a railroad that apparently no one else wanted enough to invest in. No wonder Hoxie later shook his head and declared that "the entire outfit was rotten to the core."[73]

Engineer Dey knew it was rotten as well, and when Silas Seymour, having criticized Dey's initial choice of route—on which twenty-three miles had already been graded and $100,000 spent—demanded that it be abandoned, Dey exploded. Seymour and Durant favored the Mud Creek route, essentially a detour in the form of an oxbow, which would add nine miles (and $144,000 in government and company bonds; 115,200 acres of land grants; and unspecified construction profits) merely to avoid only moderate grades. When Dey learned that the Doctor sided with Seymour he reached the breaking point and resigned early in December.[74] In a final letter to an unsupportive General Dix, he explained his action:

> My reasons for this step are simply that I do not approve of the contract made with Mr. Hoxie for building the first hundred from Omaha West, and I do not care to have my name so connected with the railroad that I shall appear to endorse the contract.
>
> I look upon its managers as trustees of the bounty of Congress. I cannot willingly . . . swell the cost of construction.

"You are doubtless informed," he continued, "how disproportionate the amount to be paid is to the work contracted for." Terminating this clear testimony to a clear conscience, Dey lamented sincerely, "I have resigned the best position in my profession this country has ever offered to any man."[75]

Two weeks later, as if on cue, Colonel Seymour filed his official report on the first portion of the route, requesting that the government approve a change to the Mud Creek line because of supposed grading angle of ascent. With no one present to challenge Seymour's judgment, the report was forwarded to Washington for approval. Almost a full year later, in November 1865, the Mud Creek route was accepted in place of Dey's earlier path, despite openly expressed doubts on the part of a special government inspector, Colonel James Simpson. By that time, however, the Mud Creek route had been in full operation for some time. Durant and Seymour, bones in their teeth, were not content to await governmental permission.[76]

As Dey wound his way back to Iowa City and relative obscurity, the Crédit Mobilier picked up both speed and cash. Because it soon controlled almost all outstanding Union Pacific stock, the would-be construction company was attracting serious attention from serious men.[77]

Among the most serious were Oakes and Oliver Ames, whose three shovel factories and Iowa railroad projects were hemorrhaging money. Their grandfather, Captain John Ames, had started the family business, making entrenching tools and weapons for George Washington's Revolutionary army, and the Ames brothers were among the "finest families" of Massachusetts.[78] Sober types (Oliver was for decades vice-president of the state's Total Abstinence Society), the Ames boys had a great deal of influence with other wealthy investors. Oakes, at age sixty, was a congressman and served on the House Committee on the Pacific Railroad from 1863 to 1869. Further, he was something of a confidant of President Lincoln, for he had contributed heavily to the 1864 Republican campaign. A 220-pound six-footer who dressed like a Quaker, the taciturn Oakes often boasted of not having taken a day's vacation for over forty years.[79] Early in 1865, he was asked by President Lincoln to do something to help the faltering Union Pacific get under way.[80] This request just happened to coincide with the lure of the evolving Crédit Mobilier, which the Ameses were watching like hawks, and, perhaps more important, the fact that the brothers' own Cedar Rapids & Missouri River Railroad, with its tracks ending just 150 miles short of Council Bluffs, was certain to be the first eastern feeder for the Union Pacific, still isolated at Omaha. In fact, it would indeed be the first of the competing railroads to arrive at Council Bluffs (on January 17, 1867), after which the Ameses collected a half-million-dollar bonus, offered by the Union Pacific's own Dr. Durant to any railroad that could reach Council Bluffs within eighteen months. The Ameses barely made it.[81]

Clearly there was money to be made and, through the vehicle of the Crédit Mobilier, with minimal risk. A nonpracticing lawyer, like so many other men involved with the Pacific Railroad, Oliver Ames was also a former state senator. Three years younger and fifty pounds lighter than Oakes, he was even more willing than his brother to invest some of their loose millions in the construction company, and had earlier been approached several times to that end. Oliver's passions were reserved for two things; shovels and railroads. That they tended to coincide was all the better.

In February 1865, they took the plunge, accompanied by a number of other capitalists, including John M. S. Williams and William T. Glidden, clipper ship moguls from Boston. The Ameses each bought an initial $100,000 of Crédit

Mobilier stock, soon buying more, while Williams and Glidden took $50,000 apiece. Before long the list swelled as many of their business associates emulated the Ameses, and soon over $800,000 in new shares were issued; even reluctant Sidney Dillon of the Union Pacific finally cast his lot and money with Train's "idea."[82] The Ames brothers brought cash into the Crédit Mobilier, but they also brought with them financial respectability and that indefinable asset, observable optimism. They and the men who followed their example soon controlled almost as much stock as did the original "Durant group," and they would before long dominate the company—and the Union Pacific, with Oliver alone holding 10 percent of the railroad's stock.[83]

On March 15, twelve days after President Lincoln signed a bill permitting both companies to issue their own bonds for up to a hundred miles in advance of continuous track,[84] the deed was done. On that date, Durant and his financier friends assigned the old Hoxie contract to the Crédit Mobilier, a reassignment ratified on April 6 by the Union Pacific's board of directors. Oddly, the first check issued by the Crédit Mobilier, five days after obtaining the Hoxie contract, was to Thomas C. Durant, in the amount of $302,700. It has never been ascertained just what the check was for.[85] The Doctor was promptly paid off for something, but poor Hoxie was not. Claiming that the final transfer of his contract was to gain him $5,000 in cash and $10,000 in Union Pacific stock, he wrote Dodge years later that "the money is [still] due me, or rather the stock."[86] All Hoxie would derive from the misuse of his name and reputation was a post as Union Pacific superintendent of river transportation, and later assistant superintendent of the railroad.

It was now the spring of 1865. Within a month Lincoln would die, Lee would surrender, and the Confederacy would cease to exist. A wartime emergency creation, the Union Pacific had not yet spiked a rail.

THE BIG FOUR EARN $354.25

T HE Central Pacific had laid rails—in 1863, 1864, and 1865—although at a disappointing pace. The company was as usual in dire financial straits. In fact, for seventeen consecutive days in the summer of 1864 there was not a nickel in the treasury. Only another timely loan from none other than Oakes Ames, who would eventually loan the Californians $800,000, tided the Central Pacific over for some dangerous months.[87]

With the exception of the purchase of company bonds by Placer and Sac-

ABOVE: *Engineer Samuel Benedict Reed, Union Pacific construction supervisor, contemplates a Nebraska infinity in the gloomy summer of 1865. His truly was the first railroad built in advance of civilization, and in 1865 it appeared doubtful that congressionally mandated mileage goals would be met.*

TOP LEFT: *The Union Pacific's porous cottonwood ties being fed into a Burnettizer at Omaha, soon to reappear almost metalic in weight and aspect. Even after treatment in the 100-ton retort (inside the shed at the left), the Burnettized ties were clearly substandard.*

BOTTOM LEFT: *Union Pacific nabobs triumphantly inspecting the work in Nebraska at the 100th Meridian (mile 247) in October 1866. Failure to reach the Meridian (near the present town of Cozad) by year's end would have forfeited the company's Pacific Railroad status. Note the man with the rifle. Mile 247 was well within "Indian country."*

OPPOSITE TOP: *"The pendulum beat of a mighty era": Tracks thud down at the 100th Meridian in October 1866 as interested "gentlemen" look on. The gentlemen in this photograph are probably guests on Vice-President Thomas C. Durant's opulent Pacific Railroad Excursion, which generated marvelous publicity for the company.*

OPPOSITE BOTTOM: *Carmichael's Cut, at mile 785, in Wyoming's Bitter Creek Valley. This difficult cut, hacked through oil-oozing shale, was 100 feet long and up to 60 feet deep, and often caught fire from locomotive sparks and cinders, illuminating the flat plains for miles around.*

ABOVE: *Payday in Wyoming. The gandy dancers gather around the heavily guarded paymaster's car, called by name and paid individually by the two clerks inside. Note the several Confederate Cavalry uniforms. Not far away lurked opportunity to spend the hard-earned greenbacks at a "Hell on Wheels."*

OPPOSITE TOP: *A Union Pacific work camp in the Bitter Creek Valley in 1868, near mile 783. This camp was built for workers who labored for months on a series of cuts demanded by government commissioners to maintain the straightest possible line. The cuts, however, filled with snow during even minor storms, delaying traffic.*

OPPOSITE BOTTOM: *The impressive and controversial Dale Creek Bridge in Wyoming at mile 550. Instead of a cheaper and more secure fill, Dr. Durant ordered this expensive, overly complex, unsafe bridge. It was 700 feet long and 126 feet above the almost dry creek and swayed dangerously in even modest winds, attracting charges of undue expense and corruption.*

LEFT: *Mormon artisans sculpting massive tunnel timbers near the bore of Echo Tunnel, at mile 972, in the bleak Utah hills. Without the labor of thousands of sturdy Mormons, both the Union and Central Pacific would have been delayed many months. Mormon leader Brigham Young was thus a man to be courted.*

BELOW: *Technology and proud of it. While the Central Pacific almost ignored construction machinery, the Union Pacific was quick to adopt any new methods or tools. Skilled workers pose proudly with their new steam shovel in Echo Canyon, Utah, 1868.*

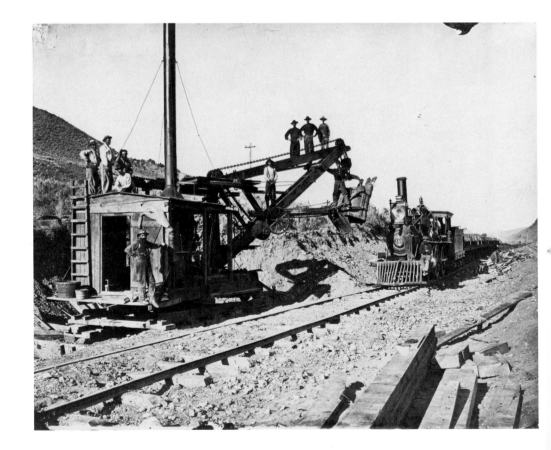

RIGHT: *Perhaps the worst of a bad lot, the Bear River City Hell on Wheels in 1868 near the Wyoming-Utah border. The scene of a bloody riot that year, the town, like most Hells on Wheels, did not exist at all a year after the work crews moved on.*

BELOW: *Testing the Devil's Gate Bridge in Weber Canyon, near Ogden, Utah, in early 1869. It was not tested sufficiently, however, and flood damage to the structure in early May embarrassingly forced Union Pacific leaders to cross the bridge on foot and arrive at the Promontory Point ceremonies in a common train pulled by a common locomotive.*

TOP: *The showdown at Fort Saunders, near Laramie, July 26, 1868. Presidential nominee Ulysses S. Grant stands in civilian clothes in front of the birdcage, General William Tecumseh Sherman offers his handsome profile, Sidney Dillon glowers on the far left, and a chastized Durant sulks against the railing (sixth from the right). The latter at this meeting had lost his right to supervise engineering and construction.*

BOTTOM: *The last spike is driven, May 10, 1869, at Promontory Point, Utah, the Central Pacific (left) and Union Pacific (right) at last meeting. The two men shaking hands are the chief engineers Sam Montague (left) and a slightly seedy-looking Grenville Dodge. On the cowcatcher of the Union Pacific locomotive, with two bottles of champagne in his hand, is legendary engineer Tom Cahoon, who had lost his scalp in service to the company.*

ramento counties, not a penny in aid reached the Central Pacific in 1863 or 1864, yet by California law local expenses, mostly for buildings and labor, had to be paid out in gold.

Gold was not easy for the Big Four to acquire, for the company's enemies redoubled their efforts to cripple the Central Pacific in 1864 and 1865. San Francisco business interests, frozen out by their own choice, wanted the Big Four to fail, and their control of the city's newspapers ensured a constant stream of anti–Central Pacific invective.[88] The stage and freight lines fought the company, as did the Placerville Turnpike and other toll roads. Shipping interests cast their stones as well, and even the Sitka Ice Company joined in, fearing that a railroad through the Sierras might cheaply provide ice to the state's cities, destroying the company's Alaska enterprise. Most influential, however, were California's other railroad barons, some of whom wanted their own lines to be the western part of the Pacific Railroad.

One of these lines was the newly organized San Francisco & Washoe, owned by Charles E. McLane (who also owned the short Placerville & Sacramento Valley Railroad), L. L. Robinson, and several other associates.* They planned a trans-Sierra rail line from the Bay area, through Placerville and Carson to the California border via Johnson Pass, south of Lake Tahoe, to Virginia City's enticing mines. If they could cross the Sierras first, their road and not the Central Pacific's, might become the western arm of the Pacific Railroad.[90] McLane and Robinson began a slander campaign, based in part on the venerable Dutch Flat Swindle, which soon degenerated into accusations of personal corruption. So effective was this libelous assault that the Placer County Board of Supervisors appointed two of its members, A. B. Scott and D. W. Madden, to go to Sacramento to investigate the Central Pacific's books and other records. Placer County, after all, had a quarter of a million dollars in Central Pacific stock, and Robinson and McLane claimed it was being defrauded.

In the summer of 1864 the two men worked their way through the company's records and could find no evidence whatever of peculation: "We found the books of the company kept in a clear, plain, legible manner," they reported. The company's directors, they noted, had *not* given themselves lands—in fact, no land patents had yet been issued by the government. Certainly the Big Four held Central Pacific stock, but they had bought it. The contracting procedures and cost of the line were also found to be legitimate by Scott and Madden, who concluded that the false charges against the company were "evidently a machination of the brain of some individual who has no regard for the true interests of Placer County," or the truth either, and was merely out to ruin the railroad

*Robinson, an eclectic entrepreneur, had also recently created and was president of the first West Coast explosives company, the Giant Powder Company, of Santa Cruz. That the Big Four did not buy powder from him may have added to his deep animus.[89]

company.[91] Scott and Madden were destined to be the only outsiders ever to scrutinize Uncle Mark's books.

The company faced some other contretemps that spring and summer of 1864. While the state legislature finally agreed to guarantee the interest on $1.5 million of Central Pacific 7 percent bonds, only a handful could be sold before a suit was again brought on grounds of unconstitutionality. While the suit was won by the company, bond sales were blocked until early January 1865.[92] Since by the summer of 1864 the Central Pacific only had thirty-one miles of track in operation, the Big Four did not qualify for government aid, which was to be paid out for forty-mile segments. After the July railroad act they did qualify for the first twenty-mile portion of the road, but Huntington, despite his imprecations, received no federal bonds at all until May 12, 1865.[93] Creed Haymund, later the company's general counsel, was merely stating the facts when he later carped that the government "never issued to the company a bond at the time at which that bond was earned and due."[94] The Central Pacific, to Mark Hopkins's chagrin, actually found itself forced to pay interest on loans guaranteed by these tardy bonds—a total, according to Haymund, of $426,000 much needed dollars. In part, the delay in issuance of these bonds stemmed from President Lincoln's unexplained slowness in naming the Central Pacific's three government commissioners. Without those gentlemen on the scene to inspect and approve the tracks laid, no aid could be forthcoming.[95]

McLane and Robinson in the meantime returned to the attack, perceiving the vulnerability of the Central Pacific. This time they struck in Nevada, which would become a state in the Union on October 31. To that end the Nevada legislature was meeting in July to frame a constitution, and one paragraph in that document was to address the railroad issue. The two railroad men and their chief engineer, F. S. Bishop, through their newspapers and by personal letters bombarded Nevadans with anti–Central Pacific propaganda and, in fact, outright lies. Claiming that the Big Four's chosen route was virtually an engineering impossibility, the McLane group asked the legislature to proffer aid to the first railroad to reach the state line, rather than guarantee it to the Central Pacific.[96]

By the time the legislature sat and began discussions on the railroad clause, which might entail some $3 million in state aid, it looked as if McLane and his cohorts would have their way. Enter former governor Leland Stanford, who had lately done little work for the company beyond hosting excursions. The "compleat" politician barely arrived in time, when the railroad aid package was in full and florid debate. By virtue of his rank, he addressed the legislature on July 13. He lucidly explained that his competitors were openly lying, that the Dutch Flat Swindle was pure poppycock, and that aid offered to the "first" railroad to enter Nevada would touch off a ruinous race and, incidentally, even further degrade the value of Central Pacific stock and bond issues. Basically, the message was that if Nevada wanted rail links with the outside world in the near future, it would

have to support the one company then seriously building in the mountains.*
Cagily, Stanford made no mention of the company's own all but empty treasury.

He proved an eloquent guest, as always. And a persuasive one, for a Mr.
DeLong of that legislature recalled that there was "no earthly doubt that if
Governor Stanford had not come over here, this Nevada Constitution would
have contained a clause providing an appropriation of three million dollars for
the first road that reached our state line."[97] With the Central Pacific once again
teetering on the brink, one of the Big Four had leapt across the chasm.

Not, however, that McLane and company gave up. Hardly. They continued to
peddle the Dutch Flat Swindle, and would continue to do so until that town, at
mile 67, was actually passed by Central Pacific tracks on July 4, 1866. In early
February 1865, they loosed a pseudotechnical broadside at the Central Pacific.
Robinson, himself a civil engineer, wrote the Nevada legislature to plump for his
own railroad and route, which had recently been fully surveyed by engineer
Bishop. Robinson, viciously attacking the Big Four, protested that Judah had
never really surveyed the Central Pacific route and, suspecting that the proposed
line was an impossible one, had allowed himself to be bribed into silence by the
Big Four. He continued:

> I could not conceive any set of men would seriously undertake to construct
> a railway over such a country . . . a railway across the Semmering Alps, from
> Vienna to Trieste is a mere bagatelle as compared with the projected line
> via Dutch Flat. . . .

Warming to his outlandish tale, Robinson, admitting that it just might be possible
to build along his rivals' route, nevertheless warned the Nevadans: "My firm
conviction is, that the CPRR will cost $250,000 to $300,000 a mile before it is
completed to the Truckee."[98] One mile, it turned out, would cost over $300,000.

All the attacks, both subtle and blunt, were to fail, but all took their toll on
aid packages, bond and stock sales, and, of course, the company treasury. Had
this not been the case, far more work could have been accomplished, for the
winters of 1863–64 and 1864–65 were by far the mildest of the decade. Despite
perfect weather and hence working conditions, the Big Four could hire only as
many men as they could pay, and that was sometimes none.[99]

Still, Crocker's eighteen miles were completed satisfactorily on February 19,
1864, and the Central Pacific entered Junction (Roseville), linking up with the
different-gauged California Central. Four months had passed since the first rail
was spiked to its ties at Sacramento. Charlie Crocker was not about to stop at
Junction. The small work crews pushed doggedly on, for Crocker had been
awarded another contract, this one for thirteen miles, from Junction to Newcastle.[100] Many doubted that he'd make it.

---

*In any event, Nevada was never to give aid of any sort to the Central Pacific.

When the rails reached mile 22, Stanford, always the gracious host, led a special excursion down the tracks. Some two thirds of the state's legislators, many with their wives and children, as well as other notables and reporters, were whisked to track's end at a steady and respectable twenty miles an hour. He had taken other, smaller groups out on the line before, but this was a true public relations maneuver, and it no doubt helped influence the legislature's vote a month later to guarantee Central Pacific bond interest.[101] It was—on the surface—a festive, champagne-washed, gala, well covered even by newspapers inveterately hostile to the company, such as the *Alta California.*

As the track slowly punched on through the foothills that spring and summer, the Central Pacific faced yet another vexing problem. Labor had long been scarce in California because of the lure of mining. With new mines and alluvial strikes being discovered weekly, even men who signed on to work (for wages much higher than normal, up to four dollars a day plus board) were skipping out from end of track for the mining camps.

By early 1864 Charlie Crocker found himself actually importing workers from New York and Boston, often Irish immigrants barely off the boat, and shipping them west at terrific expense. He was also petitioning the War Department for five thousand Confederate prisoners of war while trying to dragoon immigrants from Mexico as well. When he managed to get a gang of new workers on the line, he found he could rarely keep them there: some nineteen hundred out of a two-thousand-man crew he hired that summer lit out for the Nevada mines as soon as they had had a warm meal at the company's end-of-track camp.[102] Those who for some reason remained with the company were not always the best type, and there was much drunkenness, many strikes and slowdowns, and enough disputes over wages and conditions to drive Acting Chief Engineer Montague half mad.[103] Clearly, thought Charlie Crocker, another way would have to be found. Civil War veterans? Newly freed slaves? Chinese?

Despite all the agonies, the Central Pacific announced on April 25 that it had commenced *regular* passenger service (and would soon begin freight service) to Junction, with three trains running daily in each direction. In the first week of service, 298 passengers clambered aboard and the company could boast its first, horrendously modest, earnings: $354.25.[104] At least for a change this amount did represent earnings. In 1864 the company would take in $113,413 from passengers, the mails, and fourteen thousand tons of freight.[105] As yet there were no tunnels, and thus no light at the end of them, but it was a beginning.

Newcastle (mile 31), a town far more populous than Junction, was reached by iron in the first week of June, and both passenger and freight traffic increased dramatically after regular service to that town began on June 6.[106] Unfortunately, it was at Newcastle that the company came to a grinding halt because of lack of funds. Some few miles beyond the town, on the edge of the difficult Sierra country, lay Bloomer Cut, the first major engineering hurdle, a hurdle that was absorbing five hundred kegs of blasting powder a day (more than most major battles would), at an average of five to six dollars per keg. The cut, which when finished was over eight hundred feet long and up to eighty-five feet deep, was simply too expensive for the Central Pacific to handle.[107] Nevertheless, in the meantime, Crocker wangled an extension of his contract, all the way to the state border.[108]

Operating capital, if not actually in hand, was, however, at long last on the way, and not only from local and federal agencies. On June 14, the Dutch Flat and Donner Lake Wagon Road opened for what would be a most prosperous trade. With one-way traffic permitted free for a week to familiarize teamsters with the road's quality, the road—an excellent one that soon ruined the Placerville Turnpike—was soon choked with wagons. Although the project had cost about $350,000 at a difficult time, before long it would be doing a million-dollar-a-year business, helping to replenish the Big Four's depleted personal fortunes.[109] That the road ultimately would connect with the Central Pacific at Dutch Flat ensured greater traffic and profits for the railroad as well.

That and the impending arrival of pledged aid moneys gave the Central Pacific a fighting chance, but, for the moment, the company was in limbo. From the arrival of track at Newcastle in June to the end of 1865, only slightly more than twenty miles would be added to the Central Pacific line, although grading and other work would be carried out well beyond, in the Sierras.[110]

Despite an utter lack of funds in late 1864 and, as Huntington was wont to brag, an average of about $1 million worth of equipment in transit at any time, the Central Pacific managed to acquire in November half the rolling stock of the California Central (which it had to retool to the Central Pacific gauge); four locomotives and four passenger, three box, and twenty-three platform cars. California Central President Sam Brannan (an early Central Pacific stockholder) was paid $105,000 in discounted Central Pacific stocks and bonds for the equipment.[111] The Big Four's ability to build and purchase without money continued to be remarkable.

A week before the new rolling stock was purchased, E. H. Miller, Jr., printed a report on the condition of the Central Pacific. While showing earnings, it revealed no improvement in stock sales, with a scrawny $723,800 subscribed by individuals, in addition to the holdings of Placer and Sacramento counties. Essentially, admitted Miller reluctantly, there was no cash on hand.[112] Since Miller apparently preferred to dwell on trivia rather than on the global problems facing the company, this report is a marvel of minutiae. Thus those who read it learned such momentous facts as the average speed of Central Pacific passenger trains (22 miles per hour, including stops) and freight trains (15.5 miles per hour), and that there had only been one "minor" accident on the line, when employee Frank Brady had been run over and killed. Miller's report did nothing to instill the confidence of investors, for the questions a capitalist might ask were pointedly not addressed.

Sam Montague's annual report, published a month later, announced that Bloomer Cut had at last been finished (but not yet tracked) and that the railroad had cleared net earnings in gold of $47,268.37, after deducting operating expenses and taxes. He also pointed out the high quality of the company's depots and other buildings along the line, and he advised readers that the 396,800 acres of land grants (as yet ungranted) would bring in far more than the government-mandated minimum price of $1.25 per acre (for a total of $496,000) because it was for the most part superb agricultural land and peerless vineyard acreage. Even more heartening was his assertion that, based upon his own continuing survey work, Judah's original route could be somewhat shortened, and several tunnels omitted, with consequent savings in time and money.[113]

All in all, it was an upbeat report, while still being somewhat more realistic than Judah's previous flights of fancy. But there was one thing Montague omitted that a restricted-circulation annual report did not. Construction costs for 1864 had exceeded estimates, surpassing $2 million. Added to the $947,058 spent in 1863, the total—for a mere thirty-six miles—was almost precisely what Judah had expected to spend for the first *fifty* miles. And the difficult construction was yet to come. In fact, as the railroad ascended into the Sierras, each mile tended to be more expensive to build than the previous one, and not a single tunnel facing had yet been started. The same report also noted that late in the year the legislature had approved a boost in the company's capitalization to $20 million (by 1868 it would reach $100 million), yet no more stock had been sold.[114]

At this moment, with its stock selling—if at all—for nineteen cents on the dollar and its bonds for half of par,[115] the Central Pacific faced grave difficulties, despite the promised aid. Crocker, who admitted that he had acquired severe insomnia along with his construction contracts, tossed and turned all night long. He was later to recall of this period; "I would have been glad, when we had 30 miles of road built, to have got a clean shirt and absolution from my debts; I would have been willing to give up everything I had in the world, in order to cancel my debts."[116] In the entire construction phase of the Central Pacific Railroad, late 1864 was the financial and psychological nadir for the Big Four, a time of virtual panic. Yet they plodded ahead despite the grim prospects.

Huntington later remembered: "I have gone to sleep at night in New York when I had a million and a half dollars to be paid by three o'clock on the following day, without knowing where the money was coming from, and slept soundly."[117] That spirit, evident in varying degree in all of the Big Four, explains better than anything how the Central Pacific became reality.

Relief would come in 1865, and with it a host of new problems.

6

THE CHINESE FACTOR AND
THE INDIAN THREAT

THE BIG FOUR FIND MONEY AND MUSCLE

EVEN though a veritable army of Arabic laborers was making good progress on the Suez Canal, January was to be a good month for the Central Pacific, which had laid thirty-six miles of working track to the California town of Auburn by New Year's Day. Had there been sufficient money, work would have been going on full-blast throughout this extraordinarily mild winter, for the company had some twenty miles of iron available, but neither cash nor labor was to be had. Years later, in 1887, an irate Collis P. Huntington was to angrily tell a congressional investigating committee that if Washington had only provided its promised bonds when they were due in 1864, that winter might have been profitably used and the Central Pacific could have made contact with the Union Pacific as far east as Cheyenne, rather than Promontory Point.[1]

Still, January was a propitious month, despite the founding of the Ku Klux Klan in Pulaski, Tennessee. On the seventh, promised state aid was released—interest on the $1.5 million in company bonds—in addition to the first installment on the half-million-dollar gift from the legislature. Unlike other Central Pacific paper, the state-guaranteed bonds were an instant success on the market, pouring funds into the starved treasury of the company. Also, increasing revenues from the all-weather toll road were coming in, as well as moneys from regular rail service, and Huntington was expecting the overdue government bonds momentarily.[2]

With unusual confidence, Charlie Crocker, whose work gangs counted only some six hundred men, advertised for five thousand more laborers.[3] One of the things that made January a good month was Crocker's hiring of a construction boss, really a super-foreman. The man he chose was the formidable Irishman James Harvey Strobridge ("Stro" to his equals, of whom there were precious few). Born at Albany, Vermont, in 1827, Strobridge worked on New England railroads from age sixteen. A 'Forty-niner, he dabbled in prospecting (meeting Crocker in the Placer County mining district), farming, freighting, and even hotel management before working as construction foreman on the Placer County Canal and the San Francisco & San Jose Railroad.[4]

Strobridge, like most of the Central Pacific leadership, was a teetotaler by conviction, a workaholic by nature, and possessed the inclinations of a scorpion and the tongue of a pit viper: "His profanity and temper were spectacular," noted one author.[5] The mountains were to ring with his savory epithets. A large, muscular man, he could and often did physically intimidate and verbally abuse the men he bossed, and his Oriental workers, according to one authority, "feared him in their hearts as much as they did the Chinese devil."[6] He habitually carried a pick handle as a "persuader," and often negotiated with his fists. The hard-driving, uncompromising, and profane Mr. Strobridge within two years would boss the largest single concentration of labor on the continent. No one could have guessed this in 1865, however, for even with military demobilization, labor was still appallingly scarce, especially in California, where the mines seductively beckoned.

So scarce was labor in early 1865 that a number of schemes were bruited about to solve the problem. Henry V. Poor, writing in his *American Railroad Journal,* thought he might have the answer to both companies' labor shortage. In an article entitled "The Negro and His Uses," he urged that black Civil War veterans be put to work on the Pacific Railroad. "Retain them under military discipline, and military pay," he importuned, as this "would be an act of kindness as well as justice to the Negro . . . and would also be the most economical method of constructing the roads." Unskilled former slaves and veterans could be "schooled with economy and self-reliance," earn the gratitude of the nation, and be rewarded with public lands along the right-of-way. Contemplating "the employment of two or three hundred thousand men," Poor promised in full-capital letters that "ONE HUNDRED MILES A MONTH MIGHT BE CONSTRUCTED!"[7] Nothing came of the editor's probably unrealistic plan, but the Union Pacific did employ several hundred black workers on the Plains, and a hundred miles a month was often approached by the two companies together in the latter stages of construction with much smaller crews.[8]

Strobridge, to his dismay, was to find that the vast bulk of the men he bossed were Chinese, called "Celestials" by most Californians, after the "Celestial Kingdom," a name by which the Chinese referred to their homeland. When

Crocker called for five thousand workers that January, only a handful responded. A spate of new silver (and a few gold) strikes drew able-bodied men into the hills, their eyes gleaming with avarice. Why break your back on a railroad work crew twelve hours a day when there were millions to be made in the mountains? Every Californian could name someone who had struck it rich in the mines.

In 1865 California's Chinese community numbered close to fifty thousand,[9] at least 90 percent of whom were young men—one careful study indicates that at one point the ratio of males to females reached twenty-seven-to-one.[10] While Chinese were valued as houseboys, launderers, truck gardeners, and even cooks, there were among them many merchants and tradesmen, cigar makers, fishermen, and a surprisingly large number of miners. Those in this last group, because of their race alone, paid a stiff miner's tax to the state and were restricted even then to tailings that had already been worked, tailings they mined with patience and care, managing to turn a tidy profit.[11] The Chinese were not made welcome in California. Present since the fall of 1848, they were increasingly discriminated against—denied citizenship and all its rights, unable to testify in court, barred from certain professions and, in 1858, banned by the legislature from entering California at all (although the ban was poorly enforced).[12] That year there were bloody anti-Chinese riots—virtual pogroms—at Folsom and elsewhere,[13] and Orientals were subjected to vicious attacks by the xenophobic California press. Pamphlets such as one by Arthur B. Stout, M.D., *Chinese Immigration and the Physiological Causes of the Decay of a Nation,*[14] set the tone, dwelling at absurd lengths on such supposedly innate Chinese characteristics as syphilis and "mental alienation."

Still, to America they came, for their native land was in bloody dissolution. In the 1860s China was simultaneously lashed by the horrendous T'ai P'ing Rebellion (1851–64), the decade-long Triad Uprising (1854–64), and the sporadic Punti-Hakka feuds, which erupted in 1859. Cycles of famine, constant corruption by officials, and the pressures of overpopulation also drove many to leave the soil of their ancestors and sojourn at least temporarily among the "barbarians."[15]

When the emperor legalized the recruitment of Chinese workers in 1859, the number of immigrants swelled, most of them recruited—almost like indentured servants in early America—by brokers in Hong Kong, Macao, and Canton. A broker paid for the passage to America (often for entire gangs of young men) and advanced forty dollars or so in gold coin to each worker. The recruit then worked for a set period (four or five years), paying off his debt, with interest, in installments. With the debt paid, he could remain in America working solely for his own profit, or he could return. Many brokers guaranteed to return to China the remains of any recruit who died in service.[16]

Most Chinese in California, both before and after 1859, came from Cantonese villages and from around Hong Kong, with a sprinkling from the colony of Macao, at the time still a Portuguese enclave. They spoke for the most part Cantonese or Szeyup dialect rather than classical Mandarin, the tongue spoken by those few Americans who could speak any Chinese.[17]

In California they dealt with and relied upon the Chinese Six Companies (The Chinese Consolidated Benevolent Association), which offered them secure banking services, medical help, and legal aid. One's company could also be relied upon to arrange shipment of mortal remains back to China, transmit mail, and handle indenture accounts; on a more mundane level, these companies were also conduits for such gastronomical "necessities" as pressed duck and dried squid.[18] Run by respected merchants, the companies were neither Tongs (fraternal organizations of overseas Chinese) in the true sense nor criminal societies like the Mafia, but, wrapped in silence, if not total secrecy, they excited the fears of white society, a society that for some reason could philosophically accept as normal the occasional "highbinder," or true Chinese gangster.[19] Acting, as Thomas W. Chinn has noted, "practically [as] the Supreme Court of the Chinese," the companies provided what white society did not or would not provide.[20]

Two bilingual newspapers served the California Chinese (Mark Twain, impressed, noted that "all Chinamen can read, write and cipher"),[21] the Sacramento triweekly *Oriental* and the San Francisco monthly *California China Mail and Flying Dragon*. The former's first issue, dated January 4, 1855, noted with almost paranormal prescience that a future transcontinental railroad "will be scattered with busy lines of Chinese builders of iron roads, that shall link the two oceans."[22]

There had been some Chinese in segregated gangs among the work force that had built the San Francisco & San Jose Railroad in 1863, but while they worked well, they were used more as strikebreakers than as labor per se, and as such they were bitterly resented.[23]

In February, a month after his all but fruitless call for labor, Charlie Crocker met with Strobridge and raised the question of hiring Chinese, a score or so of whom had worked on the Dutch Flat and Donner Lake Wagon Road to good effect. Stro was horrified. He was afraid that the whites then working for him would stomp off the job; and, after all, what did these slender, almost effeminate-looking, blank-faced Orientals know about railroad construction?[24] "I will not boss Chinese!" roared Strobridge, to which Crocker replied, "But who said laborers have to be white to build railroads?"[25] Reminding his construction boss that a race which had invented gunpowder and had built the Great Wall of China just might be able to build a railroad, Crocker insisted and a compromise was agreed upon. A skeptical Strobridge was to hire fifty Chinese, whom he could easily find at Auburn, and try them out for a month under white labor supervisors. Crocker, who later testified before Congress that he "preferred white laborers to Chinese, til he could not obtain white labor," was willing to try anything to get his railroad moving again, and, while surprised by the notion, his partners swiftly agreed.[26]

Fifty Chinese were hired and put to work under Stro's demanding gaze. Diminutive Orientals in their baggy, pajamalike work clothes, their pigtails flopping on their backs, worked with a steady, rhythmic cadence. Paid regularly, and in gold—twenty-six dollars that month[27]—the Celestials worked uncomplainingly, while white crews jeered and hooted. The "Terrestrials," however, soon found that they had to pick up their own pace to match that of the silent newcomers.

At the end of the month Strobridge grudgingly admitted that the Chinese had performed superbly. Especially proficient at rock work and blasting, they worked perfectly as teams, took almost no breaks, and remained remarkably healthy: according to Ping Chiu, "Their quiet efficiency was astounding."[28] Engineer Montague, reviewing their work, highly praised the Oriental laborers in his 1865 annual report. "The experiment," he wrote, "has proved eminently successful."[29] And so it had.

As soon as the first Chinese gang had vindicated its race to the prejudiced construction chief and his white workers, Stro and Crocker sent men through the mining districts to entice more Chinese to work for the Central Pacific, offering twenty-eight dollars, thirty dollars, and finally, thirty-one dollars a month (with no board). Crocker turned also to a labor contractor in San Francisco named Koopmanschap, and instructed him to scour the state for two thousand more "coolies,"* and even import them from China itself if necessary.[30] Before the end of 1865, as many as seven thousand Orientals were at work on the line, along with just under two thousand whites, and a contract had been made through the San Francisco firm of Sisson and Wallace† to import labor directly from China.[31] Stanford, who while campaigning for the governorship had routinely railed against the "dregs of Asia" and "that degraded race," now found himself actively supporting Chinese immigration and unblushingly (did he or Huntington *ever* blush?) suggesting that it would be good for California if half a million more Chinese were promptly brought in.[32]

By midsummer, the Central Pacific's labor problem was well on the way to being solved and the Chinese "system" was in place. Crocker hired Sam Thayer, who spoke several Chinese dialects, as interpreter, and he in turn was soon instructing selected Chinese in the English language. The Chinese were organized into gangs of about twenty men, one of whom was their elected headman, and another the gang cook. The headman collected all wages, and the cook drew upon the gang's treasury to buy provisions through Chinese merchants in Sacramento and San Francisco. Other amounts might be deducted for

---

*A nineteenth-century American generic term for cheap, Oriental labor.
†Crocker's younger brother, Clark, was a minor, and soon a major, partner in this firm.

such necessities as clothing and, occasionally, opium. At the end of each month the remaining wages, usually twenty dollars or more per man, were handed over to each worker.[33] Normally, each gang had a white (often Irish) boss, or over-seer, and in general whites monopolized the specialized, or skilled (hence better-paying) work, such as trestling, masonry, and actual rail laying. The Central Pacific's "chattering Mongolian phalanx" was turned loose to grade, cut and fill, blast, fell trees, and perform other common labor.[34]

The Chinese remained in remarkably good health, and few days were lost to illness (and probably none, unlike their white counterparts, to hangovers). A glance at their diet shows why. Mark Twain marveled in Nevada at such oddities as pressed duck and paste-covered eggs imported from China,[35] but this does not even hint at the healthful variety of foods the Chinese took for granted. An often repeated list is to the point: "The Chinese menu included dried oysters, abalone and cuttlefish, dried bamboo sprouts and mushrooms, five kinds of vegetables, pork, poultry, vermicelli, rice, salted cabbage, dried seaweed, sweet-rice, crackers, sugar, four kinds of dried fruit, Chinese bacon, peanut oil and tea."[36] Rounding out the menu were various beans, salted fish, dried shrimp, peas, and "small articles for Chinese chow chow."[37] In short, the gang cook's order books read like menus from a good Chinese restaurant today. By compari-son, the white laborers, whose food was purchased and paid for by the company, wolfed down mammoth portions of beef (usually salted), potatoes, and bread and often rancid butter, washing these down with drafts of brackish water, strong coffee, or raw whiskey.[38] Also, on the line, while white workers dipped suspect water from greasy pails with communal dippers, the Chinese drank only boiled (but tepid) tea, poured from small kegs slung from the backs of the appointed "tea boys" who prowled the construction sites.[39]*

The Celestials had few vices. They almost never drank whiskey, they rarely quarreled or fought—at least with outsiders—and they were scrupulously hon-est and religiously clean. As B. S. Brooks wrote in 1870: while the white man "has a sort of hydrophobia which induces him to avoid the contact of water . . . the Chinaman is accustomed to daily ablutions of his entire person."[41] After a grueling, twelve-hour day, "John Chinaman" was wont to fully bathe, or at least take a sponge bath and change into clean, non–work clothes before sitting down to eat with his comrades.[42]

The Orientals did, however, love to gamble. Mark Twain did not feel he was exaggerating when he wrote from observation that "about every third Chinaman

*So, at least, go conventional accounts. Documents relating to the Union Pacific, however, indicate that the diet of whites was more rounded, certainly if the workers chose to buy additional fare. Stores run by the company kept pace with demands of the work crews, and were surprisingly well stocked with fish and salted codfish, peaches, cherries, raisins, currants, apples, tomatoes, eggs, beets, turnips, pickles, spices such as cinnamon, ginger, and allspice, and oceans of Worcestershire sauce.[40]

runs a lottery."[43] Fan-tan was his favorite pastime, but, with limits on losses usually set by the headmen, debts, bankruptcy, and consequent bitterness and disunity were rare.[44] Many Chinese also, on occasion, enjoyed a long pipe packed with fragrant opium, a drug introduced to China by British merchants earlier in the century. Receipts and shipping records from Sacramento, Dutch Flat, and other railroad communities invariably mention opium, but no records have been found testifying to actual addiction by Central Pacific workers.[45] "They do not stupefy themselves with opium," wrote Mr. Brooks, an ardent defender of Chinese Californians: "You do not see them intoxicated with it . . . rolling in the gutters like swine," as one saw so many whiskey-soaked whites.[46] Instead, the Chinese would smoke a pipe or two on quiet Saturday nights, their eyes glazing over peacefully in their tents, causing no problems for their fellow man. Strobridge and Crocker detested the narcotic but never interrupted its use. It was a tranquil and tranquilizing vice, and they let it be. They also permitted "odd" Buddhist shrines along the right-of-way. "Crocker and Strobridge weren't sociologists," wrote Robert West Howard, but they were content to leave the Celestials a bit of cultural leeway.[47] Strangely, Horace Greeley, who thought he *was* a sociologist, or at least a keen observer of men, wrote in 1859 that the average Chinese was "an inveterate gambler, an opium-smoker, a habitual rum-drinker, and a devotee to every sensual vice."[48] This description jars with virtually every other firsthand account, and might just be an example of the politician playing to the crowd.

There were few other diversions for the Oriental workers, save on their few rare winter days off because of storms. There were some prostitutes, to be sure—women who, in the prim words of anti-Chinese activist Augustus Ward Loomis, had been "brought for vile purposes" to America, some of them kidnapped.[49] These, however, were few in number and mostly plied their trade among whites in major cities or wealthy mining camps such as Virginia City.[50] During hearings in 1878 concerning immigration restrictions, longtime California politico A. A. Sargent told the Senate about a typical Chinese prostitute's "contract." One An Ho received from one Yee Kwan $630 in advance (with no interest charges) to go to California, turn tricks for four years, and send him most of the proceeds. After the four years, she was free to return to China or remain in the United States, practicing her ancient profession or any other line of work. Should she fall sick for a period of ten days or more, another month would be added to her obligations to Yee Kwan.[51] That the same sort of arrangement was common among American prostitutes of the time was conveniently ignored by the Sinophobes.

Despite the very small number of troublemakers, criminals, and prostitutes in California's Chinese community, Chinese were generally suspected of depravity and looked at askance. An interesting comparison can be made with the state's small Chilean community, which, being white, attracted little attention or discrimination. According to the 1860 census, there were 1,970 Chileans in the state, of whom 600 were listed as female. A surprising 105 were openly labeled "prostitute" or "harlot," but since only about half of the women bothered to list their "occupation," the actual proportion must have been considerably higher. This unusual demographic characteristic resulted in little opprobrium in California, and the United States Senate never heard of a "Chilean Problem."[52]

The labor bottleneck was swiftly being solved by the Celestials, no matter what society on the whole thought of them, and eventually almost twelve thousand Chinese were working for the Central Pacific. In 1865 one journal reported graphically:

> They are laying siege to Nature in her strongest citadel . . . the rugged mountains look like stupendous ant-hills. They swarm with Celestials, shoveling, wheeling, carting, drilling and blasting rocks and earth, while their dull, moony eyes stare out from under immense basket hats in shape and size like umbrellas.[53]

The spring of 1865 brought other good news. On March 3, President Lincoln signed an amendment to the railroad act permitting the companies to issue their own common bonds for up to a hundred miles in advance of continuous track. Fruit of more successful lobbying, this amendment allowed a potential maximum (in mountainous terrain) of $4.8 million (at par) in new issues. As the Central Pacific's capitalization had just been raised, the amendment was a welcome one in Sacramento, even though company bonds were selling at debilitating discounts.[54] The Union Pacific was equally happy.

At almost the same moment, the Big Four received permission to build the Western Pacific, a line that would run from Sacramento to San Jose, through a subsidiary they had been quietly buying into.[55] Construction of the Western Pacific began late in the year and was finished in 1869, by which time the Big Four completely controlled that line. Almost unnoticed at the time, California entrepreneur and railroader Lloyd Tevis and several associates chartered the Southern Pacific Railroad Company, which was to become the linchpin of the Big Four's West Coast system.[56]

More important, the first San Francisco bonds were released to the Central Pacific. This $100,000 in city bonds, however, brought only $75,160 when sold to the public.[57] In April, with unusual gall, even for him, Collis Huntington filed a general work-route map with the secretary of the interior covering the entire area from the California border to the Great Salt Lake. This he did in spite of the clause in the 1864 act limiting the Central Pacific to a 150-mile penetration of Nevada.[58] This, however, was not to be Huntington's most audacious and ambitious piece of cartography. The Big Four hardly stopped with such shenanigans. Supposedly impecunious if not actually bankrupt, they organized an irrigation company, purchased water rights, and began work on a reservoir near Merced, later expanding their project. This Merced operation was a costly one, for it entailed tunneling and a great deal of culvert work, but, as with most of the Big Four's enterprises, the irrigation company flourished.[59] This scheme, and others like it, was in large part Charlie Crocker's brainchild—perhaps fruit of his sleepless nights—and he was the major partner. The redirected, pure mountain water would soon open huge new California vineyard lands, something that Crocker was always proud of.[60]

On May 10 the Central Pacific's first work train huffed into somnolent Auburn, at mile 36, and two days later, in Washington, Huntington at last took delivery of the company's first government bonds: $1,258,000 worth of government paper (if sold at par). Dimming his pleasure a bit was the knowledge that they had long since been fully borrowed on.[61]

During the hectic spring of 1865, the Big Four asked engineer George Gray to make a thorough inspection of the completed line and the grading and other work beyond. Gray was known to be a rigidly honest man, as well as one of the nation's best railroad engineers. The Big Four knew that he would unflinchingly criticize the work, both finished and projected, if he found it wanting. They were taking a chance by turning him loose, but, having gambled so often already, they were prepared to do so again; in fact, it was becoming their nature to gamble. A favorable review by so eminent an engineer would be splendid propaganda, and they needed that. With a wagonload of instruments and a small team of assistants, Gray headed into the mountains in late June.[62]

While Gray was in the Sierras, so was Speaker of the House and future vice-president Schuyler Colfax of Indiana. Colfax toured the work of the Union Pacific in July, and then he and his party, including influential journalists and a strong cavalry escort, continued across the sweltering, grasshopper-infested Plains to Denver. Ben Holladay loaned Colfax his posh new Concord coach (with fully stocked bar), and the Speaker toured in style, halting from time to time to swish a fly rod in a stream or shoot something interesting.[63]

In August the Colfax party reached California, and Stanford, never a man to miss a chance to politick, invited the Speaker and his people to travel with him to end of track, then at mile 50, just short of the village of Illinoistown, at an elevation of 2,242 feet. A savvy public relations coup, the trip was replete with the state's finest wines and brandies, and the best food the Central Pacific could muster. Stops were made to inspect the tracks, trestling, and culverts, and the exotic Chinese workers as well. As the *pièce de résistance,* Illinoistown, soon to be reached by iron, was renamed Colfax.[64] The Big Four wanted to keep its friends in Congress, and, better yet, make more of them. Enthusiastic reporters filed with the media back east enthusiastic stories about the Central Pacific and

the "dynamic" Leland Stanford, and would wax even more eloquent after George
Gray tendered his official report.

After a most thorough investigation, the contracted engineer wrote a report
that he immediately sent to the president, secretary of the interior, and Central
Pacific headquarters.[65] It was so glowing that the company gleefully published
it as a pamphlet in late July and widely disseminated it. Describing the line, Gray
found it of "first quality throughout," from the seating of its bridges and the
quality of its brickwork, to the spacing of its ties (a cautious and laudable
twenty-six hundred ties per mile) and construction of its depots. To the Sacramentans' immense relief, Gray had no reservations whatever. That the report
boosted the confidence of investors is clear, and it perhaps soothed some
skeptical officials in distant Washington as well.[66] A few months later, the
Railroad Record was heartily endorsing Central Pacific bonds as "among the
most desireable securities."[67] Gray, for his part, almost immediately accepted
a position as the Central Pacific's consulting engineer.[68]

While Gray was writing his kudos to the company, Montague (with whom
he would work in harmony) was receiving regular reports from survey teams
he had sent to Donner Lake and as far east as the Truckee and into Nevada.
He was also recalculating Judah's data and discovering anomalies and inaccura-
cies. To the Big Four's relief, he now stated that he could shave several
miles off Judah's line and, better yet, eliminate two tunnels and perhaps a
third.

In the meantime, the company's gross earnings showed a healthy growth in
local-traffic revenues, from $11,040 in January to $22,939 in May to $32,000 in
June.[69] They would continue to grow nicely. That same summer of 1865, long
after the steamer *Sultana* exploded on the Mississippi, killing at least seventeen
hundred, and Anheuser-Busch began bottling beer in St. Louis, the Central
Pacific, its progress threatened by the mountains, was spending a fortune on
blasting powder. The powder at least was less expensive than it had been during
the war, and, in fact, Crocker was able to obtain a great amount of government
surplus powder; but the sheer volume of explosives needed meant large cash
outlays. Crocker at this point had a special explosives railcar built at the company's expanding Sixth and E Street shops. It had thick iron sides and a tin roof,
and its sliding doors were lined with heavy strips of India rubber. Called the
"sparkless," this car alone was permitted to haul explosives to the work sites,
and it never suffered an accident.[70]

Still, powder, used in such large quantities by the Central Pacific, was not
always easy to come by; the local, West Coast product was noticeably inferior,
and even the finest was minimally effective against Sierra granite, albeit adequate
for blasting cuts through shale, limestone, and other soft rocks. Strobridge began
looking about for an alternative, and he soon found one he could begin using in
1866. It was a newfangled liquid explosive called nitroglycerin.[71]

INTO THE PRAIRIE, HALTINGLY

A S STROBRIDGE and Crocker put together their "Mongolian phalanx" for the assault on the Sierras, the Union Pacific resembled a painting that could have been entitled *Still Life, with Durant.* Grading in earnest had begun and equipment was finally starting to arrive, but not a rail was laid that first half of 1865. Survey teams were far afield, charting the void, yet their results were disappointing. Hezekiah Bissell, assistant to engineer Ogden Edwards, later wrote that "the work along the Platte Valley was generally light," yet progress was slothlike. Part of this slow pace was the result of confusion, lack of experience, and general inefficiency, but there was, psychologically, a great sense of unease about—and perhaps even fear of—the vast, empty Great American Desert. Edwards, wrote Bissell of his highly regarded boss, "was the hardest drinker I ever saw. His regular drink was two pony glasses of straight whiskey."[72] In fact, there were many hangovers in the Platte Valley in 1865 and succeeding years, for, as another Union Pacific surveyor noted the year the Civil War ended, "This is a terrible Country, the stillness, wildness and desolation of which is awful."[73]

It was not merely the ubiquitous rotgut that retarded the company's course through the valley, nor the crushing scarcity of financial resources. Taking its toll on all levels was pandemic peculation and outright theft of company property. Durant spent a considerable portion of the year fighting court battles in Omaha to keep for himself some of the lands donated by that city and county to the Union Pacific.[74] Colonel Seymour, it was rumored, made deals to get fat commissions from crosstie contractors (he himself was awarding the contracts), and in the valley itself, wrote Bissell, "Although it was on a small scale, there was some of the most bare-faced cheating on that early work that I ever saw."[75] The Central Pacific might have been faced with the Sierras, but the Union Pacific confronted a problem of mammoth dimensions—a problem that, unlike mere mountains, would not someday be left behind.

Then there was the Indian threat, which, while genuine, inspired caution to the point of torpor among the men doing the physical work. Diaries of men like Bissell and Arthur N. Fergusen reveal their constant fear of Indian attack—a virtual paranoia. All survey parties went into the field well armed and protected by an escort of United States Cavalry or Infantry. Fergusen slept with a carbine by his side and a "loaded revolver at [his] head." In late 1865 he noted in his diary that even the cavalry detailed to guard his party of surveyors could not be counted upon: "In the midst of the worst Indian country in the West, & liable at any moment to meet with a war party, & here I had an escort of about thirty soldiers, well armed & equipped, but they had shot all their ball & powder away at wild game." Worse for the surveyor's confidence, the soldiers had not felled a single animal.[76]

Fergusen's fears were hardly groundless, for there was great anger in the camps of the Sioux and other Plains tribes in 1865, glowing hotter than the coals of the cooking fires. The Indians were defending themselves and their way of life, and it was increasingly common for various tribes to forget their animosities and join forces against the moving white frontier. "Every tribe, from the headwaters of the Missouri to Texas, appeared in the Spring and Summer of 1865 to have commenced merciless depredations against the white man," according to one authority, and their hostility was to be the Union Pacific's greatest obstacle in the Platte Valley.[77]

To greet the new year of 1865, on January 7 some thousand Sioux, Cheyenne, and Arapaho attacked the tiny settlement of Julesburg, on the Nebraska-Colorado border. They easily captured the hamlet, killing fifteen soldiers of the small garrison and an unknown number of hapless civilians. A month later they struck the desolate village again, with equally thorough results, leaving only after having razed almost every building.[78] Ben Holladay lost hundreds of thousands of dollars (and thirteen employees) that year. As Ralph Andrist wrote in his masterful *The Long Death,* "Every ranch between Fort Kearney on the Platte in mid-Nebraska and Julesburg on the South Platte in northeast Colorado had been abandoned—and, in most cases, burnt to the ground."[79] Fergusen's fears had palpable substance.

An emigrant party of thirteen was caught in the open by the Cheyenne near Plum Creek; nine were killed and the others—women and children—carried off to virtual slavery in the Cheyenne's lodges.[80] In the western part of the valley, in June, "2,000 Indians of different tribes attacked the Platte River Bridge Station," according to General Grenville Dodge, who was then on campaign against the Indians in that area. A number of soldiers and civilians were killed there, including Lieutenant Casper Collins (for whom Casper, Wyoming, was named), who "was horribly mutilated; his hands and feet were cut off and his heart torn out. He was scalped and had over 100 arrows in him" when his body was recovered. Since arrows were treasured by the Plains Indians, the Cheyenne were clearly sending white society a message.[81] Ominously, the *Omaha Weekly Herald* reported that some of the Indian raiding parties were being led by "white rebels."[82] The whites, never patient with Indians, struck back blindly and savagely. In November 1864, the unstable Colonel John Chivington, leading bloodthirsty Colorado militia, had perpetrated the infamous Sand Creek massacre of a Cheyenne-Arapaho village, killing mostly women and children and creating the impetus for this new and even more brutal round of Indian depredations. In late 1865 and well into 1866, almost every town between Julesburg and Denver was in flames, and the latter city, isolated from the rest of the world for months by the Cheyenne, reported dangerous famine.[83]

More and more troops were assigned to the Plains—twenty-five companies were now stationed along Holladay's stage routes alone[84]—but the Indians barely slackened the rhythm of their raiding. In addition to allocating more troops to the threatened region (many of whom were "galvanized Yankees," or, former Confederates), Washington convened a dozen or so peace talks. Most of these were temporarily successful at best, for the needs of white and red were fundamentally opposed. Henry Morton Stanley, then a young newspaper stringer, saw this clearly as he wandered through the Plains, writing after witnessing one powwow, "The Indian chiefs . . . were asking the impossible. The half of a continent could not be kept as a buffalo pasture and hunting ground."[85] Yet that was essentially what they were demanding. Nor, with the advent of white "civilization," could that half of a continent support the traditional Indian way of life.

Luckily for the Union Pacific, the first 150 miles west of Omaha, although occasionally raided by the Sioux and Cheyenne, was Pawnee country. The Pawnee, a relatively unsophisticated tribe, had helped Coronado and his men in the sixteenth century, and since then had only rarely evinced hostility toward whites.[86] "The Pawnees were normally friendly," wrote surveyor Bissell in 1865, but also "more degraded in their habits and ways of living than almost any tribe" on the Plains.[87] Too lazy to work, according to the diarist, the Pawnee preferred to subsist on the refuse left behind by the railroad gangs, and migrated westward with the tracks, their few possessions strapped to the backs of their scrawny dogs, which themselves often served as food.[88] From the viewpoint of the railroad, however, the Pawnee had one good and one better trait. They were ancestral enemies of the Sioux, Cheyenne, Arapaho, and other tribes, *and* they were willing to kill them for pay. The railroad would soon come to rely on these painted, "degraded" folk for much of its own security.

Perhaps more debilitating to the Union Pacific than its burgeoning Indian canker in 1865 was the confusion and indecision in its top field ranks.[89] When Peter Dey resigned, the Doctor named Seymour acting chief engineer, a position light-years beyond his competence.* Worse was the fact that Seymour had already alienated most of the company's best young engineers with his arrogance and lack of talent. His chief assistants, B. B. Brayton, D. H. Ainsworth (both of whom soon resigned to work for a more professional boss),[91] and Jacob House, ignored Seymour as much as possible, while senior engineers Samuel Benedict Reed and Jason A. Evans paid attention only to orders emanating from 22 Nassau Street.[92]

*Seymour, one of a score of engineers consulted by the government in 1865 to recommend standards for the Pacific Railroad, uniquely touted lightweight, fifty-pound rails and a continuous "bearing" under the track rather than crossties.[90]

In part this disunity stemmed from Durant's inability to attract war hero General Dodge to take over as chief engineer. The (brevet) major general, who had been so useful to both Grant and Sherman, though interested in the position and in almost constant contact with the Doctor, in February, despite Durant's lucrative and flattering offers, patriotically accepted the post of military commander of the Department of Missouri, at the request of Grant, commanding general of the United States Army.[93] Dodge's Fort Leavenworth headquarters was soon responsible for all military operations in Nebraska, Kansas, Colorado, and Utah,[94] with the specific injunction "to remove all trespassers [Indians] on land of the Union Pacific Railroad."[95]

Dodge, his practiced eye sweeping the Platte Valley—"I looked this country over pretty carefully for the purpose of seeing what the ravines produced in the way of timber which we could use in building railroads" and for the best bridge sites[96]—was, during his tenure as Indian fighter, really an unsalaried Union Pacific engineer.

This, however, failed to satisfy the Doctor, who continued almost weekly to beg Dodge to shed his uniform and become chief engineer. Durant not only renewed his offer to the general but also attempted to convince Grant and Sherman to release Dodge so he could perform a more important service to his nation,[97] and had other parties pressure the engineer. Dodge's diary records (among others) a Peter Reed writing him in 1865 at the Doctor's urging, asking him to quit the army "and take hold of the UPRR," but once again, Dodge demurred.[98]

He did, however, solve a major problem for the Union Pacific, even while unsalaried. Following a spirited Indian campaign along the Powder River, he set forth with a small party of cavalry to reconnoiter the Platte Valley and beyond, well into the Black Hills. While Jason Evans was again searching for a feasible route into Denver and Sam Reed was surveying near Salt Lake City (dreams die hard), Dodge and his escort were exploring into Wyoming (then part of Dakota Territory). Preliminary surveys, including one by Dodge, had not located a pass through the glowering Black Hills under 9,000 feet in elevation, nor one with a grade less than the 116-foot maximum, and even the best would require numerous switchbacks with tight curves and a tunnel 1,500 feet long. Just the year before, Evans had reported that the best route through the Black Hills would require grades of up to 147.84 feet, which would necessitate yet another change in the railroad act.[99] On his current investigation, Dodge was desperately seeking a better pass.[100]

He found his pass, and the pass he found saved his life—at least according to his own, rather romanticized recollection. Pursued with only a few men by a Sioux war party one day in early November, Dodge galloped up a long, gently sloping ridge, on which stood a single pine tree, visible for miles. Even as he was riding for his life he knew that he had blundered onto a superior route through the Black Hills, and a few days later he calculated that "Lone Tree Pass" (later called Sherman Pass) plunged through the mountains with a peak elevation of only 8,236 feet. More important, no tunneling would be needed, and the grade (albeit a very long one) would not exceed a comfortable 90 feet per mile. Mentally renaming his discovery Sherman Pass, he kept its existence a secret for months. Consequently, construction contracts were let at a very high per-mile cost, based upon use of the expected and more difficult route. It is possible that Dodge and Durant were in cahoots to increase construction profits.[101] The future chief engineer kept his good news to himself; engineers Reed and Evans did not do the same with their sad tidings.

While Sam Reed had been able to get assurances from Brigham Young that Mormon labor would be made available for surveying, grading, and tunnel work,[102] his report made it clear to Nassau Street that a route south of the Great Salt Lake through the Mormon capital was out of the question. A plethora of engineering hurdles was compounded by an extreme scarcity of potable water. The route would have to pass north of the lake, through sleepy little Ogden instead. Best not to inform the Saints of this just yet, decided the Doctor, and perhaps plan on a narrow-gauge line from Ogden south to Salt Lake City. So parched and desolate did Reed find portions of Utah—one sixty-mile stretch held no water whatsoever—that he recommended that Durant authorize the purchase of camels for any future work there.[103] Jefferson Davis, who had bought camels for surveying in the Southwest in the 1850s, would have understood.

Survey engineer Jason Evans bore equally unwelcome tidings. There was no question: rich Denver would have to be bypassed to the north by 100 miles or more. If not, there would have to be an exceedingly long 116-foot grade, a pass (Berthoud) at a daunting and oxygen-poor 11,304 feet above sea level, and an impossibly long, 3.1-mile tunnel, which would consume a fortune and many years of labor. Evans's report was, like Reed's, marked "private" and shelved.[104] Yet another survey team was sent into Colorado in 1866 by the ever-optimistic doctor, but its report was even more negative than Evans's had been, and Denver, with deep regret at 22 Nassau Street, was deleted from the Union Pacific's main line. Instead, the rails would have to traverse isolated, unpopulated, seemingly sterile Wyoming.[105]

Although both the Union and Central Pacific decided in 1865 that Salt Lake City would not lie upon the main route of the Pacific Railroad, and while both put off telling Brigham Young of their decisions until 1868, various railroad maps published in 1866 and 1867 (some by the companies themselves) clearly showed the line passing north of the Great Salt Lake through Ogden. Could the Mormon leader really have been aware of the truth?[106]

Money was still a desperately scarce commodity for Union Pacific directors in 1865. The company was hard-pressed to pay its few hundred graders, and it appeared that it might have to renege on orders for its first major batches of equipment.

An all-out attempt to push company stock failed miserably that spring, and only the Ames brothers and their associates coming into the Crédit Mobilier gave Union Pacific officials a brief surge of optimism. Banker John Pondir, at the request of his good friend Secretary of the Treasury Salmon P. Chase, did make a financial commitment to the company in May. He and some business associates loaned the Union Pacific just over a million dollars, accepting as collateral unissued government bonds at 90 percent of par.[107] Prior to this infusion of funds, Durant had been driven to pay a staggering 19 percent interest on what smaller loans he could ferret out.

With the Ames boys aboard the Crédit Mobilier and Pondir associated with the Union Pacific, the Doctor's operation acquired a respectability and credibility it had not enjoyed before. In fact, as the stars of Durant and Train faded and those of more stable financiers with more stable personalities came into focus, the Union Pacific found it increasingly easier to attract capital, although not buyers of its stock.

Rhode Islanders Rowland and Isaac Hazard, already involved with the Crédit Mobilier, were the next to step forward. Paragons of financial probity and hence solid advertisements for the railroad, the Hazards pumped hundreds of thousands of dollars in loans into the company in 1865, and more in succeeding years.[108] In 1867 Rowland would be elevated to the Crédit Mobilier board, from which position he railed mightily against Durant.

This newly available capital at last permitted the Union Pacific to move, and, now that the war had ended, labor (except on the West Coast) was hardly scarce. With minimal publicity, nameless workers laid the first rails at Omaha on July 10, and were spared the deadly speechifying that normally accompanied such symbolic moments. Cutting corners—in the manner of Seymour—the Union Pacific was laying substandard fifty-pound-per-yard rail, six pounds lighter than the act's mandated minimum, and using forty-five-pound iron for the sidings. Only after mile 440 were the barely adequate fifty-six-pound rails used, along with more effective fishplates to hold them together instead of the less reliable, cheaper "chairs," simple, fifteen-pound iron supports, not bolted to the rails. By contrast, the Central Pacific's lightest rails were sixty-pounders, and fishplates replaced chairs at mile 115.[109] It took the track layers eleven full days to lay the first mile out of Omaha, an indication that the company's stated goal of sixty miles by Christmas would not be met.[110]

If Union Pacific iron was not up to standards and easily worn out, its crossties were even more shoddy. Durant had ordered 300,000 ties to be delivered at Omaha before the first rail was in place, but when he saw what these cost, he almost lost his vaunted composure. Hardwood ties of good quality (oak or walnut), cut and shaped in Michigan or Wisconsin (or farther east) cost as much as $4.50 apiece, delivered.[111] Thus ties alone would cost the company $11,250 a mile—at the time an unacceptable burden. Asked a few years later to explain his reliance on unreliable cottonwood ties, Durant snapped, "If there were any [hardwood] ties in that road in the first two sections that did not cost the company $3 each it was because they cost $5 as they lay in the roadbed."[112]

On the Doctor's orders, ties were cut from the soft local timber, mostly porous cottonwood and some lightweight cedar. Unfit for use as crossties, the cottonwood was subjected to a newly available technological wonder: the Burnettizer. Purchased at St. Louis, the first Burnettizer retort, a huge one-hundred-by-five-foot, fifty-five-ton cylinder, was sent to Omaha by steamship. The cylinder was crammed with some 250 cottonwood ties, air was pumped out of it, and a near vacuum created. This opened and drained the wood's millions of pores, after which a high-pressure flooding of the cylinder with a zinc solution coated each tie and penetrated the pores. Then came heating and drying, and the ties were—in a manner of speaking—ready. The result was a wooden tie that looked metallic and had the weight of a ferrous metal, but did not last nearly as long. Nowhere nearly as reliable as a hardwood tie, the Burnettized cottonwood made a decent, temporary support and was far cheaper, costing the company a mere sixteen cents each to be processed into quasi-metal.* [113]A similar treatment, called "payanizing," which used a chloride-of-lime solution, was also tried. Although it made the ties heavier, more durable, and "almost incombustible," the process was much slower than Burnettizing, and hence rejected.[115] Utilizing one of its few natural advantages, the Central Pacific used superb ties of redwood and tamarack, cut locally and delivered for an average price (within California) of fifty cents each.[116]

To make the most of his economizing, Durant instructed Sam Reed, now construction supervisor, to use the available hardwood ties sparingly—one under each rail joint and three under every spur switch. The rest of the ties would be of the lucent cottonwood variety.[117] Thus, in the short run, the Union Pacific saved some of its precious money, but in time the company would have to spend far more. In 1870 alone, on one three-hundred-mile stretch of Platte Valley line, over 300,000 of the crumbling Burnettized crossties had to be replaced.[118] Once in Wyoming and beyond, better ties could be cut locally and at a reasonable cost, but thanks to the Colonel and the Doctor, corruption wildly escalated those prices as well.

A Burnettizer—there were soon three at Omaha—could, if worked around the clock, process five loads of cottonwood a day, perhaps half a mile of ties. Construction boss Reed was soon hiring lumberjacks in Michigan to scour the Platte Valley for stands of cottonwood on land-grant acreage and contracted with

---

*There is debate as to when the Burnettizer began operation. Many secondary sources assert February or April 1866, but an on-the-scene report described it as functioning in June 1865.[114]

private landowners to cut their timber as well. He was forced to pay his ax-wielding recruits forty-nine dollars a month, plus board, and a bonus of twenty-nine cents per tie per day over the first fifteen.[119] Much of the valley was soon stripped of its riverbank cottonwood and cedar groves, which fostered erosion, which in turn was to play havoc with the Union Pacific when flooding occurred. Cottonwood too narrow to be used as ties was harvested for locomotive fuel, for coal was not yet in vogue. Even the locally gathered six-foot lengths of fuel wood, however, cost the company a painful one hundred dollars a cord.[120]

Using light rails linked by undependable chairs seated upon shining ties, the Union Pacific moved forward at last. With a million bricks (for buildings and culverts) ordered for summer delivery, locomotives coming in from Baltimore and Philadelphia, rails from half a dozen Pennsylvania foundries, passenger cars from Fort Wayne and Chicago, and labor from demobilized Union and Confederate armies, the Union Pacific was a complex organization.[121]

By September 1, despite the "distressingly languid delivery of materials," according to Wesley S. Griswold, a thousand men were working in the field, their pay in arrears from the start.[122] Two hundred of these were grading some thirty miles out of Omaha (tracks reached mile 11 on September 25). The graders were using three new, ungainly "patent excavators," large, flat, and heavy scrapers, each pulled by eight yoke of oxen. On the flat valley topography, where literally no rock work was needed because no rock existed, the excavators and their crews could grade over a half-mile daily, a rate then considered heroic.[123] The Union Pacific, unlike the California line, was always willing to experiment with new machinery: the first Burnettizer, first excavators, first steamshovels, and more. With the exception of steam pile drivers and nitroglycerin (which the Union Pacific also used), the Central Pacific's leaders almost ignored technology in favor of human muscle.

In the early fall, about the time the first train robbery occurred in wild and woolly North Bend, Ohio, the Union Pacific's government commissioners went out on the line to inspect the company's progress and quality of work. Commissioner Springer Harbaugh, who wrote the official report, was somewhat relieved, and even impressed, despite the "economizing" in rails and ties. He found grading complete to mile 53, just beyond Fremont, although ballasting of good quality (gravel) was in short supply and easily washed out sand had been used in many places. "With the slight exception of two or three culverts and a few drains near Omaha," he found the quality of the work to be superior.[124] The editors of the *Railroad Record,* however, while publishing Harbaugh's findings, took exception to them, lashing out at the company as well as the work it had done. "We confess that *we* are not satisfied . . . neither is the country, with the performances of this company. The country has a right to expect more vigor in its construction," wrote the editors, who blasted the Union Pacific's sloth and poor-quality construction, calling them "an insult to the generosity and magnanimity of the American public."[125] Born in controversy, the Union Pacific was condemned to be hounded by it.

Controversy be damned; the Union Pacific was moving west, reaching mile 16 on November 2 and gathering momentum, now speeding its equipment and crews to end of track on its own flatcars. The sound of the shrieking steam whistle was at last competing with the howling of coyotes in the broad valley. Work gangs at Omaha were busily Burnettizing, building company shops and readying rolling stock; survey teams prowled hundreds of miles into Indian country; graders prepared the way to Train's magical Columbus; burly workers, often Irish, laid and spiked track on the lonesome prairie; other large crews worked the company's four steam-powered sawmills outside Omaha; lumberjacks neutered the ravines and hollows of the Platte and its affluents; masons and carpenters patiently constructed culverts, trestles, drains, and bridges. "A little too thick to swim in and not quite thick enough to walk on," in the words of a contemporary traveler, the Platte and its tributaries would have to be bridged many times,[126] the work taking place far in advance of track. William F. ("Buffalo Bill") Cody all the while was collecting a princely $500 a month to provide buffalo meat for all who could tolerate it.[127]

Not all was physical labor that summer and fall. At a board meeting in New York in late July, the Doctor was narrowly elected president of the Crédit Mobilier, which did not sit well with the Ameses and their New England group of investors. The fact that director Oliver Barnes—now one of Durant's cronies—was elected both secretary and treasurer also stuck in their craws, for they distrusted the motives and business acumen of both men.[128] In fact, that July election marked the beginning of a major feud between the two interest groups, a feud that would result in lawsuits, public invective and slander, government investigation, and America's most gaudy business scandal.

The Ameses and their allies might have liked Durant's and Train's ideas about making money, but they detested the Doctor and Train and did not trust them, feeling that they were detrimental to the progress of the Union Pacific. Just a few months after Durant's contested election, William Glidden and John M. S. Williams of the Boston group wrote him, open in their suspicions and questioning his handling of finances and his constant demands for more money, neither of which was followed by observable results. In November, Williams wrote the Doctor again, demanding that he be kept better informed about company finances and asking for access to Durant's and Oliver Barnes's books.[129] An example of the convoluted schemes for which Durant used company funds was his loan to the rival UPED of some half-million dollars, at a time when his own workers were going unpaid for months. It seems that in return for his generosity with company funds, Durant controlled a large block of the rival line's bonds; this might have been a sound move, for it did give Durant a loud voice on the other railroad's board of directors.[130] The chilly atmosphere in the Crédit Mobilier boardroom was soon to become as hostile as the Great American Desert.[131]

In November, with less than twenty miles of track spiked, the Doctor decided it was time to host a modest "excursion" to end of track. A few flatcars, pulled by the locomotive *General Sherman,* lurched out of Omaha with Durant, his special guest General Sherman, and a score or so of others, most of them seated on heavy nail kegs and constantly flicking cinders and sparks from their hair and beards. Not Durant's finest publicity coup, the brief trip failed to inspire the major general, who is reported to have remarked of the work he toured, "I hardly expect to live to see it completed."[132] The Doctor managed to make something of a media event out of the outing in any case.

George Francis Train was also hyperactive in late 1865. With his characteristic and boundless enthusiasm and magnificent hyperbole, the "Chevalier Train," as the press often labeled him, was raising money through his Crédit Foncier to erect buildings throughout his satrapy on the Plains. Lecturing a group of prospective investors in Chicago, he told them that he was "about to go out and build a hundred cottages at Omaha . . . and initiate an enterprise in the Far West, which would make a hundred Girards and Astors of the Chicago capitalists, would they invest money in it."[133] He was at least moderately successful with those and other capitalists, writing a friend in December, "Am off to build one hundred cottages at Omaha for the Chinese Mandarines when they come through on the Pacific Railway." In fact, in 1866 he did build more than a hundred of his four-room cottages in that town, although it seems clear that few "Mandarines" ever stopped over in them.[134]

Omaha at this point was truly booming, and not entirely because of Mr. Train and his imperial dreams. In 1865 alone, the town's population more than doubled, to some fifteen thousand, largely because of the Pacific Railroad, and a resultant building boom was frantically under way.[135] Late that year, the *Omaha Weekly Herald,* in an article entitled "The Poor of Omaha," lamented the new "urban" underclass that was now so in evidence, and actively solicited contributions from its readers to aid the indigent poor.[136] It would not be long before another Omaha newspaper was railing against another urban blight: a proliferation of whorehouses and flagrantly cruising prostitutes.[137]

GRANITE LIKE STEEL

THE summer and fall of 1865 must have been a period of numbing doubt and strain for the leaders of both Pacific railroads, for the problems they faced must have appeared overwhelming. The Union Pacific, laying its first rails in its three years of existence, was running out of time. It had just short of a year to reach mile 100, and it was in chaotic financial circumstances, bedeviled by lack of engineering leadership and cowed by the enervating shrill of war whoops in the Platte Valley.

The Central Pacific faced far worse. On September 1 its tracks reached Colfax, at mile 54, 2,242 feet high in what were still mere foothills. The next thirteen miles to Dutch Flat were murderous: an ascent of 1,200 feet, broken terrain, two major bridges, numerous cuts, the granite monolith called Cape Horn to be circumvented, and the extremely difficult clearing of the right-of-way to be done. It would take a full year to reach mile 67. Far worse lay beyond Dutch Flat. From Dr. Strong's village to Cisco was only some twenty-five miles along the Central Pacific's projected line, but the elevation increased a remarkable 2,485 feet; there was far more blasting, cutting, and filling to be done, another precipitous gorge to be bridged, massive redwood stands to be cleared, numerous tight curves to be plotted, and the first three of the railroad's fifteen tunnels to be cut through the planet's most stubborn rock: Grizzly Hill Tunnel (mile 77), Emigrant Gap (mile 84), and Cisco (mile 92.25). At Cisco, the Big Four would still have thirteen miles and another 1,132 feet of elevation to conquer before reaching Summit, where, at mile 105.5, the worst of its tunnels—1,659 feet long—would have to be gouged out, followed by six more tunnels in less than two miles. Montague's talents had by now reduced the number of tunnels from Judah's eighteen to fifteen, but the task facing the Central Pacific was not merely improbable, it was unique in engineering annals. So rugged was the land after Colfax that the cost of grading alone on some portions would exceed $100,000 per mile.[138] Tens of thousands of tons of granite and other durable stone would have to be chipped and blasted from the mountains every month. How ironic, for the Union Pacific, in a prairie swept clean by glaciers millennia before, desperately needed stone.

It would have been somewhat easier had it been possible for the Central Pacific to face its problems consecutively. Unfortunately, Crocker, Montague, Strobridge, Lewis Clement, and their host of Oriental workers would have to take on the worst problems simultaneously.

It is worth detailing the stark tableau faced by Jim Strobridge that summer and fall. With track laying assuming a low priority in the face of preparing the ground for iron, he and the omnipresent Charlie Crocker divided his growing pool of labor five ways. The largest of his work crews—some five thousand men and six hundred teams of draft animals—were sent ahead four miles east of Colfax to work on Cape Horn, an immense spur of granite rising some 3,800 feet above the American River.[139] Another thousand or so were detailed to the backbreaking and dangerous work of clearing the right-of-way, and smaller teams of three hundred to four hundred men each were put to work farther east boring entrances for the first three tunnels.

The huge gang sent to Cape Horn, which soon resembled a giant anthill swarming with Celestials, faced what appeared to be the most impossible of a number of impossible tasks. Somehow they had to create a roadbed along the almost sheer sides of the granite monster, some 2,200 feet above the roiling river below—a sharply curving roadbed at that, whose curves would hug the monolith and, worse yet, ascend. For decades, trains going in either direction would stop at Cape Horn for a few minutes so travelers could marvel at the work accomplished and admire the splendid, vertiginous view.

In early September, Strobridge turned his Celestials loose on Cape Horn with their picks, drills, shovels, tiny wheelbarrows, and blasting powder. The "crumping" of explosives reverberated through the valley below as the Chinese—who either were not susceptible to acrophobia or possessed a singular wealth of fatalism—began to sculpt the mountain, great chunks of which were blasted or pried loose to tumble earthshakingly into the American River so far below. Hundreds of barrels of black powder were ignited daily to shear away the obdurate granite and form a ledge on which a roadbed could be laid; but no matter the volume of explosives, progress was too slow to suit Stro and his boss. While as many as half that work crew was engaged in building two massive retaining walls just above the emerging ledge (one a hundred feet long, the other two hundred feet), Montague suggested to Strobridge a new tactic, to which the Chinese headmen agreed. Beginning amidst the chill winds of late October, as snow swirled over the higher peaks in the distance, scores of Chinese were lowered by ropes from Cape Horn's summit to the almost vertical cliff face. There, nestled in flimsy-looking but strong woven baskets, the workers, sometimes swaying and swinging in the wind like ornaments on some bizarre outdoor Christmas tree, bored holes in the cold rock with their small hand drills. Dangling, they tamped in explosives that had been lowered to them, set and lit the fuses, signaled the men above by jerking a rope, and, wrote Thomas W. Chinn, "then scrambled up the lines while gunpowder exploded underneath."[140] This was a hazardous business at best, and some of the Celestial acrophiles were not agile enough to escape the blasts or were hit by flying rock and followed the chunks of granite into the valley below. Notwithstanding the casualties there was no lack of volunteers, and to the surprise and relief of all, the basic work on Cape Horn was completed before winter's rather tardy fury forced a four-month halt to outside work. Track would be laid around Cape Horn the following May, well ahead of schedule. Most Cape Horn Chinese were shipped back to Sacramento for the winter, with a few score experienced rock men sent up the line to the tunnel facings.

The basketmen faced danger every time they swung out on their lines from the summit of Cape Horn, but the crews clearing the right-of-way were even more exposed to injury or death. Their task was to clear an avenue a hundred feet wide on either side of the roadbed. At least twenty-five feet on each side had to be completely cleared and leveled, stripped of all rocks, obstructions, and vegetation. Past Colfax, this growth included some of the world's largest trees, timeless redwoods hundreds of feet high. How different from clearing the right-of-way in the Platte Valley, where the largest impediments were prairie-dog villages.[141]

One three-hundred-man gang spent a full ten workdays clearing a single mile of right-of-way. The trees were felled (many of them shipped to sawmills to reappear later as ties and trestling), and then the stump and root complex had to be blasted from the soil. Some of the stumps were so massive and stubborn that ten barrels of powder were needed to break their grip on the earth. With every explosion came zinging chunks of rock and lethal redwood, tamarack, and pine splinters: mortal missiles fired back by nature at the army invading it. The road-clearing crews also had to contend with boulders and outcroppings, and often had to precipitate landslides to create a level and safe right-of-way. In any one week they used as much explosives as did Lee and McClellan at Antietam. Clearing a mile often cost Charlie Crocker $5,000 or more. When the snow accumulated to three feet that autumn, most of the road crews were sent down the line on furlough until spring.[142]

It was tunnel work, however, that was given the most attention, and cost the most money in 1865 and succeeding years. Those dark holes severely tested the ingenuity, patience, courage, and physical resources of every Central Pacific worker from Charlie Crocker down to the lowliest Chinese tea boy.

Immediately beyond Colfax an unusually hard form of volcanic granite and, estimated one observer, "even harder porphyritic rock" were encountered. Henry Root, who worked with Lewis Clement, now a tunnel engineer, recalled that "the rock was so hard that it seemed impossible to drill into it to a sufficient depth for blasting purposes."[143] Another observer wrote that against such geo-logical eccentricity "gunpowder seemed almost to have lost its force."[144]

In the early fall, teams were scratching and blasting away at the portals of Grizzly Hill, Emigrant Gap, Cisco, and the more distant Summit tunnels, finding to their chagrin just how secure nature was in "her mightiest fortress." A distant, but knowledgeable observer, writing of the Central Pacific's assault on the Sierras, noted optimistically that the workers were "accustomed to pulverize quartz and reduce mountains in a manner which would have astonished Hanni-bal," and felt that the company would conquer the mountains in two and a half years, "if there [was] any virtue in gold, gunpowder or nitro-glycerine."[145] There was very little gold in the Sacramentans' treasury and as yet no nitroglycerin, but by late 1865 as much blasting powder as the workers could handle was available.

While the Union Pacific faced no rock excavation at all in its first five hundred or so miles,[146] the Big Four's chief tunnel engineer, John R. Gillis, found that his hardworking Chinese gangs at the Grizzly Hill facing (and elsewhere) were progressing an average of a pathetic seven *inches* in an exhausting day of dangerous labor. The best day's record at Summit Tunnel in two years of work, using powder, was twenty-seven inches on one facing.[147] The Central Pacific had to order specially tempered steel for its drills in hundred-ton lots because the granite eroded the grooves so swiftly.[148] Up to three hundred kegs of blasting powder a day was going up in smoke on Summit Tunnel alone by 1866,[149] and the powder bill, according to engineer Clement, often ran from $53,000 a month to a high of $67,000 just for the tunnel work.[150] Henry Root later explained that "more powder was used by the rock foremen than was economical," but they used it so lavishly because they were told that time, not money, was of the essence.[151] The one benefit from all this blasting, chipping, and drilling was that the company found that it could use the small shards of granite for superior ballasting of the tracks, while the larger chunks, shaped or not, could be sold to construction companies for good money. According to the *Railroad Record,* high-quality, construction-grade granite, formerly imported from China, was thus made available by the Central Pacific to American builders at an acceptable price.[152]

Still, with only inches a day tallied by the Celestials and their picks and hand drills, the prospects were not cheering, for railroad tunnels, even if single-tracked (most of the company's were), are by nature large undertakings. On average, a Central Pacific railroad tunnel was sixteen feet wide at the bottom, sloping gently upward and inward to a height of at least nineteen feet. All tunnels were at least partially lined with stout timber—some, like Emigrant Gap and Tunnel Spur, were entirely timbered—and all were roofed with boarding almost three inches thick. The tunnels' side timbers (braces) were commonly twelve-by-twelve-inch, or even twelve-by-sixteen-inch, redwood—heavy, hard-to-maneuver supports that were held to the walls by long three-quarter-inch-thick iron bolts. The Central Pacific had twenty sawmills working full time on tunnel supports and crossties.[153] To complicate matters, most of the Sierra tunnels were set on both curves and grades. It was nightmarish for the Chinese to labor in candlelight or by lantern in the increasingly foul, dusty air, and the engineers themselves had a hellish time plotting accurate lines under such conditions. Given the circumstances, it is remarkable that the tunnels run so mathematically true.[154]

In view of the snaillike progress in the tunnels, the Big Four and their technical staffs made a number of decisions in late 1865. Work would continue on the tunnels throughout the winter, despite the weather conditions, from both their east and west facings. The very long Summit Tunnel would have to be pierced from above as well as from both ends so that four facings could be attacked at once. And newfangled explosives would have to be experimented with.

In late September, Crocker headed into the Sierras, which were already dappled with the season's first snows.[155] The years of late, mild winters were no more. Up the line to Summit Tunnel churned Charlie Crocker, inspecting every foot of the way. He gave orders to establish permanent work camps on both sides of the Summit and ordered round-the-clock drilling, blasting, scraping, shoveling, and hauling by the Chinese. After all, he figured, there is no day or night within a gloomy tunnel. There would henceforth be three eight-hour shifts on each tunnel face, Crocker's only concession to those Chinese selected to work throughout the winter. As soon as the weather permitted, a steam power plant would be brought to the Summit to help haul the heavy detritus from the new shaft being sunk vertically, midpoint on the tunnel's line.[156]

Some 90 percent of the Chinese work force was paid off for the winter, however, for there was little they could do in the frigid Sierras. Working outdoors was impossible because of the heavy snows, and since only a handful of men could work at one time on the constricted tunnel faces, a mere five hundred or so men were kept at work on the tunnels in gangs of approximately twenty men. Some of these would freeze to death that first Sierra winter, but that was only a harbinger of the next winter's toll.[157]

Despite what was believed at the time and has been thought since, the Big Four did *not* recruit great numbers of Chinese from China itself. In fact, in 1866 and 1867—key years for the construction of the Central Pacific—more Chinese left California than entered, a reversal of traditional immigration patterns.[158] Stanford was probably unaware of this odd exodus of Celestials just when they were most needed by his railroad, for early in 1866 he wrote to Crocker in the field: "We have the assurances from leading Chinese merchants, that under the just and liberal policy pursued by the Company, it will be able to produce, during the next year, not less than fifteen thousand laborers."[159] Whether fifteen thousand were indeed made available, the Central Pacific hired only eight or nine thousand that year.

Tunneling, under wretched conditions, continued through the winter of 1865–66, even when fourteen feet of snow lay on the ground and drifts towered to thirty feet and more. While not an especially severe winter compared with those to follow, there were five feet of snow on the ground by the first of December.[160] Other work stopped, although in the East Huntington, who tried to work eight months in advance of Crocker's needs (from pick handles to locomotives), was putting ten thousand tons of equipment in transit every thirty days or so.[161]

Tunneling, clearing the right-of-way, grading, and track laying were not the only occupations of Central Pacific personnel. The company also employed about five hundred specialized artisans, mostly masons and carpenters, to build bridges (under master bridge man and architect Arthur Brown), company depots, and other buildings, and stone and brick culverts (ultimately, 375 miles of them) seated in hydraulic cement. The bridges were major engineering works in their own right, each one perched on solid granite piers. The first bridge, across the American River, had trestling nearly a mile long, for it not only spanned the seven-hundred-foot-wide river, but adjacent, spongy floodmarsh as well. Most of the trestling and actual bridgework was made from massive Puget Sound pine and redwood, but, as these deteriorated within a decade or so, they were to be replaced with fill (embankments) or iron-and-steel structures. The men who did such work were paid handsomely, for they were both in short supply and critical to the railroad's progress. This they realized, and they demanded and received— on time and in gold—wages of from three dollars to five dollars a day, with most employed year-round.[162]

As the snows began in the Sierras that fall, another facet of mountain life became apparent. Even before the first heavy snowfall, patterns of drifting and avalanches had been recorded by Lewis Clement and other engineers. As the *Railroad Record* noted in November, "For several miles the track must be roofed, to slide off the snow."[163] It was not clear at the time, however, that this would entail the labor of thousands, some $2 million in additional expenditure, and thirty-eight miles of heavily roofed and protected track.

In December, as the lonely, freezing tunnelers made the mountains shudder with their granite-shattering explosions, and while artisans plied their specialties in the company's expanding Sacramento shops, the leaders of the Central Pacific took stock. The railroad had fifty-four miles of working track to Colfax, less than twenty of which had been spiked in 1865. These few miles, however, according to the company's annual report, had cost an astounding $6 million, which, when added to the previous two years' outlay, came to a depressing $9 million. Disappointingly, only $3,363,300 in stock had been subscribed (not all paid in)—mostly by the inner circle—and only one initial block of government bonds had been received. The company had dramatically expanded its rolling stock and reported a significant increase in earnings, grossing some $405,581 for the year. Net profits were in the neighborhood of $280,000, a rather impressive net-to-gross ratio.[164] About twice as much revenue was derived from freight than from passenger service, and only $6,500 from carrying the mails. Anticipated revenue for 1866, according to Leland Stanford, was almost half a million dollars from freight and just over $200,000 from passengers, plus a rather grandiose increase in receipts from carrying transshipped Nevada freight to and from the mines, as well as an expected large sum from the sale of timber on the company's best lands—a sum, like all projections concerning future benefits from the land grants, that was wildly exaggerated.

7

THE UP GETS AN ARMY; THE CP
GETS A RACE

THE DOCTOR AND THE GENERALS

O N THE surface, and for the nation as a whole, 1866 promised to be a good
year indeed. The Civil War was over, easing tensions and releasing hundreds of thousands of able-bodied young men. Immigration increased
dramatically after the guns fell silent, and Northern war industry, boosted
mightily by the demands of the last four years, slipped effortlessly into full-time
civilian production. The Thirteenth and Fourteenth Amendments to the Constitution guaranteed full citizenship to America's blacks and promised to reduce
racial suspicions, and the first transatlantic cable linked the United States to the
Old World. Jack Daniel distilled his first sour-mash whiskey in Lynchburg,
Tennessee, and Americans in general, not at all sapped of their energies by the
Civil War, turned their attentions to their vast interior. It was a propitious time,
and from the boardrooms on Nassau Street and the office over the grocery store,
railroaders exuded confidence to the public—a confidence they did not personally feel.

Durant's concern at the beginning of the year was to get the Union Pacific
moving, and swiftly. The forty miles he had in place (with its light rails, zinc-
soaked ties, and sand ballasting) had to become, by congressional mandate, one
hundred miles by June 27 or the company would lose everything. But, depending
upon the weather—and the Indians—work might not be resumed until March,
or even April.

On Christmas Day, 1865, the Doctor had promoted the quiet and efficient

Samuel Benedict Reed to become overall superintendent of construction, a position analogous to Strobridge's on the Central Pacific.[1] But despite Reed's efficiency, the contractors and subcontractors out on the line were undependable, incompetent, absent, thieving, or all of these, and a yawning void was still present in the upper echelon of the engineering department. Durant was all too aware that while Silas Seymour could be a valuable asset financially and politically, he was at best a quarrelsome and mediocre engineer. The aging General Dix, with his superb military and political contacts, had taken a leave of absence as company president to ply his fluent French as ambassador to La Belle France, and had been replaced by the eminent, credible, prestigious, and wealthy Oliver Ames in November. Ames, to Durant's perpetual irritation, understood railroading and actually desired to direct the Union Pacific.[2] A major stockholder, Ames refused to take a salary as acting president, but he worked at the job full-time, which severely limited the Doctor's "discretionary powers."

There were both good and bad portents that make-it-or-break-it winter and spring. Durant was seriously negotiating for top-level new talent, and was in contact with both Grenville Dodge and the Casement brothers of Ohio, who were first-rate construction men. On the other hand, the knowledgeable Henry V. Poor had stated verbally and in print his belief that "not over one mile of rails [could] be laid in a day upon a continuous line."[3] If Poor was correct, the June 27 deadline would not be met. Also, the Indians were on the warpath again in the Platte Valley, spreading death and destruction even before the snows had begun to melt. Until the end of the Civil War no major waves of white settlers had penetrated what was considered to be Indian country, but as Richmond and Atlanta lay in ruins, emigrants and fortune seekers poured into the prairie, touching off an almost continuous war with the Indians. The 1862 Homestead Act, so generous with federal lands, became a magnet drawing people to the Plains.[4] Conflict was inevitable.

Peripatetic Henry Morton Stanley, who leisurely traversed Nebraska in 1866, wrote of encountering in one thirty-mile stretch of proposed Union Pacific line "no less than ninety-three graves; twenty-seven of which contain the bodies of settlers killed within the last six weeks. Dead bodies have been seen floating down the Platte."[5] Farther out on the Plains the men running survey lines were also running grave risks. Arthur N. Fergusen, nervously noting in his journal that thirty-five whites had recently been killed by Indians in the Powder River area, wrote woefully from his guttering campfire about his party: "We were but a handful of men, poorly armed, in a strange, wild and desolate country."[6] General Dodge, leading his regiments against the Indians at that very moment, was sorely troubled, for conditions were so harsh and dangerous that two of his units had "mutinied openly" while on campaign.[7]

But General Grant, commanding general of the army, was ferociously protective of the Pacific Railroad, writing in 1866 that "the completion of these roads will also go far towards a permanent settlement of our Indian difficulties." He allocated every company he could spare to ensure unmolested construction on the Plains.[8]

During the Powder River campaign of 1865, Dodge had acceded to an idea proposed by a Major J. P. Becker, Indian agent for the Pawnee. Soon a hundred Pawnee warriors were (figuratively) in uniform, toting shiny, new government-issue carbines.[9] Led by Captain (soon Major) Frank North, a Pawnee-speaker who had been a licensed trader with the tribe, the Indian scouts performed valuable services for Dodge. Soon promoted to battalion status, though they had not increased in number, North's mounted warriors were posted along the railroad line in the Platte Valley, under a handful of white officers. They were so effective in detecting, thwarting, and occasionally defeating Sioux and Cheyenne war parties that in 1867 they were formally inducted into federal service for a three-year hitch.[10] North, a personal friend of Dodge, would later "manage" the Indians in Buffalo Bill's traveling Wild West Show. For the time being, however, he used his painted troopers as if he and they were Union Pacific, rather than federal, employees.[11]

On the bright side, government inspectors approved the company's first forty miles. The bonds, of course, were hardly issued instantaneously, nor were the land patents. On January 25, to the delight of Nassau Street, the *Railroad Record* reported that the Union Pacific, like its California counterpart, had twenty sawmills working night and day, and gave rave reviews of the company's growing physical plant at Omaha, writing of its buildings: "They are of brick, and for symmetry, utility, and elegance, have no superiors in the country, and only a few equals."[12] Indeed, within a year, the machine shops at Omaha, powered by a stationary seventy-horsepower engine that had been hauled across Iowa at considerable expense, would be producing several excellent railway cars daily in addition to performing routine repair and maintenance work.[13] Meanwhile, gathering further publicity for the company, Durant had named the first four of his locomotives after famous Union Civil War heroes, the first being the *General Sherman.*[14]

A pro-railroad pamphlet appeared in January and was widely distributed, its text a speech given by an Illinois politician before the New York State Chamber of Commerce. In addition to praising the railroads as "simply the agents of the American people," the speaker hinted at the commercial possibilities of the Great American Desert, so thinly settled. The quartermaster at Fort Leavenworth, a Colonel Potter, had informed him that he had just sent 33 million pounds of military freight westward the previous season. This had required him to hire almost two thousand wagons, three thousand horses, and fourteen thousand mules, at tremendous expense. In short, Colonel Potter—and other frontier officers—needed a railroad, and would be happy to provide a great deal of paying traffic for it.*[15] Similarly, that spring Dodge noted: "General Myers, Quarter-Master at Omaha telegraphed me that he had two million pounds of freight ready to go over the road and all the freight going to the Plains would be sent our way."[17] Under the terms of the 1864 act, there was plainly money to be made just from government contracts.

While Dodge calculated freight tonnage, on February 8, after two months of negotiations, Durant made one of his soundest moves. He wrote John Stephen Casement from his New York offices, accepting Casement and his brother Dan's "proposition in regard to track-laying."[18] "Jack" and his brother, both in full red beards, were put in charge of track laying and far more, and would soon march a civilian army across the Plains. Disciplined, armed, specialized, and often working to drum rolls, the Casement Army would prove Henry V. Poor a poor prophet, for in their first 182 working days they would spike almost 250 miles of track.[19] Diminutive Jack Casement (five feet, four inches) was a bundle of kinetic energy. Born at Ontario City, New York, in 1829 of immigrant parents from the Isle of Man, he moved to Michigan at age fifteen, and began working on railroads two years later. Rising from common laborer to foreman by 1851, he and his younger, shorter ("five feet nothing") brother by the late 1850s were doing virtually all the contracting for the three-hundred-mile-long Sunbury & Erie, and 150 miles of the Erie & Pittsburg.

Enlisting as a major in the 7th Ohio Infantry in 1861, Jack went off to war, leaving Dan behind to finish their construction commitments. Distinguished in action, Jack was soon a regimental commander of the 103rd Ohio, and by war's end a brigadier general. Demobilized a few weeks after Lee's surrender, he wired his wife: "I am on my way home, Bag and Baggage"; but his plans to become a cotton broker were thwarted by depressed international prices.[20]

An obsidian-hard man of barely repressed violence who habitually carried a long bullwhip and a fancy, engraved .44 pistol,† Jack had an innate faith in discipline and obedience. He was, in short, a hard case. Dan, a more silent, but equally hyperactive sort, was a natural, though similarly inflexible, organizer and bookkeeper. Jack stayed in the field, Dan kept the accounts and the order books straight, and both, in their distinct ways, knew just what railroad construction was all about.

Jack later wrote: "I took the contract for laying all the track of the Union Pacific Railroad, and doing the better part of the grading," but his responsibilities were destined to be far broader, and he would become the most demonic force driving the railroad across the Plains. He laconically recalled of his Union Pacific

---

*In fact, in 1862 the government paid the firm of Russell and Waddell alone over $6 million to convey freight from the Missouri River to the forts on the Plains.[16]

†The pistol, on display in the Union Pacific Railroad Museum in Omaha has grips of engraved ivory—many accounts say mother-of-pearl—with raised relief eagles so sharp that it must have been painful to grip.

years: "It has been sufficient work to keep me out of a great deal of mischief."[21] He would, in fact, create some of his own. Imperturbable in the face of a furious Durant, screaming Indians, or financial collapse, the little general could cooly write his wife: "I am still here on a grid iron. Things look awfull bad," and "Don't be alarmed for I don't think we will go to the Poor house."[22] Jack could face adversity and feed on it.

While the Casements were packing their bags, Durant was still doggedly pursuing Grenville Dodge, who now wore two stars on his shoulder boards. Sometime in early 1866, the Doctor had again talked with generals Grant and Sherman, asking them to release Dodge from service so he could get on with a greater work. According to Dodge, the generals "had told [Durant] that if I went at the head of the concern, I would have their full support," but apparently they themselves refused to pressure their colleague to resign.[23]

The Doctor met with Dodge at St. Joseph on April 24, and after a round of flattery, an offer of a handsome $10,000 a year, and various other assurances, Dodge agreed to ask for a leave of absence from the army to take on the new challenge. Not, however, before the general told the sly doctor bluntly, "I would not accept and be responsible for the road unless I was given absolute control . . . there must be no interference."[24] Such, of course, despite Durant's assurances, was not to be the case.

Dodge, who at least normally received his salary when due and received it in full, later admitted that he, like his friend Hoxie, was another of Durant's victims: "In addition to my salary as Chief Engineer, I was to have an interest in the construction company [Crédit Mobilier] as part of my compensation, which was never given to me."[25] The fact that he said this before a congressional committee investigating the Crédit Mobilier smacks a bit of sophistry, for in this and other testimony the engineer constantly strove to disassociate himself from Durant, from the Crédit Mobilier, from disbursement of funds, and from almost everything else the congressmen were interested in. Asked about the indisputable and all but public links between the Union Pacific and Crédit Mobilier, Dodge flatly lied, ingenuously and blandly responding: "Well, I knew nothing of them at the time."[26] The dullest man on his grading crews knew a great deal about them. Also, it is known that a hundred shares of Crédit Mobilier stock were held in his wife's name, and, in the summer of 1869, he was actively attempting to sell $10,000 in Union Pacific stock profitably, stock that was most probably collected as part of the Crédit Mobilier's indecently large—and premature—dividends in 1867.[27]

In any event, Sherman granted the engineer an open, or indefinite, leave of absence in early May,[28] and some two weeks later he appeared at Omaha to assume his duties. By then, the situation, thanks to the Casement boys, was well in hand.

Jack and Dan lost no time after winning their contract in February. They were on the scene within weeks and, with an almost ruthless efficiency, organized their work force and equipment and began earning their pay. A thousand men and a hundred wagon teams were signed up by the brothers and before February was over, the Union Pacific shops were working furiously on four huge "house cars," designed by the Ohioans to be the nerve centers of their operation. These special cars were eighty-five feet long, ten feet wide, and eight feet from floor to ceiling. They were so long that they were swaybacked, and were commonly called "sows" or "sowbacks." One car was divided into the Casements' twelve-foot-long office, a twenty-foot kitchen, and a forty-seven-foot-long dining room. Another was half diner and half bunkhouse, with three tiers of bunks along each wall, while a third was entirely a dining car and the last a bunkhouse. In the field, even the dining areas were used for sleeping. Each windowless car was equipped from the start with rifle racks in every convenient spot, and a thousand weapons were normally carried in the four cars, with small mountains of well-placed ammunition.[29] Also, when the Casements set forth from Omaha, a herd of five hundred cattle was driven in their wake, for the brothers never considered buffalo fit food for white men.[30] Work, food, sleep, defense, and more would revolve around the house cars, a self-contained community and command center on wheels.

The men chosen by the Casements were an odd lot, mostly (though, despite the legends, hardly all) of Irish extraction. In addition to the many "gandy dancers" and bog trotters among them, as one source correctly notes (and extant photographs clearly indicate), one finds a "crowd of ex-Confederates and Federal soldiers, muleskinners, Mexicans, New York Irish, bushwackers, and ex-convicts," with a sprinkling of blacks thrown in.[31] The Casements wanted only strong, hardworking men who could and would learn a job and stick to it with military precision and discipline. Postwar America was awash with such men and the Casements took their pick.

Each man was instructed in a basic task: unloading rails and equipment from flatcars, placing the ties or rails, ballasting, tamping the ballast, bending the rails, spiking, setting the chairs or fishplates, installing the switches, and so on. Specialized, the brothers' men could do their work like automatons. Flatcars were loaded individually with precisely the right mix of ties, rails, spikes, chairs, switchplates, and associated gear necessary to complete a specific section of the line. When the cars were pushed forward to end of track, precisely the right amount of gear was transferred to waiting work cars or wagons and brought to where the gangs were stationed, waiting to put the material in place. There was little wasted time or energy: pure economy of time and motion.[32]

The Casement Army moved out past the hamlet of Fremont before April began, and progress was swift from the beginning.

An admiring General Dodge, arriving in mid-May, was impressed by what he saw. "It was the best organized, best equipped, and best disciplined work force

I have ever seen," he wrote. "I used it several times as a fighting force and it took no longer to put it into fighting line [armed] than it did to form it for its daily work."[33] In his diary he noted that Casement had other than purely construction-related responsibilities: "His force were all armed and I depended upon him to carry out my orders as to the policing of the line whenever it was necessary to use any force that I could not obtain from the military."[34] With the armed trackmen, Major North's Pawnee Battalion, and several regiments of regular troops all looking out for the interests of the Union Pacific, it is no wonder that hostile Indians, while always a dangerous annoyance, were never a true threat.

One beautiful spring day, hoping to accelerate the pace of his crew, Jack Casement strolled the advance work areas, offering each man a pound of fresh tobacco for every day they laid a mile or more of track. According to Bissell, who was there, "This they did easily." About a month later, Dan walked the line. His offer was time-and-a-half pay for a mile and a half or better of new track, and, wrote Bissell, "This was done." Dan went out once more, in the early summer, and upped the ante to ensure that the Union Pacific reached the 100th meridian before any other line. He offered, and sometimes was happy to pay, double wages for two-mile workdays, which swelled the bankrolls of his men, then paid a standard thirty-five dollars monthly, plus board.[35] No wonder that Henry Morton Stanley was impressed by these workers, "who display an astonishing amount of enthusiasm" for their jobs.[36]

The crew did not average two miles a day but it did build far faster than Henry V. Poor and most others believed possible. The Union Pacific had initiated freight service at mile 28 the previous fall when its tracks reached (and a station was built at) Elkhorn, which served a large German immigrant community strung along the fertile Elkhorn Valley.[37] By the time the tracks reached mile 100 on June 16 (just eleven days before the deadline), nine miles past Train's fanciful new national capital of Columbus, traffic was significant and growing daily. The Union Pacific then had ten stops and had built a number of water tanks and fuel depots as well as three three-thousand-foot-long sidetracks.*[38] In August, following a sustained burst of double-pay-induced energy, the Casement Army spiked track to a point opposite Fort Kearney past Grand Island, at mile 191, which vastly increased the military freight business. Mile 191 was also a new terminus for Ben Holladay's Overland Stage Line, which also helped boost railroad revenues.[39] Unfortunately, having reached mile 191 also meant that the track crew was in true Indian country, and it was here that the Casements' men were introduced to their first—albeit short-lived—"Hell on Wheels."[40]

---

*Sidetracks would in total length eventually equal 10 percent of the Union Pacific's total mileage, and 7.5 percent of the Central Pacific's.

A FIRST WALK ON THE BAWDY SIDE

—

T HE young men of the Union Pacific were themselves hardly pacific. They brawled, screamed, drank, and occasionally murdered their way across the Plains, not quite the "advance guard of civilization" that Fergusen wrote so glowingly about in his diary.[41]

The company's base was incredibly rowdy. In 1864 Omaha was home to 127 saloons, 25 "temples of vice," 10 "full-fledged gambling establishments," but only 20 places of worship.*[42] The brawny young men spiking and tamping their way west along a route that Stanley found littered only with animal carcasses[44] constituted "the closest thing to the Foreign Legion you could find" in postwar America,[45] and after weeks of brutal labor, lashed by the elements and threatened by the Sioux, these men sought diversion. Their pockets full of time-and-a-half and double-time greenbacks, they found absurdly little to spend them on amidst the tumbleweeds, save for the efforts of the occasional itinerant whiskey seller who would furtively pop up in the night, dispense his overpriced wares, and skedaddle. The Union Pacific's work force sought vice and, lo and behold, vice followed the men into the forbidding void. Yet another component of Fergusen's "civilization" was on the move.

The entrepreneurial spirit that guided, dominated, and built nineteenth-century America was not about to permit thousands of young men to roam the sagebrush with so much change rattling so seductively in their pockets. So by the time the men reached Kearney they were being followed by "a carnivorous horde hungrier than the native prairie grasshoppers," ready, able, and willing to nibble on wads of Union Pacific greenbacks.[46]

Setting up their rude tent cities (later some had more upscale, prefabricated, wooden buildings) from Kearney to Corinne, Utah, and a dozen places in between, the sin sellers did a brisk trade out of their "mobile Gomorrahs" from the beginning.[47] Engineer Bissell, impelled by his revulsion to use more words than he usually did, noted that the Hells on Wheels were "used by the sporting fraternity as temporary centers for all sorts of vice, and they were tough places. . . . Vice, often without any gilding, exploited itself without restraint."[48] Another observer wrote of the phenomenon: "It could almost be said that the UP was built on whiskey," and that whiskey watered the weed-choked gardens of prostitution, gambling, and general mayhem and depravity.[49]

Hundred-proof concoctions such as "Red Dog," "Blue Run," and "Red Cloud"

---

*Five years later the number of saloons had shrunk to a mere thirty-eight (and five liquor wholesalers), but so had the number of churches—to six—for a population of twenty thousand.[43]

could pop skulls and lead even the most callow youth to the gaming tables and the knock shops,* with resulting fleecing and running pustules. Drunken track-men blended with painted whores, knife-wielding pimps, and shifty, Derringer-toting gamblers to form a brew more volatile than Red Dog, and one even more prone to explode. The result was a trail of hangovers, bruises and contusions, festering sores, and corpses stretching out behind the Union Pacific like survey stakes.[51] The rather puritanical Dodge and Jack Casement, his "enforcer," were willing to tolerate this unique phenomenon, but only when it did not get out of hand and affect the railroad. When it did, they would strike back, and viciously.

"There is not a virtuous woman west of Cheyenne," wrote one S. D. Page in 1868,[52] but for Cheyenne one could substitute Kearney, North Platte, Jules-burg, Bear River City, and other towns, and for 1868, 1866 or 1867, and not be far off the mark (excepting the Mormon communities). In truth, before there were settlers, one could find a "little bordello on the prairie." When the railroad crews moved on so did the purveyors of vice, for the region's only other inhabitants, prairie dogs, made poor customers. In 1869 Kearney, once bursting with dissolution, was described in the *Great Trans-Continental Railroad Guide:* "Now, we are told, the inhabitants consist of but 'our old cat and another one,' though what number of people that expresses, we are unable to determine."[53] It was there, in 1866, that the Union Pacific's raucous young men blew off their first raucous steam.

COLLIS P. HUNTINGTON GETS HIS RACE

THE Central Pacific's Sinic work force, rebuilding its ranks in Sacramento, Auburn, and Colfax in February and March of 1866, would spread no such debauchery through the Sierras and the Nevada flatlands. Sated with whatever sin they had been able to locate and afford in their several months off, and with their leather opium bags bulging, the Chinese were ready to work.

So was Collis Potter Huntington, and his task that spring was a dual one. With the pressure of supplying Crocker and his men, and often anticipating their needs with something like clairvoyance, Huntington was spending more and more time in New York, talking with bankers and investors, ordering equipment, and arranging for the requisite shipping. With the one small portion of his highly

---

*Raw whiskey commonly retailed for a mere fifteen cents a quart in towns and for ten cents a drink in the fanciest hotel bars, and—often adulterated—could be had at a Hell on Wheels for perhaps a dollar a quart.[50]

organized brain reserved for his and Hopkins's hardware business, he was also ordering stock for the store, often in fifty-thousand-dollar lots. Much of that stock, in turn, the partners were to sell to Crocker's construction company.[54] Huntington and Hopkins were, however, in the process of selling their business to their employees, and by late 1867 they would retain only a 20 percent share and their names over the door.[55]

Few things escaped Huntington's attention, and he would not buy a single axhead unless it was being sold at what he knew was a good price; he prowled the city in search of bargains. On April 4 he wrote Hopkins from New York, jubilant that the price of gold dollars in relation to greenbacks was holding at 145⅜ (it had been as high as 199 in 1865). So relieved was he that he had just bought $50,000 worth of "small" supplies for the company, including 250 kegs of nails at, he bragged, only $6.50 per keg.[56] At other times he would boast to his partner that he had ferreted out a true bargain on 517 dozen pick handles and 300 kegs of nails, with cut-rate shipping charges as well.[57] In short, Huntington would buy almost anything, and in volume, if the price was right, regardless of the construction schedule.

But that winter and spring, the Californian had a higher purpose. Perhaps because he was the company's East Coast lobbyist (Richard H. Franchot, friend, ex-congressman, and Union army general, would be hired to assist him in 1866), Huntington had deeply felt the sting of the 1864 act's limitation of the Central Pacific to 150 miles beyond the California border. He later claimed that he was never really worried about that clause, for he knew he could have it struck anytime he wanted; but could he? It was time to find out.[58]

It seemed ludicrous on the face of it. How could he even talk seriously about such a thing in Washington when his company was stalled at mile 54, with most of the worst construction still ahead? As the Casement Army made double time across the gentle Plains that spring—and many believed that the Central Pacific would need a decade to blast through the Sierra fortress—Huntington, back East, turned on the charm, and perhaps a great deal more.

There is no question that he and Franchot lobbied furiously that spring. They carefully explained to congressmen that they were not seeking more aid. What they wanted, said Huntington and Franchot, would cost the government nothing. All they desired of Congress, they importuned over dinner and drinks, was equal opportunity—the right to compete fairly. Was that not the American way? Huntington put it more bluntly to some: he wanted an end to congressional discrimination against the Central Pacific Railroad Company. There should be no mileage limit to its construction. While he later wrote to a friend that he was willing to bribe Secretary of the Interior James Harlan with as much as $100,000, it seems he never found it necessary to do so.[59] This was not always to be the case, for in the 1870s and beyond, he openly wrote in his letters about bribing officials. A good example is contained in a letter to Hopkins written on May 7, 1877, concerning a bill introduced into Congress by Florida senator Simon B. Conover: "It costs money to fix things so that I would know that his bill would not pass. I believe with $200,000 I can pass *our* bill."[60] His letters after 1869, in fact, make Oakes Ames's later controversial missives to Henry McComb appear rigidly honest by comparison.

Years later, Charlie Crocker ruminated about the Big Four's influencing politicians: "If the legislatures and legislative bodies of the country had let us alone, we would have been only too glad to have kept entirely out of politics . . . we have always tried to prevent the passage of those laws that were going to ruin us just as any man would throw a bucket of water on a fire that had attacked his house."[61] Like Huntington, apparently Charlie Crocker was more than willing to spend money to defeat "evil," as he defined it. He saw political influence as a purely defensive tactic.

In influencing legislation, the Big Four's most useful employee was Richard Franchot, a civil engineer and man of great influence and considerable charisma (and the only general on the Central Pacific payroll). An exceptionally smooth fellow, he more than earned his twenty-thousand-dollar-a-year salary* and gargantuan expense account, dispensing information, cash, good cheer, and favors to "flexible" congressmen and journalists. In fact, he may well have glad-handed as much as $5 million or more during his fruitful work for the Californians.[62] In a later investigation, horrified members of a congressional committee learned that for all the cash funneled through Franchot, the Big Four had neither asked for nor expected a single receipt.

Perhaps because of the logic of his position, Huntington managed to get bills introduced into both houses of Congress that would scrap the geographical restriction and throw the entire route open to the swiftest. There was remarkably little debate in the world's greatest deliberative body, and, surprisingly, Durant and Ames made no serious attempt to block the bills. The Union Pacific leadership simply believed that many years would pass before their California counterpart could break loose from the embrace of the Sierras and participate in any race. In any case, on June 19 the Senate approved its bill by a vote of thirty-four to eight, and a week later the House assented, ninety-four to thirty-three. Most people saw no valid objection to giving both companies equal treatment. This amendment also permitted the laggard UPED to link up with the Union Pacific at any point between the 100th meridian and Denver (they eventually did at the latter), receiving full federal aid.[63]

Most congressmen realized that by removing the geographical restriction on

---

*It is worth noting that he was the only company employee to receive the same salary as the Big Four paid themselves. Even E. B. Crocker and E. H. Miller, Jr., received less.

the Central Pacific, they were likely to accelerate the pace of construction by both companies; this they thought was in the national interest, and it certainly did act as a goad. While Congress arrogated to itself the right to name the exact site where the two lines would ultimately connect, that determination would have to await the results of what Congress now hoped would be a genuine race.[64] The amendment was signed into law by President Andrew Johnson on July 3, and a jubilant Huntington returned to New York to conduct company business, leaving Franchot to mind the store in the capital.

While Huntington was weaving his magic spells in Washington, Charlie Crocker and Jim Strobridge were lining up and dispatching the largest work force in America, which by May would number over ten thousand men, of whom some eight thousand were Chinese. The first crews sent into the Sierras that April— aside from the tunnelers—spent weeks just shoveling the snow, which was up to ten feet deep on the right-of-way and much deeper around the tunnel bores. Boss track layer Henry H. Minkler had his men spiking in early May up and around Cape Horn's vertiginous ledge, and Arthur Brown, a competent and very foulmouthed Scot who would later design and build Crocker's and Stanford's opulent private mansions, took charge of the company's trestling, timbering, and bridging, sending a thousand men to fell trees, shape timbers, and drive piles for bridges at Secrettown Gap (mile 62.5), Butte Canyon (90.5), and Lower and Upper Cascade (98.5 and 99).[65]

Charlie Crocker, with the energy of a far slimmer man, spent most of his time that spring on the line, and later fondly remembered, "Why, I used to go up and down the road in my [hand] car like a mad bull," inspecting, criticizing, and at times roaring with rage.[66] That spring he also roared at Jim Strobridge, at whom no one normally roared. Crocker ordered his pickax-toting construction boss to be less harsh on his men, to which Stro bellowed back, "They are not gentlemen; they are about as near brutes as they can get!" Crocker soon deferred to the profane Strobridge, telling him that he could, after all, "rule them with an iron hand."[67]

The headquarters train that followed the track gangs that spring—eventually, all the way to Promontory Point—had an unusual addition. In a standard passenger car made over into a three-bedroom home on wheels lived Hanna Maria Strobridge and the adopted Strobridge progeny, all six of them. The only woman who moved with either line, Mrs. Strobridge had an awning fitted to her "front porch," and when the train was halted she hung house plants and a canary in an ornate cage around the entrance. People wiped their feet before they entered Hanna's domain, even Mr. Strobridge. He alone had a family life on the line. Despite that domestic bliss, his foul temper was singularly unmoderated.[68]

Well before the snow was melting around the workers at Summit Tunnel, steps were being taken to speed their labor. A small, old Hinkley locomotive, the *Sacramento,* was being cannibalized in its namesake city. The body of the

locomotive was stripped away and the power plant was winched aboard a reinforced freight car and hauled to end of track. There, a colorful and exceptionally
profane muleskinner known only as "Missouri Bill" was waiting. He was cheer-
fully taking on his ultimate challenge: to drag the ugly, twelve-ton engine, now
known as the "Black Goose," from end of track to the Sierra Summit, some fifty
miles away as the crow flew. But the "Black Goose" was no crow, and Missouri
Bill would have to drag it over some seventy-five miles of twisting, ascending
mountain trails.

Workmen wrestled with the "Black Goose" and strapped it onto the largest
wagon available, one especially equipped with mud-sled wheels two feet wide.
Pulled by ten yokes of straining oxen, shaken out of their natural lethargy by
Missouri Bill's shrieking invective and long, snapping whip, the "Black Goose"
made painfully slow progress. Even as Chinese workers were drilling and blasting on both sides of the tunnel and from above, deepening and widening their
shafts, Missouri Bill and his helpers were forced to pause and build thick cordu-
roy roads everywhere they encountered soft and spongy ground. It was an
unusually wet spring, recalled Strobridge later, turning much of the Sierras into
a swamp, and the "Black Goose" had to halt frequently.[69] Also, because approaching horses, singly and in wagon teams, were made skittish, if not driven
half mad by the sight of the creaking, lumbering metal monster, the muleskinner
had to post one of his men ahead to put blinders on them before they caught
sight of the behemoth.[70]

Going downslope was a biblical labor. Blocks were put under the wide wheels
while heavy logging chains were secured to the largest trees nearby and, with
a few feet of slack, attached to the wagon. The blocks were then knocked out,
the wagon and its precarious cargo slid a yard or so, and the process was
laboriously repeated. Blocks and chains were needed on steep ascents as well,
all slowing progress to a crawl.[71]

For six awful weeks Missouri Bill lashed his oxen onward, bullying them with
his stinging whip and stentorious, blaspheming voice, which competed for attention with the regular, crackling explosions from the tunnel faces above. At last,
in late May, the "Black Goose" was perched atop the Sierras; the tunnelers now
had their hoisting engine to pull the massive granite chunks away and the equally
massive and ungainly tunnel timbers into place. Work on the vertical shaft, which
would be eight by twelve feet wide and almost seventy-three feet deep, progressed more smoothly.[72] The old engine, snorting the steam and soot of the
Sierras' first pollution, gave notice to all that the Central Pacific would not be
halted by either geography or geology.

In recent times, a movie company tried to duplicate Missouri Bill's feat, using
a smaller engine and the best modern equipment to move it. Recently, one
scholar wrote that "the movie makers hauled their burden five hundred yards
and gave it up as a bad job."[73] The Hollywood experts failed, but Charlie Crocker

did not. His men were soon hauling standard locomotives, and indeed, entire trains and hundreds of tons of supplies over and down those mountains, by sheer man and animal power.

THE DUTCH FLAT TRUTH

SOME of the granite-shattering explosions heard by Missouri Bill as he goaded his oxen on were not being caused by traditional blasting powder, for in 1866, frustrated by the Sierra's unique, almost indestructible rock formations, Strobridge decided to innovate, and began to use nitroglycerin on the Summit Tunnel and tunnel number 8.

Invented in Italy in 1847 by Signor Ascanio Sobrero, nitroglycerin had been refined by demolitions engineer Alfred Nobel in the 1860s. His "blasting oil" ($C^6H^5O^{18}N$) was five times more powerful by bulk than powder explosives, and, according to the *Railroad Record,* thirteen times more destructive.[74] That same publication erred somewhat when it praised nitroglycerin's supposed stability, reporting that "its storing and transport involve no danger."[75]

Master tunneler John Gillis was especially captivated by the idea of a powerful liquid explosive, for it might well prove to be the breakthrough that he sought. He hired an itinerant Scottish chemist, James Howden, to mix it for him. Shipped into the mountains in inert, binary form, the explosive was 96 percent pure when Howden finished brewing it in a special reinforced and partially buried log "factory" built by the company near Donner Lake. Gillis had perhaps not read deeply enough into the literature, for despite the *Railroad Record*'s encomiums, at precisely 1:13.5 on the afternoon of April 16, 1866, a shipment of nitro (not in inert form) ordered by Huntington from the East erupted at a Wells, Fargo office in San Francisco. Twelve people were killed outright, and scores were injured. Nitroglycerin is a fickle explosive: only one of the shipment's two boxes exploded, while the other, a mere yard or so away, was found intact amidst the rubble. A few days later, the freighter *European* blew sky high at Aspinwall, Panama, its California-bound nitroglycerin disintegrating at least fifty people and four hundred feet of new, expensive pier.[76] A subsequent investigation revealed that the explosive had been falsely labeled "Glorain Oil," a nonexistent substance.[77]

Despite these tragedies, nitro and chemist Howden were working in the Sierras by June. The light, oily yellow liquid was inexpensive, costing only some seventy-five cents a pound in its active state. Howden's brew, however, was probably too potent, for there was soon a major, fatal accident in tunnel 8. Irish workers then declined to handle the blasting oil, but the Chinese were fatalistic enough to accept the risk and for a while it continued to be employed with some success.

It was poured into holes drilled fifteen to eighteen inches into the granite, capped with a plug, and fired by a slow match or a percussion cap. It did increase tunneling progress in Summit Tunnel by some 54 percent, according to Gillis,[78] and did a far better job than blasting powder of thoroughly shattering rock, but it was indeed fickle. In one accident, after a number of charges had been set off simultaneously, Chinese pick-and-shovel gangs were sent in to the face to widen and clear the new fissures. Unfortunately, some charges simply had not gone off—that is, until a Chinese worker hit one with his pick. Then it exploded and Celestials were blown up along with the granite.[79] While no one recorded how many accidents occurred with nitroglycerin, its use was halted when Strobridge lost an eye as a Celestial's pry bar hit an unexploded batch.[80] One can only guess what happened to the Chinese. Shortly thereafter, Stro bawled out, "Bury it," and the unstable liquid was supposedly not used again on the Central Pacific, despite over two thousand successful blasts and the fact that in 1868 and 1869 the Union Pacific used it to advantage in the Wasatch Range.*[81] Oddly enough, Alfred Nobel perfected dynamite in 1866, and despite Gillis's awareness of that stable explosive, it was never tested or used by the Central Pacific.[83] Despite the cost in dollars and in time, the company largely reverted to tried-and-true blasting powder, although the *San Francisco Union* reported in 1867 that the Central Pacific was about to "contract with Colonel Schafer, the nitroglycerine man," for more Sierra blasting.[84]

There were other men at work in the mountains that spring. Isolated groups were doing preliminary grading and clearing as far as Donner Lake in the High Sierras, at mile 117, while much larger Chinese crews were gnawing at the terrain around the tiny (population three hundred) village of Cisco (mile 94), whose elevation, at 5,911 feet, was just a few hundred feet less than the summit of Mount Washington, New Hampshire, the highest point in the Northeast.[85] Cisco was the natural staging base for the assault on the highest portion of the line and the tunnels situated there. Other parties, under survey engineers Butler Ives, William Epler, and S. M. Buck, were spread out from the Truckee River, just inside the California line (named for one of Frémont's Indian guides) all the way across Nevada to Humboldt Wells and beyond. Those lonely men sent back grim reports of the country the Central Pacific hoped to traverse. Its only advantages were billiard-table flatness and a 172-mile stretch that would not require a single bridge.[86]

Not far from what would become Reno (mile 154), according to one who

---

*This is probably an apocryphal story. Stro did lose an eye to nitro, but one source contends that Howden was still mixing his brew at Donner Lake in 1869, and that its use saved the Central Pacific $1 million.[82]

wandered the region, "desolation [began] to assume its most repulsive form
. . . miles on miles of black, igneous rock and volcanic detritus . . . outcrops of
lava, intersperced with volcanic grit," with only sparse growths of greasewood,
artemisia, and sage giving testimony that life could exist there.[87] Another who
was familiar with Nevada wrote that it was "so destitute of vegetable and animal
life, as not to rise to the rank even of a *howling* wilderness."[88] Virtually water-
less, this desert was dotted with the bones of thousands upon thousands of draft
animals who had not made it to California, and a few offspring of Jeff Davis's
camels, searching patiently for water. It was also Indian country.

While the Union Pacific was led in the field by generals, protected by generals,
and worked by armed veterans of every rank, the Central Pacific, spared the
threat of Indian depredations, had little need of the military. The primitive
Digger Indians of that part of the Sierras being pierced by Strobridge's men
were—through epidemics—mere memories.[89]

Descending from the Sierras to the Truckee and the flatlands below, however,
the Central Pacific's surveyors encountered Indians neither primitive nor mere
memories. Here lay the lands of the Paiute, Shoshone, and several migratory
branches of the ferocious Apache. In 1863, by the Ruby Valley Treaty, various
tribes had assented to open their lands (at least a very narrow strip of them)
to be used for and by the railroads—a vaguely understood concession to the
right of eminent domain—and, for the most part, they had remained peaceful.[90]

The Central Pacific, which was granted permission by the Nevada legislature
to build through the state only in 1866,[91] was taking no chances. In that year
the company signed its own treaties with the dreaded Apache subtribes, Paiutes,
and others—treaties replete with generous "gifts," better defined as bribes.
Some of the Indians, notably the Apaches, did not, of course, become converts
to philosophical pacifism, but their warpaths seldom intersected the path of the
railroad, with which they had a satisfactory arrangement. Not dependent upon
the buffalo for their way of life, Nevada's Indians had less to fear from the
railroad than did the Indians of the Plains. In fact, the company was to encounter
only one potentially dangerous Indian problem along its entire route from Sacramento to Promontory Point and that passed without much bloodshed.[92]

Peaceful or not, the Indians along the Central Pacific right-of-way did little to
inspire confidence among whites, from Frémont in the 1840s to George Crofutt,
who wrote in his 1869 railroad guide of the "Shoshones and Piutes [*sic*], two
tribes who seemed to be created for the express purpose of worrying immigrants, stealing stock, eating grasshoppers, and preying upon themselves and
everybody else."[93]

In addition to giving the Indians interesting gifts, the Central Pacific soon had
"any number of Indians" on its payroll,[94] and, as workmen were tracking the
alkali flats of Nevada and Utah, the company permitted Indians to ride the trains

for free. As Huntington recalled, "They were given government passes to ride in first-class cars, in the Shoshone country," and all along the line company employees had orders "to let the Indians ride and treat them well. . . . We always let the Indians ride when they want to,"[95] said Huntington, and the company's regular passengers felt they were witness to a Wild West show.

Work continued apace, and the day after President Johnson slipped the Central Pacific's leash by signing the 1866 amendment, the company's crews finally spiked their way into Dutch Flat, at mile 67. The event was the cause for a grand celebration (shared in by Dr. Strong) for that no longer isolated community of two thousand souls.[96] It was July 4. It was indeed a day to celebrate, for in the midst of all the backslapping, Stro and Crocker (who was almost living in the work camps now) received word from tunnel engineer Gillis that his Chinese borers had broken through the headings at Grizzly Hill. It would take another month for that 498-foot-long tunnel to be widened, half of it fitted with timber braces, and made ready for tracking, but July 4 *was* a memorable day despite the company's continuing penury.[97]

Perhaps more memorable for the Big Four personally was July 5, as their track crews began to spike their way out of Dutch Flat, for with every hammer that rose and fell, another blow was struck at the Dutch Flat Swindle and its propagators. The *Railroad Record,* reporting on the progress of the Central Pacific, whimsically prognosticated that "the travel on the Pacific Railroad by Europeans who shall visit California on tours of pleasure and discovery only, will be ample to pay the expenses of the road."[98] Would that it were so, sighed Mark Hopkins.

DURANT HOLDS AN EXCURSION; THE INDIANS HOLD A WAR

WELL before the Casement Army spiked its way into Kearney in August, the good doctor was working on a publicity stunt of enormous magnitude and cost. Progress on the line was one thing, but explaining it advantageously to the public was quite another. After such long delays, the Union Pacific (and Durant) needed good press and new, influential friends and investors. He planned a large, opulent excursion across the Plains to end of track, an excursion he meticulously planned, orchestrated, and controlled.

While Mr. Train was lavishing $60,000 on construction of the lavish 120-room Cozzens Hotel at Omaha,[99] Durant made a dry run up the line with General Sherman and other distinguished military guests. Not a luxurious trip west, it was still a far cry from sitting on nail kegs on an open platform car dodging sparks on a forty-mile run. Sherman, congenitally taciturn, did not overflow with praise and bonhomie, but he was impressed by the amount of work that had been done in such a relatively short time. Perhaps he would live to see the road completed after all.[100]

Durant's publicity stunt was planned for October, and a big show it would be. Formal invitations were sent out to at least three hundred people, including President Johnson and the diplomatic community in Washington, and all were cordially invited to bring their families. Johnson, his cabinet members, and most diplomats declined the honor, but a large and prestigious party was put together nonetheless.

In all, 202 guests and two musical bands sallied forth on the Union Pacific into the wildest west. The party included Durant himself, Sidney Dillon, Orville Lambard, John R. Duff (a company director), Dodge, Seymour, Webster Snyder, Hoxie, and Train and his wife (and her mother and her maid). Also aboard were Congressman John B. Alley (Crédit Mobilier linchpin); Dan Casement; government commissioners Generals Samuel Curtis and James H. Simpson; government director Charles T. Sherman, the general's brother; John E. Sherman, another family member; Nebraska governor Alvin Saunders; Major General Philip St. George Cooke; four senators; fifteen congressmen; two French diplomats; a bevy of colonels; the Earl of Arlie; four clergymen; five doctors (including a naval surgeon); two official photographers; C. L. Jenkins with his portable printing press, which would publish the *Railway Pioneer* en route; the late president's son, Robert Todd Lincoln; and George M. Pullman, who had loaned Durant his finest rolling stock for the occasion.[101]

Few of the company's guests realized that everything that happened during the gala expedition to wild and wooly Nebraska had been carefully planned by Durant and his subordinates, from the superb cuisine to the "accidental" prairie fires. Nothing was left to chance, for the Doctor wanted these notables to have an unforgettable outing that they could brag about to friends.

With luxuriously appointed passenger cars and a mail car thoughtfully converted into a bar car waiting for them at Omaha,[102] the excursionists gathered in mid-October in New York City. As guests of the Union Pacific they went by rail to St. Louis and transferred there to two elegant steamboats leased by the company especially for the occasion. Aboard, the cuisine was positively Lucullan, arranged from appetizer to desert by H. M. Kinsley, "the Delmonico of Chicago," under temporary contract to Durant.[103] The October 20 luncheon menu aboard the steamer *Colorado* reveals the pains Durant took to care for his guests, listing two soups, chicken gumbo and oyster, trout à la Normande, baked pike with oyster sauce, six varieties of boiled meat, seven of roast meats, ten cold-meat dishes and twenty-nine "entrées," including "Rabbit sauti a-la-Chasseur," "Supreme de Volaille aux Champignons," and "Canard braise, aux Ofiace."[104] The truly gluttonous could also sample antelope, venison, bear, duck, grouse, quail, rabbit, and wild turkey, eleven vegetables, seven relishes, twenty pastries, and thirteen desserts, all to be washed down with an impressive selection of wines, beers, ales, and stronger spirits.[105] The Doctor was clearly taking no chances. He would impress his guests even if it bankrupted the company.

The excursionists were already wending their way west when Dodge learned of Durant's scheme. As Dodge remembered it, while the elaborate luncheon was being served, Durant cabled his chief engineer that "a large number of Eastern capitalists and their families" were on the way. Durant said "he would like to have some Indians camped near so that the party could see them, without going far . . . he also wanted, if possible, to give the party a chance to shoot at buffalo." Dodge immediately sent men to prepare proper campsites and contacted Major North, requesting him "to select about 50 or 60 of the best [Pawnee scout] Indians, put them in their war paint and bring them there and I would come after them at night, take them into the camp and give the people a surprise."[106] Happily for the Doctor, Dodge enjoyed such games. Certainly the Pawnee did.

The excursion left Omaha on October 23 and spent the next day at end of track, "observing the process adopted by those great *trackists,* General and Daniel Casement," whose men had orders to work furiously and well while under the visitors' gaze. Photographs were taken of individuals and groups posing with the track layers, shooting contests were arranged, and "a sumptuous game dinner" was served at the Hoxie House Hotel in North Platte, followed by a band concert; remarked Colonel Seymour, "a general *abandon* seemed to pervade the entire party."[107] In the next few days the visitors were frightened witless by a mock dawn attack put on by Dodge and the Pawnee scouts, a war dance was held, and a fireworks display supervised by Seymour and Snyder lit up the vast Plains, "much to the amazement, no doubt, of the distant savages and wild beasts." There was also "an interesting lecture upon phrenology . . . amusingly illustrated by a reference to the head of Mr. George Francis Train, the *humorist* of the party."[108] There was considerable hunting in the nearby hills (under armed escort), a formal review of the cooperative Second Cavalry, tours of prairie-dog cities, searches for moss agates, and, on the way back to Omaha, a staged prairie fire at night: "The train was immediately halted, and time given for all to drink their fill of the sublime spectacle . . . what surprise awaits us next?" asked Seymour rhetorically.[109]

The "Great Pacific Railroad Excursion," although it almost scraped the Union Pacific's coffers clean, was a roaring success. The money was well spent, for the publicity it generated was the best received by the company since its inception, and a pamphlet written by Seymour describing the event became something of a best seller.[110]

October brought the company other good tidings in addition to continued swift progress across the Plains. Government inspectors Curtis, Simpson, and William White gave their approval to another two sections of the Union Pacific's completed work. Paid ten dollars a day while on the line and ten cents a mile as an inspection fee—and permitted by the Doctor to use the truly elegant "Lincoln Car"*—the inspectors scrutinized the track and the company's attendant labors and pronounced everything first-rate.[111] General Curtis, that venerable champion of the Pacific Railroad, "died very suddenly" just days after the inspection, a sad loss to the company, which had found him unusually undemanding and amenable.[112] On October 10, Dodge, almost to his surprise, was "elected to Congress by the largest majority ever given" by the voters of his Iowa district.[113] Although he was to almost totally shirk his political responsibilities,† Durant and his friends were happy; it was highly politic to have the chief engineer in politics.[114]

Less than a week after his election, Dodge made public the details of the Sherman Pass route and officially recommended it as the route through the Black Hills; the directors accepted his recommendation the following month.[115] Dodge also dispatched a team to Salt Lake City with orders to try to obtain Brigham Young's help in supplying guides and manpower for surveys west of the Mormon capital, all the way to the California border. After all, a race was now under way, a race that, with the Union Pacific spiking in a month what the Californians did in a year, Dodge was certain to win.[116] He also hired a former sheriff of Denver, James A. Brown, "to do our prospecting" for gold and other precious metals, and directed company geologist David Van Lennep to scour Wyoming and Utah for coal deposits. Brown was totally unsuccessful, but the geologist found rich seams of coal very near the projected right-of-way in Wyoming. This was to prove first a boon and later an embarrassment.[117]

There was yet more good news on the way. The Ameses' Cedar Rapids & Missouri River Railroad was picking up speed and it appeared that it might indeed win Durant's five-hundred-thousand-dollar bonus by reaching Council Bluffs by February. This would remove one of the company's most vexing and costly logistical problems, even though there would be no bridge between Omaha and the Iowa city until 1872.[118] Also, as Silas Seymour noted, the company's progress was not to be measured solely in trackage, for "all along the road, where the company has established its stations, settlements are springing up rapidly," like Grand Island, North Platte, and Elkhorn.[119] So rapidly was Nebraska attracting emigrants that that territory acquired sufficient population to become the thirty-seventh state the following year, much earlier than had been expected.

---

*Built as a luxury car for the president, it was used by him only once, when his body was brought back home to Illinois. Durant then purchased it for the use of company directors.
†He arrived in Washington only in December 1867, yet Congress had convened in March.

By November, as Canadian winds gusted across the flatlands and tracks approached North Platte at mile 291, the board of directors, on Dodge's recommendation, announced that the Union Pacific would bypass Denver. However, as soon as possible, it would build a narrow-gauge branch line 112 miles long between the Colorado mining center and Cheyenne, Wyoming.[120] The board was also interested to learn of continuing financial setbacks inflicted on the UPED in Kansas, caused in part by the constant harassment by Indians. So strapped for funds was the former rival line that it was dumping its land grants on the market for prices as low as a dollar an acre—twenty-five cents lower than the government's own minimum price.[121] The UPED was even willing to grant a five-year period for payment or a substantial discount to those who could pay for the land outright. The race to the 100th meridian had been won by the Union Pacific in October, but the board wanted a monopoly of Plains traffic for as long as it could be had.

The Hoxie contract, carried out by the Crédit Mobilier, had expired at the 100th meridian, before the end of 1866. While the Ames brothers and many others assumed that future construction contracts would automatically end up in the hands of the Crédit Mobilier, Durant had other ideas, and, acting alone, he implemented them.

On November 10, as vice-president of the Union Pacific, he signed a contract for construction with one L. B. Boomer, an acquaintance from Chicago who had built bridges for Durant and Henry Farnam in Iowa. The contract, let at a very modest $27,500 per mile (plus bridging expenses), covered the expanse from the 100th meridian to mile 400, between Julesburg and Sidney, Nebraska. Boomer in turn sold his contract to an N. A. Gessner, perhaps realizing that there would be very little profit at $27,500 per mile.[122]

The Union Pacific directors, however, were outraged that the Doctor had contracted sub rosa, and vetoed the Boomer contract on January 6, 1867, while Durant was absent in the field. Instead, it voted—over the objections of government director Jesse L. Williams—to merely extend the fifty-thousand-dollar-a-mile Hoxie contract to cover mileage already in place beyond the 100th meridian—fifty-eight miles of track. It was now Durant's turn to become apoplectic, and he soon obtained a legal injunction against the board's decision, an injunction he soon dropped, for he realized that it stood in the way of his own large portion of resultant profits. So the construction company received $1,104,000 in profits for the fifty-eight-mile stretch, and the Doctor, holding more than one fifth of the stock, pocketed more than one fifth of the profits. Somehow, road construction in 1867 would have to proceed without a contract.[123]

In the meantime, Union Pacific surveyors in the field were beginning to relax. Remarkably, the Indians of the Platte Valley were relatively quiescent in the second half of 1866. There was one attack on a train by the Sioux in August in which a freight car was burned, but Dodge himself led a counterattack of trackmen and drove the Indians off.[124]

Instead of Indian trouble, there was a severe drought that fall, as well as other problems. As Arthur Fergusen recorded in western Nebraska, "To-day the air seemed perfectly alive with grasshoppers . . . a snowstorm of insects," which made it difficult to work, or even see.[125] There were drunken, often fatal, brawls in the surveyors' isolated camps, and one of Sam Reed's brothers, a company physician, was kept busy on the survey lines patching up the maimed.[126] Hezekiah Bissell, also in the field surveying, did more complaining in his diary about the infantry escort than about the Indians, singling out its commander, a Lieutenant Vogdes, for censure. The lieutenant, a harsh martinet, "would hang men up by their thumbs until half dead" for minor infractions. No wonder morale was so low among troops posted to the Plains.[127]

In November, William Tecumseh Sherman, ranking general in the West, in a report to the secretary of war, wrote that to guarantee the safety of those building the railroads across the Plains, the Kiowa, Cheyenne, Arapaho, and other tribes would have to be held south of the Arkansas River, while the Sioux should be blockaded north of the Platte. "This," he explained, "would leave for our people exclusively the use of the wide belt, east and west, between the Platte and the Arkansas, in which lie the two great railroads, and over which pass the bulk of travel to the mountain Territories."[128] With deep disdain for the Plains Indians, he had ordered the army to construct a new barrier of forts, including a chain of them north from the Platte into Montana, along the ill-fated Bozeman Trail. It was this expansion of the army's presence that woke the Sioux from their unaccustomed lethargy.[129] Peace with the Indians lasted only until the end of the year. On December 21, just sixty miles north of the Union Pacific's advanced grading parties, the Fetterman massacre took place.

Captain William J. Fetterman had built a fort on the Bozeman Trail in Wyoming just south of the Montana border and named it for himself. Regarding the Indians as stumps in the road of progress, he had earlier boasted publicly that with eighty men he could cut his way through the heart of the Sioux nation. On December 21, with precisely that number of men (including four heavily armed civilians), he attempted to cut his way a mere two miles into Sioux territory to rescue some ambushed woodcutters. He and all his men were slaughtered and horribly mutilated by a war party of some fifteen hundred Sioux.[130] While hardly a crushing defeat for the United States Army, the Fetterman massacre chilled public opinion more than any such battle before Custer's larger, repeat performance a decade later. It also unnerved Union Pacific workers, who realized that it probably signaled a new and perhaps worse round of Indian war. Investors also turned tail, and Union Pacific stock again plummeted in value.[131]

Well before Fetterman tempted fate, winter was upon the Union Pacific.

Fergusen, surveying near Ogallala, a few miles from Julesburg, recorded the first snow on November 12. The thermometer fell so fast that just two days later he wrote, "The river is nearly frozen over."[132] The surveying parties were soon recalled for the winter, and by December 1 most graders as well, but Casement kept his men spiking track, despite the worsening conditions, until the day of the Fetterman debacle. That December 21 all work stopped on the line and Dan and Jack took stock. It had been a marvelous run. They had laid rail to O'Fallon's Bluff, at mile 305—a total of about 260 miles in 182 working days,*[133] or a daily average of almost a mile and a half. Winter headquarters were established at North Platte, a town Dodge himself had laid out, or "platted."[134] For its skeleton work force, the company provided knock-down, prefabricated buildings, each part of which was numbered for easy reassembly. Called "Claytonvilles" after track foreman D. B. Clayton, the clusters of company structures stood uneasily alongside loopholed sod huts, settlers' rough-hewn cabins, and the fragile tents, lean-tos, and knock-downs of the hardier sin merchants who hunkered down to winter with the company.[135] The Casements and their men would use the winter months to stockpile material for the big push west in the spring. Unlovely North Platte, thriving in 1866 and 1867, would be described a few years later as consisting of "25 wooden and log buildings . . . a jail . . . three stores, nine saloons, three hotels, and—that's all."[136]

A REAL WINTER HITS THE SIERRAS

WITH the race on after July 3, the Big Four and their lieutenants increased the tempo of their work in the Sierras. In August two-shift grading began above Emigrant Gap, where a huge masonry shelf was being built to widen the narrow roadbed. Night crews worked in the flickering light of large bonfires spaced fifty feet apart and as welcomed for their warmth as for illumination.[137] Leland Stanford hosted another excursion that month, a huge, company-funded picnic at the end of track, demonstrably beyond Dutch Flat.[138]

In September, the month that Orville H. Browning was serendipitously named secretary of the interior,[139] with the company's explosions jarring the mountains as rapidly and regularly as heartbeats, the Emigrant Gap Tunnel (271 feet long) was pierced, and even though it had to be lined every foot of its length with thick timbers, trackman Henry Minkler's rail layers were working within it on September 21. Tunnel 2 had been overcome (but thirteen remained), and so had mile

---

*Some sources say 290, others 282, but if rails reached Fremont then 258 miles were constructed in 1866.

84.[140] Meanwhile, pigtailed Orientals were working steadily on both faces of Summit Tunnel while driving the vertical shaft from above. Charlie Crocker, constantly roaming the line, personally paid his workers that autumn, dispensing their wages from saddlebags, one bulging with gold coin, the other with silver.[141]

The Central Pacific, which had been earning good money in gold from local traffic since it reached Junction, saw a much needed increase in revenues upon entering Dutch Flat and connecting there with the Big Four's own wagon road. Had it not been for the railroad and wagon-road traffic, the company probably would have collapsed under the strain of its massive negative cash flow, for only $1.6 million in bonds were received from the government in 1866, and these brought only about $1.1 million in the marketplace.[142] Nor was much money forthcoming from selling land-grant acreage, for only a portion of those lands was composed of tillable soil, and there were depressingly few buyers at the company's minimum price of $2.50 an acre ($10 for timberlands).[143] Prospective buyers, with a 20 percent downpayment, had four years to make additional payments—of course, in gold—to receive their title. Future land-sale prospects were even more dismal, for beyond the Sierras lay only the desolation of Nevada, and, with luck, Utah. As Creed Haymund, later the company's general counsel, bitterly remarked of the supposed boon of government lands, "The grant to the Union Pacific was of a garden; that to the Central Pacific of a desert." In fact, by 1887 the value of Central Pacific's land sales was only about one fifth that of the Union Pacific's.[144] Well into the 1890s the Sacramento company still held some 8 million acres, mostly of desert wastes.[145] Charlie Crocker later claimed that only about 200,000 acres of California grants were usable or salable by the company.[146] So it was a case of doing what could be done with the slender available revenues, and, as usual, putting the rest on the cuff. At that, the Big Four were masters.

As the weather acquired a bite and the first flakes of snow fell in the High Sierras, it was decided, according to engineer Lewis Clement, "no matter what the cost, that the remaining tunnels should be bored in the Winter."[147] It was further resolved that as soon as the mountain snows precluded tracking and grading, large gangs should be sent ahead, down the eastern slopes of the Sierras to the more temperate weather, to do as much grading as possible before spring. This proved to be a most important move. The Central Pacific could no longer afford to give its men the winter off, no matter how expensive their retention might be or how harsh the weather. Surveyors would continue their charting, and Chief Survey Engineer Butler Ives would be sent east again with his team, this time to survey all the way to Ogden. Disappointingly, his reports indicated that Salt Lake City simply could not be included on the main line (should the company be lucky enough to get there first), and would have to be bypassed to the north.[148] For a company whose tracks did not reach mile 90 after four years of work, that was, to say the least, an optimistic call.

As the first storm raged through the Sierras in late October, the company shops at Sacramento finished work on a gigantic snowplow, the first of many to be constructed or purchased to company specifications.[149] Snow would be, despite Judah's predictions, the Central Pacific's most consistent and debilitating enemy, far more savage and costly than had been its detractors in the media.

Higher and higher toiled the Celestials, until on November 29 Cisco was at last reached and snow brought a halt to track laying.[150] At this juncture, Crocker, who would spend most of the winter floundering along the line on horseback, dispatched a thousand of his Chinese over the Sierras to the Truckee Valley, sending another two thousand to join them in December.[151] Hundreds more men were sent to reinforce the crews scratching away at the Summit and six other tunnels as well.

On December 19, as "the Homeric Winter of 1866–1867" began in earnest,[152] Summit Tunnel's deep vertical shaft was completed, although at first it was barely wide enough at the bottom to accommodate crews working both faces.[153] This would be a winter to try men's souls, one of the worst on record, with storm following storm and dropping a total of over forty feet of snow; as late as May, there were places in the High Sierras where as much as twelve feet of snow and ice remained.[154]

Storms almost invariably swept out of the southwest, and after several days of blizzard, the temperature normally rose, bringing rain or sleet or a layer of wet, cloying snow. This created a thick, hard crust, which made surface movement difficult and dangerous. Horses' legs were lacerated to the bone as they crashed through the glasslike top layer.[155]

Under this unceasing pounding, work did not halt; it merely burrowed down. As the base of snow built up, wrote Thomas W. Chinn, "the Chinese lived practically entirely out of sight of the sky that Winter, their shacks largely buried in snow. They dug chimneys and air shafts and lived by lantern light. They tunneled their way from the camps to the portal of the tunnel to work long underground shifts. A remarkable labyrinth developed under the snow."[156] In the snow tunnels leading to the work faces windows were cut to provide light, ventilation, and egress for rock scraps and garbage, and many of these eerie passages had scores of carefully carved steps leading up to the work.[157] The men sent over the mountains to the Truckee were the lucky ones, for the cruel work in the tunnels grew increasingly dangerous and claustrophobic. Snowslides were frequent and took a ghastly toll. Near Donner Peak Tunnel (mile 106.75), an avalanche carried away twenty Chinese caught in the open. They were swept so far down between two ridges that only cursory attempts were made to find the bodies. With the spring thaw, their corpses and others were at last recovered and buried in a temporary Chinese cemetery provided by the company. Their remains were eventually returned to their homeland.[158]

Chinese and white froze to death, singly and in groups, as temperatures reached −20° and gale-force winds razored through the mountain passes. Many simply disappeared. As Thomas W. Chinn has written, we shall never know the actual death toll that grim winter, but without doubt "loss of life was heavy."[159] Other workers, such as Henry Root, found themselves snowed in for weeks at a time in isolated cabins, their "provisions got down to cornmeal and tea,"[160] and they actually feared starvation. Some work gangs endured such stark privations (Frémont would have understood) that Crocker, hardly oversensitive, reluctantly evacuated them from the mountains.[161]

While mail was delivered to the workers sporadically by a Norwegian with the decidedly un-Norwegian name John Thompson, who glided to them on cross-country skiis,[162] supplies were always short, for once a thick crust formed on the snow, packhorses were useless, and small sleds had to be used, dragged by manpower alone. It was even difficult to get basic supplies as far up the track as Cisco, and, as Root described the procedure, a large plow preceded the supply train, pushed by a number of locomotives: "A Push Plow loaded with pig-iron to hold it to the rails, with the engines behind, would back up and take a run at the snow and keep going until it got stuck, and then back up and take another run."[163] It could and often did take a full day to cover the last few miles to Cisco, even with the help of large shovel crews, and there the supplies were off-loaded onto sleds for the trek to the tunnels.

Yet the work continued, although efficiency was much reduced. Snow tunnels were cut, braced, repaired, and filled with Chinese, who kept patiently hacking away at the mountains.[164] Aided by Arthur Brown, Lewis Clement, when not supervising the work at Summit Tunnel, spent time designing what he hoped would be effective snowsheds to protect the most vulnerable tracks. Both men underestimated the strength that the sheds would have to possess to survive the Sierra winter and how many miles of protection would be needed (at an expected cost of $15,000 a mile).[165] Brown, in overall charge of bridging and general timberwork, was also building the first of the Central Pacific hostelries, the Railroad House Hotel at Colfax. In later years the architect would specialize in hotel design and construction and win for himself a superb reputation, building, among others, the extremely elaborate Del Monte Hotel in Monterrey, California.[166] Stanford and Hopkins grimly built Clement and Brown's cost projections for snowsheds into their own, broader ones, and ordered Brown to make the sheds a top priority as soon as weather permitted work on them. Brown, in turn, immediately sent orders to the company's already overburdened sawmills.[167]

In the last weeks of the year the exhausted Central Pacific leadership looked back. While the company's New York and Boston stock agents, (Harvey) Fisk and (Alfred) Hatch, reported to investors that their clients had spent some $15 million on the first ninety-four miles of the line and would probably spend a similar amount on the next fifty-three mountain miles, the company's own annual report indicated that nearly $10 million had been spent in 1866 alone, which brought total expenses since groundbreaking to at least $19 million.[168] The $10 million spent in 1866 had resulted in a pathetic twenty-seven miles of new track—plus, of course, much grading, tunneling, clearing, masonry, bridging, and other work. Unfortunately for the Sacramentans, it was miles of track in place that impressed investors. Fisk and Hatch waxed eloquent about the ratio of net to gross profit and the fact that by late 1866 the company had issued $8,580,600 in stock, but failed to explain that this was due less to the stock's popularity than to its issue (at well below par) to the Crocker Contracting Company as partial payment for the work.[169]

Investors were unimpressed, for they knew that the race from the east and west was on, and the Central Pacific looked a good deal like a tortoise.

8

WAR WHOOPS ON THE PLAINS
AND THE OCTOPUS IS BORN

THE CASEMENT ARMY MARCHES

JACK and Dan Casement had done a marvelous job of stockpiling material for construction at North Platte during the harshest phase of the winter of 1866–67. Their daily work and progress reports in the spring of 1867 show an average of 220,000 crossties on hand (70 percent of which were cottonwood) and enormous amounts of spikes, chairs, and rails.[1] It is worth noting that their brother, E. H. Casement, worked for the company as a labor foreman in 1866 and 1867, and then became a subcontractor for the railroad in the Omaha firm of Hall and Casement.[2]

Had the weather permitted, they could and would have unleashed their legions in February, but that month and most of March were unusually cold and blustery, and they sat and fidgeted at North Platte. Worse, this weather was followed by a precipitous rise in temperature. The consequent rapid thaw displaced rails and buckled large sections of the newly ballasted line. Then, as work crews were rectifying that problem, the rains came in early April. These were rains of biblical proportions, slashing down in sheets for days on end; adding to the moisture of the rapid thaw, they brought the worst flooding in many years.

Sand ballasting and, on some portions of the line, shoddy construction, gave way before the rising waters. More than twenty miles of the road east of Grand Island simply ceased to exist. The repair work that followed added heavy expenditures and complicated the Casements' ability to continue work west of O'Fallon's Bluff. General Jack reported of the flood damage, "We are all in a heap generally," and every available worker was dragged from both east and west of the most severe flooding to literally stem the tide, save what was threatened, and repair or rebuild that which had been lost.[3] Prairie Creek Bridge near Grand Island was swept away by the normally sluggish tributary, and the expensive fifteen-hundred-foot-long Loup Fork Bridge at mile 84 almost followed suit, sustaining structural damage that would cost the company almost $50,000 to repair.[4] Fergusen wrote on April 17 that the road was still broken despite huge repair crews, and that his survey party was detained, bored and useless (but paid) at Omaha.[5] When public criticism of the delays in westward construction was aired at Omaha and elsewhere, the Doctor felt constrained to telegraph Nebraska Senator John M. Thayer: "I will pledge myself to complete two miles a day for the first one hundred working days after the frost is out of the ground."[6] This from a man ensconced in one of New York City's most opulent office suites. Pure confidence-building his telegram was, but it did manage to counteract some of the negative commentary. Given the previous year's burst of track laying, Durant's specious pledge was taken seriously by some.

By April 20 the line was again whole and the Casements led their army west. Their assault force that spring consisted of about 3,500 graders—some working as far as two hundred miles in advance of track—450 trackmen, 350 of the "train force," and another 400 or so masons and bridge builders, plus 100 surveyors. To that force in the field must be added (although they were not under the brothers' orders) several thousand tie cutters and lumberjacks, some floating their products hundreds of miles from the distant Black Hills, and as many as a thousand shopmen and uniformed personnel. The Union Pacific had grown to become only slightly less large and complex than its California rival.[7]

Durant's friend L. B. Boomer reemerged from obscurity early in 1867, and received the contract to build the company's bridges and supply the lumber for its other construction projects until completion of the line. Boomer at this time was owner of the Chicago Howe Truss Bridge Company, so at least this contract was a logical one. It became routine for him to arrange single shipments of 150,000 board feet of twelve-inch-by-twelve-inch-by-sixteen-foot lumber, mostly sent out from Chicago.[8] Most of the bridges he built in 1867 and succeeding years were shipped from Chicago factories in prefabricated sections, usually accompanied by the factory's own technical experts and construction labor.[9]

By late April, Dodge's surveyors were scattered across the prairies, or, as Fergusen described them, "these vast Plains which seem just released from the hand of their Maker."[10] Dodge's men were hardly basking in the fragrant spring breezes, for it was an unseasonably cold May in the western Platte Valley: "Ice stuck in our water pail" on May 21, according to Fergusen, and "the ground was perfectly white with snow" six days later.[11] This was not deep in the Black Hills, where such things might be expected, but a scant hundred miles past O'Fallon's Bluff, at an elevation of four thousand feet. Game was scarce and, judging from Fergusen's diary, the surveyors and their military escorts were laughably poor marksmen in any case. On May 5 Fergusen recorded glumly of the situation that he and his crew "had dinner of bread and Platte River water."[12]

Despite Fergusen's lean cuisine in the field, the floods, damage to the line, and ensuing delays, the Union Pacific was in fighting trim and its leadership was optimistic that spring, in part because the Central Pacific was still bottled up in the Sierras. Durant, Dillon, and Oliver Ames toured to end of track in the Lincoln Car to inform Dodge that he should begin surveying the land grants and devise a method of swiftly and profitably selling them, a task falling outside his usual repertoire.[13] While with Dodge, the visitors learned to their pleasant surprise that receipts—mostly from freight—were averaging almost $7,000 a day. A single train left Omaha in this period carrying freight that grossed for the company $5,000 in revenues.[14] Further, company geologist Van Lennep was discovering more rich veins of coal near the railroad's route through Wyoming, although he reported that the coal's sulfur content was distressingly high.[15] The Casements were happy with their new, more lucrative annual contract (signed February 15),[16] supplies were moving more smoothly and cheaply since the Cedar Rapids & Missouri had reached Council Bluffs, and General A. A. Augur, new commander of the Department of the Platte, had sent boy wonder George Armstrong Custer on the warpath with the freshly mustered Seventh Cavalry.[17] The company's mood was so upbeat that one of its pamphlets cheered: "The railroad, like a great artery full of blood, pushes its settlements" and civilization steadily toward the Pacific.[18]

The signs were good—so good in fact, that for the first time the Union Pacific offered its own first-mortgage bonds to the public in addition to its poorly received stock. They did so in an unusual manner. Issued in thousand-dollar denominations, at a rate of sixteen bonds per mile, each of these bonds would carry a bonus of a thousand-dollar share in the Crédit Mobilier. Thus one received a bond and a share worth, on paper, $2,000 for half of that price. A ploy to guarantee the symbiotic relationship between the two companies, it worked well, for almost instantly $1,250,000 in new money flowed into the Union Pacific's vaults, with more to follow monthly.[19] A high proportion of the preferred bonds was purchased by the same men who already held large amounts of Crédit Mobilier stock, and it might well be said that it was the Crédit Mobilier's first "dividend," awarded not by that company but by the Union Pacific, which was dominated by the same cabal. The logic was tungsten-hard: a man holding bonds of the Union Pacific was unlikely to raise questions about construction practices and prices if he also held Crédit Mobilier paper.

A NEW WAR

EANWHILE, out on the Plains, the Sioux and their various allies were preparing to halt the Union Pacific in its tracks and the spread of white settlement along with it. Angered by the Bozeman Trail forts and other army posts, made nervous by the increasing tide of emigrants through their lands, suspicious of prospectors who sought precious metals throughout the Great American Desert, and intuiting that the Iron Horse was related to all these things and more, the chiefs of a score of tribes and subtribes readied their warriors. The martial Union Pacific, with its generals and privates, well armed and disciplined, was at last about to go to war.

On January 11, before the campaigning season of either white or red, the *Omaha Weekly Herald* ran a front-page story entitled "The Indian Policy: Fighting vs. Feeding." Claiming that for every hostile Indian killed "there has been an outlay of cash of more than Five Hundred Thousand Dollars!," the article went on to bewail: "This is a large sum to pay for the decease of any individual." Hardly a staunch advocate of Indian rights, the newspaper did raise serious economic and humanitarian questions about the government's traditional Indian policy, which, it claimed, created, rather than quelled the tribes' hostility.[20]

In the same month, General Sherman wrote Dodge, "I regard this road of yours as the solution of the Indian affairs and the Mormon question, and therefore [will] give you all the aid I possibly can."[21] The engineer was relieved to have such assurances, for his good friend General Augur had admitted that he had too many responsibilities and too few troops at hand. He would give protection of the railroad and its crews first priority, but he warned Dodge that his uniformed resources were scarce indeed.[22]

In April, as the Casements' track layers made the valley resound with their spikes, mauls, and curses, the Sioux, Cheyenne, Arapaho, and other tribes shrugged off their winter blahs and began to flex their considerable muscle. This flexing, and that of the Kiowa and Comanche farther south, released increasing violence throughout most of 1867, and would for a time threaten to bring the Union Pacific to a halt.

On the first of May, a four-man mail party was wiped out just west of Laramie by the Cheyenne.[23] Actually, the opening, albeit casual, rounds had begun a month earlier, but were directed against Ben Holladay's stage lines. The aggrieved magnate later told Congress that from April 1 to August 15, his lines had been almost ripped to shreds by hostile Indians, who stole at least 350 head of livestock, burned twelve isolated stage stations (with their grain, hay, and other supplies), destroyed three expensive coaches, killed more than a dozen of his employees, and seriously wounded a number of passengers.[24] It is hardly coincidental that Holladay would soon sell out his previously profitable business to Wells, Fargo and Company.

The Indians, ranging their Plains in small, guerrilla-like bands of from twenty to two hundred warriors, but occasionally in the thousands, struck viciously at Holladay's installations, for they were concrete symbols of white encroachment and threat. So was the Union Pacific—a threat writ large upon the prairie.

The surveyors and grading parties were most at risk, despite their army escorts, for the soldiers were rarely swift enough to detect, prevent, or defeat an Indian raid. At best they could blunt it once begun or pursue the retreating hostiles (more often than not in vain). Also, for firepower, the army of 1867 relied on Civil War surplus single-shot muskets and carbines, which were slow to load and inaccurate. On the other hand, the Indians were often armed with the latest-model civilian repeating rifles and carbines: Sharps, Henrys, and Winchesters. Engineer Bissell observed this discrepancy with dismay, writing that the Indians "at that time were well supplied with rifles and pistols using metalic [sic] cartridges." The only saving grace, according to Bissell, was the fact that the Indians were normally short of ammunition.[25] However, it was just that shortage which often drove the Indians to raid vulnerable civilian whites, who often carried the same weapons.

On May 18, Arthur Fergusen, who had long worried about the Indians, was introduced to the problem. After a hard day of siting and pounding survey stakes west of Ogallala, he saw an Indian war party sweep by; it "pulled up one mile of Railroad stakes in sight of the party," and blithely cantered away without loss.[26] Just two days later the chief engineer, aware of the increasing incidence of violence, wrote Sherman, pleading for more protection, for the day before the Sioux had "cleaned out two of our subcontractors [a few miles south of Julesburg] of everything they had and scared the workmen out of their boots, so they abandoned the work and we can not get them back." They had also raided tie men in the Black Hills, killing several, and had hit Percy Brown's survey team, killing a soldier of the escort and a surveyor. Dodge complained that work was being slowed and warned that the mails might not get through. General Augur, he wrote, had only two slim companies of cavalry to patrol the line and eight infantry companies "to protect 300 miles of opened work." The issue was an urgent one for Dodge, for "no white man or train, except government, will travel the route this year," if the army could not effectively guard it. Protecting the reputation of his railroad—and the value of its stocks and bonds—he admitted to Sherman, "[I] have smothered all the recent attacks and kept them out of the press."[27] Perhaps this was easier to do than it might appear, for the Indians were constantly cutting the telegraph line, not to interrupt communications, but because the shiny copper wire was easily made into flashy jewelry.[28]

Less than a week later came more ill tidings. Indians had struck the company at various points on May 25, 26, and 27. A work train was derailed near end of track, sixty-five miles west of North Platte and four Union Pacific workers killed, while company livestock was rustled at a number of stations;[29] and ten miles west of end of track five of a six-man section gang were killed and scalped, while another war party was killing four graders just a few miles away.[30]

At that point, Dodge was traveling to end of track himself, in company with three government commissioners, who were to examine the most recent twenty-mile section. After inspecting and approving two sections (miles 305 to 345), the party reached end of track, where the construction crew was wolfing down its heavy lunch. Just as Dodge and his party arrived, the engineer later remembered, "A large body of Indians, one hundred or more, swept down on the grading parties, in plain view of us, cut out several of their mules and horses and got away with them before the graders could get to their muskets, which were stacked along their work." There was a great deal of noisy, smoky blazing-away at the distant Indians, but to no avail.[31] Later that day the crackle of gunfire was heard in the distance. Seven more graders were killed and others wounded. At least the commissioners had experienced, in graphic terms, the Indian threat and now knew that it was not exaggerated by the Union Pacific.

The volume of blood shed on the Plains increased in June and would increase further in July and August. The agony of the Union Pacific had just begun. Indians slaughtered five ranch hands near the railroad just west of North Platte, after which many of them crowded onto the rails to try to stop the cinder-blowing monster they could see approaching. The engineer, one "Dutch" Frank, also looked far into the distance and saw the knot of warriors, and he fed his boiler all the steam pressure it could tolerate. Roaring down the track, he rammed through the assemblage at high speed, his locomotive throwing Indians in every direction. "The entire front was plastered with blood and bits of flesh," according to one account.[32]

Farther west, Fergusen received the scare of his life, recording in his diary events of June 2:

> This morning, shortly after sunrise the camp was aroused by the cry of here they come! here they come boys! and for the next few minutes the interior of our tent presented a lively picture—the soldiers, Mr. Boyd and myself grasping our arms, and regardless of our clothing and everything else we rushed out of the tent and there we saw the Indians charging down upon us from the northern bluffs . . . it was an exciting time—some of our men almost naked.

It was not, apparently, a serious attack, for within minutes the Indians, a few of them wounded, retreated, whooping and screaming. Fergusen, elated by the action, was somewhat disappointed that one Indian who had been wounded quite close to the white men managed to escape, for "we lost the chance of getting a fine scalp." After the skirmish, "one of the engineers captured from the Indians a white woman's scalp, which was quite green, having been killed but a few days." One man's scalp is another man's horror. Fergusen later learned that all but one Union Pacific survey camp in a twenty-mile radius had been attacked that morning, some suffering casualties.[33]

About the same time, near Ogallala, Indians removed a section of newly laid track and successfully derailed a train, killing and mutilating its engineer.[34] This was probably the incident described by Hezekiah Bissell, who recorded that the Indians discovered bolts of brightly colored cloth in the wreckage. Some Indians "tied one end to their horses' tails, then run them across the prairie in all directions, making a very comical display."[35] One developed a macabre sense of humor in western Nebraska.

There was nothing comical about what happened to Senior Engineer L. L. Hills, who was leading ten surveyors and six cavalry troopers in northeastern Colorado. A highly regarded engineer, Hills was surprised in the mountains by an Arapaho war party, cut off from his men, and killed on July 20. When recovered, his body was bristling with nineteen arrows and bore five bullet wounds as well. Fortunately, he was his party's only fatality.[36] Fergusen was sent the following year to exhume Hills and bring his body back for proper burial—a horrifying experience for the young man.[37] On July 23, Percy Brown and his survey team, pursued by Sioux, became widely separated. Painfully gut-shot, Brown was found later in the day, but soon died in screaming agony.[38] The Union Pacific could not afford to lose many such men as Hills and Brown.

Nerves were stretched taut. Survey parties such as Fergusen's began fortifying their nightly camps like Roman legionnaires in Gaul, and digging trenches for their campfires so the light would not attract attention from the Indians they sensed were lurking nearby. "One of the men in Welch's camp shot a horse last night which he mistook for an Indian," recorded Fergusen in late July. It was indeed a tense time on the Plains.[39]

Sherman and others became angry, for the Indians were delaying the national work and seemed to taunt the understrength army, which numbered less than thirty thousand and suffered from a desertion rate as high as 25 percent a year. The general wrote at this time that conciliation would not work: "The more we can kill this year, the less will have to be killed in the next war, for the more I see of these Indians the more convinced I am that they all have to be killed or maintained as a species of paupers."[40] There is little question which alternative Sherman favored. A few days later, on August 3, government commissioner Jesse L. Williams, equally apoplectic, wrote Dodge in a similar vein: "I fear I shall become an Indian hater. Has not the race fulfilled its mission on the earth?"[41] Apparently not, for many more Union Pacific employees were destined to be killed. August, in fact, was to provide a greater number of martyrs than had any previous month.

On the eighth of that month a character known as "Dick the Hunter" wandered into Fergusen's barricaded camp near mile 460 to report that "the bodies of ten or eleven men had been found scalped by the Indians" just a few miles away. Fergusen's morale, already shaky, sank.[42] Three more Union Pacific graders died near Big Sandy, Nebraska, the following day.[43] It is clear that Dodge was unable to "smother" all news of Indian attacks, for the *Omaha Weekly Herald* almost delighted in recounting them in all their grisly details. Also in early August it was learned that Indians had derailed a train and killed "a number" of people near Ogallala,[44] and that the Plum Creek massacre had taken place.

On August 4* a band of Cheyenne appeared at dusk at an oft-used ambush site near Plum Creek, at mile 230, where the rugged terrain afforded easy concealment. Their movements were not very covert, however, for they cut the telegraph line and used it to bind a number of railroad ties atop the rails. They then sat down to wait. An hour or so later they were rewarded, for a six-man telegraph repair crew, led by recent British immigrant William Thompson, came speeding down the track in a large handcar, rocketing along so fast the men rammed into the railroad ties before they had time to stop. Thrown from the car, they scattered, pursued by gleeful Cheyenne. Thompson, the only one to survive, told of being chased, weaponless, by a mounted warrior who shot him in the arm, rode him down, "and clubbed me with his rifle. He then took out his knife, stabbed me in the neck, and making a twirl round his fingers with my hair, he commenced sawing and hacking away at my scalp." With Zenlike self-control, Thompson, though in agony, "knew enough to keep quiet.

"After what seemed to be half an hour," his scalp was simply ripped off by the impatient Cheyenne—"it just felt as if the whole head was taken off," he later remembered. Lying there, dazed and bleeding profusely, the formerly red-haired Briton somehow noticed that as the Indian remounted, his scalp fell with a "plop" to the ground, unnoticed. When the warrior at last galloped off, Thompson retrieved his scalp and stumbled off in search of help.[46] Later, "he showed a gaping wound in the neck, and a bullet-hole in the muscle of his right arm," according to Henry Morton Stanley, the first journalist to encounter the stunned survivor. He wrote that "in a pail of water by his side, was his scalp, about nine inches in length and four in width, somewhat resembling a drowned rat."[47]

Transferred to the company's Omaha hospital, Thompson convinced two doctors to "reset the scalp on his head," almost as if it were prairie sod, but the painful operation failed, to his great disappointment.[48] He gave his scalp to one of the doctors, who later gave it to the Omaha Public Library, which in turn loaned it to the Union Pacific Railroad Museum of that city. There, it can now be seen, perched on a Lucite skull.

---

*On the same day, according to the *Omaha Weekly Herald,* the white population of Nebraska dipped bizarrely by one when two young ladies at Paint Rock poured molten lead into their sleeping stepmother's ear![45]

The night's work was hardly over for the elated Cheyenne. They chanted and sang for hours and then piled additional impediments on the rails in hope of bigger game. At about two in the morning, with a groggy Thompson watching from a hilltop, a five-car, westbound freight ran full-tilt into the barrier, derailing, and one of its cars burst into flames. The poor fireman, Gregory Henshaw, pinned in his cab, was slowly and hideously roasted to death, screaming continuously, much to the amusement of the attentive Cheyenne. Engineer Brookes Bowers, thrown from the locomotive and badly injured, was soon dispatched out of his miseries. After ransacking the wreckage and extracting a keg of quality bourbon, the Indians set fire to all the cars, threw Bowers's body into the flames, and again sat down to await more visitors. They had, after all, wrecked a train and killed seven (they believed eight) white men, with no loss to themselves.

By this time, Thompson was staggering eastward along the tracks. Encountering another westbound freight, he warned it off and was taken aboard as it sped in reverse back to Plum Creek Station. Dodge, who happened to be there, led a force to the ambush site the next day and the Cheyenne, feeling—unlike Thompson—no pain, wisely melted away. The chief engineer recalled the incident fondly in later years: "When I called upon them to fall in and go forward and retake the train, every man on the train went into line, and by his position showed that he was a soldier . . . they went forward as steadily and in as good order as we had seen the old soldiers climb the face of Kenesaw [*sic*] under fire."[49] Dodge's only regret was that the Indians did not stay to put up a fight.

According to Stanley, the burned bodies of Henshaw and Bowers were brought back for burial in "two small boxes, thirty by twelve inches . . . both together would weigh about thirty pounds." Strong of stomach, Stanley inspected the contents of one box, finding "a charred trunk about two feet in length, resembling a half-burnt log."[50] They were buried with as much ceremony as tiny Plum Creek Station and its personnel could muster. Shortly after the Plum Creek massacre, General Sherman remarked sarcastically, but only half in jest, that "so large a number of workmen distributed along the line will introduce enough whiskey to kill off all the Indians within 300 miles of the road."[51]

Whiskey may well have debilitated the Cheyenne and Sioux, but it was the Pawnee scouts of Major North who created a respectable and verifiable body count. These "irregular" soldiers knew how to fight an irregular war and were in perpetual motion, often attacking the hostiles when they were most vulnerable—at night or in the winter. In September, Fergusen saw a contingent of Pawnee who had seventeen fresh scalps hanging from their belts, and a few days later referred to a single Pawnee scout who passed through the camp "with 9 scalps—a pretty good haul."[52] Effective as they were (it certainly did not cost the government $500,000 for each scalp they took), the Pawnee were too few in number to adequately protect the railroad.

In September a number of chiefs met for a peace parley with government commissioners at North Platte,[53] but little of substance came of the meeting and the cycle of depredations continued across the Plains. From the summer of 1867 onward, "passenger cars were then equipped with overhead racks containing loaded rifles," at no additional charge to the paying public.[54]

The Indian problem hardly stopped the Union Pacific, but as it increased in the optimum track-laying months of summer, it certainly slowed progress, and Durant's promise of two miles per working day could not be kept. April flooding contributed to the slowness, for only a single mile of new track had been laid that month.[55] The Union Pacific was off its stride.*

SIN ON THE PRAIRIE AND IN THE BOARDROOM

NOT all of the Union Pacific's problems—or casualties—that summer were Indian-related. The Hells on Wheels also took their toll. Infamous Julesburg, reached by trackmen in June, immediately began its tawdry hour in the sun. At the Colorado Nebraska border, on the banks of what Mark Twain unenthusiastically described as "the shallow, yellow, muddy South Platte,"[57] Julesburg boasted a score of rude huts before the rails hove into sight, but it was then "the wickedest city in America . . . a champion of iniquity."[58] An appalled Sam Reed wrote in June that the town "continues to grow with magic rapidity. Vice and crime stalk unblushingly in the mid-day sun."[59] "Whole battalions of whores and gamblers," in the words of Richard O'Connor, descended upon dusty Julesburg in June and July to ply their nefarious trades, and by late in the latter month, with the company using the town as a major base camp, some four thousand people crowded its tents and knock-downs, and business went on round the clock.[60]

Peripatetic Henry Morton Stanley, thirsting for more Western vignettes and human interest for his readers, found a wealth of both in Julesburg. He wrote wonderingly of its inhabitants that "mostly every one seemed bent on debauchery and dissipation." By comparison, he wrote, North Platte had been "a quaint frontier hamlet."[61]

The town *was* a sinner's nirvana, untroubled by vigilantes, for here, by sheer numbers, the hell-raisers (and their rowdy clients) utterly dominated the "settlers." This "whirlpool of sin," where "the civil law is yet too new to be an impediment to the unwashed," was a turbulent, dangerous town,[62] where hang-

---

*So was the UPED, which was even more ravaged by Indians. Somehow, however, this line was earning surprisingly high revenues from local traffic.[56]

outs like Jake Eel's Saloon on Sedgwick Street falsely advertised "unadulterated liquors," and the local (but itinerant) newspaper, the *Frontier Index,* had to be picked up at the post office, because, according to its editors, "the boys are too negligent to be trusted as carriers."[63] Not only the town but the graveyard grew with "magic rapidity," for Julesburg was a town where "not a day passes but a dead body is found," and even the women went around armed; "these women are expensive articles, and come in for a large share of the money wasted. In broad daylight they may be seen gliding through the sandy streets in Black Crook dresses, carrying fancy Derringers slung to their waists."[64] It was almost equally dangerous in the workers' and surveyors' camps (see the Fergusen entries below), and even Jack Casement, no stranger to violence, wrote his wife about one of his chief assistants, blandly noting, "Robert had one of his eyes kicked out a few days before I got here it is too bad."[65]

Apprised that "Julesburg was a much harder place than North Platte"—which had horrified him earlier—General Dodge visited the town in July.[66] Dan Casement one night took the wide-eyed engineer on a tour of some of the town's sleazier "night spots." As Dodge later remembered of the largest saloon he saw, "The hall was crowded with bad men and lewd women. Such profanity, vulgarity and indecency as was heard and seen there would disgust a more hardened man than I."[67] It must have indeed been rough to elicit that observation from an officer who had marched with Sherman to the sea!

Dodge decidedly did not like what he saw that evening, or for that matter in the daylight hours, and he was none too happy that many of his men were losing their earnings or worse to the riffraff at the gaming tables and bawdy houses. He especially bristled at the fact that this un-Christian behavior was taking place on Union Pacific property—property granted the company by the Congress he was now absent from and ignoring. The final insult was that most of this legion of shady characters were squatting on company land while conducting their trades. This would have to stop, he informed Jack Casement. The high rollers would have to buy or rent the land they occupied or move on, and pronto!

Later that month, following several fruitless attempts to convince the "sporting fraternity" to settle up with the company, a morally indignant chief engineer wired General Jack, he later recalled, "to take such of his force as was necessary and go back to Julesburg and clean the town out . . . this was fun for Casement."[68] The little general promptly gathered and armed some two hundred of his most reliable and toughest men, descended upon Julesburg, and demanded that all who had not bought or rented their "business" properties assemble at once.

When they did so—a murmuring, armed, cynical mob—Casement, flanked by his eager gunslingers, harangued them about their moral turpitude and their obligations to the company. This, of course, impressed not one of the surly crowd, and some became verbally abusive and unruly, which lit the trackman's short fuse. Jack, a decisive man, to say the very least, then bellowed to his men to fire into the crowd, "not caring whom he hit," and they did so with abandon, as if there were a bonus to be earned.[69] The issue, never in doubt, went in the company's favor. Some report that thirty died in the street in "this bare-faced lynching,"[70] while others claim a higher death toll; but a few days later, Jack took his boss on a stroll through the newly expanded cemetery, sweeping his arms grandly and proudly proclaiming, "General, they all died in their boots and Julesburg has been quiet since."[71] And so it was. A year later, at Bear River City, another massacre would take place, but at that squalid little village, it would be Union Pacific men killed.

Not as bloody as that Bear River City shoot-out, the Julesburg massacre—obviously one facet of the "policing" duties given Casement by Dodge—did tranquilize the town. Hardly all the "bad men and lewd women" were killed by the track crew, but many moved on and the remainder practiced their vices with at least a modicum of decorum, and on land they paid for. Not long afterward, Julesburg was "completely deserted, except as a point for receiving military supplies for Fort Sedgwick," a few miles south.[72] The sin merchants were off for Sidney (mile 414) and Cheyenne, to repeat their bizarre metamorphosis of a new town.

Not all the action took place on the Plains. Some of it, equally savage and immoral, occurred in the burled walnut boardrooms on Nassau Street.

If the editor of the *American Railroad Journal,* Henry V. Poor (who was proving an unreliable prophet), could write unblushingly that spring that "there is nothing connected with the Union Pacific that is not wonderful," it is only because he was not at the time privy to the vicious infighting among its (and the Crédit Mobilier's) directors and principal investors.[73] The company's own propagandists, who touted the Union Pacific as being "as profitable as it is grand," knew better.[74]

The break between the Ames group and Durant and his friends had become a yawning chasm, crossed only infrequently by bridges of dollars. In large part the estrangement came about because, simply put, the former did not trust the latter, especially the Doctor's peculiar manner of handling other people's money. From early 1867, according to Dodge, Crédit Mobilier board meetings "were very stormy,"* for the Ames group was actively attempting to oust Durant from leadership.[75] In late January, after convincing the board to increase the company's capital stock by a million dollars, Oliver Ames immediately—with help from his friends—began buying up the new certificates, a blatant maneuver by the New Englanders to control more voting stock than the Doctor did. In February, a final increase in capital stock was agreed upon and another $1,250,000 was issued. To spur new sales, a bonus of a thousand-dollar Union

*Of course, this suggests that Dodge knew a great deal more about the Crédit Mobilier than he was later to admit.

Pacific bond would go to those who bought ten shares of Crédit Mobilier stock. Once more, the goal was symbiosis.[76] For some reason, at about this time, Durant sold $100,000 of his own Crédit Mobilier paper, reducing his personal influence in the company just as the Ameses and their friends were buying to increase theirs.[77]

On March 1, John M. S. Williams submitted a construction bid from mile 247 (past which the Union Pacific had already built) to mile 515, where Cheyenne was destined to sprout that summer. He would be paid $42,000 per mile for the first hundred miles and $45,000 thereafter; he, in turn, undertook not only to build the road but to drum up $1.5 million in new Union Pacific stock sales. It was understood by the inner circle that he would immediately transfer his contract, once signed, to the Crédit Mobilier, as Hubert Hoxie had done.[78] Such was not to be.

The Union Pacific board accepted the contract with alacrity, despite Durant's anguished cries, but then had to back down when the Doctor obtained an injunction from a New York judge on the grounds that part of the contracted mileage had already been constructed and, in fact, had already been approved by the government commissioners. He did *not* mention that he thought the price per mile too low for sizable profits. The board rescinded Williams's contract, and, when he tendered a similar proposal in June, a similar charade was played out with similar results.[79] The Doctor was not a man to give in.

He could, however, be levered out, for he now controlled less Crédit Mobilier stock than did the Ames faction. On May 18, at a Crédit Mobilier board meeting in Philadelphia, his vulnerability was tested. He was voted out of the presidency, membership on the executive committee, and his directorship. Sidney Dillon took over the company's helm, while Ames supporters Rowland Hazard and Congressman John B. Alley were elevated to the executive committee (replacing Durant backers John M. S. Williams and G. G. Gray). Oliver Barnes remained as treasurer, secretary, and director, but essentially the Doctor was no longer influential in the Crédit Mobilier boardroom.[80] He would have to amuse himself with and profit from the Union Pacific.

A few days after the meeting, Oliver Ames, in a somewhat alarming tone, wrote Dodge at Omaha, informing him of the palace coup and warning him to pay no heed to orders from the now "powerless" Durant: "He is now in open hostility to the Road." A bit naïvely, given what had transpired at the May 18 meeting, Ames whined, "I cannot understand such a change as has come over the Doctor—the man of all others who has from the beginning stolen wherever he had the chance."[81] While hardly averse to illegal gains, Durant was deeply offended by his ejection from the Crédit Mobilier. He also intimated to the engineer that Durant would probably take legal action to thwart the further progress of the Union Pacific.

Efforts to buy Durant out of the Crédit Mobilier came to nothing,[82] but a major miracle of finance was just breaking. The Union Pacific's bonds, first offered to the public that spring, were an almost instant success. In charge of hawking the first $10 million worth (beyond the bonds attached to Crédit Mobilier stock), Cornelius Bushnell took out advertisements all over the East and hired a corps of agents to sell the first mortgage paper at 90 percent of par. So popular were the bonds (and the Crédit Mobilier bonus) that when an astonished Bushnell raised the price to 96 percent, they still sold. "My most sanguine expectations were realized," testified Bushnell to a congressional committee in 1872. "In less than six months I sold ten millions [of dollars] of bonds.*[83] In a transport of delight, Ames was soon informing Dodge, who was at end of track, "We are now selling from 15 to 20,000 dollars of our bonds daily."[84] At the same moment, the *Railroad Record* was editorializing that those Union Pacific bonds were "the safest and best investment at the same price in the country. Their *security is absolute!*"[85] From the summer of 1867, then, the Union Pacific, despite its boardroom brouhahas, was basically solvent. The bond prices were the direct result of the railroad's rapid progress in construction, its nearness to the mountains, which when reached, would mean $48,000 in bonds per mile, and the respectable leadership of the Ames faction. The company was at last solvent—or it should have been.

On July 28, with no lawsuits yet filed by Durant and with money flowing in, Oliver Ames wrote his chief engineer—now a close confidant—urging him to proceed full-steam for the mountains. The quality of the work was secondary to the speed with which it was to be accomplished. "Make it as perfect as possible consistent with the rapidity of construction demanded," wrote the shovel tycoon, and Dodge, who did pause to warn Ames that pell-mell building (no matter the quality) would dramatically escalate costs, took the man at his word.[86]

REARRANGING THE SIERRAS

THE mountains still glowered down at Charlie Crocker and his Celestials and the granite still mocked them as 1867 emerged from the detritus of 1866, and snow thickly blanketed all of the Sierras, down to the lowlands. With only a few breaks it stormed and howled throughout February and March (there was a total of forty-four storms), and with the snow came bursts of subzero weather and lethal mountain winds.[87] Montague had warned the Big Four that a major push during the winter would add some 50 percent to construc-

---

*Actually, it was closer to $7 million by year's end, with far more to come in 1868, but it was a godsend.

tion costs (an underestimation), but they told him to forge ahead and he, like Dodge, did, for he understood all too well that the company's survival hinged upon miles of track laid and volume of bonds received from Washington.[88]

So the work gangs, like snow moles, toiled in harsh beauty and splendid isolation. It is a marvel that through all that brutal winter train service to Cisco was interrupted for only three days, as huge gangs of men stationed along the line at regular intervals repeatedly cleared the tracks with their broad, wooden-bladed shovels.[89] At times the shovelers worked during and through a storm, heaving snow off the right-of-way just a bit faster than nature could deposit it there. When the situation became critical, these men were supplemented with drafts of more Chinese from the tunnels, explosives men with their steel shovels and minuscule two-wheeled carts. The line was kept open, and it is good that it was, for the men laboring in the bores in double shifts were consuming supplies, especially explosives, as if they were opium. More than a million dollars' worth of blasting powder and nitroglycerin would eventually be exploded before the Sierras conceded the battle to the puny, swarming mortals.[90]

The men on the Sierras' eastern slopes had desperate needs of their own. That winter, said tunnel engineer Gillis later, "these storms were grand," and many in the mountains adopted snowshoes for moving about, or the newfangled "Norwegian skiis," "each a strip of light wood ten to twelve feet long, four inches wide," and with the aid of poles and the superb mountain declivities, adversity was at times transformed into sport. Gillis waxed prolix about downhill speeds of twenty-five and even thirty miles an hour, and the mountains sometimes rang with the workers' huzzahs.[91]

Sometime during that unforgettable winter more than the usual supplies were sent to the three thousand men grading on the eastern slopes and in the Truckee Valley. A heroic undertaking, attempted by nameless, forgotten men, had begun. For upward and over the Summit and down the treacherous eastern defiles (some ninety miles as the oxen lurched) came iron rails, spikes, fishplates, switches, tools, and other material. On special snow sledges and sleds came the rails, each one weighing six hundred pounds. It is not known how many thousands of those ungainly iron ribbons were dragged, pushed, and slid across the Sierras before spring, but well before April 1, Charlie Crocker's men were laying track in the Truckee.* The Central Pacific launched their trans-Sierra attack even though it would generate no bonds as long as the gap in the Sierras (closed only in mid-1868) resulted in an uncontinuous line.[92]

Crocker was also doing some experimenting on the eastern slopes. At Prosser Creek, near a cluster of company sawmills that worked full-blast through the winter, he created the Summit Ice Company, to break the monopoly of the Sitka

---

*Much more massive loads were sent the following winter, but because of the amount of track laid in 1867, they had less distance to travel.

Ice Company in the cities of the Pacific Coast and to turn one of the mountains' curses into an advantage. Ice was cut into blocks and hauled by sledge—perhaps the same ones that hauled the material and rails eastward—to end of track and thence to California's urban centers. Curiously, although the Summit Ice Company operated for three years, it did so at a loss, even after the entire route was tracked, and in 1870 Crocker closed down his pet project, one of the very few that did not turn a profit.[93] Perhaps the 1867 purchase of Alaska from Russia allowed the Sitka Ice Company to remain competitive.

Along Prosser Creek, Crocker also had a number of huge, long flumes constructed to shoot tree trunks from the logging areas in high altitudes to the creekside sawmills. These flumes could handle thick trunks up to forty feet long.[94]

The tunnels—still thirteen of them to finish—consumed the labor of perhaps five thousand men that winter, and the lives of scores, if not hundreds. "Snow slides carried away our camps and we lost a good many men" that season, reported Charlie Crocker.[95] Others simply wandered off forever in the dizzying whiteness, while yet others cut fuses too short, miscalculated charges, or moved more slowly than the spinning shards of exploded granite. Two Oriental workers clearing the tracks disappeared in an avalanche in March, but "there, in Spring, their bodies were found, standing upright, with shovels in their hands,"[96] wrote one observer admiringly of the dedication of the Chinese, which appeared to last even beyond the grave.

The Chinese—"a lazy one does not exist," wrote Mark Twain[97]—bored, crimped, tamped, and blasted under infernal conditions. So bad did those conditions become that at tunnels 8 and 9 (between miles 106 and 107), the crews were evacuated for two months while the worst storms raged.[98] At one point, Crocker and Strobridge, desperate to finish the tunnels, hired—at exorbitant wages—a team of experienced Cornish miners, supposedly the world's best, and sent them into the Sierras, hoping to pick up the pace. They were also curious as to whether these men were, as they bragged, better miners than the Celestials, who had by now truly learned the art. As Crocker retold the story, "We got some Cornish miners and paid them extra wages," putting them to work on two Summit Tunnel faces. "We measured the work every Sunday morning, and the Chinamen without fail, always outmeasured" the Britons.[99] The Cornish experts were soon paid off and the Celestials, never again challenged, confidently continued their labors.

Oddly, the Central Pacific, with its strange faith in muscle rather than technology, never used steam drills, even though many California miners swore by them and the Union Pacific relied heavily upon them in the Black Hills and Wasatch Range. Crocker was personally in favor of them and more than willing to buy a batch, but Strobridge was adamantly and profanely opposed.[100] Also, the company's technique for bending rails was quaintly archaic. Normally, a rail to be curved was placed with precision over a fulcrum of some sort (a log, a rock, another rail), and, under the keen eyes of a supervisor, one or more men would jump on it, or use a heavy maul to change its curvature. Rail-bending machines were available, but unlike the Union Pacific, the Californians preferred to rely on "line of sight methods."[101]

Thousands of barrels of explosives were used where steam drills might have done better work, and the mountains, truly besieged, trembled, roared, and flamed. One man who witnessed the impressive pyrotechnics described the blasting at Donner Peak Tunnel, overlooking the primordial lake:

> Through the gathering shades of night, immense volumes of fire and dense clouds of smoke broke from the mountainside, as if a mighty volcano was rending it to atoms. Huge masses of rocks and debris were rent and heaved up in the commotion; then anon came the thunders of the explosion like a lightening [*sic*] stroke, reverberating along the hills and canyons, as if the whole artillery of Heaven was in play. Huge masses of rock rolled far down the steep declevity [*sic*], and pieces weighing two hundred pounds were thrown a distance of a mile. Sometimes the people at the [lakeside] hotel, a mile from the scene of destruction, were obliged to retire to avoid the dangers from the falling fragments.[102]

Not only did the Celestials do most of the destruction that winter, but some of the actual construction as well. Due to the massive widening of the Emigrant Gap ledge and construction of an increasing number of vast retaining walls, culverts, drains, and bridge supports, several hundred Chinese were selected and trained as masons. White artisans were in short supply. Those selected received higher wages and performed as well as they had in other lines of work.[103]

In the early spring, with company agents recruiting throughout California, the first Chinese hired (by Sisson and Wallace—and Crocker) directly from China arrived in the mountains. Brought from Hong Kong, they were immediately dispersed among veteran work gangs to learn the ropes, and put to work. While more workers were recruited in China that year and the next, recent immigrants were always heavily outnumbered on the Central Pacific by Chinese hired locally.[104] The Big Four were not responsible for a major influx of Chinese, as it was (and is) often claimed, and there were always far more Chinese involved in California mining than in railroad work.[105] In 1867, two years after Crocker forced Strobridge to hire the first fifty Orientals, two hundred more Chinese *left* California than entered. The next year 11,081 entered, but only 4,475 left, and in 1869 the same ratio prevailed; but it is clear that only a small proportion of the newcomers were specifically brought over the Pacific to work on the railroad.[106] The *Railroad Record,* as early as 1866, recognized that without tapping the Chinese labor market in California, the work "could never have been this advanced," and urged a big campaign to import Chinese coolies, a campaign that never came to pass.[107] The Central Pacific, both then and later, had to explain to the prejudiced California public its rather limited role in sparking Chinese immigration and, wrote one observer, dispell "their apprehension that the four hundred million inhabitants of the Chinese Empire were about to be poured into our state."[108]

The Big Four, however, were always keen to turn necessity into profit. One should not be surprised to learn that to this end they invested in the Pacific Mail Steamship Line, which carried most Chinese immigrants into California, and later, at least Charlie Crocker was a (the?) major stockholder in the new China Mail Steamship Company. A congressional investigation of the "Chinese Question" in 1876 revealed that through the steamship companies, Crocker personally profited from each immigrant who booked passage.[109]

On May 3, at one o'clock in the still frigid morning, the second shift on Summit Tunnel's four facings roared in triumph. After almost two years of frustrating, dangerous labor, they had finally broken through the last few feet of dark gray granite: the Summit was pierced! Engineer Clement, responsible for the 1,659-foot-long bore, no doubt with great trepidation, took readings and measurements. He too must have bellowed with joy, for that sloping, curving tunnel, at an elevation of 7,042 feet—the highest on the company's route—was less than two inches off true center. As one J. O. Wilder, who was present, understated: "It was a wonderful piece of engineering."[110] It would be another seven months before the tunnel was tracked, but a major psychological barrier had been shattered along with the granite.

The spring thaw in April and early May in the higher altitudes was more damaging than had been expected, with avalanches and minor flooding, which caused tracks to settle, buckle, and even collapse,[111] but there was good news from the East. In the field a record eight continuous months, Butler Ives and his colleagues had mapped from the California border eastward across all of Nevada, and Ives had personally made a thorough survey of Echo and Weber canyons, east of Ogden, a survey that seemed hilarious to Union Pacific surveyors who were working from those same canyons in the other direction, who believed the Central Pacific would be stuck in the mountains for years.[112] Based on Ives's reports, Huntington hand-carried a formal location map to Secretary of the Interior Orville H. Browning on April 25, detailing the company's proposed route from the California line to Humboldt Wells, Nevada, a 407-mile stretch (to mile 526). Perhaps because of the slow progress in the mountains (at least in terms of actual miles of track) and the large gap in the Sierras, Browning did not actually approve the map until January 1869.[113]

There was other good news. Several companies had been formed at Santa Cruz to produce blasting powder, while along the Truckee River twenty-four "first-class" sawmills were roaring and buzzing night and day, each spitting out an average of twenty-five thousand board feet of lumber daily.[114] Crocker had earlier told a local sawyer, Allan Towle, to build a few mills at the Truckee to provide ties and timbers for the railroad. Towle, unwilling to take such a financial risk, had declined, so Crocker went there himself and oversaw construction of two large mills. With the feat accomplished, Towle, now interested, was permitted to buy the new mills from Crocker at a reasonable price (he was permitted to build others on his own account), on condition that he supplied lumber *only* to the Central Pacific, and at a set price. He agreed and prospered, and so insatiable was the company's need for lumber that a dozen other entrepreneurs built mills nearby.[115]

By May, at least eleven thousand Celestials were working for the Central Pacific (Crocker later claimed no more than ten thousand),[116] as well as twenty-five hundred whites, and over a thousand draft teams. Track was being laid out from Cisco and both east and west from the Truckee; the tricky 116-foot grade was being finished just beyond the Summit, and work was progressing in all the remaining tunnels, a labor that tied up perhaps eight thousand men. But the company would still starve for government aid. As construction entered its most cruelly expensive phase, federal aid was still unavailable because of the Sierra gap, and no new bonds could be issued at Sacramento either for lack of a continuous line.[117]

This was a time when the world was awash in newfound wealth; huge diamond fields were discovered and opened in South Africa, and gold was blundered upon in Wyoming, yet the Big Four faced the rest of 1867 realizing that no amount of muscle on the line or finagling in the halls of Congress would result in government aid when they most needed it. It was a fact of life, like the Sierras themselves. They would essentially have to get through 1867 on credit. That they pulled it off and actually *bought* more railroads at the same time must rank as America's greatest essay in financial wizardry.

Secretary of the Interior Browning, an odd man who counted Huntington a fast friend, at this juncture had an odd idea. In an attempt, as he said it, to "be fair" to both companies, he informed Congress on Valentine's Day that both companies should effect a meeting of their rails precisely 78.295 miles east of Salt Lake City. His engineers had informed him that that location was exactly halfway between Omaha and Sacramento. This would ensure that half of all government aid went to each company.[118] Congress, wrestling with the ongoing issue of Reconstruction and pummeling President Johnson for "obstructionism," ignored the secretary's unusual plan and instead dealt with matters of black civil rights and military rule in the obdurate South.*

There was perhaps more to Congress's inaction on Browning's proposal than

---

*Johnson and Congress were at odds on almost every issue, the latter (soon to impeach Johnson) even granting Nebraska statehood over the former's veto.

immediately met the eye. The Union Pacific's leadership, using all of its effort to impel the Casements' mad dash across the prairie, was utterly certain that it could carve its way at least entirely through Utah (and, with luck, Nevada as well) before meeting the Californians' rails, and their astute lobbyists were busily convincing congressmen that this was so. Conversely, despite an almost messianic faith in themselves and their mission, the Big Four, still mired in the mountains, were more than willing to accept half of a very large pie rather than settle for a single piece. If it could be governmentally mandated and guaranteed that the company could build to eastern (or even central) Utah, the Central Pacific would have most of its problems solved. The pressure of the race with the Union Pacific would be relieved, lessening construction costs, and a ready market could be found at last for its none too popular securities. The secretary's plan looked mighty appealing from Sacramento.

Huntington, who had managed to convince the major brokerage firm of Fisk and Hatch to popularize and sell Central Pacific stocks and bonds (which they eventually did with great success), was spending more and more time in Washington, and it is highly likely that it was he who whispered 78.295 miles in Browning's ear. He later admitted that he had been willing to spend a lot of company money to achieve a "breakthrough" in Washington that year.[119] He had two well-placed allies to help him sway the secretary: John Bloss, chief clerk in the Department of the Interior, and the secretary's new law partner, Thomas Ewing, Jr.*[120] Working with General Franchot (so well salaried and provided with expense accounts), Collis Huntington himself had generous (by any standards but Durant's) disposable funds, and he probably did dispose of both money and favors. Referring to the cost of "informing" and "educating" public officials at this time, Huntington admitted later that "most of our expenditures . . . [in Washington were] to keep Congress from robbing us of our property."[122] The *San Francisco Chronicle,* following one congressional investigation, put it another way: "The railroad company found that the silver throat and the golden tongue come high."[123] Clearly something was afoot in Washington in 1867, for Franchot was spouting money like a surfacing whale blows water, and Huntington was wearing ruts in the Capitol's corridors. Since they were not seeking a new railroad act, or an increase in actual aid, it is likely that they were simply out to stymie the Union Pacific. What better way to do so than to settle the issue of juncture at a "fair" location: say 78.295 miles east of Salt Lake City?[124] After all, as Henry W. Farnam has sarcastically written, "Huntington's fertile brain was marvelously creative," and his company and his own financial future were in great jeopardy.[125]

While Huntington and Franchot were casting their golden spells in the East,

---

*Ewing had been secretary of the treasury under Harrison and Tyler, and secretary of the interior under Taylor, both for brief periods.[121]

an only slightly less devious Leland Stanford was becoming the Warlock of the West. As the 1898 congressional investigation revealed, "Stanford had taken charge of the corps of explainers in California, and the witness [Huntington] did not know much about them except he thought Stanford sometimes paid too much for what he got. Mr. Huntington said that Stanford was a liberal man, while the witness always tried to be just first and generous if there was anything left."[126] Still, the "explainers" (lobbyists) achieved the company's goal.

Huntington probably planted the 78.295-mile seed, but he failed to sufficiently water it, and it wilted in Congress. The race was still on.

While he and Franchot were feeding the silver throat in Washington and "educating" the golden tongue to speak their language, bizarre maneuvers were taking place in Sacramento. The Big Three (plus Huntington by telegraph) and company counsel E. B. Crocker, already carrying a truly epic debt, were beginning to purchase railroads. Essentially, what they wanted—and got—was a monopoly of West Coast railroads, as if they realized that John R. Robinson and Frank Norris would someday sit down and write flashy exposés of their business practices.[127] They already held the short Sacramento Valley line that Judah had built, and had acquired much of the rolling stock of the California Central, and now, in April, they were after the Western Pacific, founded in 1862, but somnolent since. The Western Pacific, owned by William Cass, was to stretch 120 miles, from Sacramento to San Jose, through some of California's best farm and wine country. Only some twenty miles were actually tracked, but the line clearly had great potential. It was Stanford who pushed the purchase. Huntington seconded the idea by telegraph, but Hopkins—who knew the books—was at best tepid in his support, and Charlie Crocker outright reluctant. A deal could have been struck with Cass as early as January, but the dissenter and the doubter delayed the issue, an unusual occurrence among the Big Four.[128]

During the first week of April, Stanford and E.B. drew up the articles of agreement, which were instantly accepted by Cass. On April 10 a worried Hopkins wrote his partner in New York:

> Stanford arranged for Western purchase subject to your vote which will control mine. We get 20 miles completed RR, 20 miles unlaid iron, 10 locomotives, all other gear except lands and Govt. bonds. We assume Rensalaer iron contract and pay gold $60,000 within 60 days, 17,000 within 6 months, 43,000 within 12 months and 31,000 in currency within 2 years.
>
> P.S. Stanford is certain we can raise money here on W.P. securities.[129]

For only $151,000, they could have what would become one of the state's longest railroads. Huntington jumped at the chance and Uncle Mark dubiously cast his vote—and his fate—with his partner. Charlie Crocker also finally assented to the new risk, although not with the best of grace. Legal transfer was effected in June and officers were elected. Stanford, a man born to be chief executive, was made president; Hopkins, born with a green eyeshade, was named treasurer; and a C. W. Sanger was elected secretary. Aside from those three, the board of directors comprised only Crocker and his brother, Huntington, and Asa P. Stanford. It was a savvy transaction. The rolling stock, much needed, and soon churning down the Central Pacific line, was itself probably worth the railroad's purchase price.[130] For years, however, the Big Four would lament their failure to buy the Western Pacific's land-grant acres, which Cass was willing to part with for a mere $100,000 extra. As Creed Haymund later bemoaned, failure to buy this prime land was a grievous mistake, for "it was in fact worth many millions."[131] Apparently the Big Four could not stretch their almost nonexistent resources any farther.

Nor was the Big Four's acquisitiveness sated with the purchase of Cass's railroad. With Stanford again in the lead, the Sacramentans immediately began negotiations to buy the twenty-two-mile-long (and largely unbuilt) Yuba Railroad from veteran Colonel C. L. Wilson, earlier one of the leading detractors of the Central Pacific. The details were finally ironed out and the short railroad was acquired in October, in the name of the Contract and Finance Company, which was just a few days old.[132]

The Sacramento shopkeepers had grander visions yet. They were ogling the fifty-mile-long San Francisco & San Jose, also known as the Southern Pacific (which they added to their holdings in February 1868), the California Central, and the California & Oregon (acquired in 1870), on which Congress had lavished 3.2 million acres of superb land grants.[133] Tight money and pressing priorities, however, delayed adding further tentacles to the octopus in 1867. Despite what must have appeared delusions of grandeur—to say nothing of progress being stalled in the Sierras—Fisk and Hatch by mid-1867 were advertising Central Pacific bonds at 95 percent of par, and were finding at least some takers.[134]

The Big Four's new acquisitions brought up a new issue, that of a western terminus. Both San Francisco and Oakland across the Bay were reluctant to grant adequate waterfront property to the company, so the Big Four instead filed intentions with the state government to acquire Yerba Buena Island (commonly called Goat Island) in San Francisco Bay. They planned to link the island terminus to Oakland by a causeway for the trains, and connect with San Francisco via ferry. The state was willing, but, unfortunately, the island was a federal military reserve, so recourse had to be made to Congress.[135] This, seemingly a simple matter, was to be a long and frustrating business, destined to fail. Instead, they would have to eventually turn to Horace W. Carpentier, a sharklike businessman, who owned most of the Oakland waterfront.[136] They would not at all enjoy doing so, but to ensure success, they would have to work closely with Carpentier in the future.

In the aidless year of 1867, with money gushing out but trickling in and the largest business debts in United States history to date, the Big Four, despite the strains and differences of opinion (as in the Western Pacific acquisition), did not fall out, nor did they fall apart. If any period of time was likely to cause divisiveness, it was 1867, yet none occurred. Instead, the Big Four, and increasingly E. B. Crocker, worked in an atmosphere of resigned, utter trust. Each did what he was best suited to do by inclination, experience, and aptitude: Huntington, the East Coast huckster; Stanford, the West Coast politico; Hopkins, the quiet accountant; Charlie Crocker, the gruff leader of men; and E.B., the legal prestidigitator. They were five parts of a puzzle that fit together perfectly, and they worked both together and as individuals exceedingly well. Their common goal was riches—and respect.

E. H. Miller, Jr., intimate of all (insofar as that was possible), wrote tellingly that "there probably never were five men associated together that worked so much in harmony."[137] He hardly overstated the case. They trusted one another with proxies, with power of attorney, and with each other's precious reputations, and they never let one another down. The contrast with the conniving, predatory leadership of the Union Pacific could not be more striking. With, as Huntington wrote, "a floating debt of seven millions before we got across the Sierra Nevada mountains,"[138] they conducted their business by sheer faith: "There were no written understandings" between them, because no need for such was ever felt.[139]

Yet they were not at all personal *friends*. The voluminous correspondence they exchanged is curiously—no, singularly—devoid of friendly jibes, humor, or any elements indicating closeness as people. Almost every letter begins with the formal "Dear Sir," as if they were strangers, even those between Huntington and Hopkins. They were an extremely reserved lot, and their letters reveal almost nothing of the inner men. Asked his opinion of Stanford years after the Central Pacific was built, Collis Huntington blandly responded, "Leland Stanford is a nice man," utterly damning him with the faintest of praise.[140] Under oath in 1898, the aging Huntington (last survivor of the Big Four) said of Stanford when questioned, "He was as straight a man as there was in California in all matters with which he was connected, outside of politics"—a revealing last phrase and a gratuitous insult.[141]

One of the rare testimonials to *any* warmth or friendship displayed by any of the Big Four is an observation by outsider Lewis Clement: "J. H. Strobridge was very intimate with Mr. Crocker";[142] but he must have been referring to construction matters, for any personal friendship remains unconfirmed by all other sources. Coolness and trust worked for these men, and, not content to be building an epic railroad, they now determined to build an empire, and to do so without cash.

As the summer sun melted the deep Sierra snows, and the Union Pacific was reeling under the blows of the Plains tribes, thanks to Huntington, the company was "sending out iron by nearly every ship leaving New York for California,"[143] iron whose price was mercifully and finally falling. But, although rails could now be had at the San Francisco wharves for seventy-five dollars a ton, the Central Pacific, very nearly bankrupt and strangled by debts, was on the verge of collapse.

9

INTO DARKEST WYOMING AND THE SIERRAS SURRENDER

GENERAL DODGE GOES FOR A RIDE

ENERAL Grenville Dodge, who had personally platted Cheyenne (mile 516) on July 10 when Union Pacific track stood at mile 395, and who greeted the first settlers to arrive there a week later,[1] should have been in Washington looking after the interests of the citizens of western Iowa. His diary indicates a bit of guilt about his negligence, but it hardly overwhelmed the man. This is not to imply that he was buried in the minutiae of railroad work. Hardly. He had decided to take a ride, a fourteen-hundred-mile-long ride, and that takes time.

While in the West Dodge took advantage of an obligation and an opportunity, represented in the persons of General Grant's chief of staff, General John A. Rawlins and government director and engineer Jacob Blickensderfer. Rawlins, seriously ill with consumption, was being sent on a tour of the clean mountain air by Grant, who personally requested that Dodge squire him around the frontier. Blickensderfer, the Union Pacific's only civilian government commissioner, came west by orders of President Andrew Johnson. His task was to ascertain exactly where the eastern base of the Black Hills began—where bonds of $16,000 per mile magically tripled to $48,000. The president was not about to trust the company to make that important determination, so Blickensderfer was to be trusted to make an honest and impartial scientific judgment himself.[2]

Dodge, a thorough outdoorsman, could not pass up the chance to help the commanding general—it was already rumored that Grant would run for the presidency in 1868—and he also felt that he personally should be the one to show Blickensderfer, who was unfamiliar with the terrain, just where the mountains began. Politics (as in his vacant congressional chair) would have to wait.

Hence Dodge rendezvoused with Blickensderfer and Rawlins along the Union Pacific line, and they were in Cheyenne (where they were joined by Seymour) when that town was officially created. The chief of staff gave a rousing patriotic speech, and the applause had barely ceased when Cheyenne Indians halfheartedly attacked the new town. Had there not been two companies of cavalry escorting the general, Rawlins might have been the victim of a most embarrassing massacre.[3]

After several weeks in the vicinity of Cheyenne, which was mushrooming in anticipation of receiving tracks and temporary Hell on Wheels status, the Dodge party headed west. They moved at a leisurely pace, stopping to admire the scenery and to hunt and to fish, and taking time for Dodge to indulge himself in naming various geographical features. One of these was a beautiful freshwater spring that he named Rawlins. If Blickensderfer's name had been a syllable or two shorter, Dodge would have been happy to honor him as well.

For a month the party dallied and zigzagged into the Salt Lake Valley, arriving at Camp Douglas near the Mormon capital on August 31 to catch up to their mail and telegrams. Among messages for the chief engineer were several from Oliver Ames, all in the same tenor: "Our reputation today depends upon rapid construction. When the road is completed, we can improve the grades and curves, though it will be at a heavy additional cost."[4] Ames should have been haranguing the hardworking Casements, or Jason Evans, not the wandering Dodge.

At Salt Lake City the sojourners were treated royally by Brigham Young. Dodge, who scrupulously avoided even hinting that he had decided to take his road north through Ogden, left the leading Saint with his illusions. Dodge was, on the other hand, pleased and relieved to hear from Young that the Prophet, some of his sons, his brother Elisha, and a posse of bishops were able and even eager to supply large numbers of men for grading, lumbering, freighting, and any other work the Union Pacific might need.[5] The Mormon population, in part owing to continual emigration of newly converted British Saints, was burgeoning. There were more Mormons in the valley in 1867 than there was work, and an influx of cash wages would be a boon to the isolated community, which was forced more and more to rely upon barter transactions. "The Mormon Prophet puts a good face upon the invasion of Utah by the Pacific Railroad," noted a contemporary journal,[6] and, indeed, the insular community desperately needed connection with the outside world to prosper. It was a beneficial arrangement for both. Brigham Young, still a Union Pacific director, had the manpower, and the company seemed to have the cash.[7]

The Mormon leader had another idea, or proposition, to offer Dodge. Why not build a line north from Salt Lake City through Ogden to the Green River and Snake River Valley, then northwest to the middle valley of the Columbia to Portland, and perhaps Seattle? The Mormons would be willing to help build it. That way, figured Young, Salt Lake City would have two lines open to the Pacific, while the Union Pacific would have its own doorway to Asia, exclusive of its ties to the Central Pacific.[8] Dodge was skeptical but interested nonetheless, and his retinue was soon cantering north along the suggested route into Idaho. The engineer liked what he saw, and immediately recognized that the route was a feasible one, and he recommended the Prophet's idea to Oliver Ames.[9] Calling it "a route that Nature has intended for a railroad to the Pacific," he asserted that if the money was available he could build to Portland from Utah in a mere eighteen months.[10] In a strange coincidence, a pamphlet appeared at this time taking Dodge to task for not building most, if not all, of the Union Pacific on such a route, north of the present line, terminating at Puget Sound. "We must conclude that the General is a very poor interpreter of the designs of Providence," the writer noted, for building through the sterile Platte Valley.[11]

The chief engineer then had an inspiration. Dodge had planned for engineer Percy Brown to do all of the location work of the Utah Division of the Union Pacific. With Brown now a martyr of the Indian wars, why not offer the Utah position to the obviously competent and "neutral" Jacob Blickensderfer, despite his government directorship? He did so, and the presidential investigator accepted with almost indecent haste, for he loved the country he was exploring, and he liked Grenville Dodge as well.[12]

Once the conflict of interest had been sealed with a handshake, Blickensderfer finished his calculations and telegraphed Washington that the eastern base of the Black Hills began six miles and a few hundred yards *east* of Cheyenne, a point no one else had suspected. Like Charlie Crocker before him, Grenville Dodge was a man who could truly move mountains.[13]

With exquisite leisureliness, Dodge, his new friends, and Seymour, headed east in late September, passing through a rapidly transformed Cheyenne. No tent village now, Cheyenne boasted fully a hundred thriving saloons and two hotels, one of them built for Train by the Crédit Foncier. A rowdy little city whose newspaper, the *Leader,* ran a daily column starkly labeled "Last Night's Shootings," Cheyenne, like Julesburg earlier, offended Dodge with its open licentiousness.[14] Before leaving town, in fact, the engineer had to call upon the soldiers of nearby Fort Russell to evict some of the seamier transients at bayonet point. The troopers were to be called back more than once.[15]

As they passed on toward the east, Dodge's sensibilities received another lashing. The next "town" down the line, little Sidney, Nebraska (mile 414), was in the terminal stages of Hell on Wheels debauchery. Despite the outflux of hardcases for Cheyenne, that fall the only civilized place in Sidney (which a year later would claim only a druggist, seven saloons, and Company K, Eighteenth Infantry)[16] was the new Union Pacific Hotel, and that was just barely civilized. Although Sidney was designated by the company as an eating stop, "passengers were not allowed to detrain there" because of the danger. So many shots were fired randomly into passenger cars stopped at the station that even remaining aboard was risky. Webster Snyder was forced to issue an order stating that until Sidney calmed down (in other words, until vigilantes outnumbered troublemakers), "the trains would not be halted at Sidney" at all, a distinction granted no other frontier town. After all, the company had a responsibility to its paying customers. Sad little Sidney's population would soon fall to about two hundred.[17]

By the time that Grenville Dodge reached Omaha, he had missed one entire session of Congress and most of another, sessions of violent debate over such important national issues as civil rights and impeachment of the president. No matter; the war hero took his seat in Washington on December 2, answering one of only three roll calls in his absentee career. With his friend General Grant now acting secretary of war, Dodge would not have to be just another freshman congressman. He could remain a railroader, and within days he was bragging about having his "engineering office in the Interior Department." This special suite of offices, conveniently distant from his seat in the House, was not only conveniently at the elbow of Secretary Browning, but equipped with Dodge's own personal telegraph line. He was in a good position to influence the secretary and perhaps frustrate the Central Pacific's lobbyists as well.[18] Neither was to be the case.

MR. AMES TAKES A CONTRACT

DODGE proved himself no babe in the political woods in 1867, but once again, what was transpiring in the boardrooms was more unruly than what was happening at the Sidney railroad station. America in 1867, as Lucius Beebe and John Clegg have written, was smitten by "a national orgy of finance,"[19] and some of the wildest bacchanalia of all took place not in frontier tent saloons but in company offices on sedate-appearing Nassau Street.

On August 16 Congressman Oakes Ames wrote with stiff formality to the

Union Pacific board of directors: "Gentlemen: I propose to construct for your company 667 miles of your road, commencing at the 100th meridian westward"—almost to Utah. He pledged to do so for $42,000 per mile for the first hundred miles (many of which were actually already built), $45,000 for the next hundred, $96,000 for the third, $80,000 for the fourth, $90,000 for the fifth, and $96,000 for the sixth hundred. An additional $7,500 per mile would provide machinery, shops, and equipment (but neither bridges nor tunnels), making an average per-mile tender of $71,837.[20] The board, no doubt less than thunderstruck with surprise by the offer, instantly accepted Ames's $47,915,000 contract (by far the largest in America to that time), and referred the issue to the executive committee.[21] That body rapidly concurred with the board, on the condition that speedy completion "was the essence of the contract."[22] Ames would be credited with work already done past the 100th meridian (about 167 miles), but would not receive any bonds for those miles, since they had already been issued and obligated.

The contract was officially accepted on October 1, one hectic day before the annual election meeting of Union Pacific stockholders. The executive committee, which would put its case to the stockholders, consisted of Oliver Ames, Bushnell, Durant, government director Springer Harbaugh, Orville Lambard and Dix (both absent in Europe), and John R. Duff, who flatly refused to give his assent, on the ground that the 167 miles tracked west of the 100th meridian made the contract patently illegal.[23] Apparently Duff alone expected the government to raise cain about the contract. He was mistaken.

The maneuvering on the eve of the election meeting was Byzantine. With the help of Wall Street buccaneer Jim Fisk, Durant began to subscribe huge blocks of Union Pacific stock to boost his clout at the meeting. Oliver countered by invoking a minor provision in the company charter requiring full (not 10 percent) payment as a prerequisite for voting, knowing that neither Durant nor Fisk could come up with that much money. Next, the Doctor put up his own slate of officers, without Ames supporters, and politicked for them. The Ames men then put up their own slate, without Durant men, and then levered from a crooked judge an injunction to keep the Doctor from voting at all. Durant, in his wily turn, wangled an injunction of his own, against Ames, and round and round they went.* The October 1 meeting was declared void, and on October 4 another meeting was held and a compromise agreed to.

The most important part of the deal that ended the deadlock was that Oakes Ames would immediately reassign his contract to seven trustees (Durant, Oliver Ames, Alley, Dillon, Bushnell, McComb, and ex–attorney general B. E. Bates—

---

*At this point, especially in New York City, judges were all but openly selling injunctions, much as priests sold indulgences in the Middle Ages.

three of the Doctor's people, four of Ames's). The board of directors was reshuffled by election clearly in the Ameses' favor, with Alley, Glidden, Bates, and F. Gordon Dexter (a fence sitter) replacing Dix, Cyrus McCormick, Lambard, and Charles Tuttle. The executive committee would have three men from each camp: Oliver Ames, Duff, and Glidden and Durant, McComb, and Bushnell, the seventh member being government director James Brooks.[24] Thus neither side was likely to cry foul, create bad publicity, or run for their lawyers.

On October 15 Oakes signed over his huge contract to the seven trustees, who agreed to pay the profits (less a three-thousand-dollar annual retainer each) to stockholders in the Crédit Mobilier (which, of course, they were) who, as Union Pacific stockholders as well, had given permanent proxy rights to the trustees. The ultimate profits, to be distributed each June and December, would be paid in proportion to the amount of Crédit Mobilier stock held by individuals as of the date of the contract's reassignment.

The actual cash to construct the railroad would be paid by the Union Pacific to the Crédit Mobilier, which would then loan it, with interest, to the trustees. The Union Pacific, further, paid the Crédit Mobilier a lump sum of over a million dollars to cover the differences between the per-mile figures of $27,500 (from Boomer) and $42,000 (from Ames) for the fifty-eight miles between the 100th meridian and O'Fallon's Bluff built prior to December 31, 1866.[25]

Thus, without awarding another contract to the Crédit Mobilier, the trustees would divide profits from the Ames contract among that company's shareholders. The Crédit Mobilier in actuality was merely a conduit of funds, linking the railroad and the trustees, and a marvelously profitable middleman it would be. Hubert Hoxie, recently promoted from the Omaha wharves to be Webster Snyder's assistant superintendent, could only weep with envy.[26]

There was, of course, some dissent. John Duff again voiced his doubts, objecting that because Oakes Ames was serving as a congressman there was a glaring conflict of interest that was bound to attract attention.[27] In Paris, John Dix had a fit. The general, who had drawn a comfortable $8,000 a year for doing little more than looking like a railroad president, had been replaced by Oliver Ames at the October 4 "compromise" meeting, and he bitterly resented his ouster and his replacement on the board. Even though his five hundred shares of stock had been partially bought for him by Durant in 1864, he did control them, and, he thought, he had another lever to use: in his prestigious position as ambassador to France, Dix was well placed to damage railroad stock-and-bond sales in Europe.* Bushnell was told through Dix's lawyer that the former president of the Union Pacific might very well launch a vendetta against the company unless his stock was purchased by someone, and, *at par.* Realizing that they

---

*While they were hardly booming on European markets, there were high hopes that they soon would be.

were being taken, and certainly no strangers themselves to bribery, the members of the executive committee dashed off a check for $50,000, and the ambassador and his threats faded into the background.[28] Would that all the company's problems could have been resolved in so forthright a manner.

Government director Jesse L. Williams—an accomplished civil engineer himself—was one of the few men connected with the Union Pacific to smell a rat at this stage. An honest man despite his proximity during these years to Durant and other board members, Williams saw corruption festering in the new construction contract, later writing Dodge in the field that "whoever of our Directors suggested the plan of letting the work to themselves at such enormous prices, thus making the company poor, did the mischief. No company can long have the public confidence in that way."[29] He would, reacting to the Ames contract (and its bald emphasis on rapid, rather than quality, construction), do his thorny best to keep the company honest, to Durant's dismay and discomfort. Dodge, for his part, was to swear that he did not even learn about the true mechanics of the new contract until a year had passed. Even then, he admitted that he could find no fault with it.[30]

With all these convolutions, the maneuvering did not come to an end on October 15 with the signing over of the Ames contract to the trustees, for as the snows lashed the crews west of Cheyenne (well into the forty-eight-thousand-dollar-per-mile bond zone) the men paying them decided to begin the pleasant task of distributing profits—profits that would soon ring alarm bells in the halls of Congress and beyond.

The trustees of the Ames contract met on December 12 and initiated the allotment of construction profits to the Crédit Mobilier faithful. For every ten shares held, $600 (at par) of Union Pacific first-mortgage bonds and six shares of the railroad's stock were awarded. The bonds were selling very near par, but the stock rarely topped 30 percent. The total disbursement of Union Pacific paper was $2,244,000 in bonds (at par value) and 22,440 shares of stock.[31] Three days after Christmas the executive committee of the Crédit Mobilier itself declared a dividend of 6 percent for both 1866 and 1867, to be paid on January 3. This dividend, which was said to represent interest on stockholders' investments, was paid not in cash but in more plentiful Union Pacific stock. The 12 percent return on investment was calculated on a basis of stock being worth 30 percent of par, so that each holder of ten shares of Crédit Mobilier stock received four shares of railroad stock. Because the par value of the railroad stock was so low, the actual return on investment (often inaccurately calculated at par, or as 40 percent) was indeed the relatively modest 12 percent the executive committee claimed.[32]

Nor were the shenanigans over. Sidney Dillon, Crédit Mobilier chief executive, had discovered 650 shares of the construction company's stock that, although they bore the Doctor's name, had never been paid for. Probably not at all surprised by this, which in any other company would be considered an "irregularity," Dillon took the stock in trust, and in October 370 shares were reassigned in trust to Durant (who had demanded all), and 280 to Oakes Ames. Those few shares given to the congressman were to cause the greatest problems the Union Pacific would ever face.

Union Pacific trustee Henry McComb, who would later scare up a legal hornet's nest and congressional inquisition, angrily informed Dillon that 375 shares of the errant 650 were rightfully his, although his logic was twisted even by Durant's standards. Still, Oakes, correctly sensing trouble, loaned him 500 shares so that he could collect the January 3 dividend, hoping that McComb would be somewhat mollified. Ames flatly refused to *give* McComb a single share. McComb was unmollified.[33]

It was at this point that Oakes—who apparently had no faith at all in human nature—made the first of what were to be two catastrophic mistakes. Perhaps fearful that Congress would someday begin questioning the latest construction contract, he decided to broaden the company's support beneath the Capitol dome. At least five congressmen (Alley, Ames, and Samuel Hooper of Massachusetts, Benjamin Boyer of Pennsylvania, and James W. Grimes of Iowa, Republicans all) already owned stock in the Crédit Mobilier. Alley had been in the company from the beginning, and three of the others had bought their stock directly from Ames himself. In November, Oakes decided to hawk more, and so did Durant.

In the last two months of 1867, the Doctor sold 150 shares to Congressman James Brooks of New York, while Congressman Ames peddled blocks of ten, twenty, and thirty shares to each of nine representatives and two senators, disposing artfully of a total of 160 shares. With the exception of Brooks, every congressional holder of Crédit Mobilier stock was a Republican. Among the eager purchasers were presidential hopeful, and soon Grant's vice-president, Speaker of the House Schuyler Colfax (20 shares); future president of the United States James Garfield of Ohio (10), then the chairman of the Committee on Military Affairs; and Senator Henry Wilson of Massachusetts (20), who was to become Grant's second vice-president. Ames attempted but failed to interest Maine's James G. Blaine, a presidential aspirant of known avarice, Senator Roscoe Conkling of New York, and several others.

To the purchasers, nothing appeared amiss. They did, after all, pay full par value for the stock, when it was selling under par in the marketplace. True, advance credit given them for the December 12 and January 3 dividends brought the actual cash outlay down to well under half the paper value of the transaction, but buying on "insider's tips" was common practice on and off Wall Street in those unregulated days. What did look suspicious was the fact that for several years the congressmen's stock remained in Ames's own hands and name, even though dividends were paid (through him) to the actual owners.

Still, had it not been for McComb's almost self-destructive anger and three overly candid letters he received from Oakes, the whole affair might have been buried and forgotten in the bustle of postwar America.[34]

MEANWHILE, OUT ON THE PRAIRIE

WITH the boardroom brouhahas as loud as the fighting on the Plains and the blasting in the Sierras, one could easily lose sight of what was transpiring in the foothills around Cheyenne. There, actual work was being done.

Despite the Indian menace—the Crow nation now went temporarily on the warpath—the Casement Army did not permit itself to tarry and lick its wounds. With 127 miles of new track in place by the end of July, the spikers would secure another 120 before year's end.[35]

Not only was track laid, but a team of engineers dug a canal to change the channel of the Lodge Pole River that summer,[36] and by early autumn coal seams discovered by Van Lennep near mile 650—appropriately named Carbon—were being worked by the company, which was soon dragging a hundred tons of acceptable coal from the soil daily. With wood running $100 a cord on the Plains, the coal became economical fuel for those locomotives built or modified to use it.[37] There was timber as well, good timber, and the company soon had large gangs of tie and trestle cutters dangerously deep in the Sioux's Black Hills. The timber they cut was floated part of the way and then teamstered to end of track.[38]

That fall, the price of rails delivered to Omaha dipped to $97.50 per ton, but as Hezekiah Bissell cynically remarked, Omaha was by then so far from end of track and corruption was so rife among the contractors that "it cost nine cents per pound to haul [the rails] out there."[39] At sixty pounds a yard and twenty-eight to thirty feet per rail, the cost was stupendous, even if Bissell did exaggerate. Almost everything was expensive on the Laramie Plains and beyond. Locally hired teamsters with their wagons and animals asked and received twenty-five dollars a day, and common corn was fetching twenty times its point-of-origin price. In 1873 John B. Alley, former Union Pacific government director, major stockholder, and still on the company's board of directors, would with reason complain of this period that "we were plundered."[40]

With trains averaging thirty-four miles an hour on the Plains, and up to fifty-five miles on certain stretches of the line, accidents were bound to occur, especially given the shifting properties of sand ballasting. There were a number of derailments and a few minor, low-speed rear-end collisions, but there were more serious accidents as well. As Arthur Fergusen recorded on September 3, "A severe accident has occurred on the road in which seven persons lost their lives & quite a number were wounded."[41] Although that accident cost the same number of lives as had the Plum Creek massacre the previous month, not a word of it popped up in the Omaha press. Perhaps Dodge suppressed news of the wreck, just as he tried to cover up the company's Indian problems. That same month, however, the press did note that shipping live cattle on the Union Pacific had begun, predicting it would provide a steady source of income for the company.[42] No one predicted that Omaha would soon be a meat-packing center second only to Chicago, and the phrase *Omaha steaks* would become a hallmark of quality throughout the land.

By mid-September, ice was forming in the ponds of the Black Hills, and the first snowstorm of the season, a moderate one, breezed in on October 21.[43] By then Cheyenne was attracting emigrants and hell-raisers by the hundreds. Fergusen visited the frontier town in early October and noted with surprise, "Cheyenne is quite a town & much larger than I expected," with some three thousand inhabitants.[44] He was there on one later occasion when troops "were called out to quell [a] disturbance," a gunfight that left two dead, several wounded, and a house in flames.[45] Cheyenne was "quite a town" before it received its rails, as Dodge had seen to his disgust. It was crowded with saloons (The Magic City of the West Shaving Saloon offered the lowest whiskey prices, and probably the lowest quality as well), wholesale-liquor emporiums, billiard parlors, a tenpin alley, a "Prairie dog and pet dealer," and soon a Union Pacific hospital and engine house; there also was "Mrs. J. Adams, Physician," one of the West's pioneer female practitioners.[46]

Trackers reached the town on November 13, to a suitably lusty and roaring welcome, and, as the track gangs stopped work for the season just twenty-two miles to the west, at mile 538, Cheyenne would be the company's sin-laced winter headquarters.[47] The weather (and, earlier, the Indians) had kept the Union Pacific from its goal of 280 miles in 1867, stalling the rails just 10 miles from Sherman Summit, a still laudable 233 miles from O'Fallon's Bluff. On December 2, a few days before Laramie was officially platted in the snow, government inspectors, swifter than usual, accepted miles 490 through 510, certifying them as first-class.[48]

But while track laying ceased, lumberjacks worked year round, as did the sawmills, and a force of eighteen hundred stumbled through three feet and more of snow in the Black Hills, until a particularly ferocious storm drove them too to cover.[49] A fleet of six large and twenty-four smaller snowplows were put to work to keep the line open, and the first snow fences were erected; but even then there were interruptions in service.[50] In part this was because government commissioners had mandated that Dodge hold the grade to as few feet per mile as possible, and he had grudgingly had a number of deep cuts made in the Laramie Plains rather than have the track follow the contours of the land. That first winter, the cuts became snow traps for huge drifts, severely complicating the traffic problem.[51]

Downtrack, the work never stopped. On its forty-acre Omaha tract, the Union Pacific's workshops literally hummed "when 850 sinewy men were busily engaged in manufacturing and repairing cars." A huge blacksmith shop was opened, with forty special forges designed by shop manager John Congden, and the railway cars produced under the stern supervision of master builder George E. Stevens were said to be superior in most respects to those purchased from Fort Wayne and Chicago.[52] Roundhouses and shops were also built, or were being built that winter at Grand Island, North Platte, Sidney, and Cheyenne (the last two towns also boasting company hotels), and would later appear in eight other towns farther west.[53]

With an unusually cold fall and a bitter December blocking westward progress, the company began building eastward from Omaha. Workers actually spiked rails to the ice of the thick-frozen Missouri River to connect with the Council Bluffs railhead. At last, albeit for only three months, there was continuous rail service to the east.[54] Trains were now regularly making the trip to Omaha from distant Cheyenne in a mere forty-two hours.[55]

The Union Pacific in 1867 added a significant operating profit to its burgeoning land sales, bringing in a gross of almost $3.5 million, which yielded a clean and clear net of just over $2 million. That December, with some pride, the company printed and distributed a formal, public report targeted at investors: *The Union Pacific Railroad from Omaha, Nebraska, Across the Continent . . . Its Construction, Resources, Earnings, and Prospects.* Painting a roseate picture that estimated future profits in the neighborhood of $17,664,000 a year, the report also contradicted critics who complained that the company was expending too much money per mile for construction. Ridiculous, said the company; major railroads are by nature expensive. The B&O cost an average of $66,000 per mile, the New York Central almost as much, and the Erie Railroad a whopping $80,000. That was about as much as the Union Pacific expected to spend on its most difficult sections.* Further, stressed the broadside, the company was receiving mammoth federal aid, and, aside from the grants of good farmland, should realize at least $5 million through the sale of town lots alone. With (the company claimed) $10 million in stock now sold, and half of it supposedly already used to cover construction costs, the Union Pacific, wrote the pamphleteer, obviously already had the confidence of the

---

*So why had the Ames contract quoted one hundred-mile stretch at $96,000?

American capitalist. The end of the year found the Union Pacific possessing fifty-three locomotives, eleven hundred freight, ten passenger, five baggage, and sixty handcars.[56] Now there was stability.

STRIKES, A NEW COMPANY, AND AN INDIAN TREATY

I N THE summer of 1867 the impossible happened in the Sierras, and it happened just as the Big Four were once again on the brink of bankruptcy. On June 24 some three thousand Chinese tunnelmen, graders, and road clearers laid down their picks, shovels, drills, and axes and walked off the job. As the Big Four had remarked earlier, the Chinese rarely struck, and when they did, it was in an orderly fashion. This June walkout was almost gentlemanly. Peaceful, patient, and respectful, the Celestials squatted silently along the track or returned to their camps, while several chosen headmen confronted Strobridge, their "one-eye bossy man." The Chinese politely demanded two things, a raise to forty dollars a month and an eight-hour day: "Eight hours a day good for white man, all the same good for Chinaman."[57]

Strobridge, close to a homicidal rage, was hardly sympathetic. In any case, he had no authority to grant demands, and he sent for Crocker, who, true to form, came "charging up the line like a bull." Berating the Chinese spokesmen, he swore that he would never give in to the strikers' demands, and told them to get back to work or pack up and head back down the line—on foot. They did neither. The Celestials seemed determined to wait Crocker out, and probably sensed his utter need for continued construction. Crocker, for his part, while no "sociologist," probably sensed that he could never "wait out" a Chinese. Habitually angry, Charlie Crocker flew into a towering rage. Cabling Huntington "about the feasibility of importing 10,000 Negroes" posthaste to replace the strikers, he also stopped the flow of provisions to the idle Chinese. With no dried abalone or Chinese chowchow, the Celestials within a few days moderated their terms. Exactly what transpired is not known, but the inflexible Charlie Crocker (perhaps urged by Stanford or Hopkins or both) apparently bended just a bit. While the twelve-hour day remained in effect, the workers' monthly pay was increased by two dollars to thirty-five dollars.[58] Crocker, who used to boast that "we had a friend in the camp of the enemy" spying on the Union Pacific, was, and remained, convinced that the Chinese work stoppage was caused by agitators paid by the rival line.[59] There would be a number of minor strikes—especially by the tunnel gangs—in the future, but the June stoppage was the only one serious enough to pose a threat to the company.

Aside from impending penury, the company faced another, blessedly brief, confrontation that summer, also from an unexpected quarter and also resolved by Crocker, who showed an unexpected diplomatic tact. With more men working east of the Sierras and grading into Nevada (according to one observer, "The invading army of Mongolians emerged from the mountains"),[60] the company was brought into increasing contact with Indians, not all of whom were content with promised free passes for train rides. These were not the fierce, proud, and warlike horsemen of the Plains but, as described in 1868 with a disdain reminiscent of John C. Frémont's, "the most abject of the human race—living on roots, and grasshoppers, and even the worms that were washed up in furrows" along the shores of Nevada's alkali lakes.[61] Almost all of these contacts were harmonious, if at times irritating, despite the fact that less than a hundred miles south of the Central Pacific's projected line serious Indian wars erupted with regularity. One day late in the summer, however, as Huntington remembered the story, a band of Paiutes rode up to a Chinese grading crew, and as the Orientals scattered in blind fear, opened fire. One grader fell wounded, but there was no answering volley of gunfire, for the Central Pacific had not armed its men. At once it appeared that the company's fragile, blessed, peace with the Indians was at an end. That is, until Charlie Crocker arrived on the scene.

A few days after the incident, and fully aware of the implications of Indian hostility, Crocker met with the Paiute chief whose warriors had used the Chinese to so little effect for target practice. With some patience and sophistication, and only a few basic threats, he told the Indian that he, Charlie Crocker, was also a chief. In fact, he was a "big chief," with thousands of yellow and white warriors at his command. As a big chief he would deign to sign a special treaty with the Paiutes, pledging eternal friendship. Both men then signed the "treaty," a large, resplendent document, "with a great big railroad seal to stamp on it." That done, and the chief committed by the fancy, if symbolic, sheet of paper, Crocker told him that "it was death if he broke the treaty." Then it was time to celebrate, with the stoutest of the Big Four providing the whiskey. Charlie and the chief (and their men) downed a great deal of bourbon that day, and, as Huntington related, "It was a drunken row."[62] With a fancy stamp, a keg of whiskey, and a few judicious threats, the Central Pacific had avoided a potentially crippling Indian war as adroitly as it had earlier sidestepped financial collapse.

Sidestepping the financial crisis of mid-1867 would require adroit footwork indeed, if it could be done at all. The Big Four's debts towered as high as the Sierras, through whose tunnels at least light could by now be seen. There must surely be a limit to how much even they could put on the cuff. When would the day of reckoning come? It could come at any time. Still locked in the mountains, with painfully modest mile-per-month gains and horrendous cost-per-mile outlays, the Central Pacific was not attracting investment moneys, despite Fisk and Hatch's glowing advertisements. Nor was the company generating government

ABOVE: *The "swarming" Celestials and their handcarts, creating the great embankment and cut at Sailor's Spur at mile 80 in the High Sierras, 1867. By this date some eighty percent of the Big Four's work force was composed of Chinese, who endured the harshest of conditions and dangers in return for fair pay—in gold—regularly disbursed.*

ABOVE: *A Central Pacific work train squeezes through Bloomer Cut, just past Newcastle, at about mile 39. The first major engineering obstacle, Bloomer Cut absorbed 500 kegs of blasting powder a day for many weeks and, when finished, was 800 feet long and up to 65 feet deep.*

OPPOSITE: *By late 1866, another obstacle had been overcome: Long Ravine in the High Sierras. An unusually massive structure of great strength, the Long Ravine Bridge was 878 feet long and 120 feet above the floor of the ravine. It stood for many years.*

ABOVE: *Another view of Long Ravine Bridge, showing the magnitude of the work. Designed and supervised by structural engineer Arthur Brown, the bridge consumed the output of a dozen sawmills and the energies of hundreds of skilled carpenters for months in 1867.*

RIGHT: *A Central Pacific train halts on the ledge gouged out of the granite of Cape Horn (at mile 57) so that passengers can admire the vertiginous view of the valley 2,000 feet below. This heroic sculpting of a mountain, completed in the early spring of 1866, overcame but one of a series of unprecedented engineering hurdles that faced the company in the mountains between Colfax at mile 54 and the 1,659-feet-long Summit Tunnel at mile 105.5.*

ABOVE: *The Central Pacific's first tunnel (of thirteen), Grizzly Hill, at mile 77. Work was directed by tunnel engineer John R. Gillis and jack-of-all-trades Lewis Clement, and the tunnel's two headings met July 4, 1866, the same day the company's tracks reached Dutch Flat, ten miles west.*

LEFT: *A wood train eases through Bloomer Cut, with Chinese workers and their white supervisor. The Chinese, while treated fairly, were almost entirely restricted to common laboring positions. This shipment of wood, one among many thousands, is probably destined to be used as locomotive fuel in treeless Nevada. Shipping wood hundreds of miles into Nevada congested traffic on the single-line railroad and added greatly to the company's routine expenditures.*

ABOVE: *A visual testimony to the need for snowsheds. Winter at Cisco provided scenic splendor but logistical horrors. That Sierra town registered forty-four distinct blizzards in the winter of 1865–66, drifts sixty feet high were not uncommon, and snow often lay on the ground in May and June.*

RIGHT: *Snowsheds located near Cisco, at mile 92 in the High Sierras. A total of thirty-eight miles of sheds and galleries were constructed, at an estimated cost of over $2 million. Designed by Lewis Clement and Arthur Brown, the sheds and galleries required an awesome 65 million board feet of exceptionally stout lumber. Used to cover the most exposed sections of the mountain line against some of the world's deepest average snowfalls, the structures held up well, with a few still standing in the mid-twentieth century.*

ABOVE: *Nevada's version of infinity. As the Central Pacific worked northeast toward Utah, it faced a different host of problems in the "howling wilderness" of the alkali desert: lack of water, potentially hostile Indians, and a total dearth of construction material, which had to be shipped over the Sierras at immense cost. On the other hand, Nevada's blessings included table-flat land, few bridges, little grading, and no tunnels.*

LEFT: *Accidental artwork. Sunlight filters through a snowshed in the High Sierras. Gaps were left between the boards forming the outer covering of the snowsheds for ventilation purposes, lest passengers in the rearmost cars run the risk of asphixiation. Over the years a number of snowsheds caught fire from locomotive sparks. A few were destroyed, but most were easily repaired.*

TOP: *Central Pacific engineer Lewis Clement and Union Pacific counterpart Jacob Blickens-derfer huddle beneath a buffalo robe on a cowcatcher in chilly Nevada. They were members of a bipartisan inspection team sent by Secretary of the Interior Orville Browning in February 1869 to assess the quality of the construction. An earlier inspection had revealed grave deficiencies on the Union Pacific line.*

BOTTOM: *A Central Pacific track crew laying some of the last yards of iron at Promontory Point, May 1869. They are posing next to the railroad car used as a studio by the company's official photographer, J. B. Silvis, who did a booming business at Promontory Point selling his photographs of the Sierras' grandeur. (Courtesy of the Denver Public Library Collection)*

aid, for it was having trouble putting together a twenty-mile stretch of continuous line. The tracks being laid near the Truckee were not continuous with those being spiked out of Cisco, and not a single aid-worthy twenty-mile stretch of track would be finished out of that town in 1867. It was the company's ill luck that its line east of Cisco had thirteen tunnels within twenty miles, with a total of more than a mile of bore.* Further, the experimental snowsheds were proving to be far more expensive than the company had anticipated. Thus even $960,000 in government bonds for a twenty-mile segment was denied the Central Pacific just as it was spending upward of $200,000 to complete each mile in the Sierras. As the company's general counsel Creed Haymund later irately put it: "I have grown sick and tired of hearing of the generosity of the Government," for even when it did deliver its promised bonds, they never brought their par value in cash. "We built it for them, and in return they gave not money, but their depreciated credit," and lands so generally unappealing that at the present rate of sales it would take 160 years to unload them all on the public.[63] The Big Four quite simply were out of money and saw no prospect of acquiring any.

Collis P. Huntington, who slept like a babe despite carrying debts larger than those of many nations, thought he might have the answer. New York banker William K. Garrison, who had loaned money to both of the Pacific railroads, was well aware of the Central Pacific's impecunity. He urged Huntington to convince his partners to organize a new construction company (patterned after the Crédit Mobilier) to build east from the California border, where Crocker's construction contract ended. Garrison assured the Californian that, given the Big Four's reputations, a new company, open to the public, would attract a great deal of Eastern capital—probably from the Vanderbilts and their powerful friends, men who shied away from investing in railroad companies per se.[64]

Back to California sped Huntington in September, and on October 28 the Contract and Finance Company, with an initial capitalization of $5 million, was legally incorporated. Not surprisingly, Charlie Crocker was president. However, Huntington, Hopkins, and Stanford—as Central Pacific officers—did not become board members of the construction company; they and E. B. Crocker owned it, with Asa P. Stanford a minor stockholder.[65] Not at all by plan, the Contract and Finance Company became a closed corporation, for to the Big Four's (and Garrison's) surprise and horror, there were no Eastern capitalists eager to invest in it. Garrison and Huntington had erred, and the Easterners turned a deaf ear on their pleas.

In an act of desperation, but with no other available options, the Big Four and E.B. pledged to build from the state line eastward, splitting all financial obligations and responsibilities equally—as well as future profits, which must have

---

*In fact, *seven* of these tunnels (totaling 3,894 feet) were in a single 2.25-mile stretch (miles 105 through 107.25).

seemed chimerical at this point. The impecunious company and its penurious owners then awarded themselves the contract for the work eastward to whatever point at which the Central Pacific and Union Pacific should meet. For each mile built, the Contract and Finance Company would receive $43,000 in cash and a like sum (at par) in Central Pacific bonds.[66] While hardly as convoluted as the Union Pacific–Crédit Mobilier symbiosis, the Central Pacific–Contract and Finance Company union had been not so much sought by the Big Four as thrust upon them. As Creed Haymund, congenitally out of sorts, later explained, "It is said that the Directors ought to have contracted with other parties than themselves to construct this road. There was no one to contract with them. The enterprise was [still] looked upon as wild and visionary" by large investors.[67] They *had* tried, said Haymund. "They had hawked the contract through the money markets of the world and had failed."[68] Dismissing that latter hyperbole, one must admit that Haymund was largely correct.

The Contract and Finance Company was incorporated the same month that the Big Four, financial illusionists par excellence, bought the California Central Railroad and started negotiations for several others.[69] If it is true that the more heads one cuts off the Hydra the more they proliferate, it appeared in 1867 that the less money the Big Four had, the more they spent. Could they, however, come up with the tens of millions of dollars they would need to build across Nevada and perhaps into Utah as well? Mystifying everyone, they did.

PULVERIZING AND "HANNIBALIZING" THE SIERRAS

THE first snow fell in the Sierras on September 14,[70] by which time every tunnel had been pierced (but only five finished), and some ten miles of experimental snowsheds built.[71] Actually, there were two forms of roofed track. Snowsheds proper resembled covered bridges of immense length and solidity, with sharply pitched roofs. Snow galleries had only one (exterior) wall, with a roof slanting down from the mountainside. To be effective against massive snowfall, avalanche, and rockslides, the sheds and galleries had to be extremely strong, and some of them were protected by large masonry walls designed to stop or channel avalanches and falling rock.[72] The framework timbers were stouter than telephone poles, the roof planks up to five inches thick, and the gallery roof supports were bolted deeply into the granite cliffs. Vexingly, but unavoidably, both galleries and sheds had to be frequently sprayed with water inside to prevent their catching fire from locomotive sparks, and, despite the dampening, a number did burn down in 1868 and 1869.[73]

The first sheds and galleries, just below Cisco, were built in June and July by Arthur Brown from his and Lewis Clement's designs. These were purely experimental, and after several collapsed the following winter, those designs were modified and the sheds and galleries improved and strengthened. In 1868 and 1869, almost thirty-eight miles of sheds and galleries were constructed, at a cost of approximately half a million dollars. According to Brown, who oversaw the work, these structures consumed over 65 million board feet of the stoutest possible lumber, and some nine hundred *tons* of bolts and spikes. About fifteen hundred men worked on the sheds and galleries in 1867, while twenty-five hundred were so employed the following year. These, according to the man in charge, were paid exorbitant wages because carpenters and other needed specialists were in short supply, and his orders were to save time, not money. Paying four dollars a day for carpenters and just a dollar less for "common" labor was an additional burden for the company's treasury, while its sawmills were so taxed that rough, hand-hewn trees were often used as vertical supports.[74]

The sense that time was running out permeated everything that autumn, and Mark Hopkins, like Charlie Crocker, tossed and turned restlessly in his bed. The latter's mood turned from testy to as foul as the Sierra weather. On one occasion he fired a senior foreman for accidentally delaying a work train loaded with equipment. As he later remembered, he informed the unfortunate fellow, "Mc, a mistake is a crime now."[75] Tension was building.

While he was chastising others for making mistakes, Crocker himself again went far out on a limb. The Summit Ice Company had been, and was, a disappointment, its potential profits melting in the Sierra's stark sunlight; but there were other ways for a sharp (although cash-poor) operator to make a few dollars on the side. In late 1867 Charlie Crocker had moved more seriously into the irrigation business. His new company operated in California, for the sheer magnitude of watering Nevada's alkali flats was beyond even his contemplation. He began near Merced, channeling streams, boring long flow tunnels, building aqueducts, and creating a network of small reservoirs to capture the annual Sierra runoff. Over the years, Crocker's irrigation business (it was in his name) prospered mightily, opening huge new tracts (some of them, fortuitously, Central Pacific acreage) for vineyards. It added to the prosperity of Charlie Crocker, the Big Four, and, incidentally, the state of California.[76] It was, however, a painful drain of cash at the time, the desperate time of 1867.

With the snow drifting in the High Sierras, presaging a halt to track laying and outside work there, more Chinese and Caucasian workers were sent east to the Truckee Valley, along with mountains of equipment. At end of track (Soda

Springs, mile 102, reached in mid-November), just a few miles from the work at Summit Tunnel, everything necessary to build and run a railroad was unloaded, strapped on special sleds, and hauled by oxen along the fully graded right-of-way, with the caravan making arduous cross-country detours around uncompleted tunnels and several unfinished bridges. An astonishing forty miles of iron (sixteen thousand rails), forty freight and platform cars, and three standard-size locomotives (three times the size and weight of the "Black Goose") crossed the Sierras that winter. The heavier items, such as the locomotives, had to be frequently rolled on logs across difficult ground, and, at Donner Lake, everything was shifted to reinforced wagons for the trip down to the Truckee. As James McCague has written, "It may be that nothing like it had been done since Hannibal led his war elephants over the Alps," millennia before.[77] Hannibal actually had had it comparatively easy. This labor was truly epic, carried out by as many as a thousand forgotten men, and it was expensive at a time when money was all but a memory to Uncle Mark back in Sacramento. But, by December, the Central Pacific had more men working on the eastern slopes of the Sierras and deep into Nevada than it had elsewhere, and, symbolically, on December 31, its first train crossed the state line.[78]

Summit Tunnel had been completed and tracked in the last days of November, but the other tunnels, and bridges at South Yuba (mile 102) and Donner Creek (mile 118), delayed the march of the rails more than did the weather. The huge retaining walls between tunnels 7 (mile 105) and 8 (mile 106) were finished in December, by which time large gangs were quarrying quality granite in the mountains and sending it east for culverts and bridge supports.[79] The Celestials continued to grade, and track was being laid both east and west from the Truckee. Once more, the Central Pacific's progress in 1867 must be measured not in terms of miles of new track, but in obstacles overcome.

In all, the company tracked from mile 94 to 107, and from mile 110 to mile 117 (only twenty, uncontinuous miles in the mountains), and some twenty-four miles east and west from the Truckee. Under the circumstances, this was a splendid achievement, but the almost three-mile gap at the unexpectedly stubborn Pollard's Hill Tunnel (mile 107) and a seven-mile gap around Donner Lake kept the three segments of the railroad uncontiguous and the company ineligible for government (and their own) bonds.[80] The trip could be made across the Sierras that winter by stage or wagon from where the tracks abruptly ended. Later, the gaps grew by another ten miles or more, as some poorly ballasted and hastily laid track shifted and in some instances collapsed.[81]

When the news that Summit Tunnel was finished reached Sacramento, Leland Stanford decided to host yet another excursion, to boost public confidence. In December, a special train, with the company's most luxurious cars, departed from the state capital with a crowd of legislators and other luminaries aboard. The guests were excited by the magnificent mountain views, admired the quality of the company's work, and were made semicomatose by a gargantuan spread of viands and potables; but Stanford's bad luck as a host snatched defeat from the jaws of victory. Several cars caught fire from sparks, the ride was uncomfortably rough and jerky, a faulty coupling caused two cars to smash together dangerously, and, to the former governor's horror, the entire train broke down for a while inside Summit Tunnel, nearly causing blind panic among the hundreds of excursionists, who found themselves in the dark, smoke-filled bore gasping for breath.[82] With everyone grumbling and less than favorably impressed by the outing, the red-faced Stanford vowed to eschew further public relations gimmicks of this sort.

He was lucky that he and his guests were not snowed in that December, for the winter was every bit as harsh, damaging, and killing as the previous one.[83] Snowsheds collapsed under the weight of snow and avalanche, blocking the line for days; snow tunnels like rabbit warrens reappeared around the unfinished bores; a barn was buried in the mountains, killing a large number of Chinese; and, according to one A. P. Partridge, who worked in the Sierras all winter, "a good many were frozen to death," as the thermometer fell vertiginously.[84] As Partridge and others traveled along the grade in a sleigh one evening, they "stopped and found a frozen Chinese. As a consequence, we threw him in the sleigh with the rest of us, and took him into town and laid him out by the side of a shed and covered him with a rice mat, the most appropriate thing for the laying out of a Celestial."[85] Death by accident or act of God was accepted as routine along the Central Pacific line, much as death by Indian or rowdy was on the Union Pacific. The mountains were yielding, but were exacting a toll for the railroad's victory.

By year's end, the Big Four still faced financial ruin. The only good news reaching K Street was that the price of rails was still falling,[86] and of course they and Montague knew, as the *Railroad Record* reported, that "the bulk of the engineering difficulties . . . [had] already been overcome."[87] They had added forty-four miles of uncontiguous track, some tunnels, and a few bridges, but at a murderous cost. Their annual report estimated the year's expenditures at nearly $12.5 million, and that did not include the purchase of rolling stock or that of the Western Pacific, Yuba, and California Central railroads.[88] An 1869 company report asserted that the Central Pacific had spent more than $4 million to build the most difficult seventeen miles in the Sierras (at over $235,000 per mile), but that the company had only received from the government $816,000 in bonds for those same miles, and that almost a year after the work had been done and the workers paid.[89] Against the huge expenditures, the company in 1867 netted only about $870,000, on gross receipts of just under $1.5 million.[90] True, both gross and net were more than 50 percent higher than earnings in 1866, but again, while money was gushing out, earnings were merely trickling in. During that year of financial uncertainty, Uncle Mark openly complained that the company, in addition to all its other burdens, paid out almost $50,000 in state and local taxes.[91]

Also on the negative side, survey reports now made it clear that no coal existed along the entire projected route through Nevada and into Utah.[92] Complicating Hopkins's books were large, but necessary, purchases of rolling stock in 1867, increasing the number of locomotives from 19 to 51 and freight cars from 199 to 443. The fact that the passenger-car inventory increased only from 6 to 10 indicates that passenger revenues were not keeping the company financially sound.[93] At this point almost $15 million of company stock was in circulation, but, as before, most of this stock was not actually "circulating" at all, but had been paid out to Crocker's construction company at well below par. Further, land sales were depressed, and, given the nature of future acreage, they would continue to stagnate,[94] while not a single government bond had been received from January through December. It looked appallingly clear that the Union Pacific would win the race. If the Central Pacific could break free of the mountains early in 1868, the broad, flat Nevada wilderness would at least provide a fast track; but exactly when would it emerge from the Sierras? Not knowing the answer, the Big Four could only wish a hard winter on their competitors.[95]

10

BACKSTABBING ACROSS THE PLAINS AND BLESSEDLY FLAT NEVADA

THE SCENT OF SCANDAL

A S THE new year was being celebrated, the temperature dropped, both at Cheyenne and at Nassau Street in New York.

The skeleton crew at end of track recorded a temperature of 23° below zero on January 5, weather so cold the graders had to blast the earth before they could shovel it. In fact, because so many men got frostbite, most graders were sent on temporary furlough that January, and only the seemingly indestructible tie cutters in the Black Hills and Wasatch mountains remained in the field, attempting, with some success, to meet the company's goal of 200,000 hardwood ties each month.[1]

Also in the field that enervating January was Arthur Fergusen, sent to La Porte, Colorado, on a somber mission. It was at this time that he exhumed and brought back to the rail line the body of survey engineer L. L. Hills, killed by Arapaho the previous year. "Is it possible that this is what we all come to?" he pondered incredulously when he uncovered the decaying corpse. "This seething mass of corruption . . . the lipless mouth giving its ghastly, awful smile," sent a shock wave through the young man. With his grim burden in a wagon, Fergusen headed north through drifting snows. Hills was later given a proper, permanent burial by his family, and Fergusen, who had seen the disfiguring scalp and face wounds on Hills, began to truly hate the Indians.[2]

As Hills's corpse was being toted across the Colorado mountains, Grenville Dodge, in Washington, was all but ignoring politics in the formal sense, and focusing his attentions on "politicking," counter-lobbying, and running his railroad from afar. He had appallingly little success in these varied ventures, in part because Secretary of the Interior Browning (in whose department Dodge had offices) found him distasteful, perhaps because of Huntington's inuendos. In fact, Browning, a man whose ambition dwarfed his character, was virtually a declared enemy of the Union Pacific.[3]

So Dodge spent most of the winter in a distinctly hostile environment, totally unable to impose a check on the lobbying of the much smoother Collis Huntington. Isolated in the Interior Department and rarely fulfilling his duties as congressman, Dodge kept his personal telegraph key tapping—at the taxpayers' expense. He was in daily telegraphic contact with the Casements, with Webster Snyder and the company's leaders, and slightly less frequently with his engineers in the field, Sam Reed and Jason Evans. From these sources he was soon to learn that Seymour, who stayed in the field, was increasingly acting as if he were assistant chief engineer while Dodge was confined to Washington, often countermanding Dodge's instructions and making important decisions on his own. This was something Dodge determined to rectify as soon as he could again head west.

It was the chief engineer's hope that the Casement Army could resume its march from mile 540 by April 1, and in January the stalwart government commissioners, well wrapped in buffalo robes, inspected and approved the line to that mile.[4] Already the Casements had a 150-mile stockpile of iron and its accoutrements, and several hundred thousand ties, while caches of coal had been laid out along the right-of-way where company coaling depots were to be built.[5] Dodge noted in his diary in late January that the second Crédit Mobilier dividend (paid January 3), had been "a very handsome dividend" indeed. So handsome that it had driven the construction company's stock prices well past par.[6]

Indeed it had. The back-to-back and very generous dividends and rumors of more to come pleased those congressmen who had recently purchased stock from Ames and the Doctor, enriched the New England group and Durant and his allies, and had created a run on the few shares they did not control. While Union Pacific stock could barely be given away, Oakes Ames could write in February that "Mr. Bates offered his [Crédit Mobilier paper] at $300," and had no trouble finding a buyer.[7] Dodge, who held some stock in his wife's name, recorded with satisfaction that Crédit Mobilier securities carried an asking price of 350 percent of par in late January.[8] With the railroad's stock hovering around 30 percent of par and the company's bonds selling at 95 percent, Crédit Mobilier paper at 350 percent was bound to raise some eyebrows—especially as so few knew just what the Crédit Mobilier actually did. Somebody clearly knew something about their future, short-term dividend potential.

As Edmund McIlhenny brewed his first Tabasco sauce on Avery Island, Louisiana, the temperature was rising in Congress. Many congressmen—most of whom had no understanding of railroad construction—were beginning to become suspicious of railroads in general and the Pacific railroads in particular. Rumors had long circulated about the companies bribing members of Congress and other bureaucrats; it was known that there were several major conflicts of interest (those of John B. Alley, Oakes Ames, and others), and hearsay concerning the Union Pacific's various construction contracts, from Hoxie onward, was attracting serious attention at last. Wisconsin congressman Cadwallader C. Washburn, never a friend of railroads, was actively attempting to organize a proper investigation into the Union Pacific, and he was gaining support from those who wanted the construction contracts explained, who wanted the Crédit Mobilier's role divulged, who wanted to see both companies' books, and who suspected that the Union Pacific was charging uncommonly high freight rates. In short, Washburn and a growing number of his fellows were striving to become the guardians of the largesse of the American people. This was a dangerous atmosphere for men like Oakes Ames and Thomas C. Durant.

Unfortunately, Ames, who had sold stock in the Crédit Mobilier to colleagues specifically to forestall such antirailroad sentiments, put a gun to his own head. Overestimating his own charm or underestimating the wrath of Henry S. McComb, Ames naïvely wrote the latter a series of letters in January and February, letters that were to be used as damning indictments against him, his ethics, the Crédit Mobilier, and the entire ethos of Big Business America. Each letter contained rather vague but incriminating references to Ames's stock sales to congressmen. On January 25, explaining that stock should purposefully be placed with congressmen of different states across the country, he remarked that he still had a few shares to distribute, "which I shall put where they will do the most good to us." Five days later, he informed McComb that he would push for more dividends as soon as they could be arranged, to make the congressmen-stockholders happy; "in view of [antirailroad congressman from Missouri, Andrew] King's letter and Washburn's move . . . we can do it in perfect safety." A letter of February 22 simply asserts, "We want more friends in Congress," and hints that stock distribution and frequent dividends were the surest means of gaining them.[9]

McComb, festering with anger over the 375 Crédit Mobilier shares that he felt were rightfully his, simply filed Ames's letters away. He would use them as a blunt instrument with which to bludgeon the company and shock both Congress and the American public.

Cadwallader C. Washburn was probably the only reason that Grenville Dodge turned up for his second rollcall in the House. An abrasive man who suspected all railroads of skulduggery (especially those receiving federal aid), Washburn earnestly believed that both Pacific railroads were making too much money on their public services, overcharging both the government and the American people. Perhaps he had been taking seriously both companies' prospectuses. In any case, on December 9, 1867, he introduced a bill to cut passenger and freight rates on both lines. The bill died in the Pacific Railroad Committee, which was dominated by none other than Oakes Ames, creating a certain animosity between the two congressmen.[10]

Washburn, however, returned to the attack, reintroducing his bill in February, and Oliver Ames, fearing that it might pass in the House, instructed Dodge to gather all relevant statistics, find his unfamiliar legislative seat, and defeat the bill. On March 25, the engineer gave his first and last speech in the Capitol. Using detailed railroad data, he rebutted Washburn point by point, informing the House that service per mile on the Union Pacific was considerably cheaper, both for passengers and freight, than on lines east of the Mississippi. A cut in the company's rate schedules could only cause construction delays and further discourage investment. In spite of Dodge's irrefutable logic, and patriotic appeals to get on with the great national work, the bill did pass in the House, but the railroad's friends in the Senate referred it back to Ames's railroad committee, and there the shovel king buried it so deeply it was never resurrected.[11]

Dodge was on the floor one more time on behalf of the Union Pacific, this time with better results. He had asked General Sherman to provide increased protection for the Union Pacific, to avoid a repeat of the 1867 tragedies, but Sherman had been unusually cautious in his response, although he admitted that it might be necessary to hound "the Sioux, even to their extermination, men, women and children," if they remained hostile.[12] Essentially, he informed Dodge that if the chief engineer wanted increased military aid, he should obtain authorization not from the army itself, but from Congress. "We [the army] had to bear the blame of precipitating an Indian war because we tried to protect these roads" in 1867, said Sherman, so he urged his friend to convince Congress to approve greater military protection. That way, the road would be adequately guarded but the army would escape the opprobrium of going against a rising tide of sympathy for the Indians. As Dodge recorded, "On receipt of this letter, I introduced a resolution in Congress providing for this which was promptly passed giving the military full authority" to take any measures within reason to guard the Union Pacific.[13]

There were other heartening developments that winter. Durant decamped for Europe for two months early in January to market stocks and bonds. Although this was an added expense for the company, it might bear economic fruit, and his absence brought a sigh of relief from everyone save Silas Seymour, for Durant was fast becoming an embarrassment to the company.[14] The Interior Department accepted the base of the mountains where Blickensderfer had fixed it, mile 525.078, to be precise,[15] and Union Pacific bonds were moving smartly at 95 percent of par, and soon 97 percent, even though the company's stock was still moribund. With a one-hundred-million-dollar capitalization, only $8.5 million had been subscribed, and most of that, as we have seen, by a mere handful of men.[16]

To date (by mile 540) the company had spent over $30 million to build the easiest portion of its line. In the mountains, grading costs would escalate dramatically, as would bridging outlays, and tunnels would have to be gouged and a great deal of blasting done. Proximity to Black Hills forests briefly brought the price of hardwood crossties down to $1.20, but labor costs climbed with each foot of elevation, with many common workers getting $3 a day plus board.[17] Specialists were commanding a good deal more: Boomer was paying $4.50 a day for "men," and a handsome $10.50 to his several foremen, and billing the company accordingly. His contract to build all of the Union Pacific's bridges was renewed in February.[18]

The winter's work—most crews were on the line in March—also cost extra money. The weather damaged the rail line, and while sidings were being spiked and some progress was being made out of Cheyenne during the cold season, much of the work done was admittedly temporary; ties and rails were laid on ice and snow to be reset later. The tie cutters, slogging through deep snow in Indian country, received extra pay and quota bonuses, and the men constructing the enormously complicated and expensive Dale Creek Bridge (mile 550) and other spans also received bonus pay for winter work. Dodge had "estimated for the company that the extra cost of thus forcing the work during the Summer and Winter was over $10,000,000,"[19] and not all of the additional cost was legitimate, for prices for basic supplies had multiplied beyond explicable reason.

But it was speed that 22 Nassau Street demanded, not economy, and several thousand worked throughout the winter. Testifying to the harshness of the season, even the sin sellers, a hardy lot, lit out for warmer locales. To be sure, a railroad man could always abuse his system in ramshackle Cheyenne, for there were still saloons there, with faro dealers and whores hard enough or desperate enough to stay on near end of track. But ten miles or so from Cheyenne, near Dale Creek Bridge, the most advanced settlement was sleepy, ice-bound Sherman. No Hell on Wheels, Sherman, at an elevation of 8,560 feet, boasted only twenty buildings, and an engine house under construction. There was a hotel and a photographer's salon, but not a single saloon.[20]

With the vice index falling along with the mercury, and the Indians, as usual, taking the winter off, the Union Pacific was uncharacteristically tranquil. True, Sam Reed wrote Dodge in February, "Whiskey, thieves and robbers trouble us seriously," but this was a routine complaint.[21] Engineer Bissell, working on Dale Creek Bridge, wrote, "I send my laundry to Omaha, more than five hundred miles away," and added that he was looking forward to repeating a minor survey he had performed first at Sherman. There, the previous autumn, before a single building had been raised, a gambler had offered him $500 (he earned $150 a month as an engineer, and his pay was always in arrears) to stake out the future town's streets. The gambler wanted to be able to choose a prime site for his gaming establishment before land prices rose as people flocked in (they never did). It was but work of a few hours for Bissell, and the two parted company content, although it appears that the gambler made but little use of his expensive site.[22]

Charles Mansfield, paymaster of the navy's Pacific Squadron, sensing that the two companies were prepared to launch themselves into the void whenever good weather unlocked their energies, wrote that "soon from Cheyenne on the one side, and from Cisco on the other, the Chariot of fire will descend into the Great Basin of America . . . here are the gardens for the laborer, the resources of the poor, the solace of the unhappy, the outlet for the discontented . . . here is a place for the man who is afraid of Negroes."[23] "The old-time rule has been reversed," wrote the editor of the *Railroad Record,* and "the locomotive is now the pioneer of the emigrant, and, in 1869, when the through line is complete, there will be no Western 'frontier.' "[24]

The "Chariot of fire" was indeed about to descend, preceded by its Chinese and Irish hosts, but the frontier would not so rapidly disappear.

DR. DURANT FLEXES HIS MUSCLE

I N MARCH, Oliver Ames sent Grenville Dodge some very unwelcome and surprising news. The Union Pacific's board of directors, apparently afraid of Durant's penchant for making legal trouble, had on March 11 named him general agent, "with power to assent to a change in the grades and location of the road," and with a vague and sweeping mandate in various technical areas as well.[25] Dodge, who knew all too well that Durant would interpret that vagueness to his own advantage, was enraged. It must have struck him immediately that the Doctor had specifically asked for, or demanded, the authority to change grades and line locations. A man like Durant would never ask for something like that if he did not have plans. Dodge cabled Ames immediately, warning him that the Doctor would soon be meddling and trying to change everything, which would undoubtedly slow the pace of construction. He was correct, and his frequent absences from end of track left Durant and Silas Seymour more latitude than should have been the case.

Sure enough, Durant was again on his way west to "inspect" the line and confer in Wyoming with Colonel Seymour, in the process alienating virtually everyone. He arrived at Casement's work train on April 3, just a few days after the trackmen began working in earnest, claiming for himself the right to drive the highest spike on the line, at Sherman Summit, on April 5.[26] Symbolic spikes were one thing, but the Doctor's constant criticism, inane suggestions, threats, and generally insufferable pomposity soon had Jack Casement and the engineering staff on the verge of revolt, filling the mail sacks with acidic accounts of Durant's blundering interference. Samuel B. Reed, upset about the cost of raising one mountain bridge, wrote to L. B. Boomer, requesting a copy of the contract for that structure. Boomer responded only that he had "no written contract for the timber, it was a verbal order" from Durant.[27] At about the same time, a contractor named McGugan angrily wrote Jason Evans that many bridgemen were idle—but, under Boomer's contract, they still had to be paid by the Union Pacific. They said they had "no timber that Doctor Durant told them to stop shipping also that Davis and Co. would furnish all the square timber wanted—this must be a mistake."[28] A mistake it was not, but a foul-up due to Durant's reassignment of a timber contract to a dear friend, one of George Francis Train's many in-laws, who ran a small contracting firm out of Omaha. It was simply one of many easily avoidable delays.

Especially angered by Durant were the irreplaceable senior engineers, Evans and Reed, both of whom claimed bitterly that they no longer could or would work with the company vice-president (let alone under him), or his crony, Seymour. When the Doctor in early May issued what he fatuously called "Order Number 1," at Fort Saunders, just west of Cheyenne on the bleak Laramie Plains, the die was cast. His first, and last, numbered order arrogated to his good friend Seymour the power to make all engineering decisions in the absence of the chief engineer, who was all too often absent, in Washington. Since Seymour was roundly despised and the Doctor genuinely detested, and since Order Number 1 was obviously designed to undermine Dodge, Evans resigned on May 11.[29] A month later, Sam Reed followed suit.[30] Dodge, his stomach knotted with pain by the actions of Durant and Seymour, was badly jolted by the resignations of his finest talent and refused to accept them. He shifted Evans west of Durant's stomping grounds, where he would work directly under Reed, and when the latter resigned, the chief engineer made him chief of the Utah division and promised to somehow keep Durant away from the actual work.[31] He also sent a spate of increasingly angry letters to Oliver Ames, who, while certainly no friend of the Doctor, refused to address the issue.

Between the two resignations, Reed, who was in Salt Lake City, more than earned his pay. Unlike most Union Pacific personnel, or Americans for that matter, Reed had a great deal of experience dealing with Mormons—and Brigham Young personally—and did not despise them and their "social abominations."[32] He got along famously with the Saints, and, with the Union Pacific in desperate need of labor far in advance of track, he was the perfect man to negotiate a subcontract. Dealing with the Prophet himself, Reed made a contract calling for over $2 million worth of work on May 21. The agreement called for grading, cut-and-fill work, and tunneling on a 120-mile stretch of line both east and west of Ogden, with bonuses for hauling detritus and equipment, and fifteen dollars per cubic yard for tunneling. It was also agreed that the contract might later be extended to cover additional miles under the same conditions. To sweeten the pot while conserving cash, the company agreed to transport Mormon emigrants (mostly English) to Utah at much reduced fares.[33]

From the viewpoint of the Union Pacific, the contract was an utter necessity, and the terms obtained by Reed were hardly onerous to the company. The Mormons worked relatively cheaply, and Brigham Young—who soon subcontracted to a firm run by his eldest son, Joseph A. Young, and Bishop John Sharp (with Brigham a silent, 25 percent partner)—could put up to four thousand husky men into the field.[34] A steamboat, the *Kate Connor,* was swiftly constructed by the Mormons to haul ties and other lumber across the sprawling Great Salt Lake, the first such vessel on that body of water.[35] The only drawback was the Mormons' lack of proper grading equipment and tools, most of which had to be trundled overland to them at considerable extra cost. Enthusiastic Brigham Young, who at least feigned ignorance that his capital was not to be on the main line of the Pacific Railroad, was soon writing glowingly that "we fully expect when the Railroad comes through to plant the oyster, lobster and other salt water fish in suitable places in our lakes," and create a unique, inland shellfish industry.[36] Bissell at this time observed of the supposedly naïve Prophet that "President Young was fond of posing as a simple-minded old farmer when newspapermen came to interview him; but when he came down to business, he was the peer of the shrewdest."[37] Young, however, had not yet actually met Thomas C. Durant.

In the meantime, Durant was again raising cain. It appears that he was becoming angered because he felt his authority was being circumvented by Dodge, Evans, Reed, Casement, and most of the men closely connected with the work. He was, of course, correct. In a fit of pique the Doctor sought to bring a legal injunction against his own company to halt construction, following which he apparently planned to purge the engineering staff. Oliver Ames, rarely rattled, shot off a telegram to Dodge (and others), informing him that the board of directors had just stripped Durant of his "special powers," on May 29.[38] The chief engineer had hardly sighed his relief, however, when the Doctor made peace with the board again, dropped (for the time being) his legal harassment, and recouped his supervisory powers over construction, on July 3.[39] Again, Dodge screamed in protest, but it should be noted in passing that he did not resign, as the first chief engineer, Peter Dey, certainly would have done.

While Durant was neurotically impairing the Union Pacific's credibility and physical progress, actual work on the line continued, despite severe March snowstorms. Not counting the Mormons, who were not yet contracted, the

Casements put ten thousand graders and timbermen, a thousand trackmen, and a thousand teams into the field that April, the second largest work force on the continent (to that of the Central Pacific).[40] Contending with the high altitude and the lingering snow, these men ate up the miles, spiking track into Sherman, at the Summit (mile 549), on April 5.[41]

Dale Creek Bridge, which had been worked on all winter, was "completed" on April 23. Called by one skeptical engineer "a big bridge for a small brook that one could easily step over," the impressive-looking, seven-hundred-foot-long structure spanned a chasm over insipid Dale Creek, some 126 feet below.[42] This bridge, which Seymour had wrongly decided would be better than a fill, had been made in Michigan, in sections, to Boomer's specifications, and laboriously hauled to the site. Before it was finished it would cost the company more than $200,000, and many thousands of dollars more after it was in place.[43] While the Union Pacific inaugurated the structure on April 23, in reality it was far from completed. A few days later a storm nearly toppled its timbers into the creek, and only prompt action by Hezekiah Bissell and his team saved the bridge from collapse.[44] Fergusen was still working on the bridge in May, when it trembled so much in a high wind that two carpenters fell from it to their death.[45] The government inspectors, including the suspicious Jesse L. Williams, after several times refusing to approve the bridge, delayed giving even provisional approval until June, pointedly noting that despite additional supports, it still swayed dangerously in even modest breezes.[46] Just a few years later the rickety structure was dismantled and a huge fill was made, neither the first nor the last of Seymour's decisions expunged.[47] It was probably the Dale Creek incident that prompted Jesse L. Williams to investigate all the company's construction that summer.

Still, progress was dramatic. Laramie (mile 572), already sporting twenty-three saloons, a hotel (and soon a company hospital), and growing numbers of vigilantes, yet neither a school nor a church, was reached by iron on May 9, the same day Charlie Crocker named Reno, Nevada.[48] Called by the peripatetic *Frontier Index,* which soon set up shop there, "a young Nineveh," Laramie was situated near glorious natural springs set amidst scenery so grand that "the senses dilate," according to one awestruck visitor.[49] Laramie, of course, was partly owned by George Francis Train. He and his Crédit Foncier were wagering that Laramie Springs was destined to become America's premier health spa. They lost.[50]

As tracking crews almost jogged west, the campaigning season for the Sioux opened, as usual.[51] Jack Casement, who wrote his wife on April 19 that Indian raids were expected, "but I hope not enough to delay us," wrote again nine days later: "The Indians are on the Rampage, Killing and stealing all along the line, we don't apprehend any danger from them our gang is so large."[52] But large gang or not, the Sioux would indeed delay construction once again. On April 16 alone, five section hands were killed just east of North Platte, while two off-duty conductors were wounded near Sidney. One of these, Tom Cahoon, was, like William Thompson, scalped.[53] Several workers were murdered near Dale Creek the following week,[54] and Fergusen's diary for the period reads like a dime novel, so frequently does he mention Indian raids and his fear of them: "Many and many has been the days which I have proceeded to my duty at the risk of my life." He was haunted by "the wild war whoops of the Indians. I have seen them fall before our bullets . . . their day has, however, nearly ended."[55] It had, for while raids and attacks would continue, they were, as one student has noted, "simply the rattle of [the Indians'] dying civilization."[56] That rattle, however, was prolonged enough to cost the government a million dollars a week in 1868.[57]

It also impelled Dodge to leave Washington and head for a brief visit to end of track in early May. He talked with Western military authorities, and while in Wyoming met with Durant (who was almost constantly prowling the line), Dillon, and Seymour. They met at Cheyenne, where Dodge "had a very plain talk with them" about their meddling with the construction work and proposals to change the actual line itself.[58] The issue was one of just who had the authority to do what. The talk, however, was apparently not "plain" enough. Seymour, backed by Durant, had earlier on several occasions changed Dodge's (and Evans's)[59] route in the approach to the Black Hills. While time and money had been wasted in preparing Seymour's deviant lines (always longer than Dodge's), the chief engineer won his case with the board, and later experts, and his original lines were again approved, over Seymour's protest.[60] However, after Dodge returned to Washington in May, Durant with his special powers and Seymour with his untalented engineering had their way.[61]

Shortly after the May conference with Dodge, Seymour filed a route change with Durant, who immediately accepted it. Previous surveys had revealed two practicable routes westward from the Laramie River some thirty miles west of Laramie. One was a swing northward, by way of Rock Creek and was, despite sharp curves, through terrain that was both easy and fast to work, and hence inexpensive. The other, via Cooper Lake through Rattlesnake Pass, was more difficult, but had the same grades, far fewer curves, and was more direct, saving twenty miles. Evans had recommended and Dodge had approved the latter, but, as the chief engineer returned to his offices in Washington, Seymour (who agreed with Durant that additional miles were a blessing rather than a problem) opted for the Rock Creek alternative, and work began on it immediately. The zigzag route somehow was to be extremely expensive for the company, despite the easy topography, adding an outlay of an estimated $1,920,000 counting the work on Dodge's abandoned original route. It also was more costly, in bonds, to the government—some $960,000 more.[62] However, it could be built more quickly, and Durant was, as vice-president, cheered to be able to issue an extra $960,000 in company bonds, which briefly were selling *over* par, at 102 percent.[63]

Not content with changing Dodge's plans, Seymour and his mentor also ordered the company's already constructed shops to be shifted from Cheyenne to Laramie, perhaps because of George Francis Train's investment in that town. Durant later denied that this was the reason, claiming that he intended the move of company shops to help stimulate lagging land sales at Laramie on the western side of Sherman Summit.[64]

When Dodge learned of the Rock Creek route through a wire from Jack Casement, he found himself faced with a fait accompli since so much work had already been done on it. He could and did rant, but enough time and money had been sunk into the new route so that further change was unacceptable to the board of directors. Dodge's judgment was later vindicated, and in his dotage he could gloat a bit when the H. E. Harriman railroad promotion group, reengineering the line, cut out the Rock Creek zigzag and rebuilt through Rattlesnake Pass. In fact, the only rebuilding along the entire length of the Union Pacific, except for the Salt Lake causeway, took place where Seymour had displayed his imaginative engineering talents.[65]

So in early June, Dodge again followed the rails west, determined to at least halt the migration of company shops from Cheyenne and to confront the Doctor one more time. In Cheyenne, and in public, he did so, warning Durant that the company, the investors, and the United States government would not stand for further waste and fraud. In a shouting match that almost degenerated to fisticuffs, he told Durant that the shops would not be moved to Laramie, by God! He also wired both Oliver Ames and General Sherman, giving his side of the issue along with a virtual ultimatum; choose Durant or him. Ames and Sherman met in Washington, hoping to end the debilitating wrangle for good. They decided that both Durant and Dodge should meet with presidential hopeful Grant and iron out their difficulties, through the general's mediation. Grant was to attend peace talks with Red Cloud and other Sioux war leaders in July at Fort Sanders. The disputants would meet with him immediately thereafter.[66] There would be, in short, a showdown.

Despite the turmoil, Jack Casement continued doing what he did best, unconcerned about who chose what route (although he had an aversion to both Durant and Seymour as men). After all, he was paid by the mile. In May he had written his wife that he and his foremen intended to "lay over three miles every day," and while he failed to do so consistently, his progress was dramatic, and, in fact, record-setting.[67] The most vexing interference with his work was the dearth of water, for west of Rawlins there was no *potable* surface water for a full 130 miles. Much money was wasted drilling unproductive wells, and Casement's goal of three miles of construction every day was frustrated in large part because of the need to keep special water trains chugging up and down the line, overburdening an already strained logistics system.[68]

The mileposts flashed by in quick succession as the Casement Army spiked west from Laramie, a town described as containing "the hardest kind of material from which to manufacture good Christians" in the entire West.[69] Stations were hurriedly built at Wyoming (mile 586), Cooper's Lake, Lookout, Miser, Rock Creek, Como, Medicine Bow, Carbon, Simpson, Percy (a company lumbering station at mile 666), Dance, St. Mary's, and Benton (mile 697) by midsummer, almost too fast for the whores and gamblers to keep up. It was, for the most part, a depressing country: "desolate, dreary, not susceptible of cultivation and only portions of it fit for grazing. It had no inviting qualities," at all, according to one who crossed it a year later.[70]

At St. Mary's, the line made a sudden and dramatic detour on temporary, multiswitchback track, for it was here that the company was blasting its first tunnel, and the Casements were not about to call a halt to tracking and await its completion. A short, straight bore only 215 feet long, the St. Mary's tunnel would have appeared child's play to Strobridge's experienced Celestials, but there were few if any experienced tunnel men working that summer for the Union Pacific. The tunnel was finished in June by a small team of 150 Mormons, but as it had been gouged from soft and crumbly sandstone, it had to be fully timbered, and that took another fifty days.[71]

While the Mormons were fitting the timbers, the company's second tunnel, almost three hundred miles ahead of end of track (at mile 972), and their longest, at 772 feet, was begun by Young and Sharp's Mormons. That bore, however, would take almost a year and hundreds of additional, non-Mormon laborers, to finish.[72] Work in the second tunnel, through much more solid rock, was slow, and Sam Reed decided to turn to nitroglycerin. In short order the company built a nitro factory near Julesburg, a stout cabin surrounded by earthen embankments to absorb any accidental blast. The nitro was used on the second and third—and probably the last—tunnel, and the Union Pacific never had a serious accident with it.[73]

That spring, as Durant and Dodge dueled and Dodge's friend Grant and Seymour's brother Horatio prepared in advance their presidential acceptance speeches for the Republican and Democratic nominating conventions, Treasurer John J. Cisco published a slick, thirty-two-page promotional pamphlet, *The Union Pacific Railroad,* a fanciful panegyric on the fabulous potential of the Union Pacific.[74] Distributed free at the company's offices and at banks (including Cisco's) and brokerage houses that marketed Union Pacific paper, the pamphlet attracted a great deal of attention and helped spur bond sales with above-par premiums. Also, work began at last on the Missouri River Bridge, under the supervision of Mr. Boomer. An iron structure 2,750 feet long, the bridge to Council Bluffs remained for years a dream, for despite how necessary it was, Boomer was soon ordered to halt work. The board had learned, a bit tardily, that no work *east* of Omaha was eligible for government aid under the Pacific Railroad Act. Boomer shifted his crews west again, leaving only seated piles where a bridge was to have been. The Union Pacific simply did not have the resources to complete the bridge and continue the western work.[75] Construction of that bridge resumed only in the summer of 1869, and it would consume almost three years of labor and almost $2 million before East and West were permanently linked.

JESSE L. WILLIAMS SUSPECTS

A T ABOUT the time that Wyoming became detached from Dakota Territory and was made a territory in its own right because of the voting strength of Union Pacific workers, Oliver Ames was noting with a certain pride that he had been able to sell the most recent consignment of federal bonds on the market at 99.5 percent of par. Even though interest rates on loans were climbing (to 16 percent and higher on short-term notes), both federal and company bonds were producing a great deal of money.[76]

May also brought some bad news. The Central Pacific was fast closing its Sierra gap and would emerge onto the Nevada flatlands, and Secretary Browning, it was learned, was about to approve a route map from Huntington that showed a line far to the east of either legality or propriety. Huntington apparently had enough influence with the secretary that he thought he could convince him to approve as "Central Pacific territory" all of Nevada and a large chunk of Utah as well. Informed by a junior member of Browning's staff, Dodge consulted with Oliver Ames, who told him to immediately throw his own survey teams and graders well to the west of Ogden, and in the meantime use his personal reputation and all of his Washington contacts to frustrate the Californian's patently illegal maneuver.[77]

The chief engineer was resoundingly unsuccessful in the latter endeavor, for Browning had indeed already accepted Huntington's map, with its claims, all the way to Monument Point, on the northwest tip of the Great Salt Lake. This was many hundreds of miles east of any Central Pacific employee, let alone track. The secretary did, however, "temporarily" withhold his acceptance of an extension of the Huntington map that covered the area from Monument Point east to Weber Canyon, well past Ogden. The Union Pacific was already grading and tunneling there, yet the far distant Central Pacific was trying to claim it as theirs. The Big Four were attempting the railroad fraud of the century, and even the normally pliable Browning was a bit embarrassed.[78] That Huntington won most of the game is a tribute to his ability to confidently propose the impossible.

On the first of June, a government act decreed that all subsidized railroads make annual reports to the president and secretary of the interior each June 30, to conform to the government's fiscal year. This set the men on Nassau Street (and in Sacramento) scrambling to get their paperwork done by the imminent deadline. The reports were to be, unlike Sisco's exuberant pamphlet, financially explicit, and the June 1 act reflected Congress's increasing desire for more and better information about the railroads their constituents were aiding.[79] Suspicions were growing.

At least the act was applied to both railroad companies. Two weeks later Commissioner Jesse L. Williams took action against the Union Pacific alone. Increasingly disenchanted by that company's leadership and workmanship, Williams had spent part of May and June personally examining the work that had been done. He returned from the field with a heavy heart and grave reservations. On June 14 he informed Durant that, since he had seen many instances of poor grading and shoddy construction, the Union Pacific had better create, immediately, a large reserve fund to meet the obvious deficiencies so that the railroad could be certified, pursuant to the 1862 act, "first class."[80] Strongly implied was a threat that if the railroad failed to set aside such a fund, Williams would take the matter to the already inimical Browning, and then to the president.

Williams had learned that the Crédit Mobilier—with exquisitely poor timing— was about to pay another, major dividend, and the commissioner, in one of his frequent reports to the secretary, opened Pandora's box. In addition to hinting at substandard construction and collusion between the Union Pacific's management and that of the Crédit Mobilier, Williams mentioned the idea of a reserve fund and suggested that, since it appeared that Durant would not create one, the secretary himself should, by withholding "a part of the bonds due . . . equal to the cost of substituting permanent work" for the obviously temporary work done at so many points along the line.[81] He did *not* in this report refer to both railroads.

Just one day later, on June 17, as if to call attention to its bizarre financial practices, the Crédit Mobilier declared a 100 percent dividend, payable that same day, 60 percent of it in *cash* ($2,250,000). This "spasm of openhandedness" offended a great many people, and smelled of misuse of company, and hence public, funds.[82]

Williams then set out to more carefully inspect the entire line and file another, more complete report, cataloguing the Union Pacific's defects. That document, which reached Browning's desk in mid-August, was a bombshell, and the fact that its author was a man known for both engineering experience and personal integrity gave it added credence. Even before he drafted his report, Williams wired Browning from end of track in July. Deeply troubled by what he had observed, he bluntly asked the secretary to withhold further bonds from the Union Pacific without delay.[83]

He hardly exaggerated. The only question is why he and the other inspectors had not spotted the extent of the third-rate work earlier. The Casements' daily progress reports for 1867 and 1868 provide eloquent testimony to support the commissioner. For instance, on August 1, 1867, almost a mile of track was laid, but upon only 1,091 ties (the government had mandated at least 2,400 per mile), and *all* of these were Burnettized cottonwood, even those under track joints.[84] This, in addition to the common use of sand or raw earth as ballast, made for a substandard, shifting line. Some of the track near the Utah border was so unstable that a worried Durant ordered that westbound passengers be detrained scores of miles from end of track and taken on by stage.[85]

Dodge, who was still jousting with Durant and Seymour, at last realized that he could no longer control events (or even influence Browning) from Washington. On the same day of the Crédit Mobilier's 100 percent dividend, he requested an indefinite leave of absence from the House of Representatives, from which he had been so often absent without leave.[86] The chief engineer churned west to save his railroad and his reputation, not necessarily in that order.

On June 30, in accordance with the law, the Union Pacific tendered its official report on earnings and expenses for the previous twelve months. It revealed a prominent falloff in net earnings over the previous year, despite a gross that surpassed $4 million. From the company's figures, which are highly suspect, it appears that there had been an astonishing increase in routine operating expenses. "Operating expenses" is a traditional category in which to hide various outlays. The report basically lied when it asserted that net earnings were just over $1.5 million, for it soon became public knowledge that the true figure was a very disappointing $894,000. Further, the company owed nearly $2 million in interest on its own first-mortgage bonds, and almost as much on government bonds.[87] In short, the company was glaringly in the red, but tried to minimize that fact in the annual report to avoid frightening its investors.

NEVADA AT LAST!

A S THE slanting rays of January sunlight made the Chinese workers' snow tunnels eerily translucent, Crocker, Stanford, Hopkins, and Huntington faced disaster. On January 8, the fifth anniversary of the Sacramento groundbreaking, they had less than 140 miles of track in place—and average of only 28 miles per year—and these had cost an average of $200,000 each to build.[88] The editors of the prestigious magazine *The Nation* wrote that in the United States there were "650 millions of money in circulation on January 6, 1868."[89] If these figures were correct, the Big Four had spent 4.3 percent of it ($28 million), had debts of more than $5 million, and had somehow to meet a monthly payroll in excess of $450,000, and in gold. Despite all this, no government aid had been received in 1867, and it was clear that none would reach the Central Pacific in the first half of 1868, if at all that year. The Californians were at this point 600 miles from Ogden (despite the claims on Huntington's map), while the Union Pacific end of track was 500 miles east of that city. Could the Central Pacific hold on until the Sierra gap was closed and an avalanche of bonds was loosed?

Charlie Crocker thought they could survive, and he promised his partners a mile of track per working day in 1868, which would not at all have sufficed, and he ended up greatly exceeding that amount. Huntington, "working like ten beavers,"[90] concurred, sending virtual fleets of ships westward, crammed with equipment acquired by his charm and the Big Four's communal and apparently inexhaustible credit.[91] Leland Stanford must have retained his faith in their ability to survive, for in February he closed the deal to buy control of the San Francisco & San Jose Railroad (the Southern Pacific).[92] The Big Four and E. B. Crocker each gained one eighth of that railroad's stock for $360,000 in cash, bonds, and Central Pacific stock. Lloyd Tevis, one of the original Southern Pacific directors, remained on the board, holding another one eighth interest.[93] No one knows, however, what Uncle Mark Hopkins, a reserved man at the best of times, thought. Only he truly knew the books, and Huntington, receiving sheaves of dunning letters in New York, usually shunted them back to his bookkeeper partner. Hopkins alone saw all the bad news.

An example of grim tidings was a March 14 note from the rather testy Oriental Powder Company of Boston. Obviously not the first attempt to collect this overdue account, the letter notes that the company "made the last shipment of 4,000 kegs as you will recollect," in November, "upon your recommendation." Since then, they had received from the Central Pacific only $5,000, which left an overdue balance of over $23,000. Less than politely, the Oriental Powder Company requested their money.[94] Perhaps this is why the Boston concern, a giant in the explosives field, was soon to close its doors.[95] Mark Hopkins was feeling the heat, heat that would make him "cook" his books.

Despite their penury, the Big Four and their lieutenants dashed frantically ahead, as if a reduction in their activities would doom them. Stanford bombarded Crocker in the field with pleas for greater speed: "Anything less than the utmost that can be done will very likely end in defeat," he wrote that spring.[96] Similarly, Sam Montague (soon promoted at last to chief engineer) wrote Butler Ives, who was again surveying in Utah, not to worry about the truest line possible, for "the line we want now is the line we can build the soonest, even if we rebuild immediately."[97] Ives understood, as did Strobridge and their opposite numbers in the Union Pacific. Charlie Crocker, who hardly needed to be pushed, received a brief note from Huntington, who was worried as much about finances as geography, reminding him that "when a cheap road will pass the commission, make it cheap."[98] Hardly a lesson in moral certainty, the fastest railroad building in history was about to begin.

In January, the men in the Sierras, covered with fine granite dust, faced killer avalanches by the score, which they often inadvertently brought on with their constant blasting. A contemporary source noted "immense slides near the Nevada Summit, of five or more miles in extent, killing many persons and burying seven locomotives."[99] The Big Four managed to keep this and other negative news from the press. The avalanches added another severe burden to the already overburdened work crews, and with the snow in those avalanches came boulders and other track-twisting and crushing debris. Repairs on track (and snowsheds) occupied the energies of hundreds of workers.

Sometime early in the year, Huntington—who was pleased to note strong bond sales—convinced a group of German investors to loan the company half a million dollars, one of the few instances of foreign interest in either of the Pacific railroads. As collateral he had the gall to pledge government bonds that would not even be printed until the Sierra gap was plugged.[100] It is a fair bet that no word of the gap was ever mentioned to the Germans.

It was probably this (and company bond) money that he used to such effect that spring to delay the Union Pacific. Because of a nationwide railroad boom, rails were unusually scarce in 1868, and learning that Durant was planning to place a huge order for sixty thousand tons, Huntington scrambled and beat him to the punch. With some money, some credit, and a great deal of arrogant bluff, he placed a Central Pacific order with all the major railmakers of Pennsylvania, for sixty-six thousand tons. He frequently bragged later about having temporarily cornered the market on available iron, delaying the Union Pacific and discomfiting Durant. The Californian next, in a single day, arranged shipping for most of the rails, "hiring" twenty-three vessels at a shrewd, bargain price.[101]

Since, as the work crews emerged from the mountains, time was money in a very real sense, Huntington now occasionally took recourse to shipping some vitally needed material across the isthmus of Panama, despite the chillingly high prices. For one single heavy-duty locomotive, desperately needed in California, Huntington paid a record $8,100 in freight charges in order to save several weeks in transit.[102] Thus yet another strain was put on dour Mark Hopkins, the man who would have to find the money.

While Huntington hocked and huckstered in the East, Charlie Crocker had all of his men moving by early March, despite the weather. Thousands were put to work doing nothing but shoveling snow, even as it fell. The Sierra track had to be both cleared and repaired, and he even brought crews up from the vital Truckee Valley work to help disperse drifts that were up to sixty feet deep in the cuts.[103]

Strobridge was building into Nevada with a crew of about four thousand, laying every rail as fast as it came over the mountains. By May the gap was so narrow that the transfer of equipment took little time, and with good weather, the flow of rails to Nevada moved with clocklike regularity. On May 1, just two weeks before Secretary Browning accepted the Central Pacific's fraudulent map to Monument Point, Stro's burly trackmen halted for the night near M. C. Lake's run-down trading post (at what would become mile 154), a community, according to one source, with a "population of two men, one woman, three pigs and a cow."[104] Called Lake's Crossing (of the Truckee River), the "community" was located at a ford frequented by mining and freight wagons from tempestuous Virginia City twenty-one miles south. That, and the fact that much of the acreage at Lake's Crossing was to be the company's federal land grant, made the spot a natural site for company shops—a roundhouse and hotel and dining facilities—and engineers were assigned to survey the bleak terrain and stake out town lots. The line from Truckee (mile 119) now stretched to Lake's Crossing thirty-five miles to the northeast, and Strobridge, with some reluctance, sent part of his work force back into the Sierras to add extra muscle to the labor of closing the infamous, cursed gap.[105]

Crocker arrived at the growing tent city at the ford on May 4 or 5, and highly approved of its strategic location on the Virginia City trail. That and the company's announcement of their intention to make the town-to-be a railroad center would surely boost land values and pump some fresh cash into the treasury. Charlie Crocker would personally benefit as well, for before the public auction, with the survey map in his hand, he bought forty prime acres on his own account. Never one to miss an opportunity, he opened the "grand" land auction on May 9, preceding it with a small ceremony during which he renamed the site Reno, in honor of Major General Jesse Reno, a Civil War martyr killed at South Mountain.[106] The assembled speculators and businessmen flocked forward to bid on the best lots and acreage beyond. The first lot was knocked down for a healthy $600, a few sold for $1,000, and, all told, several hundred lots were disposed of that first day, and all paid for with gold, which the company so needed just to meet the next month's payroll.[107] Within days, while land sales continued, some two hundred buildings were raised,[108] and Reno a year later had a boisterous population of fifteen thousand, all of whom eagerly awaited a linkup with "the crookedest little railroad in the world," which snaked up from Virginia City under the direction of Darius Ogden Mills.[109] According to the *Pacific Coast Mining Review,*[110] the 1869 juncture of the Virginia & Truckee Railroad with the Central Pacific resulted in a decrease in freight charges between the mines and Sacramento, from $100 to $26 a ton, with daily, all-weather service. Central Pacific freight revenues were instantly and dramatically increased by "the silver traffic."

As the final work in the Sierra gap took place, Strobridge, with depleted work crews, set off northeast from Reno. It was a daunting country, beginning with a sterile, forty-mile desert, described by one who crossed it as "a purely arid plain, covered with sage brush, varied by white alkali flats, holding but little water and that bad; with hot springs here and there; lizards and jackass rabbits the principal inhabitants; no timber," and no usable stone for the company's masons.[111] From Reno to Humboldt Wells (now Wells) at mile 526, a distance of 372 miles, the terrain ranged from "horrible" to "useless" to merely "unhelpful," even the portions along the turgid Humboldt River. The only redeeming feature of those miles was their level topography. In the first hundred miles, to a point just past Oreana, the elevation rises an imperceptible 100 feet, in the next hundred only another 700 feet, and over the rest of the distance to Humboldt Wells an extremely moderate 725 feet in 172 miles.[112] Also, grading work would be very light, and there were few curves, no major bridges, and no tunneling work whatever.

Counterbalancing those advantages, though, were some gruesome realities and problems. In the forty-mile desert—and over some other stretches—there was no water within sight of the right-of-way, and men, draft animals, and locomotives consume an awesome amount of water, especially when working in a stark, hot desert. Summers are staggeringly hot in Nevada, downright dangerous for working men and animals. Also, the complete absence of timber and construction-grade stone meant that millions of pounds of ties, timbers, and granite blocks would have to be cut or quarried and shaped and then shipped down from the Sierras, for as Creed Haymund later told Congress, "There was not a tree for 500 miles of the route that would make a board."[113] Transporting these heavy items along an increasingly long line into Nevada would become extremely expensive, and it would also clog the single track with dense, often delayed traffic.

Still, the race was the thing, and in Nevada it would continue as fast as supplies could be brought up. The Chinese, who had bested the Cornish miners, now set themselves to test the polyglot legions of the Casement brothers. As they sprinted out of Reno, Collis P. Huntington delivered his fairy-tale map to Secretary Browning.

XENOPHOBIA

THE water problem was the first stumbling block in Nevada to be removed by the Central Pacific, although neither easily nor cheaply. Lewis Clement, that engineering jack-of-all-trades, got the idea after wasting effort and money vainly drilling deep test wells along a hundred-mile line out of Reno. The little water brought up was so alkaline that it was undrinkable. Instead, he started drilling into the mountainsides east of the right-of-way. More often than not his drill bits reached fresh water from internal springs. Soon there were dozens of tunnellike, slanting bores in the mountainsides, gushing water into elevated, flume-sized water pipes. A few of these pipes actually stretched from the source of the water to the right-of-way (as far as eight miles away), but most emptied into large storage tanks. Water wagons would fill up from the tanks and sway back to the crews, animals, and locomotives, some shuttling constantly between the tanks and the water towers springing up along the line to service the locomotives.[114] Despite how expensive and labor-consuming it was, the system worked. Lumber for ties and bridge timbers was brought in from the Truckee on special trains, while other trains carried only shaped granite or crushed rock for ballasting. All this was in addition to the crucial construction trains, and it took forty cars laden with rails and assorted gear to build one mile of track. The scarcity of sidings in the mountains made orchestrating the various shipments and the return of empty trains a full-time job.

Crocker's Chinese graded through the dry Nevada desert at an accelerating, metronomic pace. Since the heat at times reached 120° and men were routinely collapsing on the line from heat stroke and dehydration, Crocker authorized a hot-season pay raise for all hands.[115] Exhorted by Strobridge, the track layers not only picked up their own cadence, but devised a system to otherwise speed their work. Under this system, a first gang of tie men placed only every other tie, with a second tie gang following minutes behind to place the rest. These were followed by a crew of levelers, who jostled, kicked, and aligned and seated the ties to a more or less uniform heighth, and the track men, who were instantly followed by two gangs of spikers, one driving half the spikes and the others finishing the job.[116] Under this evolving regimen, Strobridge began hitting his stride, and enjoyed his first two-mile days.

Finally, on June 15, word was flashed to Reno and beyond that the Sierra gap was finally closed. By that time trackers were some twenty miles beyond Reno in the ghastly desert, so instantly the company became eligible for bonds covering five twenty-mile sections, most of which lay in the forty-eight-thousand-dollar-a-mile mountains, with the rest in the thirty-two-thousand-dollar-a-mile wastelands. The bonds were hardly issued with alacrity, of course, but during the second half of 1868 the Big Four would receive a torrent of them—thirteen separate issues with a total (face) value of $10,610,000. The Sierras were finally, irrevocably breached.[117]

The first trans-Sierra passenger train chugged into Reno on June 18, crammed with sightseers who marveled at the dizzying curve around Cape Horn, the steep ascents and descents, and the superb scenery around Donner Lake. One of the passengers reported the trip in the *Railroad Record,* writing that, despite the mid-June date, "we traverse continuous snow-fields and immense drifts, through which the road has been cut with shovels for the passing of the trains . . . the snowbanks rise high above the road on either side . . . the snowbanks come down so close to the track that the eaves of the cars rake them on either side. It is the closest fit imaginable." Rapturously, he continued: "Six more tunnels . . . in many of which we see great masses of solid blue ice, hanging down from the wall like stalactites," the conductor at one point bellowing, "By Heaven, we are over the mountains." On the downslope, the engineer chose to coast eastward, a thrilling experience for those on board:

> The steam is shut off, the brakes put down, and, as the eagle sets his wing and floats noiselessly down, through the realms of air toward the earth from his eyrie among the clouds, we slide swiftly and smoothly down the acclivities of the mountains into the Great Basin of Nevada.[118]

The train was greeted with considerable company-sponsored pomp and ceremony at Reno, and the passengers were ecstatic about the entire experience. But another traveler noted something distinctly "Union Pacificish" out of the corner of his eye—idle workers: "These were the hardest, roughest looking men I ever saw . . . spending all their time in gambling . . . I saw but two or three women in the place and they were apparently not much better than the men."[119]

Meanwhile, in New York City, Henry V. Poor, who had earlier waxed enthusiastic about how "wonderful" was the Union Pacific, now openly boasted that "the crossing of the Sierra Nevada Mountains . . . is the greatest achievement yet accomplished in Civil Engineering."[120] There was no need for him to blush, for he was correct.

Arthur Brown was a busy man that summer of 1868. He had some five months to construct a complex of snowsheds and galleries before the snows returned to the mountains, and others to repair. He was allotted more than twenty-five hundred men, whom he had to pay premium wages, and he ran six long, traffic-snarling work trains, whose priority passage often delayed scheduled traffic and the transit of material for the Nevada work gangs. The almost total lack of sidetracks between miles 40 and 110 caused painful congestion on the line.[121]

Some of the sheds were virtual fortresses of thick hardwood, reinforced with iron braces, supports, and rods. Basically, they were tunnels rather than buildings, and every bit as unsightly. One traveler who examined them in 1870 found them "timbered as heavily as line-of-battle ships."[122] The strongest of them, in the most threatened portions of the line, reputedly cost $170,000 per mile to construct. Although far more expensive than anticipated, the snowsheds more than justified their cost; some of the original structures were still in use as late as 1952.[123]

Hammering alone rang through the no longer virgin mountains, for the blasting had been all but completed. In a few places, where danger of rockslides was preeminent, huge concrete retaining walls were built. Rock was laboriously stacked in back of the walls until a slope was created equal to that of the

mountainside, and then a gallery was constructed, with an extra-stout roof angled
so that boulders or snow avalanches would roll off the roof and tumble into the
gorges and ravines below.[124] Although he did not complete the last of his sheds
until the following summer, Brown, in a splendid show of crisis engineering
under pressure, had roofed more than twenty-three miles of the most critical
track before his crews were paid off for the winter.[125] Not one of his new sheds
or galleries would collapse during the snows of 1868–69.

Nevada was not hospitable to the Chinese that summer. Aside from the
climate and the sometimes dangerous local fauna, Nevadans, a brawling, prejudiced folk, sincerely disliked the Celestials, many of whom worked in Virginia
City and its outlying mining camps. The Chinese were seen as foreigners, men
of a different race, worshiping in an incomprehensible religion, and competing
with Americans for jobs and the wealth of the soil. The rude Nevadans, so well
described by Mark Twain in *Roughing It,* and by Lucius Beebe and Charles
Clegg in their witty *Virginia and Truckee,* [126] often caused trouble for the Celestials, rioting against them and expelling them from a number of towns and
camps—Virginia City among them—in 1867, 1868, and 1869.[127] Augustus Ward
Loomis, who was sympathetic toward the Orientals, noted in 1870 that at least
eighty-eight Chinese had recently been murdered by whites in California and
Nevada, "and *but two* of the murderers [had] been convicted and hung."[128] A
cacophony of racism was rising in California, especially in the media, one pamphlet warning that "China torn by rebellion, poisoned with opium and starving
in poverty, must fall together in one general ruin," releasing a torrent of yellow
immigration into the United States.[129] Perhaps this vicious prejudice explains
why the Central Pacific's Orientals "liked" Charlie Crocker and Jim Strobridge,
and were so loyal to them. The two men did not mock or threaten the Celestials
or their odd customs. And they paid fair wages, on time and in full.

It was fortunate for the company and its Celestials that the route across
Nevada took them largely through terrain as unpopulated and as cheering as the
moon. Race riots were certain to have erupted in towns, and ten thousand
Chinese men could not be expected to be entirely passive in the face of constant
abuse. And while the company armed neither white nor Chinese workers, it had
tons of explosives in its various depots and had trained several thousand Chinese
to use them. Had there been riots, the cost in human lives might have been high,
and for the Central Pacific there would have been other costs as well: delays,
extra expenditures, bad publicity, and perhaps a plague of legal problems. However, luck ran their survey lines through the state's least populated regions.

Adjusting to the climate, the scorpions, and tarantulas was a difficult task made
more difficult by the local tribes, whose Indians, while generally peaceful, and
described as "humble, peaceful supplicants for food and tobacco,"[130] inspired an
almost superstitious dread among the Chinese. Paiute Indians, who thought the
Orientals a genuine curiosity, often played pranks on them, eyeing their luxuri-

ant, foot-long pigtails while making sawing motions in the air with razor-sharp knives. Joseph Graham, one of Sam Montague's assistants, told of the arrival of a recently recruited gang of Chinese at Reno. Somehow (probably by sign language), some Paiutes warned the newcomers that in the desert they would soon be working in, there lurked immense, man-eating snakes, twenty feet long, "large enough that they could swallow a Chinaman easily." Since the recruits had been taught myths from birth, hundreds of them bolted in terror and fled back along the line toward the safety of the mountains. Strobridge, caught between blind rage and laughter, had to round them up by force and have the truth explained to them by veteran compatriots.[131]

Still, the Chinese, perhaps hearing stories of Sioux and Arapaho attacks on the Union Pacific, steered clear of all Indians whenever they could. Strobridge was offered military protection by the army in 1868; perhaps Commanding General Grant felt a bit guilty about allocating so much of his resources to protecting the Union Pacific and none to the other road. The construction boss haughtily rejected the offer: "I said 'damn the military' and it was damned."[132] He never had cause to regret his decision, for the Central Pacific was never the object of Indian wrath.

As construction progressed through Nevada, the *Sacramento Union,* an off-and-on supporter of the Central Pacific and its leaders, became violently antipathetic to the Big Four and their company, printing editorial attacks on their business ethics and the quality of the work being done in the name of the American people. This bad publicity might have hurt the sale of company securities. According to Charlie Crocker, the source of the bitter diatribes was the newspaper's new owner, one Jim Anthony. He felt offended by his treatment at the hands of Central Pacific trainmen, who, following printed company regulations, had asked, then ordered, and finally demanded that the editor's dog and rifle be consigned to a baggage car. In steaming wrath, Anthony stormed off the train and the vendetta was on.[133] On the other hand, despite Crocker's version, the hostility might have had a more mundane basis, for the Central Pacific had recently switched its printing business from Anthony's shop to one owned by Crocker's brothers in San Francisco.[134]

When the *Sacramento Union* claimed, in a detailed article, that there was a portion of the Central Pacific line so poorly built as to be a hazard to life and limb, someone (a Union Pacific man?) in Washington listened, and soon a presidential inspection team was in Sacramento. President Andrew Johnson had recently been impeached, but the failure of the Senate to convict him made him a more active president than he had been since inheriting the office in April 1865.

Charlie Crocker met the team personally, wined and dined the inspectors, and put a short train at their disposal. He also "graciously" accompanied the officials out on the line. When they reached the suspect trackage, he placed a tumbler brimful of water on the coach's floor, ordered the engineer to accelerate to fifty miles an hour, and sat back confidently in his plush seat. Less than ten minutes later, his point had been made: he and the inspectors were still alive, and only a few drops of water stained the floorboards.[135]

Anthony's next challenge became one of Crocker's favorite stories. The editor charged in print that the Central Pacific had bilked the government by exaggerating the length of its first hundred-mile stretch, obtaining more government aid than it deserved. A team of military engineers was dispatched by Congress (at a cost of $10,000) to measure the line, and, after the most careful and precise calculations the Central Pacific had ever had, announced that there was *more* track in place than the company had filed for, rather than less. The first 100 miles was actually 100.34 miles in length. Immediately, "Crocker the Wronged" had Huntington file a request for the extra 500 or so yards, but the government refused to part with any additional aid.[136] All in all, while vexing at the time, Anthony's harassment generated more good publicity than bad for the company.

In June the Central Pacific was moving swiftly on all fronts. Attempting to steal a march on the Union Pacific even though it would not (at least for a while) lead to more government aid, Crocker sent engineer Lewis Clement on a risky mission. Clement was to take three thousand of his best Chinese graders and push ahead through the "arid, alkali and Arabic" desert, almost to Humboldt Wells, to the Palisades, some 350 miles ahead of track.[137] He was to commence the grading there in three twisting, narrow canyons while other grading teams handled the easy work leading to the Palisades. Thus, when the track reached those tortuous canyons, there would be no delays. Clement's Chinese, grading east, would eventually encounter the Union Pacific's newly hired Mormons, grading west from Ogden.[138] It was a bold plan, for it would cost a fortune to freight tools, explosives, and even food across the desert to Clement's men. There would be no bonds for months for this work, for grading so far ahead of track was not eligible for aid under the railroad act. Still, with bonds now flowing in for previous work, there was more money to risk, and the chance to frustrate the Union Pacific was too tempting to resist.[139]

If the gamble was to succeed, however, extra, Mormon labor would have to be contracted, and that was a delicate matter on two counts. The contracting would have to involve Brigham Young, or at least receive his overt approval, as did anything of moment in Utah. But Young was not only a Union Pacific director and supporter, but also a personal friend of engineers Sam Reed, Jason Evans, and Grenville Dodge. Worse, in May he had already agreed to provide thousands of graders for the Omaha-based railroad. Would he be willing to do the same for its rival? Second, no matter what the Union Pacific's planned route or what that company might have told Young, the Central Pacific was certainly bypassing Salt Lake City and heading for Ogden along the line located and mapped by Butler Ives. Should the leader of the Saints hear this, he would almost certainly withhold Mormon labor.

Into this fragile situation came Leland Stanford, successful in every endeavor save excursions, and, as Huntington later characterized him, "a nice man." Calling on Clement in the nearby Palisades for any necessary technical information, Stanford pulled into Salt Lake City during the first days of June and booked the best suite in the Newhouse Hotel. He would remain there almost continuously for six months.[140]

The former governor soon had a series of long interviews with Brigham Young, who, to Standford's relief, showed a greater interest in money than in company affiliation. On June 9, following a meeting with the Prophet, Stanford wrote Hopkins that since "Brigham was cold and close," the politician had "not thought it advisable to enlighten him" concerning the Central Pacific's route through Utah.[141] Neither did a succession of Union Pacific officials who passed through Salt Lake City that summer. At a time when surveyors from both companies were doing most of their work north of the lake; when location maps to Ogden from both east and west were on file with the Interior Department as public documents and others based on them appeared in popular books and magazines; and when Reed and Dodge, Stanford, and soon Montague as well, were contracting Mormon labor to grade out of Ogden rather than Salt Lake City, even the densest man should have gotten the message. Nevertheless, in a Tabernacle sermon in mid-June, Young said: "Whether they meet in this city . . . has yet to be told . . . still, I would like to hear the whistle and the puffing of the iron horse every evening, and through the night, in the mornings and through the day," but "whether the junction will be in our city or in the vicinity adjacent, I do not know."[142]

What Stanford sought was a contract for Mormon grading from Ogden both east and west, if enough manpower was available. To his immense relief, Mormon muscle was abundant, the Prophet gave his blessings, and a contract was negotiated through him with the firm of (Ezra T.) Benson, (Lorin) Farr and (Chauncey W.) West, a firm in which the leading Saint had a sizable silent interest and whose partners were all high church officials.[143] The contract called for immediate work on a hundred-mile line, grading west from Monument Point, and later, from that landmark east to Ogden and beyond. If both areas were fully graded, the contract would cost the company $4 million, but it would be worth every penny, for if the work was done, the Central Pacific would have a far stronger claim to most of the Utah portion of the Pacific Railroad.[144] Possession, hoped the Big Four, would indeed be nine tenths of the law.

Stanford produced a large sum of gold as earnest money and everyone, for the time being, was happy. Like Reed and Evans before him, Stanford found a distressing lack of proper equipment in Mormon country, and so equipment would have to be hauled enormous distances at company expense.[145] Much of the profits, and Mormon wages, mandated the Prophet, was to go directly to the Church of Jesus Christ of Latter-Day Saints or to its Perpetual Emigration Fund, which footed the bill for European converts to flock to Deseret.[146] As a gesture of goodwill, as well as from his happiness at being rescued from isolation, the expansive Young donated to both companies all the additional land they might require for stations, engine houses, and other railroad buildings.[147]

Stanford, perhaps somewhat smug, was still at Salt Lake City when Dodge, Durant, and Dillon coached in.

11

THE UNION PACIFIC DOES NOT
BEAR SCRUTINY WELL

SHOWDOWN AT FORT SAUNDERS

THE Casement Army, now truly veteran, picked up the pace of its march that summer of 1868, and Jesse L. Williams began to complain that perhaps the pace was too swift to be consistent with quality construction. The trackmen were not listening to Williams, but to General Jack. Earning bonuses, they were spiking three and even four miles a day, and the Casement brothers, whose 1868 contract provided sizable mileage bonuses to them, were as avid as their Irish "iron men" to move on.[1] Henry V. Poor saw his prophecies belied every day on the Wyoming plains, where a two-mile day disappointed everyone. In mid-July the end of track was at previously nonexistent Benton (mile 695), fourteen miles east of Rawlins, and, perhaps having taken a breath at the short-lived Hell on Wheels there, the track crews sprinted forward for a record sixty-five miles the following month.

Tiny Benton, "by day disgusting, by night dangerous," was one of the most riotous of the movable Gomorrahs, a sleazy fantasyland with no permanent buildings, no permanent residents, and not a single town lot sold. "Averaging a murder a day; gambling and drinking, hurdy-gurdy dancing and the vilest of sexual commerce," wrote one observer, "this was Benton," a sixty-day citadel of sin.[2] Another who was there noted that Benton's chief attraction was "the Big Tent," a one-hundred-by-forty-foot framed tent, "conveniently floored for dancing." Within, on the tent's north side, was "a splendid bar, supplied with every variety of liquors and cigars, with cut glass goblets, ice-pitchers, splendid mirrors, and pictures rivaling those of our Eastern cities." He marveled that the action was so continuous in the tent that "a full band [was] in attendance day and night."[3]

The scenario changed but little from what it had been in Julesburg and Sidney, and what it would be at Green River, Bear River City, and Wasatch. Dodge's "bad men and lewd women" continued to leapfrog the Union Pacific's work crews, "catching the drippings from the feast in any and every form that it was possible to reach them . . . desperadoes of every grade, the vilest of men and women . . . this congregation of scum and wickedness" trekked ever westward, harbinger of "civilization" as much as were the surveyors, graders, and trackmen who sampled their delights.[4]

A year after its sordid hour of infamy, Benton ceased to exist once more, and where the bars, gaming establishments, and houses of flowers had once done double shifts, "only a few old chimneys and post-holes to mark the spot of the once flourishing town" remained to be seen from passing railroad cars.[5] *Sic transit* transients.

Transitory as the merchants of moral turpitude may have been, their votes as well as those of the Union Pacific's workers, when added to those of the scattered settlers, were enough to qualify Wyoming for territorial status in 1868, another achievement of the Casement Army.[6]

Chief Engineer Dodge, however, saw a situation brewing that was more dangerous than an itinerant whiskey seller's cheapest popskull. Thomas C. Durant, long the bane of his existence, had become a threat to Dodge, the fundamental engineering process of the Union Pacific as well as its construction work, and to the company itself. Dillon, Oliver Ames, and other powerful figures in both the railroad company and the Crédit Mobilier were apparently unwilling or unable to put Durant in his place, so Grenville Dodge, on leave of absence from Congress, would do so himself. He would, he knew, have powerful allies.

The month of July 1868 saw a pilgrimage of notable Americans to the Great American Desert. Newly nominated by the Republican party, General Grant went west. With him on his mission to talk peace with the Sioux (and the Union Pacific leaders) went Sherman, Sheridan, and a constellation of the nation's highest-ranking generals. If Red Cloud had massacred that party he would have devastated the American high command, decapitated the Republican party, and rewritten American history. Oliver Ames had headed for Wyoming and Utah,* and so did Sidney Dillon, Durant, and Seymour. Dodge, who sped west first, sat down with Bannock and Eastern Shoshone chiefs at Fort Russell (now Warren Air Force Base) near Cheyenne to attempt to free his company from at least part of its ongoing Indian threat.[8]

---

*Ames was described by Fergusen, who guided him for a while, as a "very plain, elderly looking gentleman."[7]

Grenville Dodge's meeting with the chiefs worked out well for the company, for treaties were signed with most of the tribes attending, granting them huge reservations in return for guarantees of peace. Washakie, powerful chief of the Shoshone, was granted the entire Wind River Valley, in return for "the protection of the railroad through their country." Perhaps in imitation of the Central Pacific's ploy, Dodge promised on behalf of the company that Washakie "and his tribe should be carried over our line free, whenever they desired to go," and soon "it was not an unusual thing to see on the top of the freight cars forty or fifty Indians, with their blankets, children and squaws."[9]

General Grant had a much more troublesome negotiating session, for the formidable Red Cloud alone could unite and lead into battle perhaps five thousand Sioux warriors and large contingents of Cheyenne and other Plains tribes as well. When they met at Fort Laramie, the army brass were bluntly informed by Red Cloud that, as a basic demand, the irritating and humiliating Bozeman Trail must be closed, its forts abandoned. Few Indian leaders had made concrete demands on government and army officials and fewer still had their demands acceded to, but Red Cloud won his point in mid-July. The army backed down and appeased the great Sioux leader, despite the implied loss of face by the army and the famous presidential candidate. After all, the Bozeman Trail forts had been a great deal of trouble for the high command. Isolated and usually under light Indian siege, they had never achieved much more than large expenses and embarrassing casualties. They certainly had not protected the Union Pacific. The opposite was clearly the case, for the existence of the forts, in the heart of Sioux country, kept that Indian nation and its friends in constant, hostile motion. Perhaps the best way to protect the railroad (and settlers, and save money while avoiding bad publicity) was to simply abandon the forts and grant the Indians much of Dakota and Montana territories. By July 16 it was done, and the Indians, content, streamed home with glad tidings. This did not end raids against the Union Pacific. Red Cloud, after winning his major point, for some reason delayed ratifying the agreement for four months, and in September a train was ambushed and wrecked, with several fatalities. But the agreement did, however, deescalate the violence that had been so badly complicating construction since early 1866.[10]

Grant and his entourage did not immediately return to the East after the highly publicized peace parley with Red Cloud. First, with no publicity whatever, it would be necessary to arbitrate with the white chiefs of the Union Pacific.

On July 23, Dodge, at end of track, learned that Durant, Seymour, and Dillon had arrived at Fort Saunders, near Benton, and were awaiting Grant and Sherman. There was little doubt that the Doctor would use the occasion to attack Dodge as an incompetent, absentee chief engineer. If he could persuade Grant that Dodge should be ousted—or at least demoted in favor of Silas Seymour— Durant would have more freedom than before. It should also be noted that

Seymour's brother Horatio had been nominated by the Democratic party just two weeks earlier. While Seymour's name was not as much a household word as Grant's, he would deliver New York's massive vote. The Democratic party was resurgent throughout the country, six (solidly Democratic) states of the former Confederacy were readmitted to the Union in 1868, and Seymour's chances to win the presidency were reasonably good.[11]

Hurriedly, Dodge set off to intercept his old friend Grant in transit, and the two, along with the other generals in the party, met at Benton on July 25. It is not known exactly what was said, but it seems clear that Dodge used this "accidental" meeting to inform Grant and his coterie that Durant and Seymour were fundamentally detrimental to the Union Pacific, in terms of reputation, financial chicanery, and even basic engineering. The fact that questions were already being raised in Washington about the Crédit Mobilier and construction shoddiness no doubt strengthened Dodge's already formidable hand.[12] The deck was obviously stacked against the Durant cabal.

On July 26, on the hot, flat plain where Fort Saunders sat in tedium, the confrontation took place. Into the long, low officers' mess trooped Grant, Sherman, and Sheridan, Durant, Dillon, Jesse L. Williams, and Grenville Dodge (for whom the company station Grenville had just been named by Sam Reed, at mile 703). Seven major generals were left standing on the mess-hall porch, along with a dejected Silas Seymour—a mere colonel—despite his brother's prominence.[13] No minutes were taken, yet what transpired is hardly a mystery.

The air was almost electric inside the mess hall, and Grant immediately took charge, bluntly telling Durant to make his case. The Doctor, looking a bit seedy and exhausted (he had been out in the field for a long time and, as he himself admitted, rarely bothered to change his clothes when in the West), opened fire on Dodge. Taking from his vest a written statement, which was basically a list of charges, he attacked the chief engineer for a variety of malfeasances. Among other things, Durant claimed that Dodge ignored the advice of his consulting engineer and, in fact, rarely consulted with him; he did not press the work with vigor and was responsible for many costly delays in construction; he wasted money on unnecessary survey work; he was rarely present at end of track; he often disobeyed direct orders from Nassau Street; and somehow it was his fault that Denver and Salt Lake City had to be bypassed. Sweating profusely, Durant carefully folded his papers and sat down. He had shot his bolt in front of a decidedly hostile audience, and he must have realized it.

Grenville Dodge then took the stage and dispassionately refuted every charge made, save that of absence from end of track, and that he explained was due to a decision made by the leadership that his presence in Congress would be more useful to the company. Dodge took a few moments to launch attacks himself. In very plain language, he explained to the generals that Durant and Seymour were guilty of gross extravagances that cost the company hundreds of thousands of dollars, and explained at great length the stupidity and added expenses of Seymour's various unnecessary route changes, which bilked the government of so many bonds and acres. He also indicated in no uncertain terms that unless Durant and the consulting engineer could be kept from interfering in his work, and kept generally "in their places" (i.e., as far from construction as possible), he himself would resign.

Then, as Dodge recalled, Grant stood up, paced noisily around the long room, and "took very strong ground with Durant and Dillon, telling them frankly that the Government would not stand for any change in my lines and that they should insist upon my remaining upon the road."[14] Another source has it that the Republican nominee's final words were addressed to Dodge, while really meant for Durant: "The Government expects you to remain with the road as its Chief Engineer until it is completed."[15] End of story.

Outgunned by the army brass, Durant backed down completely, mumbling that henceforth he would support his chief engineer and not hinder him. After all, with Jesse L. Williams squalling and Secretary Browning only too happy to listen to him, it would be foolish for the Doctor to push too hard on the issue of Grenville Dodge. Deflated, Durant, a slightly embarrassed Sidney Dillon, and the other participants filed out of the building for some ritual photographs. Persuaded to pose with the others, Durant made his last point by sitting dejectedly on a fence, while all the others stood proudly and rather pompously, facing the camera. He then hastily decamped, heading back to New York and a fresh change of clothes. Dodge would be, with minor exceptions, his own man.

The same month Dodge and Durant went head to head, an excursion of "editorial gentlemen" was escorted by Union Pacific Chief Superintendent Webster Snyder on a run to end of track. The company needed good publicity more than ever now, and great pains were taken to impress the fourth estate with both the speed and quality of construction and the great variety of the company's table and bar. All the way to Rawlins (mile 710) the newspapermen were hauled, to personally witness the robotics of Jack Casement's track crew and admire the scenery. All in all, the excursion was a great success, and excellent propaganda blossomed in the press. The editors and reporters, who soon founded the Rocky Mountain Press Club, became ardent boosters of—and virtually spokesmen for—the Union Pacific.[16]

In the meantime, Dodge was also politicking. Perhaps a little bruised by his duel with Durant, he remained with Grant and the generals as long as they were in the West, acting now as their host. He wrote Oliver Ames: "As General Grant had been nominated for the Presidency, and no doubt would be elected, I took great pains on this trip to post him thoroughly about everything connected with the Union Pacific." He would continue to do so until the last spike was driven home.[17]

The Union Pacific was soon to need good friends in both politics and the press, for it was acquiring powerful enemies in both arenas. Not that director Jesse L. Williams was an enemy of the Union Pacific. Far from it. He was a friend and co-worker, and as such he was outraged that the company was neither being managed nor built correctly. Williams, it should be remembered, was the engineer who, in a report to the Board of Standards for the Pacific Railroad in 1865, said, "A railroad cannot be called complete until well-ballasted" with twelve to twenty-four inches of gravel.[18]

INSPECTING THE UNION PACIFIC

I N MID-AUGUST the meandering Dodge was again in Salt Lake City, where he met briefly with Leland Stanford, unsuccessfully sounding him out concerning a point, satisfactory to both, where the two rail lines might join in an attempt to reach agreement to avoid costly, duplicate grading in Utah. This matter was no small headache, for the proximity of the two companies' work gangs was fast breeding violence. According to Dodge, "The laborers upon the Central Pacific were Chinamen, while ours were Irishmen, and there was much ill-feeling among them. Our Irishmen were in the habit of firing their blasts in the cuts without giving warning to the Chinamen on the Central Pacific working right above them." A number of Celestials were killed in the resulting slides, and although Dodge ordered his foremen to cease such amusements, they did not—until the Chinese retaliated with blasts above the Irish, which "buried several of our men." A tense and fragile truce resulted.[19]

Stanford, as slippery in his own way as Durant and a great deal less abrasive, refused to commit himself to anything. Dodge turned next to engineer Lewis Clement, whom he met on several occasions in Salt Lake City. While there was nothing the young man could do save compare construction problems, Dodge did learn from him what he had long suspected, that the Central Pacific planned its route north of the lake and through Ogden.[20] The chief engineer probably also talked with Montague, who passed through the city at this time. Durant certainly spoke to him later, but neither apparently gained anything from Judah's heir.[21] At least when Durant or Dodge informed Brigham Young of the Union Pacific's decision to excise Salt Lake City from the Pacific Railroad's main line, they might tell him that the Central Pacific had made the same decision for the same sound engineering reasons.

It was Dodge who broke the sad tidings to the Mormon leader, and the Prophet burst into an appropriately biblical rage. As Dodge remembered it: "He would not have this, and appealed over my head to the Board of Directors, who referred the question to the Government Directors, who fully sustained me."[22] Young briefly threatened to withdraw all Mormon labor from the Union Pacific and use it to aid the Californians instead, and "he even went so far as to deliver in the Tabernacle a great sermon denouncing me, and stating that a road could not be built or run without the aid of the Mormons."[23] A week later, having obtained no solace from Leland Stanford, and assured by Dodge that the Union Pacific would build, or at least aid, a Salt Lake City to Ogden branch railroad, the Prophet returned to the Tabernacle and "told his followers that the Lord, in another vision, had commanded the Mormons to help the Union Pacific."[24] The leading Saint was used to having his way, but after a few weeks of protracted tantrum, he accepted the inevitable and merely wanted to get on with the work.

While Young was experiencing holy apoplexy, Commissioner Williams was experiencing something similar, if secular. After a very careful examination of almost the entire Union Pacific line, he informed the company—and the secretary of the interior—in his official capacity that he had personally recorded deficiencies in construction that would cost at least $3 million to rectify. A few days later, a nervous Oliver Ames, feeling the heat, wrote Secretary Browning, exceedingly careful not to question Williams's findings. He explained that since construction was still under way, deficiencies were to be expected, and that these could and would be taken care of in due course. Agreeing to establish a fund to cover all costs of "finishing" the road to first-class standards, Ames all but begged the secretary not to withhold bonds soon scheduled to be delivered to the company.[25]

Accordingly, Orville Browning was informed on September 2 that the Union Pacific board had voted to create a three-million-dollar fund to cover the needed work on the line, which, the company hoped, would defuse the situation and dampen the moral fires felt by Williams and many others. The fund was to be made up of par-value first-mortgage bonds,[26] as there was so little actual cash available. President Ames had done what he could, but the secretary, perhaps influenced once more by Collis Huntington, was neither impressed nor mollified. Instead, he formulated a plan that might have made even morose Uncle Mark beam with joy.

On October 7, Browning announced that he had appointed a special commission to reexamine the entire Union Pacific line. Its members were civil engineer James Barnes, General (and engineer) Gouvernor K. Warren, who had participated in the Jefferson Davis surveys, and, inexplicably, Jacob Blickensderfer, Utah location engineer of the company being investigated. Until he had their formal report in hand, growled the secretary, no further bonds would be released to the Union Pacific.[27] The die was cast, very likely by the invisible hand of Mr. Huntington.

Further threatening the Union Pacific, Browning the same day wrote to Williams and the company's other government personnel, instructing them to report most fully on the state of Union Pacific finances.[28] They in turn requested all relevant records from Oliver Ames, who fumed, fussed, and sweated, finally producing partial and very confusing data two weeks later.

Oliver was in a cold sweat indeed, and even Durant, who informed him on October 20 that "the Road will bear examination from any reasonable commission have no fear on that account," could not calm the company president.[29] The Doctor, himself as placid as a Nebraska pond, took the opportunity to proffer the ornate Lincoln Car to the commissioners, sending an order to commissary officers to flesh out its larder with forty pounds of butter, ten "sugar cured hams," and "1 box champagne wine."[30] Lavish hospitality had served Durant well in the past, and he fully believed that it would put his "guests" in a proper frame of mind.

Finally, on October 25, with Dodge as escort and guide, the three special investigators left Omaha for an inspection that might have a critical impact on the Union Pacific. While they crawled westward, consuming their hams and champagne, a bondless company board began squeezing its stockholders for more and more money. It was a risky moment,[31] for as Dodge wrote, "The CPRR are laying track very fast. I have had a man there a week and they lay 2½, 3 and four miles a day; work moonlight nights when they have the material," and they were not at all (for the moment) pressed for funds.[32] The "man" reporting to Dodge was probably Augustus A. Belden, who had guided the chief engineer through Seymour's route in the Black Hills the previous July. Promoted by Dodge to assistant engineer of one section of the line, Belden was mysteriously working for the *Central* Pacific by November, if not earlier, returning to his position on the Union Pacific in 1870.[33] Dodge knew that the Union Pacific could afford no delays at this crucial moment, with the Central Pacific churning across Nevada while Collis Huntington filed ludicrous, yet to the Union Pacific potentially dangerous, maps in Washington.

Dodge also took the time to dispatch an engineer named Hudnutt with a survey party to run a preliminary survey line through the Snake River Valley to Portland, for he had learned that the flamboyant and eclectic Ben Holladay had just seized control of the newly chartered Oregon Central Railroad. Holladay never did anything out of caprice, and there was no telling what he might do, so Dodge wanted his survey data in place before the "Stagecoach King" could even put parties into the field.[34] In the same vein, the chief engineer urged Durant to put more men and money into the work *west* of Monument Point, so that even if the company's construction pace slowed, the Union Pacific would have at least some claims with which to fight the Central Pacific.[35]

Dodge was certainly earning his pay, but he was no doubt somewhat rattled by a letter sent him by John B. Alley, who warned him that the Crédit Mobilier (and, by association, Dodge's railroad) was scandal-ridden. Its indecent dividends, wrote the congressman, would inevitably call down the wrath of the government and the American public.[36] He could hardly have been more prescient.

As the inspection party rolled out of Omaha, Dodge was handed another disturbing communication, marked "personal." Oliver Ames had found what he hoped was a way out of the company's "fix." No naïf, Ames had doubtlessly known for some time that his railroad was far from being first-class, despite Durant's placid assertions to the contrary. Hence, from the day Browning decided to send the inspectors out, Ames had sought a way to negate their candor. He informed Dodge now that the secretary of the inspection team, a Dr. Chaffee, was "their man." Chaffee would be the one to draft the inspectors' final report, and, added Ames, "He will make the report as favorable as the Commissioners allow and will have it promptly executed."[37] The company president must have learned something from the devious doctor after all. He also warned that a new government director, Cornelius Wendell, was openly hostile to the company. Ames feared that Wendell would attempt to delay the inspection report just to keep the government bonds in Browning's oversize safe.[38]

Despite Dr. Chaffee, the inspection report was a shock to those at 22 Nassau Street, and despite Wendell's purported efforts, it was not at all delayed, but tendered to the secretary on November 23, just a month after he had quietly accepted from Collis P. Huntington a Central Pacific route map all the way east to Echo Canyon.

The inspectors' report, presumably despite Blickensderfer's best attentions, revealed that Jesse L. Williams's criticism had been, if anything, benign. While praising some aspects of the work (general location of the line, quality of company buildings), it found much wanting, and assailed the company for having permitted too many curves, curves that were too sharp, substandard embankments, cuts too shallow ("upon portions of the road ballasting is entirely wanting"), shoddy, impermanent bridges, excessive grades, and other defects, ad nauseam.

Specifically, the inspectors concluded that to make the first 890 miles of the Union Pacific acceptable under the 1862 act and its amendments, the following moneys would have to be expended correctly:

1.	Changing certain locations	$200,000
2.	Completing embankments, filling trestle works, etc.	240,000
3.	Completing excavation of cuts	20,000
4.	Reducing grades between Omaha and Elkhorn	245,000
5.	Replacing 525,000 cottonwood ties	525,000
6.	Ballasting, surfacing, and curving rails	910,000
7.	70 permanent abutments, 26 pier foundations	144,000
8.	30,480 yards of masonry for abutments and piers	457,200
9.	8,450 lineal feet of Howe Truss bridging	380,250

10. Girders and permanent trestle works of masonry	60,500
11. Renew or replace Dale Creek Bridge	100,000
12. Enlarge stone culverts, additional waterways	100,000
13. 60 new locomotives	840,000
14. Thorough repair of 50 locomotives	150,000
15. 44 new passenger cars	264,000
16. 30 new baggage, express, and mail cars	114,000
17. 500 box freight cars	450,000
18. Complete shop complexes at Cheyenne, Omaha, etc.	350,000
19. Other shops and depots	200,000
20. Additional water stations, etc.	80,000
21. More station buildings	75,000
22. More snow fences	50,000
23. More stock fencing	30,000

The total additional expenses on the first 890 miles would be a staggering $6,489,550, according to the inspectors.

Softening the blow a bit was final praise for the Union Pacific: "Taken as a whole, the Union Pacific has been well constructed . . . deficiencies exist, but they are almost without exception, those incident to all new roads, or of a character growing out of the peculiar difficulties encountered, or inseparably connected with the unexampled progress [speed] of the work."[39]

This report was handed to President Johnson on November 30, along with Browning's annual report, which also included the financial data collected by the government directors. That information, according to Browning, indicated that the leadership of the Union Pacific–*cum*–Crédit Mobilier had already made an unseemly profit of $17,750,000. Hence, concluded Browning, "I have the honor to recommend that the issue of patents for land and of bonds be suspended until such deficiencies shall have been supplied."[40] The secretary was doing his best to stop the Union Pacific cold, and would soon issue an order doing precisely that.

Ames, Durant, and the directors were sorely embarrassed—not only by details of the secretary's report or the findings of the inspectors, but by the withholding of more than $2.5 million of government bonds and the like amount of very marketable company bonds, some of which had, in fact, been prematurely sold to the public.[41]

To avoid charges of partiality, in late October Secretary Browning had also appointed a special commission to examine the Central Pacific. Its august members were United States surveyor general for California Sherman Day, Lieutenant Colonel R. S. Williamson of the army Corps of Engineers, and railroad engineer Lloyd Tevis—the Big Four's partner in the Southern Pacific. These commissioners began their "labors" in early November, accompanied, entertained, and coddled by Leland Stanford, who lost not a moment in making the visitors comfortable.[42]

When he learned of the complexion of the team to inspect the Central Pacific, Oliver Ames (knowing that his own road would be found wanting), wrote President Johnson on October 29, and "respectfully" demanded that the Central Pacific be examined as rigorously as the Union Pacific, and by the same men. He admitted no conflict of interest in having a Union Pacific engineer inspect his rival's work. Further, he requested that the president free the overdue bonds, and endeavored to explain away the deficiencies found on his company's line. Somewhat lamely, he claimed that these were inevitable, for "no road is ever finally completed."[43] President Andrew Johnson was not convinced.

While Ames was attempting to beguile the president of the United States, Casement track crews were setting world distance (if not quality) records. They laid 4½, 5, 6 miles a day, and on October 26 an amazing 7¾ of a mile.[44] A beaming Dan Casement was proud to authorize triple wages for that effort. Milepost 900 was practically visible in the distance by early November, but December was to witness the final, harsh blows struck against the Union Pacific, blows from which it would barely recover.

FURTHER ROCKS IN THE ROAD

IN SEPTEMBER, Oliver Ames had filed a map with the secretary of the interior showing the Union Pacific's route from mile 900 to Weber Canyon, just west of Echo Canyon, on the approaches to Ogden—a one-hundred-mile line. The map was routine and legitimate, and it correctly revealed Union Pacific track to mile 847, near Green River, with grading and most bridging complete to Weber Canyon.[45] Instead of accepting Ames's map, however, Browning simply shelved it, and, good friend that he was of Collis Huntington, accepted the Central Pacific map less than a week after receiving it, on October 20. At that moment, the easternmost rail of the Central Pacific lay some 350 miles from Sacramento, another 340 from Promontory Point, and over 440 from Weber Canyon. It was patently unfair and laughably fraudulent, but of course Browning churlishly hid his decision from Ames, while the gleeful Big Four kept a carefully guarded silence as well.[46]

Finally, on December 15, perhaps because the Union Pacific pestered him so about the fate of their own map, the secretary dropped his bomb, informing Oliver of his approbation of the Californians' map. Ames, of course, and Durant and Dodge and every other Union Pacific supporter who knew of it, was stunned and then irate. For perhaps the first time genuine righteous indignation swept through Nassau Street. Dodge arrived in Washington in time to join the Ames brothers as they stormed in to see the embarrassed but thick-skinned secretary. It must have been a tumultuous get-together, for beyond Browning's unethical behavior loomed the highly possible mortality of the Union Pacific Railroad Company, so desperate for its bonds.

Orville Browning, uncomfortably aware of the "irregular" nature of his behavior, and confronted with three influential and highly agitated men, waffled, vacillated, and squirmed. Basically, he whined, the Central Pacific map he had approved was only a *route* map; that is, he had approved only a route, and not a railroad company's graven right to build upon it. To his perplexed audience he explained in the fuzziest, most obfuscatory manner that the route he had approved could conceivably be used by the first company to lay track on it. Since the Union Pacific was bound to be the first to reach the disputed terrain, that company, apparently, would be able to claim it.[47] This explanation, of course, made no sense whatsoever, for among other things Browning ignored the question of bonds and lands to be dispensed. Those had always gone to the company whose map had been accepted. Hardly reassured by the secretary's amorphous soliloquy, the three Union Pacific leaders stomped out, with Oakes Ames determined to find out exactly when the Central Pacific map had been filed (Browning could not remember) and precisely where its tracks had ended the moment it *was* filed.[48] Dodge, for his part, was ordered to gain access to the map and study it himself. After all, it was a public document.

He was soon perusing the map in question, and what he saw must have induced either a paroxysm of rage or gales of relieved laughter. The Central Pacific "map" was not a map at all, but simply a long sheet of paper with a red line across it like a recently healed wound. No topographical features marred the almost pristine blankness of the cartography—not even the Great Salt Lake appeared on the paper! It was preposterous. Even the mandatory engineering affidavits, while attached and signed, had not been witnessed and sworn, as was required. The whole thing was a bad joke, played on the Union Pacific by the California pranksters. Oliver, with a tone as neutral as he could force himself to maintain, wrote Browning in late December, to bring all of this to his attention: "The Central Pacific Railroad location must have been accepted by the honorable Secretary through a misrepresentation of the facts," he carefully asserted. The Central Pacific was in the midst of the Nevada wastelands when the map had been filed, "and yet they are allowed to file a map with no topography upon it, but merely a bare, red line, whose location no person could tell, through what mountains, up what streams or rivers" no expert could deduce. This was clearly a sham, wrote Oliver, and he wanted the secretary to revoke his acceptance.[49]

That, however, was not to be. Although on New Year's Eve Browning did release the Union Pacific's long-awaited $2,560,000 in withheld government bonds, the Central Pacific's "red line" was not rejected.[50]

To add insult to injury, the investigators' report on the condition of the Central Pacific was delivered in the last days of the year, after the *Railroad Record,* in a "scoop," had noted: "A telegraph report of their decision has been received. They speak very favorably of the road, but say it has 'minor' deficiencies."[51] The operative word was indeed *minor,* for the investigators found that the Central Pacific was so well constructed that it could be declared first-class after an additional expenditure of merely $310,000. Dodge cried out in pain that "it was a white-washing report," and he and Oliver immediately protested its findings to both Browning and the president, demanding a new and this time "impartial" investigation of the rival railroad.[52]

There is no doubt that both Huntington and Stanford had both done their work well, one with a fantasy map that actually lied about the extent of continuous grading and tracking, the other by influencing the government's special investigators. Much of this "influencing" was actually carried out by Charlie Crocker, who was getting rather proficient at hoodwinking visiting inspectors. He was also the only one of the Big Four who had a taste for strong spirits. Crocker later happily recalled guiding the inspectors along the line in a luxurious car thoughtfully provided with a variety of potables. "The train stopped, the engine took a drink, and so [did] the Commissioners. In truth, we became hilarious. Toasts were called for and drank [*sic*] with vim and enthusiasm, the desert was forgotten, and all went 'merry as a marriage bell.' " Under these conditions, the inspection of the Central Pacific was, one might conclude, less than rigorous.[53] Ames and Durant had once again seriously underestimated the Californians and overestimated their own position. Or they had for once been too honest.

December could hardly have been worse for the Nassau Street habitués, for extremely harsh winter weather and a cycle of storms completely halted tracking and impeded movement of supplies west of Laramie for two full weeks.[54] And there were other, increasingly frequent delays caused by shortages of matériel or food at end of track. Jason Evans's correspondence and telegrams reveal growing frustration over delays caused by shortages of basic supplies. At one point, Boomer's bridgemen needed "four more pile drivers [in order] to get out of the way" of the track crews. Then Evans wrote to a contractor stalled by lagging bridge building, urging him to help Boomer's crews by using "all the transportation in the country to haul bridge timber" so the specialists could get on with their work. Sam Reed angrily wired Evans at end of track in October, demanding that he do something to speed foodstuffs to his men, for "unless corn has been purchased . . . work would stop"; the long-unpaid workers were already noticeably restive. Typical of the telegrams reaching Evans, who was fast becoming the company's troubleshooter, was one from a contractor's foreman:

"Cannot find tunnel bolts. Work being detained for want of them." A few days later, in another telegram, Webster Snyder complained that no timber was reaching the bridge crews at all, and that the trackmen would soon have to stop work and await completion of several bridges.[55]

Also congealing blood in the New York boardrooms were random factors such as the avarice of government director Cornelius Wendell. Not only anti–Union Pacific, but also in search of boodle, the director told Webster Snyder that he had serious doubts concerning the quality of one twenty-mile portion of new track, and that, according to Dodge, "before he [Snyder] could get the section approved by Wendle [*sic*] he had to pay him $25,000." If he was not paid that sum Wendell threatened to personally walk every foot of the new line to find faults.[56] Snyder, well aware of the November report and the consequent bad publicity, promptly paid up, informing Dodge of this on December 18. Wendell then gave his seal of approval to the new mileage.

Dodge sharply criticized his superintendent for acceding to extortion, although he admitted that he was not entirely surprised at the display of venality from a government official. He ordered Snyder to pay no more bribe money:

> We had a similar case of this with [Chauncey H.] Snow, a Govt. Director, who was sent out on the road to make an examination and his report was brought to me for sale. I refused to pay a cent upon it. It was finally offered to me for $1,000. He had two reports—one was a very severe criticism of the road and the other was a favorable opinion of it.[57]

According to the chief engineer, the rebuffed Snow filed the critical report, but Dodge himself reported the whole affair to Browning, and officially protested it. Snow's report was ignored by the government. Oddly, there is no record that Snow really was a government director. He himself claimed to have been appointed by President Johnson on January 9, 1869, which would in any case have been *after* the alleged extortion attempt.[58] It is vaguely possible that Snow had some other job with the Union Pacific, such as building inspector or bridge inspector.

A lawsuit brought by Jim Fisk, Jr., in July finally reached the courts in December, that grimmest of months for the Union Pacific, less than a month after Henry McComb began his long and embarrassing, but ultimately fruitless, legal struggle with the company. Bad publicity piled upon bad publicity for the men at 22 Nassau Street.[59] Fisk in 1867 had attempted to purchase twenty thousand shares of Union Pacific stock, but Oliver Ames, wary of the "Barnum of Wall Street," kept putting the financier off with various pretexts, and Fisk, a vindictive man on the most pleasant of days, vowed revenge. That revenge would play into the hands of the Big Four. Early in 1868, still unable to acquire a large block of Union Pacific stock, Fisk quietly bought six shares and immediately brought suit against the company and the Crédit Mobilier in July. He claimed that he had subscribed twenty thousand shares but that they had been illegally withheld from him, and that the Union Pacific board was conspiring to keep almost all stock in their own corrupt hands.* More damaging to the Union Pacific leadership were his charges that virtually all of the profits from building the road had been turned over to the Crédit Mobilier, "a close corporation" owned by the Union Pacific directors. Further, he claimed: "The whole cost of constructing the railway has not exceeded the amount of bonds issued by the government," and that the railroad itself was poorly, unsafely, and criminally constructed. Hence Fisk asked that the management of the Union Pacific and the Crédit Mobilier "be declared a fraud" perpetrated upon the stockholders of the former (who had yet to receive a penny in dividends) and that contracts between the two "be declared fraudulent and set aside," with the Crédit Mobilier returning all the profits it had so far received from the railroad company.[60] There was just enough truth in his accusations, just enough suspicion already in Congress, and just enough notoriety to his name to ensure national press coverage. The timing was perfect for Fisk, and, as usual, perfectly horrible for the Union Pacific and the Crédit Mobilier: on July 3 (the very week Fisk's case was introduced, gaining national attention), Crédit Mobilier stockholders received another, 75 percent dividend, and, worse still, just five days later yet another dividend of 30 percent, paid in *cash*. Even without Fisk's suit, McComb's babbling, and the November inspection report, such large dividends, paid back-to-back, would have generated doubts and suspicions from Wall Street and Congress to farms in Iowa and Tennessee.[61]

Although Oliver had written Dodge in the fall that "Bushnell thinks he can buy him [Fisk] off with $50,000," and there is some indication that the money was actually paid,[62] the sum was apparently not enough, for Fisk persisted with his suit and the headlines it produced melded nicely with Williams's allegations, the investigative reports, and more. Fisk eventually lost his suit in 1869, but the whole business poisoned public faith and severely rattled Congress, which increasingly felt obliged to protect its constituents against misuse of the public largesse. In December, almost suicidally, the Crédit Mobilier declared still another dividend. On the twenty-ninth, it announced immediate disbursement of a scandalous 200 percent payment in Union Pacific stock to its stockholders— hence a real value of between 65 and 70 percent.[63]

What this means in terms of money is that a total of over $20 million in dividends (at par value) was paid out to Crédit Mobilier investors on their initial investments of $3,750,000—and all in one twelve-month period! In terms of actual market value (bonds at 97 and 100 percent of par, stock at 30 to 50 percent, and cash), the stockholders received over $13 million. Since Durant that year held about 18 percent of all Crédit Mobilier paper, he personally raked in

---

*Government regulations required that the Union Pacific keep its subscription books open until all of its stock was spoken for. It never was.

over $1.5 million, and one should not doubt George Francis Train's boast that he later had "three generations living off Crédit Mobilier."

The final boardroom trauma of 1868 concerned the construction contract. The Ames agreement officially expired when the tracks reached mile 914, just east of the Utah line, a few miles past Bridger, which they did in mid-November. Ames, reading the signs, declined an opportunity to extend the contract or draw up another.[64] Nor did anyone else rush forward with a contract bid, for there was everywhere a sense of dark and gloomy foreboding.

Not, however, dark enough to deter, dissuade, or even faze the Doctor. Even before the Ames contract was completed, he had secretly signed a new contract, from mile 914 to completion of the railroad. The name on the contract was that of George Francis Train's brother-in-law, James W. Davis, an Omaha business- man of modest means and experience, who had handled some of the company's lumber contracts. Davis undertook to build what was to be the company's final 172 miles under the terms specified in the old Ames contract, and on November 6 he assigned his days-old contract to the seven trustees, for a promised (but, naturally, not delivered) $5,000 in currency.[65] Not until late February did the Doctor deign to inform the Union Pacific board of the new arrangement,* and the Davis contract was not even submitted to a vote and legally accepted by stockholders until a meeting in Boston held on May 28—eighteen days after the Golden Spike was driven!

Little wonder that Grenville Dodge could wearily write as the year ended: "Our great difficulty in contending with the Central Pacific was that the Adminis- tration and the Departments had lost all confidence in Mr. Durant and many of the decisions made against us came on account of his interference and state- ments."[66] There was worse to come.

BEAR RIVER CITY AND OTHER MARVELS

OST of these events, of course, passed far over the heads of those in the field who were working fanatically to make the Doctor's railroad a reality.

Progress was astonishing that summer and fall. The Continental Di- vide was crossed in August,[67] and in September five- and six-mile days were not considered rarities, although there was a trade-off, for jury-rigging became the

---

*How on earth did the board think the road was being built between November and February? By charity? They must have known the truth.

order of the day, and quality, never superb, visibly declined. Ballasting was still minimal—as the investigators were soon to learn: "The track has, without exception, been laid on the bare roadway," read one report.[68] The same defect was evident years later. This was the case even though after mile 560 or so, proper ballasting material was readily available. Also, little masonry work was being done, cottonwood ties were no longer even receiving the benefit of Burnettizing, and the company's buildings were no longer being built of brick or stone, but were crudely slapped together out of wood. There was a character of impermanence about the Union Pacific in Wyoming and Utah. Speed was the thing, and speed alone.[69] Durant, to goad progress yet further, poked around (in vain) for more labor, at one point attempting to recruit two thousand Chinese workers, offering them forty dollars a month and rations.[70]

By September, work was under way on all four tunnels (at miles 680, 972, 1005, and 1005.5), and late that month Snyder reported that Weber Canyon Tunnel number 3 was being pierced at a rate of six feet a day, with boring from both faces and liberal use of nitroglycerin.[71] In the relatively soft limestone and quartzite, the liquid explosive was far more efficient than powder, and far less dangerous than when used to blast hard, brittle granite. However, despite the rapid progress, temporary tracks had to be laid in detours around tunnels 2 and 3—eight winding, roller-coaster miles of them—and all four tunnels had to be fully timbered to prevent the collapse of their straticulated roofs.[72] The relative ease of tunneling was largely offset by spiraling prices for most material. Good ties had to be hauled hundreds of miles, and Snyder watched in dismay as their price climbed again to $4.50 or more each (there was still a great deal of gouging and padding of accounts). The much larger tunnel timbers meant a proportionate increase in expense, and Evans noted that common logs, locally cut, brought a staggering $4 apiece,[73] and even hay for livestock was sold by the Mormons for what the traffic would (barely) bear; $120 a ton and more. Water, according to Jack Casement, was another heavy expense: "The country is awfull we haul our water about fifty miles."[74]

The work itself went on at full speed, barely slowed by curses that included grasshopper plagues so dense that the crushed masses of bodies on the tracks afforded no traction and a locomotive's wheels merely spun helplessly.[75] Nor did Durant's constant meddling interfere much, although Jack Casement was constrained to write, "Durant is here trying to hurry things up but he only causes delays"; nor did heavy snows, beginning on September 19, sporadic Indian raids, the sapping effects of the Hells on Wheels, or the frequent excursions foisted on the men at end of track by Nassau Street.[76]

One of these excursions involved a large group of professors of science and engineering from Harvard, Yale, and other prestigious Eastern schools. Their constant questions and requests sorely taxed Dan Casement and sorely vexed Jack, who would have preferred no visitors at all.[77] A second involved Grant's running mate, Schuyler Colfax, who had all but demanded another outing to end of track. Described by a close *friend* as "not of brilliant or showy intellectual qualities, not a genius," the future vice-president did show a certain genius for getting in the way.[78] So did future Speaker of the House, secretary of state, and presidential hopeful James G. Blaine, who, among many others, requested and received open-ended passes for himself and his family and was hardly bashful about using them.[79] In fact, freeloaders had become such a nuisance that Oliver Ames complained to Dodge that summer, "We must make some different plan about free passes or we shall get no room in the cars for anything but dead heads."[80] Snyder, who bore most of the burden of arranging the excursions, of special treatment for individual luminaries, and of the free passes, confessed late in the year, "The excursions this season have interfered with our work very much and have worn me out."[81]

What the erudite professors and Schuyler Colfax had omitted from their itineraries were the Hells on Wheels, which were becoming progressively nastier and more dangerous, the very worst being at Benton, Green River, and Bear River City. The last of these may well have been qualitatively the worst of a bad lot, and it is a pity that no Henry Morton Stanley passed through to adequately describe it. There, in addition to the normal attrition caused by barrooms, open warfare soon erupted among the Union Pacific workers, their merchants-of-mayhem friends, and what passed for a local citizenry.

A tense atmosphere and a growing cemetery had by October made Bear River City locals turn to vigilantism to protect themselves, if not actually clean up the squalid little community. As one source has noted, Bear River City was soon "governed by a vigilance committee that seemed bent upon hanging half the population,"[82] and perhaps shooting the rest. The heavily armed, trigger-happy townspeople just barely kept an unsteady lid on their village for a while, but then the Freeman brothers came to Bear River City and set up shop, their one-ton printing press carried free over the Union Pacific line by Jack Casement's order.[83] Georgians, Leigh and Richmond Freeman, owners and editors of the *Frontier Index,* were unreconstructed Civil War veterans, virulent Southern nationalists, fanatical Democrats, and open racists. Their brief newspaper, published twice a week, was often offensive to Northerners, Republicans, the reading public in general, and humanity at large. In short, a highly volatile ambience now contained an inflammatory rag. The Freeman boys, with their contorted hyperbole, began denouncing Republican candidate Grant as "a whiskey bloated, squaw ravishing adulterer [and] nigger worshipping mogul."[84] The future president was similarly depicted (and Lincoln defiled) in another issue as "the filthy, lecherous carcass of a libertine, seducer and polygamic squaw keeper . . . Booth still lives," railed the Georgians. *"Sic Semper Tyrannis!"*[85] Coming just a few years after the beloved Lincoln's martyrdom, the latter phrases were considered to be in bad taste, even in Bear River City.

to one unlucky man: "Here lyes, Jeemes Engles, hoo was kild by the Shy-An injuns. Juli 1800 and 68. He was a good egg."[92]

Fergusen, whose diary is spare, unimaginative, and often terse, was a man rarely given to passionate expression, yet he gave vent to something like raw hatred for Indians that autumn. In September he wrote that the Indians' day was done:

> Thus no more will resound the wild war whoop—no longer will the fierce flames hiss round the cabin of the pioneer, while his bleeding form and those of his mutilated wife and little ones lie around him. . . . Farewell thou Savage! Your name may still remain, historians and sorcerers may weave a fairy halo around your memory, but education and civilization will be satisfied—you cease to be.[93]

As for the maudlin politicians and Indian apologists back in the Indianless East, Fergusen was even more blunt: "I would that I could witness their destruction . . . I should be content to wrench one of their scalps off for my own gratification."[94]

By late October, when the Casements' men set their seven-and-three-quarters-of-a-mile record for a single day's work, some of the crews were laboring at night by eerie lantern and bonfire light.[95] It was then that Durant, witnessing progress beyond his wildest expectations, cabled Charlie Crocker and offered to wager $10,000 that the Union Pacific's record could not be surpassed. Crocker, whose own men were tracking four miles or better on a good day, and had exceeded six miles once, accepted the bet, bragging that his crews could spike ten miles in a working day. He told Durant that the test would come at a time and place of his own choosing.[96]

With the Union Pacific leaping west, with travelers writing back home about riding on its trains "at the rate of 230 miles a day,"[97] and with its graders working fifty miles west of Promontory Point in plain view of Clement's Celestials, there was a certain optimism among those in the field, despite their chronically overdue pay.[98]

Even the government, eying the Union Pacific with suspicion, could find some solace in the decrease in Indian hostility and the fact that the railroad was charging only 52.5 cents per mile per ton for military freight, when the wagon tariff had been $1.97. That alone would save Washington millions of dollars each year.[99] With Grant and Colfax elected on November 9, certainly things would look up for the company, if only through the medium of a new secretary of the interior after the March 4 inauguration.

Late in the year, with the weather turning vicious again, before settling into winter camps the grading crews west of the Great Salt Lake were recalled for the final push on the line leading into Ogden. Jack and Dan prayed for another thirty days of blizzardless working conditions, while Stanford and his colleagues

The Union Pacific hell-raisers were hardly ideologues, or readers
some of them decided one fair November day to put the Freer
business, perhaps permanently. They may have been a bit out of so
lynching of three of their pals by exasperated local citizens.[86] A r
than two hundred liquor-fueled railroaders, led by hulking "Bear
Smith, and in a foul mood, descended upon the *Frontier Index* offic
mauls, sledgehammers, and ax handles. The Freeman brothers
escape their fury, but their business did not, and was thoroughly

Emerging from the rubble of the newspaper office, the sated wrec
with a host of tight-lipped, hard-eyed vigilantes, armed to the tee
lantes, themselves hardly fans of the Freeman publication, never
their advantage in firepower, and when the smoke cleared, the Uni
at least fifty-three immediate openings on its work crews, and scor
wounded. The bodies were unceremoniously and swiftly heaved
grave, hastily dug and left unmarked. Almost no publicity acc
massacre, which was Wyoming's bloodiest fight not involving In
and Richmond Freeman, with a new press, later resumed their
from much safer Ogden, and Bear River City was described a
shootings as still under harsh, informal law: "If they were not ha
wearing of the green, they were for other offenses."[88]

There was nothing left of the town by 1870, but, ambling wes
Wheels did not end at Bear River City. At Wasatch, the com
terminus, one man counted forty-three graves in the new ceme
of whose inhabitants had stopped breathing from natural causes

Even engineer Arthur Fergusen found time to get shot at de
schedule, often solitary work, and rather puritanical outlook o
corded with just a hint of surprise that one day while dining at a
"quite a number of bullets whistled over my head," and that "th
afternoon, rather, a man was shot through the head and robbed
of money." It was not even safe in the most isolated survey car
14 he scratched in his diary: "While sitting on one of our cots a
a bullet entered the canvas making quite a hole through it and s
side . . . quite a narrow escape."[90] Violence was casual and ofte
wherever the Union Pacific went, and Fergusen laconically enter
one evening, "One man was shot and wounded in the knee and
No news."[91]

At least the Indian threat had abated, if not entirely disappeared
Fergusen, and Dodge still recorded raids and the killing of settler
but there was little to fear, especially after the army evacuate
Trail forts. There were depredations every month except Dec
dead rested where they fell, but the railroad was largely unaffec
stone sighted at this time near North Platte contained a final, sem

were at the same moment all but offering sacrifices to conjure up a stormy Wasatch winter, preferably one with daily snowfall.[100] No matter the various prayers and imprecations, the Casement Army drove forward until grinding to a halt in blinding storms during Christmas week. They had reached Wasatch Town, at mile 966. The Union Pacific had laid 425 miles of rails in 1868, with another hundred miles or more of more or less substantial sidings. It had, however, cost an alleged $56 million to do so, the highest one-year outlay for either company. And, as the November investigation had shown, there were millions more to spend on the part of the line already in operation.[101] As the temperature *inside* the company's ramshackle Wasatch Hotel dipped to 5° below zero and the lubrication used on its newfangled steamshovels and steam-powered pile drivers froze,[102] the Union Pacific hunkered down for the winter a scant sixty-five miles short of Ogden.

12

CARVING THROUGH NEVADA

THE BIG FOUR DIVERSIFY

THE second half of 1868 was kind to the Central Pacific, and its leaders. Poised on Nevada's flat, bleak plains, its Sierra gap at last closed, and with government bonds gushing in at last, the company could make up for lost time in the mountains and race across Nevada to meet the Union Pacific as deep into Utah as luck, the weather, and the Huntington-Browning arrangement would permit. Charlie Crocker had prophesied years before that "luck has a hell of a lot to do with it," and so it was. If luck alone could not give the company a line deep in the Mormon territory, then Huntington would have to do so from Washington. It was perfectly legal (if unproductive of bonds) to grade in the Palisades hundreds of miles ahead of continuous track, but perhaps a vague map filed with the secretary of the interior could hint at a continuity that did not in fact exist. Huntington would see what he could do.

That summer, in addition to Stanford, many of the company's engineers were in Salt Lake City, if only briefly, their presence hinting at a confidence that the Big Four did not unanimously share, and inducing nervousness among the many Union Pacific leaders who also passed through. Consulting engineer George Gray was there, helping to arrange the Mormon labor contract,[1] Clement was in and out to confer with Stanford and rush along supplies to his men in the twisting canyons, Butler Ives and his team of surveyors passed through several times while driving stakes between Humboldt Wells and the Wasatch mountains,[2] and Sam Montague was in town for a while as well. To men laboring in arid Nevada, Salt Lake City looked like a booming, sophisticated metropolis. The Central Pacific's chief engineer met at least once with Durant and probably with Dodge in August, for both of those gentlemen were intensely interested in fixing a meeting point for the rails while the Californians were still deep in Nevada. They continued to seek an end to duplicate work, but the time was not yet ripe for that or any other agreement, and in various meetings the two sets of engineers and their bosses merely exchanged pleasantries and gossiped about Brigham Young and such Mormon practices as plural marriages.[3]

On July 9 the Central Pacific's tracks crossed the Truckee for the first of five times, and the company founded Wadsworth, thirty-five miles beyond Reno, at mile 189. Wadsworth was soon to become a major railroad town, with a hotel and extensive company shops, but for decades its population would not surpass one thousand. It remained for generations a true "company town."[4] It was an excellent staging base, for from Wadsworth, the Celestials had an open avenue, a veritable boulevard, to the Palisades, where their comrades were blasting and chipping a new topography.

Strobridge was keeping about five thousand men on the move in Nevada, 90 percent of them Chinese. There really was no need for more workers on the line. Three thousand were with Clement in the Palisades and another two thousand with the work train, or ahead of it, grading.[5] Not that these workers by any means constituted the Central Pacific's payroll. Several thousand more men were engaged in finishing work in the Sierras and down to the Truckee, about twenty-five hundred worked on the sheds and those "great, gloomy galleries,"[6] hundreds were constructing company buildings from Cisco to Wadsworth, more were quarrying granite to be hauled from the mountains to the Nevada desert, at least a thousand Mormons were doing the Big Four's grading in Utah, six hundred or more men worked in the main company shops in Sacramento, several hundred worked aboard the trains themselves or took tickets, and so on. Charlie Crocker could always find something interesting for any "excess" labor to do, on the Central Pacific, on another of their railroads, in the ice company or in the irrigation business. In early August, in fact, the Big Four expanded their empire once again. They acquired another jewel, from A. A. Cohen, the Oakland Railroad and Ferry Company, anticipating the extension of the Central Pacific from Sacramento to the Bay area.[7]

On August 21, the embryonic town of Brown's, at mile 242, was reached by rails, with no fanfare and no slackening of the pace. Early the next month, consuming a hundred carloads and more of material each day,[8] the trackers laid four miles of rail on several occasions and, at least once, five. When Strobridge learned that the Casements' Irish had recently spiked six miles in one long day, he responded with offers of bonuses and his men did seven. No one on either side was counting the hours of labor. Men worked from sunup to sunset (fourteen to sixteen hours in the summer), and sometimes well beyond, with but a single hour-long lunch break. Many times the work continued until midnight, when a new shift began, in the guttering light of bonfires.[9] Oddly content, if not exhilarated by the challenge, exhausted (but well-compensated) track crews collapsed into their bedrolls too tired to argue, gamble, or fight. While the Casements increased their workweek to seven days, with double pay for Sunday work, Strobridge, even though largely employing "heathens," did not, figuring that a day off each week would keep morale high. And, throughout the fall, the Celestials kept an even pace in track laid with the bogtrotters.[10]

It was the Union Pacific's seven-and-three-quarter-mile-day in late October— unimaginable a few years earlier—that led to the Durant-Crocker wager, and the Californian exhorted his men to beat the rival's record not by yards, but by *miles*. He wanted a ten-mile day, and he assured his workers that they could do it, offering a sizable bonus for success. Durant had insisted on prior notice of the attempt at a new record, so that "impartial" (Union Pacific) witnesses could be present, and Crocker instructed Clement and Strobridge to locate the most level ground on their route, as close to the Great Salt Lake as possible, to lessen the chance that the Union Pacific might set a new record, besting their own.[11] Charlie Crocker was in no rush to do his ten miles, and he now had total faith in his experienced track crews.

While the rails crashed onto the Nevada alkali flats, themselves almost as hard as iron, the Big Four somewhat boyishly continued their shopping spree, buying the charter of the San Francisco Bay Railroad and creating their own new ferry line from Alameda to San Francisco. That fall, they also acquired the Napa Valley Railroad and the California Navigation Company, and began quietly buying into the Stockton & Visalia line, while detailing workers to do the surveys for the San Joaquin Valley Railroad, which they sought to begin constructing at the earliest possible moment. According to Samuel Brannan, who sued them, they were also secretly buying a controlling interest in the Wells, Fargo Company, by now a broadly diversified concern.[12] This all took an enormous amount of money, and even more was needed to hire two thousand new Celestials and one hundred white workers to build the line from Oakland to a junction with the slowly expanding Western Pacific (which was also absorbing labor), twenty-six miles away.[13]

The acquisition of Goat Island, perhaps the most natural Bay area terminus of the Big Four's budding railroad empire, was not progressing as had been hoped. Although Huntington had been able to get a bill introduced in the House by which the government would have donated that preserve to the Central Pacific, it stalled, and while later it did pass in the Senate, the House version was never brought to a vote. Too many congressmen were too skeptical of rail-roads—the Pacific Railroad in particular. Sensing that the Goat Island preserve might never be theirs, the Big Four turned to the California legislature for help in obtaining a logical terminus. With that body they had more luck because, with the legislators in Sacramento, they had more clout. The legislature soon donated to the Central Pacific thirty prime acres on Mission Bay, and, after buying it from Horace Carpentier at a monumental price, five hundred acres of the Oakland waterfront as well. Carpentier, with his new partners Lloyd Tevis and Leland Stanford, controlled the rest of the waterfront through the recently chartered Oakland Water Front Company. The acreage held by that company soared in value after it was publicly known that the Pacific Railroad would use Oakland as its western terminus.[14]

Further, Charlie Crocker, in a new partnership with the ubiquitous Tevis, formed the Pacific Express Company, which promptly obtained a monopoly contract with the Central Pacific for express service.[15] As the Goat Island bill floundered in Congress, the Big Four put all of their hopes for the terminus into the Oakland waterfront, beginning construction there of the immense Oakland Mole (pier) and other extensive bayside facilities.[16] Wasting no time bickering or suing one another, the Big Four (and E. B. Crocker) were busily tracing an octopus on the map of California, and they planned many another tentacle before stopping to rest. In fact, they had grandiose plans to blanket the entire Southwest with their rails.[17]

They certainly were not financing these ventures and the Central Pacific from land-sale revenues, which were almost a standing joke. The company was charging what it considered rock bottom prices $2.50 and up for good farmland, $5 and up for oak timberland, and $10 for fine pine forest land—and finding few takers. This was especially true of Nevada grants, for in that state there were precious few good farming acres along the right-of-way, and no forested land at all. In fact, the Big Four quite probably earned more money from the sale of town lots than they did from other acreage. By 1871, after five years of offering land to the public, the Central Pacific had only been able to dispose of 125,000 acres within California, and those acres were the best its federal grants had to offer. If one estimates a median price of $5 an acre, the total was a mere $625,000, most of which was paid in installments over four years' time—a dribble of cash. The Dutch Flat and Donner Lake Wagon Road produced ten times the annual revenue that land sales provided. Also, from the calculated $625,000 Uncle Mark had to deduct sizable outlays for advertising the land and having it surveyed. The resultant income was, to put it kindly, negligible, although somehow the public has been misled to believe that the Pacific Railroad land grants produced a fabulous sum of money. In Nevada, Central Pacific land sales were at a standstill. In fact, after 1869, the state actually *lost* population, as some of its mines played out, and the company, always desperate for funds, even offered to lease land if no buyers could be found.[18]

At any rate, while land sales stagnated, earnings from traffic on the Central Pacific did not, rising monthly (in July, the net profit was $260,000), while operating expenses held remarkably steady. Still, income was dwarfed by the Big Four's outlays.[19]

Meanwhile, back in Washington, Collis P. Huntington continued to win the heart and mind of Secretary Orville Browning. Thus it was that on October 14, through the medium of Browning's law partner Thomas Ewing, Huntington nonchalantly gave the secretary the essentially blank map of his prospective route to Echo Summit. This map, to the trained or untrained eye, showed only a thin red line, perhaps, but it was a *continuous* thin red line, despite the huge gap in Nevada and Utah between the company's grading parties—a gap of almost three hundred miles.[20] Ewing, who knew instinctively that the Californian's map was spurious, had urged Huntington to wait until October to submit it, for by then Congress would have adjourned for the year and its members would not be lurking around the capital to pry into the matter.[21]

Browning took the map with no protest at all, and wrote Huntington about it on October 20: "I hereby give my consent and approval."[22] Unabashedly, the secretary had, that same day, covered his flanks by discussing the map with the rest of the cabinet. Perhaps even to his surprise, its members expressed no reservations. Perhaps they believed that once officially accepted, the map would inspire the Central Pacific to work throughout the winter, speeding the completion of the Pacific Railroad.[23] Anything to hasten the work.

However, when Huntington visited the secretary a few weeks later, casually inquiring after his $2.4 million in new government bonds, Browning seemed unnaturally cautious, and even evasive. Browning, in fact, even took the map to Attorney General William Evarts for a legal opinion. When that learned lawyer somehow found it "legally sound," Browning carried the map to a full cabinet meeting, where again it was discussed, perused, and approved, with not a single dissenting voice. The map could draw no cries of outrage and was approved by all in the executive branch of government who saw it; but Browning, probably feeling exceptionally vulnerable to the charge of favoritism (who would not, holding a virtually blank map?), delayed authorizing the bonds. Though Huntington cajoled, flattered, and browbeat,* Browning continued to put him off.[25]

Other bonds continued to be issued for continuous trackage, for at the speed the Central Pacific was spiking, twenty-mile sections flashed by with great rapidity, and, at a rate of $32,000 per desert mile, each section brought in $640,000 in government paper and a like amount in company paper, both of which were selling at near par. There were times when an entire section was tracked in a week, and the bond flow was both impressive and very much needed by the Big Four. The Central Pacific was keeping its government commissioners busy in the second half of 1868, and those gentlemen evolved a peculiar, less rigorous inspection system than that practiced on the rival line.

On the Omaha line of the Union Pacific, government commissioners normally

---

*Frankly, he lied, claiming that end of track was seventy-five miles east of its actual location, and that progress was averaging over three miles a day.[24]

inspected the track while seated on the cowcatcher, seeing with their eyes and feeling with their bones the quality of the work, halting the train from time to time to evaluate a bridge or culvert, or to recess to the Lincoln Car, with its fully stocked bar. On the Central Pacific, one commissioner normally stood on the rear platform with a spyglass, scanning the rails, ties, ballast, and grade as the train meandered down the track. Another—in 1868, a Colonel Henley—merely "laid down, on the front of the car, shut his eyes and composed himself to sleep." The logic employed was that if passengers aboard could sleep, the track must be level and well spiked. A report on the method noted that "the Colonel slept profoundly, and did not wake until we overtook the end of the road just 307 miles from Sacramento."[26] The colonel's narcolepsy resulted in another segment of the Central Pacific line gaining approval. The inspection party that discovered only $310,000 in deficiencies along the entire line in December was even less rigorous.

On October 1, Winnemucca, named for a Paiute chief, was tracked at mile 325, and soon workers were erecting a hotel and company shops. Although Winnemucca Lake was merely "another stagnant pond," the tiny town was soon thriving, and served as a stage and freight center for the general Idaho traffic.[27] Within months it boasted a large, white brick brewery and a newspaper; according to one traveler, "The buildings manifest some taste."[28] The "howling wilderness" of Nevada was being tamed like the Sierras before it.

The heat was intense well into the fall that year, and a growing number of men fell victim to the combination of the sun and exertion, their bones joining those of the thousands of draft animals that littered the landscape. Strobridge and Crocker, ignoring the medical effects of the heat but realizing that shifts of twelve hours and longer were debilitating, ordered a schedule by which one shift would work from four in the morning until noon, and another from noon until eight in the evening. That was their concession to the brutal climate, and together with the Sunday day of rest, it helped increase efficiency and the number of rails laid, while decreasing the mortality among the crews.[29]

A PRODUCTIVE, EXPENSIVE YEAR

WITH startling rapidity the tracks thudded down on the hard alkali soil. Carlin was reached—and created—at mile 444, where in early December the completed grading in the Palisades began to reduce work time noticeably, marking more than a hundred miles of construction in just two months' work. And, finally, at year's end, during Christmas week, the trackmen were welcomed at Elko, exactly twenty miles beyond Carlin and almost at the Utah border. There, however, it was necessary to pause, for the winter snows in the Sierras were beginning to cause delays in the supply of basic materials, despite the miles of new snowsheds and galleries.

Central Pacific workers spent much of December erecting the rather ornate Cosmopolitan Hotel in distinctly uncosmopolitan Elko, and the town briefly became the company's only, albeit pale, imitation of its rival's Hells on Wheels. Prior to arriving at Elko, Strobridge, who detested strong drink, had prided himself on (and attributed his progress to) "the absence of the saloon" along his route. In his own quizzical words, "Don't ask me how we kept them out. It has always been a mystery." Not really. The few portable gin mills that had sprung up along the way to service the workers had been "mysteriously" put "out of business" by a person or persons unknown who often toted an ax handle.[30] But at barren Elko, the exuberance of the men prevailed, saloons and knock shops sprang up, and there were wine, women, and opium for all who cared to indulge and could pay the tariff in gold.[31] Stro would later put a stop to public debauchery, but Elko would continue to build a reputation as an "open town" for many decades to come.

Union Pacific superintendent Webster Snyder, who followed developments in the Central Pacific's "camp," kept Dodge well informed of their rival's spectacular progress. The worried general wrote late in the year, "I can see no good ground why the CPRR cannot reach Monument Point by the time we do," even without the Huntington map, and nervously noted, "The Chinamen are moving up in swarms" from California to end of track and beyond.[32] While a year earlier it had looked as if the Union Pacific would cross Utah and penetrate Nevada, it now appeared to Dodge that it would be a major achievement for his company to link up with the Californians anyplace west of Ogden: the tortoise and the hare in railroad garb.

As 1868 ended, the Central Pacific's annual report recorded amazing progress. Some 363 miles of new tracks (plus sidings)—more than triple the track mileage laid from the company's groundbreaking to 1868—had been placed, most of it in the last six months of the year. Now only about three hundred miles separated the two companies' ends of track, and weather, more than human determination, would mandate who would close the gap more swiftly. The new construction had cost the company over $27 million, according to its rather garbled statistics, but this might be a figure based upon par, rather than market values of Central Pacific stocks and bonds. In all, the company had spent nearly $57 million since its creation, and considering that mammoth outflow of money, earnings in 1868 were hardly astronomical, although they were healthy. The company claimed a gross of $2,316,465* and a net of $1,271,700. Operating expenses remained

---

*This figure is suspiciously low. There is great confusion concerning the statistics for 1868. The figure could represent the net and not the gross. Also, the Central Pacific paid no dividends until September 1873, which, while it made the company appear to be honest, certainly did not attract investors.[33]

modest, and most of the debits were due to taxes and interest payments.[34] At year's end almost $25 million in Central Pacific stock was spoken for, but the annual report once again failed to mention that most of this went to the Big Four through their construction company. Meanwhile, admitted debts totaled $37,816,498, about half of which comprised first-mortgage bonds.[35]

In Washington, Collis P. Huntington still awaited the bonds he had cadged with his blank map, and in December had a record thirty-five ships bound for California, laden with perhaps $1 million worth of matériel.[36] In Nevada, Darius Ogden Mills was driving his Virginia & Truckee Railroad north from Virginia City toward Reno, its tortuous twenty-one miles containing "a curvature equal to twenty-two full circles." When the two lines joined, Central Pacific revenues would dramatically improve.[37] The Central Pacific was also on the verge of profiting from a dramatic new tourism industry, which it had almost accidentally created. As the line wound through the Sierras, resort hotels and spas blossomed in the crisp mountain air, especially among the crystal-clear lakes. In 1868 the *Railroad Record* featured a report on "Crystal Lake, with a large hotel near it, where the wealthy Californians resort in the summertime,"[38] and Crofutt's *Great Trans-Continental Railroad Guide* and Bowles's *The Pacific Railroad— Open* touted the glories of scores of other resorts.[39]

With the government inspectors (so far) writing rave reviews of the Central Pacific (reviews soon echoed by private engineers such as E. H. Derby*) the Big Four, although without doubt grossly overextended, were content to face the new year.

*"The road bed of the Central line is wide, and all but thirty-five miles of it appears to be well ballasted with gravel."[40]

13

CROCKER'S WAGER AND THE
GOLDEN SPIKE

THE UNION PACIFIC UNDER FIRE

A S THE year turned, "lager beer and nationalism" ruled in the West, according to a minister who crossed the nation by rail,[1] while in the East, the first national Prohibition party was launched into politics. And, with the first days of the new year, both the Union and Central Pacific came under attack. Combined with a host of other problems, the new assault upon the former nearly ruined it just miles short of its still unspecified stopping point.

The Union Pacific became the target of a congeries of political and financial interests, and when Charles Francis Adams, Jr.,'s article "Railroad Inflation" appeared in the January issue of the highly respected *North American Review,* it convinced many of America's elite that the Crédit Mobilier and the Union Pacific had literally stolen from the public. Ironically, Adams, who blasted away so successfully in this influential forum, would himself in later years serve as president of the Union Pacific.[2] Within days, Congress added to Adams's charges, as a number of congressmen took swipes at the railroad or its erstwhile construction company, which had clearly given so much so fast to so few.[3]

This, however, was but a taste of what was to immediately follow. On the second day of 1869, Durant, through an insultingly terse note, fired engineer Jacob Blickensderfer, friend of Grenville Dodge and hardly a shy or callow fellow. Alleging that his work on the government investigatory commission had left him no time for the Union Pacific, the Doctor simply dumped Blickensderfer, the one man among the inspectors who had kept the report on deficiencies at least somewhat within bounds. Dodge seethed, and told Blickensderfer to ignore his dismissal and continue to work, but the fired engineer talked openly against Durant and the company's management in general, adding substantially to the bombardment of opprobrium raining down on the Union Pacific.[4]

As Blickensderfer was muttering in important places, so was Oliver Ames, who had failed in his ongoing attempts to convince Browning and the president that Huntington's map was fraudulent. On January 8 he wrote his chief engineer that the only remedy now as to "show up" the secretary before Congress as a corrupt tool of the Central Pacific. Ames no longer had any faith in the executive branch (for since Lincoln's death, Congress had essentially run the country, to President Johnson's chagrin). "Our hope is in Congress. The Cabinet will be too deferential, to the head of the Interior Department just now that its corruption is being exposed, and this action of Browning *shows* that the head is corrupt . . . there is a nigger in the woodpile somewhere."[5] Justifiably upset, Ames was singularly naïve concerning what Congress might achieve. He was to get from it something quite different from what he expected.

Corruption there certainly was, but Browning was hardly cornering the market on it. On January 9, Chauncey H. Snow, the apparently bogus Union Pacific commissioner, telegraphed President Johnson. Snow, who had earlier attempted to bilk Dodge of $1,000, bluntly advised the president: "I do not think any more money [or land] should be given to the Union Pacific until it is better constructed and managed better."[6] He followed up this message with an extensive "report" damning the company: "The interests of the country in this railroad have never been properly cared for. They have not been cared for at all!," he concluded.[7] Whoever Snow was, he must have had some influence, for he not only bombarded Johnson personally, but also wrote Grant as soon as the new president had been sworn in. Dodge remembered that Snow, after his frustrated shakedown, had next tried to wangle the major Union Pacific coal contract, to supply the trains with two hundred tons a day. He was, however, outhustled by none other than the good doctor, and therein lies another convoluted yarn that would come back to haunt the Union Pacific. Losing out once more, Snow was enraged, becoming an even more dedicated detractor of the company.[8]

In July 1868 the Union Pacific had signed a contract with Thomas Wardell and C. O. Godfrey* to supply the company with virtually all of its coal, for a period of fifteen years at a set price (beginning at a very high six dollars a ton) that would decrease over time. The railroad company was also to receive from Wardell and Godfrey 25 percent of all money earned from the sale of coal to outside purchasers. In early 1869 Wardell and Godfrey—for a consideration—turned their contract over to the new Wyoming Coal and Mining Company, John Duff, president. Duff, Durant, Oliver Ames, Sidney Dillon, and Charles Lambard

---

*The latter soon dropped out, and the deal became known simply as the "Wardell Contract."

each had 10 percent of the stock, Cornelius Bushnell 5 percent, and Train's in-law J. W. Davis 2 percent, with the remainder spread among other Union Pacific stockholders.[9] Small wonder that Snow was frozen out! The Wyoming Coal and Mining Company, known from the beginning for what it was, cast even darker shadows on the Union Pacific–Crédit Mobilier crowd, and at a critical moment. Later in the year, the always-hostile-to-railroads congressman Jeremiah F. Wilson would embark on another crusade, this one against the coal company, and Oliver Ames, lapsing into his congenitally poor grammar, wrote nervously, "He is bound to break up the Wyoming coal contract [because] he don't think Dodge has been well treated."[10] Snow's condemnatory report, replete with mention of the coal contract, would end up on President Grant's desk on March 5, the first full day of his tenure in the White House.

While all this was unraveling, the Central Pacific, also reeling under some harsh blows, struck out at its rival. There is no doubt that the Union Pacific was playing games in Utah with its "temporary" construction practices. Most troublesome to the Californians was that the Union Pacific's grade path unnecessarily intersected with that of the Central Pacific at five separate points, causing confusion, anger, delays, and, later, potential legal problems.[11] For this and other reasons, Stanford in Salt Lake City urged in January that the Big Four act. With technical details and affidavits from Clement, Ives, and others of the engineering staff, Stanford prepared and sent to Secretary Browning a report and protest, claiming with some truth that the Union Pacific was departing from its government-approved line in Echo and Weber canyons and was grading well within territory delineated in the Central Pacific map on file in Washington.[12] A few days later, on January 19, Stanford wrote President Johnson to assert that the Union Pacific had violated its location lines and was building temporary, rather than finished, trackage. He wrote with feigned indignation, "If the Union Pacific Railroad Company [had been] required to build their road in a substantial manner," as the Central Pacific had always done (!), then the California line would have gotten to Echo Canyon first. Conversely, if the Central Pacific had done "hasty and incomplete construction" like that of its rival, it would be moving so fast it would drive the Golden Spike east of the Wasatch Range.[13]

Thus a steady flow of criticism to Washington continued to drain the company's credibility and sully its reputation in Congress and among investors and banking houses. This is why, when the transcontinental was so patently close to reality, the Union Pacific had to borrow—when it could find money at all—at a staggering 2.5-percent-per-*month* interest.[14] There simply was no faith in the company, no matter where its end of track might be.

Unfortunately for embattled Nassau Street, there was worse to come, for the Union Pacific's *via crucis* was far from over. Jim Fisk was openly warning the financial community that the Union Pacific had been plundered from within and was facing inescapable bankruptcy.[15] Oliver Ames, trying feverishly to shake more capital out of the inner circle, had to admit in late January that the company was $2 million short on immediately due draft notes, with "really nothing to raise the money with,"[16] and Jack Casement, fearing strikes by long-unpaid workers, was writing, "I am afraid the Union Pacific is in a bad way. They owe an awfull amount."[17] Wages owed to the Mormon workers were so late in coming that Durant, Dillon, and a large retinue had to rumble west to Salt Lake City in January to soothe Brigham Young, while Irish and Mormon workers on one tunnel walked off the job in protest, a harbinger of serious labor troubles to come.[18] Since the fall of 1868 the company had been falling farther and farther behind in its obligations to contractors and workers, with brief telegrams like one from C. L. Frost at Salt Lake City ("Send me fifty thousand—50,000—in New York drafts immediately") landing on Nassau Street desks daily.[19]

Then a report by Jesse L. Williams estimating true Union Pacific construction expenses to November 1868 went semipublic, causing a further storm of protest in the already tempestuous capital. Basing his calculations on eleven hundred miles of line, Williams figured that, despite its own figures, the company had spent only $38,824,821, or just $34,977.32 per mile.

Over half of the outlay, according to the commissioner, was verifiable, with concrete items or services publicly contracted for or purchased. Williams calculated the other half with the assistance of a team of reputable civil engineers. In terms of *income*, the company had received a total of $29,504,000 in government bonds.* In addition, company bonds in the same amount, which, Williams calculated, had sold at an average of 92 percent of par,† yielded another $27,143,680. Each mile of track laid, then, resulted in $51,034 in income from bonds. There was, Williams blandly announced, "very ample margin for profit."[20]

Dodge, caught between a finagling Durant and a messianic Commissioner Williams, retorted that the latter had underestimated the cost of materials, especially those purchased during the war; the cost of transportation and labor, especially during the winter months; and, of course, the most recent work, which was the most expensive of all. According to the chief engineer, charged later with defending the company in public, "The actual cash cost of the road when completed . . . was between fifty-four and fifty-five millions of dollars," plus perhaps $20 million more due to heavily discounted government bonds, high interest payments on loans, commissions paid, "the cost of the New York and Boston offices,"‡ "etc."[21] Similarly, when challenged about their own stated construction costs, the Big Four, through Creed Haymund, attacked the government's much lower estimate, claiming with a great deal of truth that those figures "were

*Williams assumed the bonds always sold at par. They did not.
†Actually, this figure is low. They rarely sold below 94 percent.
‡No small item, given Durant's penchant for luxury.

not made in the storms of the Sierra nor on the desert wastes of Nevada and Utah."[22] It is worth noting that neither Williams (oddly) nor Dodge (understandably) mentioned the government land grants. Considerable acreage had by this time been sold, mostly in Nebraska, as the farming frontier swept forward.[23]

Whatever the case, Williams's figures clearly did the Union Pacific no good, and, with the commissioner's estimates soon common knowledge, Secretary Browning finally acceded to the Ames brothers' demands and on January 14 ordered the same commission that had inspected the Union Pacific to examine the Central Pacific. Huntington pointed out that, since Blickensderfer was a Union Pacific engineer, the Central Pacific should have a man of its own on the inspection team. He managed to get Lewis Clement named as its fourth member,[24] but only after he and the entire California congressional delegation had stormed into Browning's office and demanded it.[25]

It was in the field, however, that things were looking especially bleak for the Union Pacific.

PLUNDERING *OUTSIDE* THE BOARDROOMS

———

J ANUARY in the Wasatch Range was not cooperating with the Casements. Blizzards swept out of Canada and down the narrow valleys in rapid succession, and drifting snow seriously delayed the movement of materials. Had the company not erected some twenty-five miles of tall snow fences the previous year, the delays would have been crippling.[26] The weather was so horrendous that work had to be halted entirely for days on end, and when laboring, the men's cumbersome overcoats slowed their pace and efficiency.[27] One can hardly criticize the normally austere Casements for telegraphing an order for five gallons of "the best whiskey" on January 28, along with five more of the "best Sherry wine," and two demijohns of other strong spirits. A week later, as an afterthought, they ordered via express, "two corkscrews" as well.[28]

It was the company's poor luck that it had to face its worst engineering problems in its last months of construction, and the Celestials' good fortune that they could chant atonally as they worked across a still largely open plain. On New Year's day, not only were three of the Union Pacific's tunnels unpierced, but they were also untracked, and, trying Dodge's soul and spirit, were thirty-one crossings of Echo Creek, with some of Boomer's most delicate bridgework, as well as the Big Trestle over a gorge west of Ogden, one of the company's largest and most difficult.

On January 3 the headings met at Echo Tunnel, but alas, it would not be finished, timbered, and tracked for three more months, with an expenditure of 1,064 barrels of blasting powder and an unknown amount of nitroglycerin.[29] The other two tunnels would be pierced only after the last spike had been driven, and recourse had to be made to roller-coaster detour tracks until summer— detours that Huntington denounced as violations of the regulation concerning "continuous tracks."[30]

Webster Snyder was frantic by late January, with the snow, the inherent defects in jury-rigged construction, and frequent supply shortages slowing him down. On February 3 he wrote Dodge that the tracks in the Wasatch were in such poor condition that trains could not exceed six miles an hour, with four miles an hour more common. This was due to workmen having laid much track that fall on deep frost, which, as time went by, made the rails buckle, heave, and shift dangerously.[31] As if to prove Snyder correct, a number of expensive, time-consuming accidents, mostly derailments, slowed work even more.

If Bissell in 1865 had complained about "bare-faced cheating" in the early stages of the Platte Valley work, Webster Snyder harped about massive theft and cheating in Utah. He wrote the chief engineer that the situation was deteri- orating well beyond the critical point: "Six months more such plundering as we now have in the Construction Department will kill the institution so dead that no set of men can save it from bankruptcy."[32] It seemed to Snyder that every- body, from tie contractors to common workers, was out to make money on the side before the line was completed and the opportunity lost. Dodge himself was later to admit, "I never saw such needless waste in building railroads" than he found in the Wasatch, where contractors (and Durant) commonly ordered far more ties or trestles than were needed, pocketing kickbacks from grateful suppliers. Much of the theft and waste must have been due, at least in part, to the company's failure to pay its men on time.[33]

On January 15 the tracks, which were inching along, entered tiny Echo City, eight miles from the mouth of Echo Canyon; but just at this point work halted entirely as the weather grew insufferable. It is generally agreed that early 1869 witnessed the worst weather on record in the Wasatch Range. On February 17 a series of mighty blizzards screamed in, locking the company in the Wasatch and in the Black Hills as well. The Big Four's prayers were being heard. Dodge himself was frustratingly snowed in for several weeks at Laramie, with ten feet of level snow on the westward tracks and drifts of forty feet or more. Even ten large snowplows and the labor of hundreds of men could not clear the cuts enough for construction trains to move. "I have seen a cut fill up in two hours which took 100 men 10 hours to shovel out," wrote the distraught chief engi- neer. His only consolation as he cooled his heels in Laramie was news of a cholera outbreak among the Central Pacific's track crews.[34]

For a stretch of some ninety miles, from Rawlins to Laramie, the Union Pacific line was broken for three full weeks by the weather, and in the Wasatch for shorter periods. Henceforth, every westbound train was provided with "a box car with a stove in it and loaded with provisions," to be used if stranded between stations.[35] The precaution proved to be a wise one. On March 8, Jack Casement wrote his wife from Echo City that the road was still blocked by snow east of Ogden, and where the snow was not a problem, the thaw was, for "this whole country is one vast mud hole," and wagon transportation to the advanced grading crews had become all but impossible.[36]

Under these harsh conditions, in blinding snowstorms, work began on the Big Trestle in February, halting from time to time for want of material. Ironically, barely a hundred yards away, in the most ostentatious act of duplicate work and expense, hundreds of Chinese were creating the Big Fill, a long and costly earthen platform across the same gorge. While the Big Trestle was being pounded together from hundreds of thousands of board feet of thick timber, more than ten thousand cubic yards of earth and stone were being packed and tamped into the Central Pacific's Big Fill.

COLLIS GETS HIS BONDS

NOT that things were going all that smoothly for the Central Pacific as 1869 began. On November 3, 1868, Republican Ulysses S. Grant had been elected president. Though all of the Big Four were stalwart Republicans, they worried a great deal over what the new president might do when he was inaugurated in early March. After all, he was a close friend of Grenville Dodge and had used all his influence and military connections to protect the Union Pacific. At the very least he would name a new cabinet and Browning would be out, and it would be fanciful to think that his successor would be as susceptible to pressure and persuasion as Huntington's "friend" had been.

Although weather on the Nevada-Utah border was not unduly harsh, conditions in the Sierras were another matter, and all Central Pacific equipment, gear, and even food had to pass through the mountains, hundreds of miles west of end of track. The Sierra winter of 1868–69 was every bit as severe as the previous two had been, with extremely heavy snowfall, avalanches, and rockslides. While the snowsheds and galleries held up superbly, unprotected track was torn away in some areas, or warped out of usable alignment. Wrecks consequently had become distressingly common in the white-draped mountains, and both tracks and cars were costly, and time-consuming to repair. In a single night in February, a monster storm threw thirty inches of new snow on the old in the High Sierras and some of the higher cuts became clogged with forty feet of dense snow.[37]

There was also trouble, throughout the far West, with the Chinese. Dodge's spies had been correct when they had reported that Asiatic cholera (*colera morbis*) had struck the Central Pacific's work force, without respect to diet or race, killing about one third of those it infected (it was also killing tens of thousands in Paraguay). It hit the gangs at end of track most severely, and, as Dodge's informants reported, the disease for a time greatly reduced the company's manpower where it was most needed.[38]

Also, racism spread beyond the Union Pacific's crews who worked within sight of the Celestial graders. Typical of a spate of anti-Chinese pogroms was an incident at Unionville, Nevada, not far from the Central Pacific line. A telegram sent from that town to Governor Henry G. Blasdell described the situation as of January 10:

> Our town is under control of a mob. The miners league organized at seven of this Friday morning about fifty—50—strong arrived with broad axes, pistols, shot guns and Henry rifles paraded through the town with American flag fife and drum, went to all houses inhabited by Chinamen, compelled the inmates some twenty—20—in number at the peril of their lives to pack up and get into a big wagon provided by the mob and then hauled them down to Mill City on the railroad twenty—20—miles distant. Many of the Chinamen were taken out of houses built and owned by themselves on their own ground.

The Chinese wanted to return despite being unwelcome, but the sheriff of Unionville was tactfully absent and his deputy overcome by lassitude. John C. Fall, who sent the telegram, requested that the governor send the state militia.[39] The situation was soon in hand, but outbreaks of violence continued elsewhere and demoralized the Central Pacific Celestials, while frightening the Big Four and Strobridge.

It did not help matters that the Chinese in San Francisco and along the railroad line began to indulge in violence themselves, and even full-fledged Tong wars. One such war erupted between the Teng Wo and See Yup "factions" (or companies) at end of track, and hundreds of Celestials, "armed with every conceivable weapon," were involved. "Spades were handled, and crowbars, spikes, picks and infernal machines . . . several shots were fired," and at least one man was killed before Strobridge, his one eye ablaze and accompanied by some of his more massive white workers, waded into the melee. With the help of some respected headmen, he soon calmed the situation and disarmed the rowdies.[40] The violence between white and yellow and yellow and yellow did not slow the work appreciably, but it threatened to, and anti-Chinese vitriol spewed from the press—"they are but pioneers or advance guard of the masses to come," a "distinct, indigestible mass in the community," sent by "the grand slave-masters of the Pacific, called the Chinese Six Companies"—merely made a tense situation worse.[41]

The press was complaining about more than the Central Pacific's Orientals that winter; it also found space for a vicious frontal assault on the company itself. An anonymous article, datelined "Nevada, January 20, 1869," was as violently anti–Central Pacific (and as off base) as had been tales of the Dutch Flat Swindle in the past. Printed in the *San Francisco Herald* on January 22, the article was soon reprinted across the nation, even in reputable, specialized railroad journals, which should have known better.[42]

Claiming that the California press, allegedly in the Big Four's pocket (!), would never print anything negative about the Central Pacific no matter how true it might be, the author, who admitted that he could not "speak knowingly of more than two hundred miles of road, running east from Reno," attacked virtually every aspect of the railroad. "This railroad not only charges twice the freight charged by any other company in the whole land, but it is the *very worst constructed,* and I think the worst managed," he wrote, "for they have built the worst that could be constructed and be a railroad at all." Unwittingly proving that he knew nothing about the line, the anonymous sniper wrote of senseless grades of 116 feet in the Humboldt Valley—there was no grade there one third that steep—and chided the Central Pacific: "Not the least effort has been made to ballast the road . . . and I pledge you my word that a good soaking rain will make miles and miles of the road-bed run like wet soap." Further, "The management of the rolling stock is only equalled by the road itself" in lack of quality; "not one train in ten arrives at this place on time," while none could exceed fourteen miles an hour because of the shoddy and dangerous construction. "The people have paid for a first-class road," he shrilled, "and, owing to the silence of the Pacific Coast press, they think they have got it; but it is perfectly notorious along the line of the road this side of Reno, that it is built just as cheap as it can be got together . . . let us see if Congress can not be forced by the people, who are being so outrageously swindled, to cause a thorough ripping up of this whole business."[43] Although totally incorrect, this article helped stoke the fires of "reform" in Congress, spurring further investigations.

While Strobridge's men struggled with cholera, racism, and opprobrium, Collis Huntington was earning his putative twenty-thousand-dollar salary in Washington, as was General Franchot. On January 12, Secretary Browning appointed three commissioners to travel to Utah, inspect the most recent portions (and locations) of both lines, and decide finally the exact location where both should join.[44] With that move under way, it was more important than ever for Huntington to loosen the government's grip on the "blank map bonds," so that whatever the secretary's commission might announce about line, location, or juncture, the securities would be in Central Pacific's hands. At the moment the bonds, approved by Browning, the cabinet as a whole, and the attorney general, were in the safe of Secretary of the Treasury Hugh McCulloch, a man thought to be partial to the Union Pacific. So the Californian put on the pressure, wherever and whenever he could: "I got two cabinet meetings in one week outside of the regular day," he recalled, while he was at the same time wearing down the treasury secretary. "I went in there every day and asked him to give me the bonds."[45] It appeared, however, that McCulloch preferred to await the new Grant administration, which Huntington feared would be predisposed toward the Union Pacific. Still, Huntington huckstered and badgered the seemingly implacable secretary.

McCulloch, although perhaps an advocate of the Union Pacific, was receiving other intense visitors that winter, for not only Huntington and Franchot were on the prowl. Grenville Dodge was learning the dimensions of Washington as surely as he knew those of a ridgeline or tunnel bore. To protect the interests of the company, and deny the bonds to Huntington, he had hired two "illustrious mercenaries." These men were Caleb Cushing and William Evarts. Cushing was a former United States attorney general, and Evarts, a future secretary of state, had recently been named attorney general, and was, as one might suspect, an especially influential figure.[46] Moreover, also in Dodge's corner—at least so he believed—was Thomas Ewing, former secretary of both the interior and the treasury, and currently Secretary Browning's law partner. Ewing was playing both sides of the railroad, and, according to Oliver Ames, was paid $10,000 in January for his services to the Union Pacific.[47]

Dodge was learning, but time was fast running out. Secretary Browning in February ordered the Union Pacific to halt construction and all further work past Echo Summit, on the basis of the Central Pacific's "red-line map,"[48] and on March 1, just three days before Grant's inauguration, the cabinet's other members (including Evarts) unanimously directed McCulloch to release the bonds to Huntington posthaste.[49] The secretary, however, still hesitated, and the cabinet at last resolved the issue on March 3, at its last official session. That day McCulloch caved in and ordered Treasury officials to prepare bonds for the Central Pacific to Monument Point, with, for some unstated reason, the government retaining $1 million of the $2.4 million due.[50] It would appear that Huntington one last time exercised his unexcelled powers of persuasion, however, for he distinctly remembered that "a little after eight o'clock I went out and found the bonds in my room. There were $2,400,000 odd," in an untidy package on his bed.[51] Just hours before the new administration cleaned house, Huntington had triumphed, and he knew very well that the bonds, once issued, were unlikely to be taken away.

GRANT ORDERS A SITE CHOSEN

O N MARCH 4, Ulysses Grant was sworn in as president. Before the sun had set he ordered a freeze on further bond payments to either company until both had been thoroughly investigated once more. It was too late. The Central Pacific had its coveted bonds, while the Union Pacific, having ignored Browning's order to halt construction, was working on the disputed mileage furiously.[52]

Grant, personal friend of Grenville Dodge, and certainly a friend of the *Pacific* Railroad, was no enemy of the Central Pacific, nor of the Big Four. A righteous man of simple honesty, he was perturbed mightily by the case of the missing (purloined?) bonds, and deeply troubled by rumors of scandal and poor construction he had been hearing for months. He changed not only the cabinet, but replaced all government commissioners and directors serving with both companies.[53] He then made it clear that both companies must reach an agreement on the ultimate point of union for the rails, notwithstanding the commission sent west by Browning to do just that.[54] If they could not decide where to meet, he would mandate the spot himself.

To this end, Dodge and Huntington, with the approval of both companies' leadership, met in Washington. They were both unwilling to have Grant set the site for the last spike, and both were eager to staunch the flow of cash for the duplicate grading, bridging, and filling then going on. There is no question that the Californian held the upper hand. He not only held the bonds, but the bonds covered a portion of the line the Union Pacific was at that moment building. It would appear to outsiders that the Union Pacific was, at its own expense, building a part of the Central Pacific railroad! One had the bonds, the other had the track. Also, it was common knowledge that the Union Pacific was penniless, that its workers were beginning to strike and riot, and that Jim Fisk's suit might well cause its collapse.

On April 8 the two strong-willed men (plus Franchot and a number of Union Pacific directors)[55] met at the house of Massachusetts congressman Samuel Hooper. Their after-dinner negotiating session—about which neither ever spoke or wrote—lasted through the night and was resumed the next day. From it came the compromise "Treaty of Hooper's House," which resolved the most pressing questions.[56]

The two railroads would meet and connect at stark and treeless Promontory Point, overlooking the north shore of the Great Salt Lake, 690 miles from Sacramento, 1,084 miles from Omaha (some say 1,086, for a symbolic total of

1,776). The Central Pacific would permit the Union Pacific to build to Promontory over 47.5 miles of land whose bonds Huntington had collected, and, when the line was complete, the Big Four would buy those same miles of track for $4 million ($84,210.53 per mile). Also, the Central Pacific was to lease the five miles between the 47.5 miles it was to buy and Ogden for a period of 999 years. The five miles could also have been purchased, but Huntington had the rather myopic idea that a new, important, non-Mormon metropolis could and would be created just five miles north of Ogden. It was not to be.[57]

The $4 million would go far toward easing the financial atrophy of the Union Pacific, and that purchase, plus the leased miles, would expand the Californians' road to the area's only genuine settlement. All duplicate work was to cease immediately, and telegrams to this effect were sparked off to ends of track, to everyone's relief. The Treaty of Hooper's House was probably the only possible solution to the problems confronting both companies, and Dodge and Huntington parted with the shared hope that it would get both Congress and the president off the railroads' backs.[58]

Congress *was* pleased by the arrangement, because a potential investigation of the duplicate work—there had been almost one hundred miles of redundant grading, bridging, and filling—was on its agenda. Both houses heartily endorsed the compromise, and on April 10, with uncommon speed, officially proclaimed Promontory Point the juncture site. The only reservations Congress expressed concerned the purchase of the 47.5 miles of future track by the Central Pacific. It found the negotiated price too high. So a committee was appointed to study the issue and recommend a more realistic price.[59] Huntington, never bashful, later boasted, "If I had not paid the Union Pacific four millions they would have broke just about the time they got" to Promontory Point.[60] The sum actually paid was considerably less.

Congress's decision to "study" the price of the 47.5 miles was a rude blow to the Union Pacific leadership. They needed the Californians' cash, and they needed it now. On May 10, the day the Golden Spike was hammered into place, Oliver Ames wrote questioningly to Dodge: "How much will they owe us on the road west of Ogden?" He urged his chief engineer to escalate the cost per mile as much as possible to influence the committee's final award: "You must make it cost $60,000 per mile if possible," for the company desperately needed close to $3 million.[61] Despite the fact that the miles in question were relatively easy ones to construct, Dodge managed to do just what Ames had requested; but it was not until the end of the year (far too late to alleviate the crisis) that the committee awarded the Union Pacific $2,840,000, or $59,789.47 per mile. The company received its money within weeks of the award, but while the committee had been studying sums and the company's workers went virtually unpaid through the second half of the year, Nassau Street had to grapple with Jim Fisk, Jr.

FISK, BOSS TWEED, AND A CROOKED JUDGE

F OR at least a year now, financier Jim Fisk had been attempting to purchase
a major interest in the Union Pacific, to extort a sizable sum from that
company, or sue the company for every penny it had. Or all three. A born
speculator and peculator with an infamous reputation, Fisk could and did
cost the Union Pacific dearly. Cornelius Bushnell, who thought he could buy Fisk
off for $50,000, had underestimated the man, for this was the financial pirate who
had wrenched control (with the aid of New York's archetype of corruption,
"Boss" William Marcy Tweed) of the Erie Railroad from the cold and ruthless
grip of Cornelius Vanderbilt and the equally granite-eyed Daniel Drew. He *might*
indeed have demanded money from the company to end his harassment of it,
but $50,000 was not an impressive sum to such a man. Whatever he was
eventually offered he spurned,* and in March his suit began tying up company
officials in earnest in the New York courts he knew and loved so well. On the
tenth of that month, thanks to the notoriously boodle-collecting New York judge
George C. Barnard, warrants were issued for all of the Union Pacific's directors,
and eager deputies fanned out over the metropolis, dispersing the company's
stockholders at their annual meeting. Oliver Ames himself was caught in the
dragnet and had to post a twenty-thousand-dollar bond to be set free.[63] The
directors did manage to meet the following day, and they overwhelmingly voted
to strip Durant of his powers as general agent, immediately wiring Dodge and
Snyder to that effect.[64]

A week later, the venal Judge Barnard declared the Crédit Mobilier in receiv-
ership on the most diaphanous grounds (causing its bonds to crash to 65 percent
of par), and appointed The "Boss's" son William Marcy Tweed, Jr., as receiver,
with orders to sequester the company's books and all other records. Fisk had
friends indeed, something the Union Pacific did not have. On March 30, the
company's Nassau Street headquarters were surrounded by sheriffs and deputies, and on April 2 Tweed and a "posse" of beefy officers literally broke into
the Crédit Mobilier's suites and went to work on the massive safe there. As they
were working away with sledgehammers and cold chisels, Durant's personal
lawyer, Charles Tracy, filed a million-dollar lawsuit against them for criminal
trespass.

When the safe at last groaned open, Tweed was grim with disappointment,
for there was little of interest or value within, save for wads of Union Pacific

---

*There is some indication that he *was* given Bushnell's suggested $50,000 to drop his claims, and that
he reneged.[62]

first-mortgage bonds and others based upon land-grant acreage. Nowhere was there incriminating evidence or the company's books, which were, by nature, incriminating. Durant, tipped off by a sympathetic government director, had cleaned out the safe of important papers a week or so earlier. He probably realized that he was about to be ousted from his positions of power in the Union Pacific and wanted to have ammunition for a protracted fight (or blackmail).[65]

Fisk's suit ground on in the courts, but without any truly damning evidence it was inconclusive, merely keeping the Union Pacific and Crédit Mobilier in the glare of media spotlights. Fisk busied himself during the court proceedings by joining Daniel Drew and Jay Gould in a successful plot to raise the price of gold, making another financial killing. He made a host of enemies in doing so, however, and when in 1871 he repudiated a number of contracts, he was all but ejected from the financial community. He never did get a chance to savor the profits he had made from gold, for in January 1872, a disillusioned former partner, Edward S. Stokes, shot him to death for having alienated the affections of his wife. Following the shooting, which was one of the media events of the century, the courts awarded Fisk's widow a token $20,000, plus the sub-par market price of her husband's six uncontested shares of Union Pacific stock.[66] While the $20,000 was indeed a token settlement of the Fisk suit, it did seem to indicate that, even in the absence of hard proof, the court found the railroad company and Crédit Mobilier in the wrong, and was interpreted that way in the press.

The Fisk imbroglio cost the Union Pacific several million dollars through falling bond prices, about $400,000 worth of bonds that disappeared from the Crédit Mobilier safe, and an unknown sum through the panic sale of land-grant bonds at bargain prices. It also cost a great deal in legal fees and had given the company yet another black eye in the media and in Congress, despite a reasoned and rational defense of the company by Oakes Ames that appeared in the *New York Times*. Properly leery of the Tweeds, Judge Barnard, and Fisk, the Union Pacific board asked for and received permission to move their headquarters from New York to Boston that April.[67]

While all this was transpiring, President Grant received from Congress one of the few mandates they would give him in all his eight years in the White House. Tendered April 9, signed by the president the next day, the act empowered and directed Grant to appoint "five eminent citizens" to carefully examine both Pacific railroads and determine precisely how much money each would have to spend to raise its road to first-class status. The president was also to withhold government bonds and other aid sufficient to rectify the deficiencies found. Finally, the attorney general was required to investigate both companies for fraud, illegal dividends (neither company had yet paid any), and any other criminal irregularities.[68] This sounded like the death knell of the Union Pacific and a thoroughly nasty inconvenience for the Big Four, although it turned out to be neither.

The Union Pacific, beset by Fisk, Henry McComb, public antipathy, falling bond prices, a lack of stock sales, debts of some $14 million, interest payments running over $500,000 each month, and thousands of unpaid, restive workers, appeared closer to utter collapse than ever.*[69] Poor Webster Snyder and the Casements, on the "sharp end," were feeling the repercussions first-hand. General Jack wrote from Echo City in early April:

> I am still here on a grid iron. Things look awfull bad and I can't hear a word from New York. I can close up the work now and have some money left if the banks don't burst, we owe our men about $90,000, and have $160,000 in the banks at Omaha and Cheyenne. The banks are loaded with UPRR paper and if the company don't send some money here soon they will burst up the whole country. The company owe us over $100,000 . . . I have telegraphed Dillon twice but got no answer . . . the men on many of the jobs are striking.[71]

Just three days later he narrowly averted a major strike by his track crews by paying the men part of what they were owed out of his own and Dan's pockets. Still, the workers, many unpaid for three months, were surly, and General Jack feared they might tear up the roadway. Just a few weeks later, Sidney Dillon wired William Glidden in something of a panic: "We must have $500,000 to pay contractors' men or road can not run,"[72] while bridge builder Boomer wrote Sam Reed, pleading, "Could you send me $30,000. I beg you will do so."[73]

As Durant and John Duff headed west for the joining of the rails at Promontory Point, the labor problem was driven home to the Doctor in a way that telegrams from Jack Casement and others at end of track could never have done. At Piedmont, a tiny settlement with half a dozen buildings and a sidetrack at mile 916 (almost at the Utah border), trouble was brewing. A mob of armed tie cutters employed by James W. Davis stopped the official train, uncoupled the fancy officers' car, and sent the locomotive up the line. Durant's car was shunted to the sidetrack, and there at Piedmont he was confronted with what might have passed for a lynch mob. The workers demanded hundreds of thousands of dollars of long-overdue pay, and threatened to detain both the Doctor and Duff until the money was produced.†

The somewhat ruffled "bird of striking plumage" carefully, diplomatically, explained to the "kidnappers" that it might take days, even weeks, to get the money to Piedmont, and even more carefully refrained from mentioning that, as far as he knew, even the company vaults did not contain that much cash. To satisfy the workers, he telegraphed Ames in Boston, explaining the situation and

---

*While the Central Pacific was healthier, Huntington could not at the moment hawk its stock even for 5 percent of par.[70]

†One source notes that the men demanded $200,000, but most others claim that the sum was closer to $500,000, or even more.[74]

instructing him to send the money without delay. Ames, with no immediate access to such a sum, in turn wired Dodge, then at Salt Lake City, telling him to seek help from the army rather than the banks. Dodge then got on the wire himself, describing the problem to Dillon, and also wiring the commander of Fort Bridger, a few miles from Piedmont, to send a company of infantry to the rescue. Dillon himself then took to the telegraph key, countermanding Dodge, and ordered the loaded troop train *not* to stop at Piedmont, but to continue on down the line.[75] This enraged Dodge and Oliver Ames, both of whom later suspected that the Doctor (with Dillon's connivance) had planned the whole charade to force the company to pay for ties that Webster Snyder had recently decided were in excess of the number needed and that he accordingly had refused to buy.[76] It may well be that Durant was receiving a substantial kickback from Davis (Train's brother-in-law), for as Oliver had written him in January, the company was disturbed that "ties are said to cost $4 each laid on the track, when contract price is but one dollar."[77]

In any case, the money was somehow finessed out of Laramie and Cheyenne banks in sufficient amounts to mollify the tie cutters, who released their distinguished "guests" after forty-eight hours. This incident was thoroughly hushed up, and on March 7, despite labor problems and impending financial collapse, Union Pacific spikers emerged from Weber Canyon and hammered their way into Ogden, at mile 1,028.

Prim little Ogden greeted the rails officially the following day with some trepidation but as much gaiety as the Mormons could summon up, considering that the town's twenty-five hundred citizens (with their single, small hotel, two restaurants, and no saloon) were outnumbered by Casement's sweating, cursing "gentiles."[78] As Ogden's brass band bid a nervous welcome, Brigham Young was chartering the Utah Central Railroad Company, which he would use to build the thirty-six-mile Salt Lake City to Ogden line.*[79]

The workers hardly slowed to sample the "delights" of Ogden—much to the delight of its inhabitants—but plunged onward, on April 7 reaching the site of Corinne, twenty-seven miles to the northwest. At mile 1,056, Corinne was to be the first non-Mormon settlement in Utah and, for the record, the last, lusty Hell on Wheels. Bisected not only by Union Pacific tracks but also by the duplicate grading of the Central Pacific, Corinne would always be suspect—and avoided—by the Mormons, and its newspaper, the territory's only gentile periodical, was long "a perfect thorn in the side of the Mormons."[81]

Salt Lake City's own *Deseret Evening News* delighted in picking on rowdy Corinne, noting, "The place is fast becoming civilized, several men having been killed there already, the last one found in the river with four bullet holes through him and his head badly mangled."[82] The same newspaper wrote of a blasting

*Ground was broken on May 17. In 1872 Young sold the short branch line to the Central Pacific.[80]

accident that befell a four-man Union Pacific crew, one of whom "was blown two or three hundred feet in the air, breaking every bone in his body, the other three were terribly burnt and wounded with flying stones." With a certain sadistic humor the reportage continued: "Fun is fun, but standing astraddle of four or five kegs of powder and working it into the rocks with a crow bar" was *not* a good way for an intelligent man to make a living.[83]

After the April 10 announcement that Promontory Point would be the site of the joining of the rails, the Union Pacific slackened its pace and began releasing some of its now unnecessary labor. After all, Promontory was now only twenty-eight miles in the distance.

CHARLIE CROCKER WINS HIS BET

THE Central Pacific was remarkably tranquil that winter and spring—even confident. Its crews moved into Utah practically at a trot, rails magically appearing behind them. As a reporter described the scene, "Every thirty seconds came that brave 'down,' 'down' on either side of the track. They were the pendulum beats of a mighty era."[84] Thousands of Chinese were thrown forward to the Promontory Point area and beyond, and Lewis Clement oversaw a gang of five hundred men at the Big Fill, alongside the suspiciously fragile-looking Big Trestle that Seymour—in Dodge's absence—had ordered thrown across the gorge. The Big Fill, over five hundred feet long and one hundred seventy feet high, was the company's biggest single engineering feat accomplished since the men had emerged from the Sierras, and it consumed more than a month of concentrated, round-the-clock labor.[85]

As the cadenced Celestials drew closer to Promontory, more and more emigrants, not content to await the ceremonial joining of the rails, streamed across the narrowing gap between the two ends of track; they found the wagon ride a minor inconvenience, for they now considered themselves "through" passengers.[86] The Big Four, as was their habit, were still lavishing money on other projects. They agreed to buy A. A. Cohen's San Francisco & Alameda Railroad in April, began negotiations to acquire the Los Angeles & San Pedro Railroad, drew up papers for the Southern Pacific to absorb most of their lines (*the* "Octopus"), and pushed construction toward Oakland with every Chinese they could hire or spare from the Central Pacific.*[87] When one considers that in their

---

*All this with very few dollars in the treasury. In fact, on December 4, 1868, original founder Lucius Booth was unable to sell his shares in the company even when asking only 44 percent of par.[88]

last thirteen months (to May 10) the Big Four's men had built 549 miles of new tracks, some 120 miles of sidings, and a total of 615 miles of grades, the magnitude of the achievement is readily apparent.[89] They were also spending vast sums on rolling stock, and not always of the spartan variety. Leland Stanford had become enamored of the patented Palace Car, each priced at $20,000 and more and described by another devotee as "cheap at the price." The Palace Car was lauded by Charles Godfrey Leland, who traveled in one whenever he could;

> The seats, the sides of the car and the ceiling are exquisitely adorned in *marquetrie* or inlaid woods, while the gilded glass frames, in ormolu, and the general tone of color, are truly artistic. It is heated by a separate furnace beneath, and its lounges and mirrors, with every other luxury, make it in fact a rolling palace.[90]

Stanford would take his finest Palace Car to the Promontory Point ceremonies, as Durant would use his "Pullman's Best," but, unfortunately, neither would be able to flaunt his car's opulence.

Charlie Crocker had been biding his time. He still had a wager of $10,000 to contend with, and although he had agreed to the bet with Durant in October 1868, he was awaiting flat, relatively curveless ground and a smooth Mormon grade. As additional insurance, he wanted his end of track after the "ten-mile day" to be so close to that of the Union Pacific that Durant would have no opportunity to break the new record with an eleven-mile extravaganza of his own.

While Crocker had planned to win his wager on April 27, supply problems forced him to wait until the twenty-eighth. That day, before dawn, with stockpiles of equipment in place, Crocker and Strobridge selected the various teams (almost all their men volunteered) for the heroic work, promising them four days' wages in return for success. There were almost 5,000 men involved, each with his specialized job, but only 850 would do the actual construction. There were men detailed specifically to unload rails, others to place ties, more to push the handcars to end of track, teams to unload these, two eight-man teams of rail men (muscular Irishmen all), 400 Chinese tampers, 20 spikers, and so on. Backup, or relief teams were available for each operation, and large numbers of the fittest draft animals were on hand.[91] Track boss Henry Minkler would prowl the work, relieving the exhausted, and shouting orders, encouragement, and monosyllabic invective, as the occasion demanded. Crocker and Strobridge were there, as was Stanford and Sam Montague, as well as guest witnesses Sam Reed, Seymour, and both Casements, and a knot of interested army officers from nearby garrisons.[92]

Precisely at dawn, a whistle shrilled and Crocker's battalions leaped into action in the damp, chill grayness. "In eight minutes, with a noise like a bombardment," the first sixteen cars of iron were unloaded by the fragile-looking Chinese;[93] the material was carefully thrown on handcars, which in minutes, pulled by both Celestials and horses, were churning down the track to the waiting work crews. Each handcar carried sixteen rails, a keg each of bolts and spikes, and the correct number of fishplates. As the Chinese atop each car threw down the rails with concussive thumps, other Chinese doled out bolts and spikes along the roadbed and threw down fishplates every ten yards, within reach of the waiting workers.

A similar process was taking place with the tie crews, who worked some hundred yards ahead of the trackers. The ironmen, four of them working each side of the roadbed, grasped the six-hundred-pound rail with tongs, two men at each end, lurched to the exact spot, jolted it down within inches of the previously placed rail, and went back for another. Then came the rail straighteners, who perfectly fitted the rails end to end and aligned them on the ties, followed closely by the levelers, who adjusted the rails' height to gain a smooth road, and then the sweat-streaming spikers, twenty in number. Each spiker drove only one specific spike in each rail, stooping to retrieve his next spike from those just strewn along the roadbed. Ten mighty blows with the maul and the spike was set, a rigid, metronomic cadence marching across the barren plains. After the spikers came the fishplate men, carefully setting the twenty-two-pound joiners, which were then spiked by others who followed. Then came the tampers, in their hundreds, divided into three long lines, in the middle and on both sides of the ties, smashing home the ballast, each man allowed but two gravel-crunching tamps before moving on. As Crocker fondly recalled of that day: "No man stops, nor allows another man to pass him." The age of specialization had truly dawned.[94]

The Union Pacific witnesses were impressed, for from the start, the rails were advancing almost at the pace of a walking man. One of the witnesses timed the advance that morning and found an amazing 240 feet of rails laid in one minute and twenty seconds![95] On they went, with no discernable change in rhythm or speed, the material arriving smoothly just minutes before it was put in place. By six in the morning almost two miles of iron had been spiked and tamped[96]—and, the Casements had to admit, well spiked and tamped—and the trackmen were each lifting eleven thousand pounds of rails each hour.[97] Exhausted workers were pulled out of the line and replaced as needed, and the handcar horses were rotated every two hours; but the eight rail men (and many others) showed no sign of faltering, and throughout the morning they moved as smoothly, if not as beautifully, as ballet dancers.

At 1:30, with six miles of track finished, the whistle blew. Despite the frenetic atmosphere, every man took his full hour off for a hearty lunch. By lunchtime, the Union Pacific visitors knew that Crocker would win his bet. When the whistle again blasted, only seconds passed before the rails again were falling onto the ties with undiminished swiftness and sureness, and the march resumed. The advance men were now working on an ascending curve, and special crews spent the hours after lunch bending the rails, their supervisors judging by sight alone the proper curvature. On the rails flew, hour after hour, and, after a final measurement, with Union Pacific men in attendance, the whistle blew at dusk for the last time. The played-out workers hooted and howled, or merely slumped, slack-jawed, to the ground where they had been standing. They had finished ten miles and fifty-six feet of good track, which was immediately tested as Crocker ordered the heaviest of his locomotives to roar along the new stretch of road at forty miles an hour. The rails passed the test with flying colors.[98]

In all, that day the Central Pacific's crews placed 25,800 ties, laid 3,520 rails, sledged 28,160 spikes, and turned 14,080 large bolts—a record that has never been surpassed, even in the days of sophisticated machines. The reserve eight-man team of track layers was never called upon, for Michael Shay, Michael Kennedy, Michael Sullivan, Patrick Joyce, Thomas Daily, George Wyatt, Edward Kieleen, and Fred McNamara had done the entire job.[99] They had lifted and placed 2,112,000 pounds of iron that day, an incredible 264,000 pounds each. Everyone who worked that day earned his quadruple pay, but the eight Irishmen were the real heroes, for the track they laid ended a mere five miles from Promontory Point. Crocker had won his wager and the Celestials had again proven themselves.*[100] The Central Pacific, at a leisurely pace, kept working, laying their last rail (save one) at Promontory Point on May 1.

As Charlie Crocker later recalled, that evening, during the festivities, an army officer remarked with little exaggeration, "It was just like an army marching over the ground and leaving a track built behind them . . . it was a good day's march for an army."[101] By April, that is what the men had become, a weaponless, veteran army, disciplined, tested, and run by professionals. Said Charlie years later with his customary false modesty, "I knew how to manage men."[102]

"IT IS DONE!": PROMONTORY POINT, MAY 10

———

THE magic day at Promontory Point was delayed by strikes, kidnappings, the weather, the terrain, and the collapse of a shoddily constructed bridge. All of these phenomena affected only one of the companies; of course it was the Union Pacific. The falling bridge stranded Durant and his company's special train east of Devil's Gate, forcing him and his party to abandon their ornate cars and gleaming locomotive for more pedestrian transportation

———

*Fittingly, there is no record of Durant paying up.

found on the other side of the gorge. Had there not been another train on the far side of the gorge, the Union Pacific nabobs would have had to arrive at the ceremony on foot. Durant and his friends chugged to Promontory Point behind run-of-the-mill engine no. 119, and instead of occurring on May 8, the unrehearsed, and in fact largely unplanned, formalities took place two days later. Festivities at San Francisco and Sacramento, however, began as originally scheduled.[103]

Stanford was there on May 8, but had hardly arrived in the style he expected. A huge tree trunk, blasted from the Sierra soil, slammed into the train especially selected to bring him to Promontory Point, gouging and severely damaging the Palace Car he rode in and the fanciest of the company's locomotives. The Palace Car, defaced by the accident, was pulled to the site of the last spike, but by an undistinguished locomotive, *Jupiter,* which had been commandeered at Reno.[104] Sharing his beloved Palace Car was a very small party, and behind it were a number of other, everyday cars, crammed with the first genuine "through" excursionists from California and Nevada. The Central Pacific president probably did not know it, but the day after the *Jupiter* ground to a halt at Promontory Point, the last Wells, Fargo Overland Stage in history symbolically passed by less than a mile away.

About eleven in the morning, on May 10, Stanford's train puffed up to its assigned position for the ceremony, within feet of Durant's no. 119, which was already in place. According to Dodge, "It was a bright, but cold day," and about fifteen hundred people were gathered, including four companies of the Twenty-first Infantry and its regimental band, which happened to be in transit westward.[105] One witness described the scene:

> Grouped in picturesque confusion were men of every color, creed and nationality—the Indian, the Mongolian, the Saxon, the Celt, and the half-caste Mexican, some arrayed in gorgeous costumes, and some innocent of any, mingling freely with American citizens and soldiers.[106]

One such "innocent," perhaps having sampled all of Promontory Point's fourteen temporary saloons, was arrested and fined seventy-five dollars for indecent exposure.[107]

Leland Stanford, surprisingly, had with him but one company director, the patient and enigmatic Charles Marsh, present since creation. Also accompanying him were the three government commissioners, the governor of Arizona, Darius Ogden Mills's son Edgar, and three other, lesser luminaries. Montague and Strobridge were there, but the Central Pacific's party was curiously small. Durant's retinue was considerably larger, including Dillon, Duff, Dodge, Reed, Evans, Snyder, Seymour, the Casements, Hoxie, J. W. Davis, J. A. Williamson, and Hezekiah Bissell, who staked out the best seat in the house for witnessing the event, the steam chest of engine no. 119, whence he could simply look almost

directly down on the proceedings.[108] Also, but on their own hook, several congressmen, the governors of Wyoming and Utah, and a gaggle of reporters were present, along with a brass band from Ogden and three professional photographers.[109]

Oddly—ominously?—absent were the Ames brothers, John Cisco, Bushnell, Charles A. Lambard, Alley, and the other directors, as well as all five of the company's government directors. Also notable among the missing, but not ominously, were the Crocker brothers, Hopkins, Huntington, and E. H. Miller, Jr. Brigham Young stayed home—he was miffed by delays in Union Pacific funds due him—as did President Grant, who had earlier hinted he would attend.[110] Still, there were more than enough people in attendance, including twenty-one women, to make a ceremony and then a party.

The two locomotives were face-to-face, almost glaring at one another; Dodge remembered that "the engineers and trains of each company faced each other in silence like rival armies on the morrow of a battle."[111] Happily, that battle was at long last over.

One pair of rails was still to be placed, and eight Celestials, in new blue jackets and floppy trousers, stood proudly by to lay it. Unfortunately for their decorum and pride, the Chinese all bolted hysterically when they heard a word in English bellowed out by a photographer, who, trying to be heard over the murmur of the crowd, yelled, "Shoot." The Chinese scattered, but were soon back in place, having provided the day's greatest entertainment.[112] One lone tie also remained. It was a length of beautifully polished laurel, with silver straps and a silver commemorative plaque bearing the names of the Central Pacific's leaders. A gift from the company's chief tie contractor, West Evans, the tie had spike holes already drilled so that the precious ceremonial spikes would not be damaged.[113]

At about noon, Sam Reed and Jim Strobridge hefted the tie and set it in place, and the Chinese instantly positioned the rails and tapped common spikes into the common ties. Then, after a number of blessedly short speeches and a benediction by Congregationalist reverend John Todd, of Pittsfield, Massachusetts,[114] Stanford and Durant stepped forward to seat the last spikes.

These had been brought by Stanford along with the laurel crosstie, and had been provided by Californians, Nevadans, and other Westerners. Chief among these was the Golden Spike (now at Stanford Memorial Library, Stanford University) donated by David Hewes of San Francisco, the city whose capitalists had done so little for the railroad. It was five and a half inches long and a half-inch thick (just a bit smaller than a standard spike), and its eighteen ounces of California gold (then valued at $19.44 per ounce) had been worked into shape and inscribed by the Bay area jewelry firm of Schultz, Fischer and Mahling, at a cost of $15.25 (not everything was donated),[115] and placed in a velvet-lined box (another $4). Atop the spike was a large nugget of gold, from which souvenir watch fobs and rings would later be made and presented to Stanford, Oliver

Ames, the Reverend Todd, Secretary of State William Seward, and President Grant.[116] Attached to the hickory-handled spike hammer (a ceremonial maul with a five-pound head of Nevada silver) was a wire leading to the telegraph key of Western Union telegrapher W. N. Shilling. The moment the last spike was tapped, the word would be electrically flashed to both coasts and all points in between.[117]

The spike itself was engraved on three of its sides:

> The last spike. The Pacific Railroad—
> Ground broken January 8, 1863; Completed May . . . 1869

> May God continue the unity of our country as this
> railroad unites the two great oceans of the world

> Presented by David Hewes, San Francisco

Before the spike was tapped, however, other ceremonial spikes were driven into prepared holes by other dignitaries—a spike of silver from the Comstock Lode and a gold-silver-iron alloy spike brought by the governor of Arizona.[118]

Finally, at 12:30, Stanford and Durant stepped into place, the former carrying the unaccustomed burden of the spike hammer. The spike had been positioned in its hole and Stanford raised the maul to head-height and clumsily brought it down, completely missing Hewes's spike and clanging the silver hammerhead on the rail instead. In any event, the iron rail was a better conductor of electricity than the gold would have been, and the signal went out to the world, followed by Shilling's postscript: "It is done!" Durant then hefted the maul, and, to the amusement of those in the crowd who could see, also banged the unfamiliar tool into the rail instead of the spike head, then stepped aside with an embarrassed shrug to let Sam Montague and Grenville Dodge tap the spike lightly, and after them Jack Casement and Jim Strobridge. Last of all to hit the spike was Hannah Strobridge, in honor of having been the only woman to follow the work from start to finish.[119]

In seconds, the famous spikes were extracted, placed in boxes, and given to Stanford, and, in minutes, according to Bissell, the laurel tie was jimmied from under the rails and carried away to the Californians' train, replaced by one of hemlock. Souvenir hunters soon whittled that "last tie" down to toothpick size, and it was replaced, at least a dozen times that day, with other "last" crossties.[120]

Unfortunately, the one photograph taken just as Leland Stanford took his mighty, inaccurate swing was lost to posterity as Union Pacific photographer Colonel Charles R. Savage dropped the historic glass plate, which shattered on the spot.[121] Other photographs, taken by Savage and his friend Major A. J. Russell, and Central Pacific photographer Alfred Hart, permit us to savor everything except that one epic moment.

News of the completion flashed into Western Union's Washington office at 2:47 P.M. (allowing for pre-time-zone time differences), soon followed by a telegram to President Grant:

PROMONTORY SUMMIT, MAY 10, 1869

THE LAST RAIL IS LAID! THE LAST SPIKE IS DRIVEN! THE PACIFIC RAILROAD IS COM-PLETED! THE POINT OF JUNCTION IS 1086 MILES WEST OF THE MISSOURI RIVER AND 690 MILES EAST OF SACRAMENTO CITY.

It was signed by Stanford, Durant, Dillon, and Duff.[122]

In fact, a riptide of telegrams kept Shilling and an assistant busy all day: "The iron wedding is a fact accomplished," read one of the shorter messages, and "What the Erie Canal was to New York, will this great undertaking be to the United States at large," read another.[123]

While all around the nation the last blow precipitated celebrations (the Liberty Bell was rung, Wall Street closed early, there was a seven-mile-long parade in Chicago, and cannon salutes across the land), the *Jupiter* and engine no. 119 were brought to within inches of one another, the forward wheels of both on the last rails, their cowcatchers almost touching. The two locomotive engineers climbed out on the headlights, and, as Dodge recalled, "Each broke a bottle of champagne on the other engine."[124] The engineer of no. 119 was railroad legend Tom Cahoon, who had sacrificed his scalp for the Union Pacific several years before, and the photographs of that moment clearly show that he is holding *several* bottles of the bubbly. It is a safe bet that there was champagne in the engineers as well as on the engines. Soon, the *Jupiter* backed up so that no. 119 could pull its passengers a few hundred yards into Central Pacific country, and then the process was reversed and the *Jupiter* traveled a bit on Union Pacific line. The union was unified.[125]

The major figures then repaired to Stanford's elegant if contused Palace Car, which sported a complete kitchen, dining area, and bar, and, remembered an admiring Dodge, the "wine flowed freely, and many speeches were made."[126] While the companies' leaders and their guests wined, dined, and toasted, the humbler multitude also partied at the railroads' expense. That afternoon and all night long, the two railroad companies picked up the tab for all potables, from expensive wine to Red Cloud, and they also hosted a ball that chilly evening in the largest tent at Promontory Point. The ball alone cost an estimated $3,000, but on May 10, 1869, it hardly mattered.[127]

While the partying disturbed the silence of the High Plains in bleak Utah, Charlie Crocker in Sacramento, an insomniac the past six years, had a gargantuan dinner, a sedate celebration with some friends, and then he noted, "I went to bed that night and slept like a child." He would never toss and turn all night again.[128] As Crocker surrendered to unaccustomed slumber in California, Anna Judah in Massachusetts was also dreaming: "The spirit of my brave husband descended upon me, and together we were there unseen" at Promontory Point.[129]

The following day, with Crocker refreshed and exhilarated and Anna somewhat maudlin, *The Times* of London, in its "Latest Intelligence" column, reported matter-of-factly, "The Pacific Railway was completed this afternoon at half-past two o'clock" Philadelphia time.[130] On May 11, the first true "through" train of excursionists and emigrants rumbled through the arid slopes of Promontory Point, heading west, while from the other direction came a California freight carrying the first consignments of Japanese teas to the cities of the East Coast.[131] Regular through-service, inaugurated May 15, with a change of trains at Promontory (later at Ogden), made the Omaha to Sacramento trip in a comfortable five days, and people were now traveling by rail from one coast to the other for a modest one-way fare of $150, with emigrants, paying one third that tariff, crammed into steeragelike quarters.[132] Publicist Samuel Bowles, author of several tour books, wrote unblushingly in his first transcontinental railroad guide, "We used to call it the Great American Desert; it is really the great national pasture-ground of the nation; and the Platte Valley will yet prove the Northern Nile."[133] One can forgive the hyperbole, for the nation was at last, however tenuously, united.

But thousands of miles away, very close to the true Nile and another desert, turbaned workers intoning chants in a dozen Arabic dialects were almost finished with their decade of labor. In November, the Suez Canal would be a reality, and, as for centuries, the riches of Asia would reach European markets by a non-American route.

14

JUDGMENT DAY

EXIT DURANT, WITH CASH

THE hangovers suffered by the celebrants at Promontory Point did not end the pain—both financial and legal—to be experienced by both railroad companies. Nor did they mark an end to the work, for the Pacific Railroad was far from finished.

There was, in fact, a great deal of work yet to do merely on the companies' main lines, for Jesse L. Williams had been correct. Too much had been done too hurriedly to be called permanent, professional, or first-class. This was a point driven home to both the Central and Union Pacific as former Secretary Browning's four-man commission filed its report on May 14. The four, who had spent three months inspecting virtually every foot and aspect of both roads, found that while the Union Pacific would indeed need to spend almost $7 million to become acceptable, its actual location line and grades were far superior to those of the Central Pacific. Admitting that the latter company had clearly had the more difficult route from an engineering perspective, they found that almost $4.5 million (not the previously estimated $310,000) would be needed to make that line first-class, which meant that the cost per mile would actually be higher for the Central Pacific than for the Omaha-based line. The most important Central Pacific flaws were the most basic and expensive: $1.6 million for location changes and reduction of curvature and grades, and $626,800 for ballasting, proper recurving of rails, and readjustment of track. Another $400,000 would have to be expended building engine houses overlooked at various points, and

$874,000 would be required to buy, repair, or modify the company's rolling stock.[1]

Still, while perhaps embarrassing, the extra sums represented considerably less than 10 percent of what had already been spent, and both lines were generating healthy operating revenues, revenues that were now spiraling upward since through-traffic had been initiated. Also, the verdict of history has been generally kind, at least on one point. In the early years of the twentieth century, after truly exhaustive engineering studies aimed at deducing and building a more efficient route, Union Pacific President E. H. Harriman's engineers found they could save only seventy-nine miles. Of these "saved" miles, fully forty-five came from crossing, rather than skirting, the Great Salt Lake, a feat Harriman admitted had been beyond the technology of the 1860s. Of the remaining thirty-four miles, twenty were gained by discarding Seymour's Rock Creek route in favor of Dodge's original line in the Black Hills, while thirteen more came from eliminating the consulting engineer's Omaha oxbow and again reverting to Dodge's original location. This left a bit less than one mile gained from straightening track here and there along the route, "this showing," wrote Harriman, "that those railroads were originally constructed on true lines and not for land grants and subsidies." Except, of course, for Colonel Seymour's "diversions."[2]

The Union Pacific that spring faced a host of familiar and a few new problems, not the least of which concerned Thomas C. Durant. The Doctor knew that the Ames brothers and their growing circle of allies meant to oust him from the Union Pacific leadership, as they had from the Crédit Mobilier earlier. He did not really care, for, as was his habit, he rapidly lost interest in a railroad after it was constructed. He had, after all, a fortune from his 18 percent holdings in the Crédit Mobilier,* and, in part through that company, but also from the Union Pacific's formative years, he held a great deal of stock in the railroad, even if it was being quoted below par. His Union Pacific stock alone, despite its weak position in the marketplace, would suffice to keep fifty middle-class families comfortable for life.[3]

Durant had enough contacts to know that the forces arrayed against him— including many former allies—were too strong to be resisted. Hence, on May 24, the day before the rescheduled Union Pacific stockholders' meeting in Boston, he resigned from the vice-presidency, declining as well any opportunity to continue as a director. The Ames people were no doubt mightily relieved that there would be no messy fight before the assembled stockholders. There had been enough rancid publicity already. The Doctor was out, with neither a bang nor a whimper.[4]

Once the stockholders had ended their ritual get-together and were heading

---

*It will never be known just how much money he bilked from various contractors.

home, the Ames faction at long last had uncontested control of the company, with only one Durant supporter, Bushnell, left on the board. William T. Glidden, Frederick Nickerson, and (replacing Duff in August) Grenville Dodge were elevated to the board. Oliver Ames continued as president, Duff was the new vice-president, J.M.S. Williams was treasurer, and E. H. Rollins secretary and assistant treasurer. As the stockholders faded into the evening gloom of Boston, the board took its first actions, deciding to rid itself of Silas Seymour, whose contract was brusquely terminated, and to fire Webster Snyder. Seymour had basically played out his role, but Snyder had not, and he was blamed for a host of evils—although Dodge continued to defend him tenaciously—including over-stocks of material, escalating transportation costs, and labor trouble through his dealings with various contractors. Most probably, Seymour and Durant were far more to blame for these things than Snyder.[5]

The new officers of the board had a great deal of work to do, and it would almost appear that Durant's sensitive antennae had led him to abdicate at this juncture, leaving the Ames mafia to steer the *Titanic.* One problem concerned labor. Although it had been possible to discharge many workers even before the Golden Spike was driven, at least two thousand men were still needed on the line to finish construction and remove the tallied deficiencies. These men, how-ever, were causing problems, for their pay, as usual, was scandalously in arrears. Snyder's replacement, Colonel C. G. Hammond, wrote Oliver in late July that $770,090 was due workers for their labor to June 30, with another $320,000 due them a week later for July.[6] The threat of costly labor violence and destruction of company property was a sword of Damocles hanging over the board of directors.[7]

Further, nearly $3 million was owed to individual contractors—who owed most of it to their own, restive men—and considerably more than another million dollars was due Brigham Young, who was beginning to raise hell with the company. The Union Pacific had declined to build the Salt Lake City to Ogden spur, and while the Mormon Prophet was ready to do so himself, he could only begin building when the Union Pacific paid the balance of the Mormon contract agreements.

This, however, was virtually impossible for the Union Pacific to do in the summer of 1869, for the company's bonds slumped to 88 percent of par, and soon to 84. Its stocks hit bottom at about 20 percent, and its land-grant bonds sold at half of par to the few people willing to buy them. It was as if the public, scenting impending scandal or bankruptcy, were holding its breath.[8] One B. F. Ham, hired to make sense out of (i.e., arrange, clean up, and perhaps "cook") the books for the Hoxie and Ames contracts, threw up his hands in horror and confusion and quit. Nobody, according to him, could put those books in order.[9] Land sales were gratifyingly up, but the proceeds, payable in installments, were meandering, rather than rushing, in. One must sell a great deal of land at two dollars to ten dollars an acre to alleviate financial problems of the magnitude of those facing the Union Pacific.[10]

Even Dodge, his own pay delayed by months, had to scramble and on his own raise money to keep some of his men at work.[11] In fact, as early as May 29, he wrote Oliver that he was attempting to hire some of the Central Pacific's Chinese to replace whites: "As soon as we can get Chinese labor instead of Irish, we can reduce the cost of labor 50%."[12] This gambit failed, for the Central Pacific never did have any "excess" labor. The Big Four used their skilled workers to build the Western Pacific, Yuba, and their other railroads. Sam Reed, on the same day Dodge wrote about the labor issue, wired Ames from Echo City: "Have been compelled to borrow twenty thousand dollars . . . unpaid men are idle and clamorous for their money." The same was true up and down the line, wherever the Union Pacific had workers.[13] In June, Reed again wired the company's president, his tone even more serious, for, as he begged, "We must have funds . . . cannot keep men quiet long and damage will be done to the road unless payments are made" soon.[14] Even the miracle-working Casements went unpaid, and Jack complained that summer to Bushnell: "It seems to us there ought to be no further delay in your settlement with us."[15] It was to be a long time coming.

Financial wizard, banker, and Union Pacific supporter John Pondir also felt constrained to remind Oliver, rather shrilly, of a basic economic principal: "Notes must be paid when they are due," and constantly harped for payment, for he was the target of a coterie of irate capitalists whose loans to the Union Pacific he had negotiated personally.[16] Oliver and the board were fast becoming pariahs.

Some of the company's financial implosion had been caused by Dr. Durant. That is the one thing upon which all of the Union Pacific's key players could agree, although the specifics are curiously amorphous. As Dodge wrote somewhat self-servingly to Treasurer Williams in June, "I defy any man to contradict it, that all our losses, all our thieving, all our wrongs, come directly or indirectly from Durant and Seymour's orders, and it is no use trying to charge it off to any one else."[17] It certainly seems that while he was general agent in the field, the Doctor spent both unwisely and too freely. From Cheyenne to Ogden were scattered huge stocks of unnecessary supplies, mountains of equipment, ties and the like, which were "on hand" but were "never used." Although Webster Snyder had been held partly responsible for these overstocks (at least $1.5 million worth), Durant was the real culprit,[18] and Dodge, who discovered that much of the excess material had been purchased at wildly inflated prices, was convinced that the price gouging had poured a river of silver into Durant's capacious pockets.[19] Why else, wondered the chief engineer, would the Doctor order two thousand car axles at outrageous prices, when fewer than two hundred were needed? Kickbacks were the only logical answer.[20] L. B. Boomer's voluminous correspondence and construction accounts for 1868 and 1869 are filled with the notation "ordered by T. C. Durant."[21]

Strapped for funds, and with its securities selling low, the Union Pacific directors had once again to pressure company stockholders to buy more paper or come up with loans guaranteed by that paper. With over $4 million in interest payments on previous loans payable in 1869 (over $5 million the following year), in addition to other pecuniary obligations, the company found itself again in desperate straits.[22] To quiet the increasingly noisy Prophet, the company managed to send him $346,000 in July,[23] but that still left more than a million dollars on account, and the directors simply could not produce that kind of money. They could produce, however, the Doctor's excess matériel, much of it stored in Utah. Brigham Young had a railroad to build, and perhaps a deal could be struck.

Several times that summer and fall, Young's emissary—and labor contractor—Bishop John Sharp, traveled to Boston to talk with the board. The Saint's Utah Central Railroad would be long stalled if the Union Pacific did not somehow pay its debts to the Mormon community. As one writer has tersely noted of this period, there was "much unhappiness among the Saints."[24]

In tangled negotiations that included a pilgrimage by Oliver Ames to Salt Lake City to explain in person the lack of funds, a compromise was finally reached between the sacred and the profane. In late August it was agreed that the Union Pacific would pay the Mormons, over a period of months, some $940,000. Most of this amount would not be in cash, but in company securities and some equipment. The remaining $200,000 was to be held back pending arbitration by independent referees, for there was some disagreement about the actual amount owed. While this was not at all the settlement Brigham Young had sought, it was what he got, for the Union Pacific had finally convinced him that it had almost no liquid resources, especially since it had yet to receive one cent for the 47.5 miles the Central Pacific was buying from it. Months later, the arbitrators wiped the slate clean. The Mormons were to receive more equipment from the company's Durant legacy, as well as $35,000 in cash and a like amount in three-month notes.[25] The Utah Central Railroad was finished on January 10, 1870, a month before the Union Pacific notes came due.

While the company and the Mormons bickered, President Grant somewhat tardily appointed the commission of five "eminent citizens" to once more examine the railroads, as authorized by Congress on April 10. These men, all of them knowledgeable, were Samuel M. Felton (chairman), Hiram Walbridge, J. F. Boyd, and generals Cyrus B. Comstock and E. F. Wonslow. A serendipitously objective group, they were, as other commissioners before them, to ascertain exactly how much money would have to be spent to bring both lines up to first-class status. They spent September in the field and tendered their report to the president on October 30. The Big Four and the Ames group could relax, for the authoritative findings, solid enough to calm a very suspicious Congress, were laced with praise for both companies. The bottom line was that the Union Pacific faced additional expenditures of only $1,586,100 and the Central Pacific $576,650 to be accepted as finished, first-class roads. Another $206,000 would be spent, by whatever company controlled it, to correct deficiencies on the stretch between Promontory Point and Ogden. Not a whitewash, the report helped the reputations of both companies,[26] publicly vindicating their construction policies. In December the contested 47.5 miles east of Promontory Point was transferred to the Central Pacific for $2,840,000. The actual agreement was made on November 17, following months of talks between Huntington and Franchot, Oakes Ames and John Duff, and the congressional committee charged with the determination.[27] At least part of the difference between the Grant Commission's figures and those of the previous commission would appear to be the result of work done to remedy many faults between March and the final inspection in September. If that is true, a great deal must have been accomplished.

As the year ended, the Union Pacific, its head still barely above water in terms of its finances, reported gross earnings of over $8 million, but unusually high operating expenses (including taxes and large interest payments) reduced the net to almost exactly $2 million. While this was still a substantial net, the company's disturbing ratio of net to gross was carefully noted on Wall Street.[28] Never admitted publicly by the company was a litany of minor lawsuits brought by contractors—the board simply refused to honor some of the wilder deals made by Durant—and Henry McComb's continuing legal battle to obtain an injunction to halt the sale of Union Pacific paper. McComb was so troublesome in 1869 and after, that it would have been far more sensible and much less messy if the company had bought him rather than fought him. It appears that he was trying to be bought off, but for once the Ames group did not do the obvious. Hence, on September 6, 1872, Ames's three letters to McComb appeared in the *New York Sun,* causing renewed indignation, and they became a perfect issue for the Democratic party to publicize in their underdog struggle to prevent Grant from being reelected.[29] Hence the McComb letters, hardly proof positive of skulduggery, became the centerpiece in a political media event.

Also absent from the company's reports was any mention of the squawking Durant. The Doctor had been sued by Rowland Hazard on criminal charges that he had looted vast amounts of money from the Crédit Mobilier. Arrested and briefly jailed, Durant made ugly noises that reached the bloodthirsty press.[30]

On the positive side, four separate railroads now terminated in Council Bluffs, which was rapidly becoming a major rail center. Three more were winding toward that Iowa river town, and work had again commenced on the Missouri River Bridge. Although it would be several years before trains would transit the river, the end was in sight by late 1869.[31]

Eighteen sixty-nine had been a tempestuous and disappointing year for the Union Pacific, but events initiated in 1870 were to prove far worse. Dodge was quite premature when he wrote of his company in 1869, "Its future is fraught with great good."[32]

LOOKING FOR THE CENTRAL PACIFIC'S BOOKS

FOLLOWING the union at Promontory Point, the Big Four had reason to rejoice. They had achieved the seemingly impossible. Reflecting, Mark Hopkins wrote: "By engineers of repute, the scheme was pronounced impracticable; by capitalists it was ridiculed, and in newspapers and pamphlets it was denounced."[33] In the face of all the opposition, and with very little outside investment, the Big Four had gone ahead, carrying most of the load alone. Crocker, who had left his home in Indiana as a penniless teen-ager with a few possessions "tied up in a cotton handkerchief," was now building a mammoth French Renaissance mansion.[34] In 1871 he and his brother sold most of their holdings (retaining their Central Pacific stock) to their associates for $1.8 million, to be paid over a three-year period.[35] The firm of Huntington and Hopkins (the two partners retained 10 percent each) was thriving as never before, in part because the Central Pacific and the Big Four's other railroads were using it as an agency through which to purchase equipment. As Hopkins recalled, "Between the firm of Huntington, Hopkins and Company and the Central and Southern Pacific Railroads there existed from the first a close business intimacy."[36] Indeed, Huntington alone was to build many another railroad, having become smitten with the business, and in the 1880s constructed a line in Africa, from Stanley Pool to the Congo Coast.[37] All of the Big Four remained railroaders, although, as Crocker admitted, "We none of us knew anything about railroad building" in 1862. By 1878 they owned twenty railroads with 22,050 miles of working track. The Octopus had matured.[38]

In fact, the entire team stayed together except for E.B., who had become ill in 1868, "being stricken with paralysis," according to brother Charlie, "followed by softening of the brain."[39] Either E.B.'s brain regained its normal texture or the Big Four used his name as a blind, for in the late 1870s he was listed as the Central Pacific's largest individual stockholder.[40] Sam Montague stayed on to be chief engineer of the sprawling Southern Pacific, and James Harvey Strobridge built many other railroads for the Big Four, continuing to rely heavily upon Celestials for his labor. The Central Pacific, it turned out, had been something of a school for Chinese labor, and many of its graduates, now skilled craftsmen, went on to build a number of West Coast railroads, and the Canadian Pacific as well.[41] Others took their blasting skills into mining. Many Chinese truck farmers and merchants got their starts and prospered by supplying the needs of Stro's Celestials.[42] Several thousand were retained to do the finishing work on the Central Pacific and, later, routine maintenance. John Ross, traveling the railroad west in 1869 noted, "The Chinese are very numerous along the line. We were very much disappointed to find them so small and effeminate in appearance," not at all the sort of men they envisioned breaching the Sierras.[43] As the records of Ross and later travelers affirm, "John Chinaman" was there to stay.

A month after the Golden Spike eluded Stanford's hammer, Huntington and Crocker visited Boston to iron out with the Ames brothers and John Duff the terms of purchase of the Ogden to Promontory Point line. They also talked about permitting each other's trains to travel the entire distance from Omaha to Sacramento, but no agreement could be reached, and a change of trains at Ogden was necessary for years. Also on the agenda were more fruitful discussions concerning coordination of freight and passenger rates.[44] On the latter subject it was decided that the Union Pacific would charge first-class passengers seventy-six dollars (one way) from Omaha to Ogden, with the Central Pacific collecting fifty-seven dollars for the remainder of the trip to California's capital. Travelers would, of course, have to pay extra for food and drink, and, if they chose, sleeping accommodations. The normal duration of the trip was soon down to four days, with freight taking about twice as long.[45] Not quite swift enough to put Irish "fresh no. six mackerel" on California dinner plates, but a good start.

Crocker and Huntington returned to California just in time to witness the purchase of A. A. Cohen's San Francisco & Alameda Railroad. Cohen sold his company for almost half a million dollars, but would later sue the Big Four for concealing indecent profits from common stockholders, and tie them up in a long and bitter court battle.[46] Their Southern Pacific Railroad Company was beginning to assume its form as well. Its first end-of-year report, on the last day of 1869, showed $1.8 million (of a thirty-million-dollar capitalization) subscribed. Almost every penny of the investment came, of course, from the Big Four, who by now were used to owning railroads without outside interference.[47]

On March 1, 1870, however, Congressman Jeremiah Wilson, an Indiana Democrat, introduced a House bill to "Examine into the Financial Condition of the Central Pacific Railroad Company."[48] Debated endlessly and broadened in scope to include the Union Pacific, the bill was to spawn a drawn-out investigation that would smear the names of both companies and their officers, and, indeed, of Big Business and the entire business ethic of America. Somewhat naïvely, the American public was shocked by what it learned from this investigation—that "the moral level of the business enterprise [was] not up to the heroic physical achievement."[49]

While Congress had long suffered grave misgivings concerning the Union

Pacific and the Crédit Mobilier, little beyond vague rumor had reached it implicating the California company in any shady dealings. As if to prove Jeremiah Wilson correct, however, in April, Samuel Brannan brought suit against the directors of the Central Pacific for exercising "the entire control and management of all its affairs, business, subsidies, and assets, to their joint and individual benefit, profit and gain, and to the loss, detriment, and disadvantage of said last mentioned corporation, of plaintiff and the other stockholders thereof." In a classic of disinformation, Brannan (who held two hundred shares of Central Pacific stock as partial payment for his California Central rolling stock)[50] charged that the company's directors had received, in gold value, an astronomical $156,825,360 for building their railroad. He arrived at that figure by equating government and company bonds at par and in gold, setting an arbitrary and fanciful value on the as yet unsold land grants, and exaggerating in every conceivable economic category. He alleged that the Contract and Finance Company charged 200 percent above actual construction costs and that (he never explained just how) the directors had managed to pocket a fabulous $200 million. More to the point, he claimed that as owner of 200 of the 7,345 capital-stock shares ever issued, he was owed close to $6 million in profits, and some 272,213 acres of land grants. Obviously, he had nothing against indecent profits; he merely wanted his own indecent share.*[51]

Slightly complicating the issue was a similar suit brought by the Lambard brothers, early investors in the company. Although they generated a great deal of publicity by demanding a public accounting of every dollar spent by the Central Pacific since its inception, their threat was brief. They were bought off. Their two hundred shares were repurchased at 125 percent of par. Still, their suit was an uncomfortable coincidence.[53]

Brannan's suit was poppycock. But his legal action had great ramifications, for it further disillusioned many who were already suspicious of the Union Pacific, it strengthened Wilson's hand in Congress, and it led to some embarrassing court testimony.

In mid-1870 the courts demanded that the Central Pacific directors produce their books, as well as those of the Contract and Finance Company. When these were not forthcoming, Stanford and E. H. Miller, Jr., were arrested for contempt of court and hauled off to jail. The books were still not proffered, for as David Lavender has assumed, they had almost certainly been "deliberately destroyed."[54] Described by Central Pacific employees as "large ledgers and journals containing several hundred pages each, numbering in all from twelve to fifteen volumes," they were last seen by witnesses as Hopkins packed them away in several boxes.[55] Tight-lipped Uncle Mark was in poor health, but

*His figures were laughably incorrect. Over $50 million in Central Pacific stock had been issued by this date, while he claimed that only 7,345 shares in all had ever been sold.[52]

Crocker, on the witness stand, "[gave] it as his opinion that the books were destroyed by Mark Hopkins as having no value."[56] As for Crocker, he simply declaimed, "I was not familiar with the finances." This from the man who led and putatively owned the largest construction company in America.[57]

Crocker was "unfamiliar" with his own company's finances, Hopkins hinted at one point that he might have "lost" the books,[58] Huntington was conveniently unavailable in New York, and Stanford, when he did testify, put on the first of his many displays of amnesia. In fact, so bizarre was the ex-governor's behavior on the stand that his associates had him examined for insanity—no doubt to get him off the hook—but he never acted truly abnormal again, except for gargantuan and selective memory lapses each time he was called upon to testify.[59] The code of *omerta* had come west.

For more than a year Brannan's suit dragged on, generating headlines on both coasts and between, but little else. The directors won the case by default—through lack of proof of their guilt and through Brannan's nonsensical claims. The damage, however, had been done, and Jeremiah Wilson now had the bone firmly between his teeth.

While the California courts puzzled over Brannan's case of the supposedly missing fifth of a billion dollars and attempted in vain to reconstruct Stanford's memory, and as Wilson was gathering an investigatory committee, the unflappable Collis Huntington was affably writing a fellow Republican who was planning to run for reelection. In April 1871 he wrote U. S. Grant at the White House, enclosing "an annual pass for yourself and family on the Central Pacific Railroad," and offering to "furnish accommodations for yourself and party," anytime the president might wish to travel to the West Coast.[60] The "Great Persuader" rarely missed an opportunity to ply his talents.

With a little help from his friends, Huntington was also desperately attempting to block Congressman Wilson from forming his committee and to stall what he considered antirailroad bills in the Senate. One of his "friends," Thomas T. Crittenden, representative from Missouri, wrote him soothingly in 1871, urging him to not worry about the Senate, for "some of our friends will see to it that nothing else is done" about one recently proposed bill. Referring to hostile Congressman George F. Edmunds, he wrote, "We don't want to pitch into him until we find it absolutely impossible to control him or modify his views. I have treated him with the highest consideration." Of the legislative body as a whole, Crittenden bluntly noted, "I believe, however, that Congress *can be made to understand* both the facts and the law."[61] Such open admissions make Ames's letters appear mere harmless gossip.

By early 1873 the Wilson Committee was finally in place, and so was another, the Luke Poland Committee, which was directed specifically to investigate the Crédit Mobilier. Congressman Poland, a Vermonter, had long been known for his suspicions that the Pacific railroads had burgled the American taxpayer.[62]

For months the two committees summoned witnesses, took testimony, and subpoenaed company books. They did at least get a chance to marvel at some Union Pacific "books," but these revealed finances so utterly snarled that even the thick-toothed comb of Congress was soon worn out.[63] From the Californians the Wilson Committee got almost nothing, save lengthy, rather bored protestations of complete innocence. When Huntington testified under oath, he evaded with consummate skill. Asked if the "practical control" of the Central Pacific and the Contract and Finance Company was "in the same persons," Huntington shrugged innocently: "It is my impression."[64] He would not even admit to having made any money from the railroad, testifying about personal profits, "If I have received them at all it is as a stockholder in the Contract and Finance Company," which, in fact, according to the witness, was still due almost $6 million by the Central Pacific for construction work.[65] One could almost feel sorry for the poor fellow.

Huntington showed himself an astute witness, for he always managed to halt just short of actual perjury, relying heavily upon a poor memory and the vaguest of generalities to obfuscate the issue. Even the most skillful interrogators failed to extract anything of importance from Huntington, who was frequently questioned under oath between 1873 and 1898.[66] Probably Torquemada would have failed as well, and what the public was left with was twenty-five years of testimony signifying nothing. The fact that he was so often called to the witness box is testimony itself to the American preoccupation with railroads and business scandals relating to them. This preoccupation created a genuine American literary genre: muckraking.

Surprisingly, in late 1872 the Big Three (who now possessed most of the Crockers' interests), decided to sell out, letting it be known that $33 million was their asking price.[67] There were no takers, perhaps because of the growing clouds of scandal, so in early 1873 they lowered their price to a round $20 million. A consortium of San Francisco capitalists, led by Darius Ogden Mills, and including friend/antagonist A. A. Cohen, expressed enough interest so that formal negotiations were opened. The deal, which included 432,000 shares of Central Pacific stock, land grants, and stock in other companies, would lead to payment over a period of fifty-four months, with 6 percent interest on the unpaid balance. Legal papers were actually drawn up, but for some reason—probably the existence and revelations of the Wilson Committee—the purchase was not consummated.[68]

The Wilson Committee was to prove more of an inconvenience than a threat. It never could produce any "hard" data with which to accuse the Big Four, and Huntington, who remained in Washington during the hearings, managed to get the committee's secretary, one J. Hubley, in his camp, through considerable expenditures. According to the Californian, in a letter to his partner, Hubley informed the committee that "if the committee really wished to make the government safe, they had better join us in making the Central Pacific the most solid Railway institution on the continent instead of hunting for opportunities to find fault." Huntington bragged to Uncle Mark that Hubley was invaluable: *"Every word I said he will repeat to the Committee!"*[69]

Another man called upon to testify at length was General Franchot, Huntington's slick, full-time "explainer." For a man paid so handsomely ($20,000 a year, plus almost unlimited "expenses") to "explain" and "educate," Franchot was a singularly uninformative witness, even when measured against Huntington. He responded to one important question concerning influencing public officials with "I cannot say now; I have no distinct recollection of any specific thing."[70] The Central Pacific's only general certainly earned his salary that day.

But the committee did not learn much from its Union Pacific witnesses either, even from Peter A. Dey, a man of unquestioned integrity. The perceptive engineer wrote in his diary, "Spent part of the day in the House of Representatives. Pretty rough place. Not a dignified body." Given his brief tenure as chief engineer, all that he could volunteer was that he felt the Hoxie contract was inflated, but by now that was hardly news.[71] At least Dey was willing to cooperate.

Dodge simply and prudently ran for cover. In fact, the committee report frankly noted, "The presence as a witness of General Dodge . . . under whose supervision the principal part of the work was done, could not be produced," despite telegrams summoning him and a thorough search for the engineer by a subpoena-armed congressional deputy sergeant at arms. Somewhat rattled by witnesses who did appear, the committee members "believe that he has been purposely avoiding the service of the summons."[72] Dodge, of course, had always had something of an aversion to the House of Representatives. He later admitted to nothing and accused no one in public, not even the Doctor. He sidestepped the most important questions directed at him with a generic statement: "I disbursed no contractor funds, and I had no control over contract and contractors. The contracts were not even submitted to me for approval."[73] Perhaps he protested too much. Durant, more subdued than normal on the stand, was similarly unhelpful.

Wilson failed to get a bill passed that would halt the sale of Union Pacific securities, prohibit the company from declaring bankruptcy, limit its issuance of dividends, and provide criminal penalties for anyone involved in fraud,[74] but his and Poland's committees did unearth some interesting figures. While the Union Pacific, using almost random bookkeeping, claimed that it had cost almost $109 million to build its railroad, the committee's technical experts came up with a "real" figure of only $50,720,958.94, estimating that the contractors, primarily the Crédit Mobilier, had made profits of some $23 million in cash.[75] Probably both the company and the committee erred in their estimates. The true figure—which will never be known—might logically fall about midway, between $70 million and $80 million.[76] How much of this was paid out to price-gouging contractors, used for bribes, or pocketed by Durant and other company officials will remain sheer guesswork. Despite the revelation of uncalled-for profits and the surly attitude of many witnesses, the House of Representatives did not support Wilson's recommended bill.

Probably not coincidentally, the Central Pacific Railroad Company paid its first dividend in 1873. The company had done exceedingly well that year, with gross revenues of $14 million. With a net of $8,281,000, it had a pure profit (after paying taxes and interest on its bonds) of $4,767,000. Hence the directors were happy to declare a 3 percent dividend to stockholders: that is, themselves.[77]

CONGRESS AGAINST CONGRESSMEN

HE Poland Committee, or as Luke Poland himself called it, the "Inquisition," was far more direct in its approach to its goal, and it had, in truth, a more vulnerable target. It waged what was almost a vendetta against certain businessmen who had only done what many other businessmen had done. The committee's final report exonerated most of the congressmen investigated (those who had purchased Crédit Mobilier stock) because they had, according to Poland, merely bought the paper as an investment, and had not given political favors in return. The Poland Posse found two exceptions: Oakes Ames and James Brooks. Ames was accused of willful bribery, and Brooks (also a Union Pacific government director, 1867–69) was pilloried for having accepted stocks that he knew were offered "with the intent to influence the votes and decisions of said Brooks." Brooks, it turned out, also held a large block of Union Pacific stock—stock that he had purchased at advantageous rates and, worse, that he had recently transferred to his son-in-law's name. The Poland Committee resolved that both congressmen be expelled from the House in disgrace.[78] Among the committee's many witnesses, only one had come forward and actually accused Ames and Brooks of bribery and accepting bribes: Henry S. McComb! It struck some observers then that the Republicans who had bought stock from Ames should share the fate of Brooks—the lone Democrat to have done so. But the Congress of the United States in 1873 was a solidly Republican institution.

From February 24 to 27, there was truly heated debate on the expulsion resolutions, debate that halted when the House Judiciary Committee (with some dissent) decided that the House did not have the Constitutional right to expel (impeach) anyone on the stated grounds.[79] Oakes spoke eloquently in his own defense on the twenty-fifth, claiming that there was no proof whatever pointing to bribery on his part. His long speech ended with the sound of violins:

> Those then, are my offenses: that I have risked reputation, fortune, everything, in an enterprise of incalculable benefit to the government, from which the capital of the world shrank; that I have sought to strengthen the work, thus rashly undertaken, by invoking the charitable judgment of the public upon its obstacles and embarrassments; that I have had friends, some of them in official life, with whom I have been willing to share advantageous opportunities of investment; that I have kept to the truth through good and evil report, denying nothing, concealing nothing, reserving nothing. Who will say that I alone am to be offered up a sacrifice to appease a public clamor or expiate the sins of others? . . . But if this body shall so order that it can best be purified by the choice of a single victim, I shall accept its mandate, appealing with unfaltering confidence to the *impartial verdict of history* for that vindication which it is proposed to deny me here.*[80]

At the end of the debate, venerable railroad enthusiast Aaron A. Sargent of California brought forth a compromise resolution, "that the House absolutely condemns the conduct of Oakes Ames" and James Brooks—a humiliating act of official censure. On February 27, the House voted to censure Ames (by a vote of 182 to 36) and Brooks (174 to 32).[81] Both men left the capital before the third session of the forty-second Congress ended, and on May 8, just ten weeks following his censure, Oakes Ames died of a stroke, almost certainly brought on by his political mugging.[82] Coincidentally, Brooks had died a few weeks earlier.

The Poland Committee had pleased the public, for it had found villains at last, and had sacrificed them. There was self-righteous joy throughout the land. Hardly noted at the time, a brief Senate investigation found New Hampshire senator James W. Patterson guilty of bribe taking and perjury in the Crédit Mobilier scandal and recommended his expulsion, but did not press the issue, as Patterson's term expired just days later.[83]

Although exonerated, many other congressmen who had purchased Crédit Mobilier stock found their political careers abbreviated or ended as their constituents turned against them. Even Vice-President Schuyler Colfax committed political suicide. During the investigation he was openly accused: "The stock was sold to Mr. Colfax to influence him as a member and Speaker of the House, and that it did so influence his action in favor of the Union Pacific road, and incidentally in his own favor as a stock and bond holder in both companies."[84] While

---

*It is odd that he so frequently pictured himself as the *sole* victim, while Brooks shared his fate from the beginning of the investigation.

Colfax wriggled free of actual charges, his blind refusal to admit any connection with Ames and the Crédit Mobilier—when it was clear that one had existed—drove him from politics.[85]

CREED HAYMUND TO THE DEFENSE

THE Central Pacific, emerging from the Wilson Committee interlude unscathed (if faintly ridiculous because of its lack of company records), was forced to endure other investigations over the years, especially as its Southern Pacific Octopus seemed to be acquiring a virtual monopoly on West Coast rail service. Perhaps to prepare for these, the Big Four dissolved the Contract and Finance Company in 1874, dividing its proceeds among themselves.

A. A. Cohen's 1876 lawsuit against the directors of both the Central Pacific and the Contract and Finance Company for defrauding investors in both, failed, but the trial did bring to the surface some interesting financial details hitherto suspected but unproved. Among these was a court-certified list of stockholders in the defunct construction company. Of its 542,755 shares, the Big Four and E.B. held 58 percent, with Stanford having reserved another 15 percent in his own name; E. H. Miller, Jr., his brother E. S. Miller, and Moses and E. H. Hopkins (Uncle Mark's brothers) all held significant blocks of stock.[86]

Courtroom testimony was insultingly uninformative: "It appears that said Huntington not only forgot the names of the officers of the corporation, but had so far forgotten . . . his ownership of one fourth of the whole capital stock . . . it was a matter he had nothing to do with."[87] Uncle Mark expired quietly as Cohen's suit was fading away, taking with him to his mausoleum the Big Three's thanks and the secrets of their finances, and leaving them—or at least Huntington, the longest-lived—to face other serious investigations in 1884, 1887, and 1898.[88]

In the 1880s attention again swung toward the Central Pacific (or, rather, to the complex called the Southern Pacific). In part this was because of increasing public skepticism concerning Big Business, stimulated by cutthroat tactics and the ostentatious life-styles of "Robber Barons" such as James Hill and Andrew Carnegie. It was also because the Central Pacific had evolved into the nation's most successful and profitable railroad empire. As Charlie Crocker rather simplistically put it, "You can get any man to be unfriendly with a railroad after it is built."[89] Railroads, people were starting to believe, were also "public carriers," and should be regulated in order to serve the public interest. The Union

Pacific's chicanery was an old story, and now it was time for the Central Pacific to be pinned down.

Anti–Central Pacific campaigns became the order of the day in the 1880s, and no right-thinking politician passed up his chance to be quoted in the press or muckraking media. Typically, according to one printed attack, the Big Four "were almost from the date of the company's incorporation, engaged in debauching Senators and Representatives, buying up legislatures . . . [and] subsidizing newspapers and agents of the Associated Press."[90] Crocker's standard riposte was pointed: "It is a 'great monopoly' as soon as it wants pay for serving the public."[91] Dismissing public criticism so brusquely did nothing to endear Crocker to the American people.

On March 3, 1887, Congress instructed President Grover Cleveland to appoint commissions to examine the books, accounts, and technical construction records of all railroads built (or building) with federal aid. He immediately did so, and one congressional committee named by Cleveland went to work on the Big Three's empire. The committee's first meeting took place in New York in late April, with others held in Boston, San Francisco, and other cities. Their findings, tendered the following January, comprised fifty-six hundred pages, much of them testimony. The committee rendered a split decision, with the majority vindicating the railroad men, while committee member Congressman Robert Pattison found serious indications of malfeasance, corruption, and base dishonesty.[92]

There was enough smoke in Pattison's broadside to indicate fire, and the Senate put together a seven-man select committee in March 1888 to look into the matter again, and call more witnesses, if necessary. Once more, the verdict was a split one, with the majority finding no major fault with the railroad. Pinning specific charges on the Big Three was like trying to nail a jellyfish to a rock.

Some interesting information surfaced in the two congressional investigations of the 1880s, much of it coming from the Big Three's attorney, Creed Haymund, an exceptionally sharp-minded and sharp-tongued man. In his own testimony, Haymund consistently attacked, taking on individual congressmen, Congress itself, and, at times, the United States government as a whole. Instead of dwelling upon how much government aid—which was always discounted in the marketplace, or in the case of land, often unsalable—said Haymund, dwell instead upon how much money the first transcontinental saved the government, and, by extension, the American people. According to the attorney, who had a brace of his own accountants at hand, during the fifteen years from 1870 to 1885, the government saved a total of over $139 million on the movement of the mails, government freight, and the shipping of troops and other official personnel. In other testimony during the proceedings, he mentioned an even greater figure.*[93]

---

*About the freight and troop-transportation charges, Haymund may not have been far off the mark, even if he was a bit beside the point. Government statistics indicate that while army manpower following the Civil

Furthermore, said Haymund, the government bonds were going to be repaid—with interest—beginning, as agreed upon, in 1895. This was no handout, but merely a loan given in the national interest. He went on to explain in an almost patronizing manner that on operating profits of some $59 million made since 1869, the company had—since 1873—paid out semiannual dividends of from 3 to 6 percent, totaling $34,308,055. Certainly, the attorney admitted, this was a very large sum, but he reminded his interrogators that this sum came from the actual earnings of a very efficient railroad rather than from the pockets of the taxpayer. The profits were legitimate, had been spread over a period of fifteen years, and went not to the company's management but, as was proper, to those who risked their capital investing in the Central Pacific. Never once mentioning that it was the management itself that held the vast bulk of the stock, Haymund assured the Senators that no undue profits had been made by anyone, except, in a roundabout way, the United States government.[95]

This brought the feisty Haymund to another, surprising point. The federal government, he explained, owed the company money. At least $1.8 million was owed for transportation of government personnel and freight. This figure had recently been upheld in a Supreme Court case argued by the attorney, who also claimed an additional $321,152.72, which the company had erroneously overpaid and which the government now refused to return. Claiming ingenuously that the company at that moment only had precisely $13,768.19 "cash on hand," Haymund urged his listeners righteously to pay their debts.[96] In his counterattack, the lawyer accused the government of acting in bad faith: "In striking contrast to the faith kept by the Piutes [*sic*] and Apaches stands the broken faith of a civilized nation with the company."[97] If Haymund had had his way, there would not have been a dry eye in the gallery.

Stanford, again under oath, was bluntly asked if he had bribed public officials at any time on behalf of the railroad. He puffed out his chest and declared, "I state that I never corrupted or sought to corrupt any member of any legislature, or any member of Congress, or any public official, nor have I authorized any agent of mine to do so."[98] As Haymund played upon statistics (cleverly realizing that adding nineteen cents or seventy-two cents to a huge number increased its credibility), Stanford played upon semantics, for by his definition, if someone *was* corrupt, how could a man corrupt him? In one of the true classics of

---

War tended to remain relatively steady into the 1890s (fluctuating from thirty-four thousand to forty-two thousand officers and men), the army's budget was consistently shrinking. In 1867 it had been $95,224,000 and the following year over $123 million, but by 1872 it had shriveled to $35,372,000. It would remain in the thirty-million-dollar range for decades, despite major Indian wars (Custer was killed in 1876), hinting strongly at major, railroad-induced savings for transportation, with further savings from being able to cut back on the number of forts on the Plains since troops could be rapidly shifted to trouble spots by rail. These figures do *not* include massive and growing veterans' compensation and pensions (over $28 million in 1872 alone). It should be noted, however, that the Union Pacific and Central Pacific were hardly the *only* railroads saving the government money during this period.[94]

testimonial *chutzpa,* he responded to a question about company money having been used for bribes: "We will account to the government as if no such expenditures had been made."[99] In other words, the company would not bill the government for its "education" expenses!

Crocker also had his day in court and spent most of it complaining that most people did not understand railroad accounting methods. Instead, they drew their information from the company's monthly and annual reports, which, by their nature, were misleading. They were misleading, admitted Crocker, because the "net" income figures in company publications showed earnings before massive interest payments had been made. This helped attract investors, but it also made people think that "every month we are making millions of dollars." He claimed, without mentioning the time frame, that "out of gross earnings of over thirty millions, we have made clear after paying all our expenses about $1,250,000," but the public firmly believed the figure was over $20 million: "These monthly statements are a great injury to us," said the misunderstood millionaire.[100]

Charlie Crocker died not long after testifying, and a probate court made the extent of his estate public. He left behind over $20 million in assets, and a further $8.5 million in promissory notes, as well as an adopted daughter, Clara, who the next year married Prince Hatzfeldt, of Schoenstein, Germany. His will was a distinct disappointment to many, for, as one obituary noted shrilly, "Mr. Crocker gave nothing to charity, nothing to the park, nothing to public institutions of any kind."[101]

The investigation also brought out the fact that the Central Pacific had benefited very little from the government land grants. The Big Four had often said so, but information brought to light in 1887 and 1888 confirmed that, at least in comparison to the Union Pacific, land sales had been poor indeed. In all, the company had received 9,497,600 acres (the Union Pacific 11,309,844), but, by 1886 had only realized sales totaling $7,332,581.34, from which survey costs and taxes had to be subtracted. This appears to mean that in twenty years, less than 1.5 million acres (16 percent of its grants) had been sold, and those acres were probably the only ones salable. Haymund might have quoted Horace Greeley on the lands in Nevada and Utah: "There can never be any considerable settlement here."[102] In the same two decades, the Union Pacific managed to sell over 87 percent of its (largely) good farming and grazing lands, bringing in about $20 million.[103]

Muckraker John R. Robinson accused the Central Pacific of having refused to survey most of its lands, or even apply for formal government patents on them, as a means of escaping the payment of taxes for the grants.[104] If he was correct, the company's refusal probably was owing to the useless nature of the land. Anyone today driving through western Utah and Nevada along the Central Pacific route receives a graphic lesson in why those lands were not, and could not, be sold. In fact, the far luckier Union Pacific still held almost a million acres as late as 1950.[105]

The commission finally estimated that the actual cost of the Central Pacific construction to Ogden had been some $36 million. This figure represented actual cash value, legitimately calculated in gold, rather than the paper value, calculated at par, of unstable securities. It was this estimate that prompted Haymund to remind the senators that their figures had been drawn up in Washington offices, and not in Sierra snowdrifts or Nevada's alkali flats. He produced a series of expert witnesses, such as Arthur Brown, to explain the costs of building snowsheds; Lewis Clement, to portray the horrors of boring tunnels in the dead of winter; and Leland Stanford. Stanford explained that since Congress in 1866 had seen fit to turn construction into a race, and since government aid was contingent upon completing entire segments of line, the company operated year-round in all conditions, with many two-shift, twenty-four-hour workdays. This, the ex-governor said patronizingly, cost a great deal of money.[106] His testimony, and that of Clement, Brown, and others, was effective—so effective that the company, through the Crocker Printing Company in San Francisco, rushed out a thick pamphlet, a selective transcript of the Senate hearings, entitled *CPRR. Its Relation to the Government. Oral Argument of Creed Haymund, Its General Solicitor, Before the Select Committee of the U.S. Senate, March 17 and 26 and April 7, 1888.* [107] The committee did not retract its estimate of $36 million, but it did back off from pursuing the matter of precise construction costs. The Big Three had ridden out another storm, and had used the investigation to its own ends. They would have another decade to prepare before they (rather, Huntington) would be called upon again. When that happened, and the government submitted a list of specific questions for Huntington (now the Big One) to answer, his response was typical. According to the *San Francisco Chronicle,* [108] the Californian was as obtuse as ever: "C. P. Huntington professes to believe that if he sits up nights and works hard every day for the next 102 years he may be able to prepare answers to all the questions asked him today by Attorney General Fitzgerald." A fitting epitaph for the complete huckster.

NOTES

KEY TO NOTES

CPRR   Central Pacific Railroad
HL   Huntington Library, San Marino, California
LL   Lilly Library, Indiana University, Bloomington
NHHS   New Hampshire Historical Society, Concord
NSHS   Nebraska State Historical Society, Lincoln
UCB/B Bancroft Library, University of California at Berkeley
UPRR   Union Pacific Railroad

AFTER the first citation of a work in the notes section, only the last name of the author is used. When two or more works by an author are cited, then subsequent citations include the last name of the author followed by a short form of the title. For the reader's convenience, I have noted which works are pamphlets.

References to NSHS are followed by call numbers, which in some cases include specific MS numbers, series numbers, and box and folder numbers. For citations referent to UCB/B, folder and page numbers follow the name of the collection—as, for instance, 2/57 (folder 2, page 57). For UCB/B citations, as well as for those to HL and NSHS, I have included in each citation "(Dodge)," "(Bissell)," "Casement," "Crocker Papers," etc., as an aid to the reader.

1: AMERICA, THE MACHINE, AND THE IDEA WHOSE TIME HAD COME

1. Theodore Dehone Judah, *A Practical Plan for Building the Pacific Railroad* (New York, 1857), pamphlet, 8.

2. Alice Felt Tyler, *Freedom's Ferment* (New York, 1944), passim.

3. *Panama Star,* October 12, 1851, 1.

4. John Haskell Kemble, *The Panama Route: 1848–1869* (Berkeley, Calif., 1943), 188, 192–93.

5. Ibid., 206.

6. George T. Clark, *Leland Stanford: War Governor of California, Railroad Builder, and Founder of Stanford University* (Palo Alto, Calif., 1931), 125.

7. Kemble, 163–64.

8. James McCague, *Moguls and Iron Men: The Story of the First Transcontinental Railroad* (New York, 1964), 6; Kemble, 87.

9. Kemble, 23–24.

10. Ibid., 8, 23, 55–58.

11. Murdo J. MacLeod, *Spanish Central America* (Berkeley, Calif., 1973), 160–64; Kemble, 79.

12. Henry V. Poor, "Railroad to the Pacific," a paper delivered to the American Geographical Society of New York City and published as a pamphlet (New York, 1854), n.p.

13. Ibid.

14. "Old Block," *The Central Pacific Railroad; or, '49 and '69* (San Francisco, 1868), 3.

15. Theodore Talbot, *Soldier in the West: Letters of Theodore Talbot During His Services in California, Mexico, and Oregon, 1845–53* (New York, 1978), 37.

16. Neill C. Wilson and Frank J. Taylor, *Southern Pacific: The Roaring Story of a Fighting Railroad* (New York, 1952), 22.

17. Josiah Copley, *Kansas and the Country Beyond on the Line of the Union Pacific Railway, Eastern Division, from the Missouri to the Pacific Ocean* (Philadelphia, 1867), 65.

18. Ibid., 66.

19. Horace Greeley, *An Overland Journey, from New York to San Francisco, in the Summer of 1859* (New York, 1860), 272.

20. John Debo Galloway, *The First Transcontinental Railroad: Central Pacific, Union Pacific* (New York, 1950), 297.

21. U.S. Department of Commerce, Bureau of the Census, *Historical Statistics of the United States: Colonial Times to 1970* (Washington, D.C., 1975), 2:1114.

22. James V. Frederick, *Ben Holladay, the Stagecoach King: A Chapter in the Development of Transcontinental Transportation* (Glendale, Calif., 1940), 168.

23. HL, MS. film 428 (Bissell), 57.

24. Hubert Howe Bancroft, *History of Utah* (San Francisco, 1890), 557.

25. John Bakeless, *The Eyes of Discovery: America As Seen by the First Explorers* (New York, 1961), 368.

26. Wilson and Taylor, 27. See also William Cronon and Richard White, "Indians in the Land," *American Heritage* (August–September 1986), 23.

27. Bakeless, 364; John Charles Frémont, *Report of the Exploring Expedition to the Rocky Mountains in the Year 1842, and to Oregon and North California in the Years 1843–44* (Washington, D.C., 1845), 79–81.

28. Galloway, 18.

29. David Mountfield, *The Railway Barons* (New York, 1979), 50, 52.

30. Dee Brown, *Hear That Lonesome Whistle Blow* (New York, 1977), 20.

31. Mountfield, 52.

32. As quoted in Creed Haymund, *The Central Pacific Railroad Co.: Its Relations to the Government. It Has Performed Every Obligation* (San Francisco, 1888), 35, pamphlet.

33. John F. Stover, *Iron Road to the West: American Railroads in the 1850s* (New York, 1978), 10.

34. Galloway, 11–12; Brown, *Hear That Lonesome Whistle Blow,* 20; Mountfield, 52–53.

35. Brown, 23; Mountfield, 113.

36. Robert B. Shaw, "The Profitability of Early American Railroads," *Railroad History,* Bulletin no. 132 (Spring 1975), 57.

37. Galloway, 13.

38. Stover, 16; Mountfield, 56.

39. Stover, 72.

40. Albert Fishlow, *American Railroads and the Transformation of the Ante-Bellum Economy* (Cambridge, Mass., 1965), 58–62; Stover, 199; Brown, 24.

41. Galloway, 16.

42. Stover, 197.

43. Jack T. Johnson, *Peter Anthony Dey: Integrity in Public Service* (Iowa City, Iowa, 1939), 30; Stover, 190, 192.

44. Thomas Curtis Clarke, et al., *The American Railway* (New York, 1889), 4, 7.

45. Galloway, 17.

46. Clarke, et al., 8.

47. Ibid., 27, 34.

48. Ibid., 3.

49. O. S. Nock, *The Golden Age of Steam* (New York, 1974), 14; Stover, 188–89.

50. As quoted in Stover, 210.

51. Ibid., 103–8.

52. *Vincennes* (Ind.) *Western Sun,* July 24, 1830, 3.

53. Edwin L. Sabin, *Building the Pacific Railway* (Philadelphia, 1919), 15.

54. Ibid.

55. Hubert Howe Bancroft, *Chronicles of the Builders of the Commonwealth* (San Francisco, 1892), 5: 515.

56. Galloway, 29.

57. U.S. Department of Commerce, *Historical Statistics,* 2:1104; Sabin, 17; Galloway, 31; Bancroft, *Chronicles,* 5:516.

58. Papers relating to the Dubuque meeting and Plumbe, who was later a famous daguerreotypist, in HL, HM 4257–66.

59. (Rev.) Samuel Parker, *The Tour Beyond the Rocky Mountains* (New York, 1838); Galloway, 30.

60. Galloway, 61.

61. Sabin, 16; Galloway, 31.

62. Bancroft, *Chronicles,* 5:518; Brown, 28.

63. Frémont, letter to the editor, *National Intelligencer* (Washington, D.C.), June 15, 1854.

64. *Railroad Record,* August 13, 1863, 763.

65. Bancroft, *Chronicles,* 5:518; Brown, 28.

66. Sabin, 17.

67. Bancroft, *Chronicles,* 5:523.

68. *Proceedings of the Friends of a Rail-Road to San Francisco at Their Public Meeting Held at the U.S. Hotel in Boston, April 19, 1849,* pamphlet, n.p.

69. Ibid.

70. Galloway, 36.

71. "Old Block," 6.

72. Levi O. Leonard and Jack T. Johnson, *A Railroad to the Sea* (Iowa City, Iowa, 1939), 53.

73. As quoted in the *Railroad Record,* October 9, 1862, 389.

2: UNDERSTANDING THE VOID

1. Lucius Beebe and Charles Clegg, *Virginia and Truckee: A Story of Virginia City and Comstock Times* (Berkeley, Calif., 1963), 8–9; Sabin, 28; Ward McAfee, *California's Railroad Era: 1850–1911* (San Marino, Calif., 1973), 47.

2. William H. Goetzmann, *New Lands, New Men: America and the Second Great Age of Discovery* (New York, 1986), 117–21.

3. Ibid., 127–37.

4. Bakeless, passim.

5. Ralph Moody, *The Old Trails West* (Salt Lake City, 1963), 266.

6. Ibid., 271.

7. William H. Goetzmann, *Army Exploration in the American West, 1803–1863* (New Haven, Conn., 1959), 77–80.

8. As quoted ibid., 86.

9. Frémont, *Report,* 337.

10. Ibid., 365.

11. John Bigelow, *Memoir of the Life and Public Services of John Charles Frémont* (New York, 1856), 102.

12. Ibid., 103; Goetzmann, *Army Exploration,* 97, 104.

13. Frémont, *Report,* 332; Goetzmann, *New Lands,* 170–73.

14. Frémont, *Report,* 433.

15. Leonard and Johnson, 47; Ferol Egan, *Frémont: Explorer for a Restless Nation* (Reno, Nev., 1977), 297–310.

16. Charles Edgar Ames, *Pioneering the Union Pacific: A Reappraisal of the Builders of the Railroad* (New York, 1969), 3–4.

17. Moody, 282.

18. Goetzmann, *Army Exploration,* 104, 122.

19. Ibid., 116–18, 127, 153; Fishlow, chapters 1–3.

20. Goetzmann, *Army Exploration,* 220–23.

21. Ibid., 267–73.

22. Salmon P. Chase to General John A. Dix, November 25, 1863, Chase papers, NHHS.

23. Donovan L. Hofsommer, "A Chronology of Iowa Railroads," *Railroad History,* Bulletin no. 132 (Spring 1975), 72; Helen Hinckley Jones, *Rails from the West: A Biography of Theodore D. Judah* (San Marino, Calif., 1969), 24.

24. Goetzmann, *Army Exploration,* 278–92, 305, 206.

25. Ibid., 336. Scholarly Resources, Inc., of Wilmington, Del., in 1986 republished *Pacific Railroad Survey* under the title *The Pacific Railway Surveys, 1853–1855,* on seven rolls of microfilm.

26. Judah, *Practical Plan.*

27. Ames, 4.

28. Poor, "Railroad to the Pacific."

29. As quoted in Goetzmann, *Army Exploration,* 267.

30. Bancroft, *Chronicles,* 5:71. For an amusing account of this incident, see *Railroad Record,* December 14, 1865, 517.

31. Galloway, 51.

32. Jones, 45.

33. Judah's pamphlet was published in Washington D.C. as well as New York. See *Our Pacific Railroads: The Union and Central Pacific and Northern Routes; Their Character and Relative Merits* (New York, 1868), 3. Judah claimed that the Buchanan administration was strongly in favor of the Northern route, but "the financial revulsion of 1857" made it put off a final decision.

34. Goetzmann, *Army Exploration,* 375.

35. Bancroft, *History of Utah,* 557.

36. Poor, "Railroad to the Pacific," 14–15.

37. Bancroft, *History of Utah,* 512–42.

38. *Arguments of the Hon. William M. Gwin on the Subject of a Pacific Railroad, Before the Senate of the United States, April 8, 1858* (Washington, D.C., 1860), pamphlet, n.p.

39. Haymund, 44.

40. Bancroft, *History of Utah,* 522–27; Frederick, 173; McAfee, 19–20.

3: "CRAZY" JUDAH, THE BIG FOUR, AND THE PACIFIC RAILROAD ACT

1. Biographical material taken from the Anna Judah papers, UCB/B, C–D 800, folio 3. See especially page 1.

2. Ibid.

3. Ibid., 4–5; Jones, 11–12.

4. Estelle Latta, *Controversial Mark Hopkins* (Greenberg, N.Y., 1953), 18.

5. Jones, 24–27.

6. HL, MS film 721 (Dodge), 702. A surprising number of Sherman's kin would become closely tied to the Pacific Railroad.

7. Jones, 44–45.

8. Wesley S. Griswold, *A Work of Giants* (New York, 1962), 9.

9. Jones, 53.

10. Ibid., 60–61.

11. Edgar W. Martin, *The Standard of Living in 1860* (Chicago, 1942), 71.

12. David Lavender, *The Great Persuader* (New York, 1970), 387n.

13. Stover, 165–67.

14. Jones, 71–72; Griswold, 10; and Salmon P. Chase to General John A. Dix, November 25, 1863, in Chase papers, NHHS.

15. McAfee, 41–44; Jones, 74–75.

16. Robert West Howard, *The Great Iron Trail: The Story of the First Transcontinental Railroad* (New York, 1962), 112; Jones, 81–84.

17. Bancroft, *Chronicles,* 5:316–19.

18. Anna Judah papers, UCB/B, C–D 800, 3/3–6.

19. *Congressional Globe,* January 5, 1861.

20. *Central Pacific Railroad Company of California,* San Francisco, November 1, 1860, pamphlet.

21. Hopkins papers, UCB/B, C–D 749, 5/11.

22. John Patterson Davis, *The Union Pacific Railway: A Study in Railway Politics, History, and Economics* (Chicago, 1894), 137.

23. Stuart Daggett, *Chapters on the History of the Southern Pacific* (New York, 1922), 15.

24. Hopkins papers, UCB/B, C–D 749, 1/7 and 5/11.

25. As quoted in Johnson, 186.

26. Lavender, 95–97.

27. *Congressional Globe,* December 21, 1860.

28. Lavender, 93.

29. Jones, 94–95; Huntington papers, UCB/B, C–D 773, 8/13.

30. Jones, 97, 108.

31. Bancroft, *Chronicles,* 5:96.

32. Ibid., 19–22, 23.

33. Huntington papers, UCB/B, C–D 773, 2/21.

34. Ibid., 2/47.

35. Ibid., 2/38.

36. Ibid., 2/49; Bancroft, *Chronicles,* 5:37–40.

37. Huntington papers, UCB/B, C–D 773, 2/48.
38. Ibid., 2/64.
39. Hopkins papers, UCB/B, C-D 749, 1/46.
40. Ibid., 1/5.
41. Ibid., 5/2.
42. Ibid., 5/10.
43. Ibid., 1/45.
44. George Kraus, *High Road to Promontory* (Palo Alto, Calif., 1969), 57.
45. Huntington papers, UCB/B, C–D 773, 2/57.
46. Clark, 17–18, 35–36, 43–55.
47. Ibid., 69.
48. Richard O'Connor, *Iron Wheels and Broken Men* (New York, 1973), 69.
49. Clark, 69.
50. Ibid., 90, 111.
51. Kraus, *High Road,* 297; Wilson and Taylor, 83–85.
52. Crocker papers, UCB/B, C–D 764, 1/45.
53. Ibid., passim.
54. Ibid., 3/9.
55. Ibid., 1/48.
56. McCague, 44.
57. Bancroft, *Chronicles,* 6:35–52; Daggett, 13.
58. Kraus, *High Road,* 21; Greeley, 135.
59. Clark, 173.
60. Griswold, 12.
61. Huntington papers, UCB/B, C–D 773, 2/9–10; McCague, 22.
62. Ibid.
63. As quoted in Jones, 101.
64. Daggett, 19; *Central Pacific: Articles of Association, June 27, 1861,* pamphlet, n.p.; Lavender, 97; Wilson and Taylor, 11.
65. Bancroft, *Chronicles,* 6:212.
66. *Central Pacific: Articles of Association, June 27, 1861,* pamphlet; Wilson and Taylor, 11; Lavender, 101.
67. George Kraus, "Central Pacific Construction Vignettes," in David E. Miller, ed., *The Golden Spike* (Salt Lake City, 1973), 46.
68. Daggett, 20.
69. Ibid., 19.
70. Lavender, 96–100. Judah's official report a year later almost perfectly duplicated this 1861 prospectus. See CPRR, *Report of the Chief Engineer,* issued at Sacramento, October 22, 1862, pamphlet, n.p.
71. Sabin, 59; Jones, 115.
72. Lavender, 107. One source claims that Judah actually did distribute some $66,000 in stock, but later stockholder lists do not even hint at this.
73. Ibid.
74. Ibid., 102; Jones, 122, Clark, 204; Kraus, "Central Pacific," 47.
75. Judah notebook, UCB/B, C–D 575, vol. 2, n.p.
76. As quoted in Kraus, *High Road,* 41.
77. McCague, 28–29; Jones, 127–29.
78. Lavender, passim.
79. Jones, 129.
80. Johnson, 107.
81. Bancroft, *Chronicles,* 5:542.
82. Henry V. Poor, *Poor's Manual of the Railroads of the United States, for 1868–1869, Showing Their Mileage, Stocks, Bonds, Cost, Earnings, Expenses, and Organizations; with a Sketch of Their Rise, Progress, Influence, etc.* (New York, 1868), 67.

83. Ibid.

84. Stover, 103; Frederick A. Cleveland and Fred Wilbur Powell, *Railroad Promotion and Capitalization in the United States* (New York, 1909), 250.

85. *Aaron A. Sargent to the Senate, April 9, 1862,* pamphlet, n.p.

86. Ibid.

87. Bancroft, *Chronicles,* 6:82.

88. Ibid., 85.

89. As quoted in O'Connor, 37.

90. Salmon P. Chase to General John A. Dix, November 25, 1863, NHHS.

91. *Railroad Record,* September 11, 1862, 337–38.

92. Clark, 233. There is no evidence that money changed hands. It might have been the Central Pacific's bribe to a potential rival railroad. There was no lack of foes of the company and this might have bought one off.

93. Griswold, 24.

94. Lavender, 117; Hofsommer, 73; Keith L. Bryant, Jr., *History of the Atchison, Topeka and Santa Fe Railway* (New York, 1974), 5–10.

4: THE FIRST, FAINT STIRRINGS

1. As quoted in McCague, 30. See also Joseph Nichols, *Condensed History of the Construction of the Union Pacific Railway* (Omaha, 1892), 15–16.

2. Ibid.

3. *Railroad Record,* September 11, 1862, 338.

4. Ibid., 339.

5. Ibid., 341.

6. Nichols, 56.

7. *Railroad Record,* September 18, 1862, 351.

8. Griswold, 45.

9. George Francis Train, *My Life in Many States and in Foreign Lands* (New York, 1902), 284.

10. *Railroad Record,* October 9, 1862, 385.

11. William Kennedy, *O Albany! Improbable City of Political Wizards, Fearless Ethnics, Spectacular Aristocrats, Splendid Nobodies, and Underrated Scoundrels* (New York, 1983), 80–87; Howard, 20–26.

12. Johnson, 128.

13. Johnson, 39, 49, 64; Leonard and Johnson, 17–19; Henry W. Farnam, *Memoir of Henry Farnam* (New Haven, Conn., 1889), 55–56.

14. Griswold, 93.

15. Leonard and Johnson, 8–17.

16. *Railroad Record,* January 25, 1866, 83.

17. Brown, 6–10, 13.

18. Ibid., 17.

19. Train, ix.

20. Ibid., x.

21. As quoted in Johnson, 120.

22. *Omaha Weekly Herald,* May 3, 1867, 1.

23. O'Connor, 41.

24. Train, 283.

25. Ibid., 293.

26. *Omaha Weekly Herald,* May 3, 1867, 4.

27. Train, x.

28. Henry Morton Stanley, *The Autobiography of Sir Henry Morton Stanley, G.C.B.* (Boston, 1909), 193.

29. Brown, 13; Ames, 99–100.

30. As quoted in Johnson, 48.

31. Oddly enough, many sources, including the *Dictionary of American Biography,* say that Dillon was working on the railroad as a waterboy when he was seven (1819?), which was more than a decade before it was built!

32. Train, 286; Allen Johnson, Dumas Malone, et al. (eds.), *Dictionary of American Biography,* 26 volumes, New York, 1943.

33. Alfred D. Chandler, Jr., "Henry Varnum Poor, the American Geographical Society, and the Pacific Railroad," in Wilfred Webster, ed., *The Golden Spike: A Centennial Remembrance* (American Geographical Society Occasional Publication no. 3, New York, 1969), 1–2.

34. Ibid., 3–5.

35. Johnson, 16–66.

36. Grenville M. Dodge, *How We Built the Union Pacific Railway* (Washington, D.C., 1910), 5.

37. Jacob R. Perkins, *Trails, Rails, and War: The Life of General G. M. Dodge* (Indianapolis, 1929), 29–30; Nichols, 146, quoting Dodge; Farnam, 56.

38. Perkins, 85; Griswold, 231, 268; Dodge, 3–11.

39. Brown, 15; Martin, 405.

40. Quoted in Perkins, 52.

41. Moody, 1.

42. Frederick, 247.

43. *Life Story of George L. Colegrove, Pioneer California Stage Driver and Railroad Man, as Told by Himself* (typescript, n.d., n.p.), UCB/B, 76/83C.

44. *Railroad Record,* November 9, 1862, 341.

45. James L. Ehernberger and Francis G. Gschwind, *Smoke Across the Prairie* (2d ed., Cheyenne, 1975), 14.

46. Henry V. Poor, "The Proposed Pacific Railroad," printed version of a speech by Poor to the American Geographical Society of New York City, June 1863. 2–3.

47. UPRR, *Report of Jas. A. Evans of Exploration from Camp Walbach to Green River, dated Jan. 3, 1865,* pamphlet, 2.

48. Kraus, *High Road,* 51, 54.

49. McCague, 54; Gerald D. Nash, "Government and Railroads: A Case Study in Cooperative Capitalism," in Miller, ed., *The Golden Spike,* 121. Some batches apparently went for as much as $267.50 a ton, according to Sabin, 98.

50. Sabin, 98; Nash, 121; Arthur Pine Van Gelder and Hugo Schlatter, *History of the Explosives Industry in North America* (New York, 1927), 290–96.

51. McCague, 54.

52. Sabin, 99.

53. Kemble, 112.

54. Lavender, 411n.

55. Sabin, 51–52.

56. Kraus, *High Road,* 54.

57. Sabin, 100.

58. Crocker papers, UCB/B, C–D 764, 2/29; Griswold, 26.

59. Lavender, 129.

60. Jones, 135–36.

61. Ibid.

62. Kraus, *High Road,* 64.

63. Huntington papers, UCB/B, C–D 773, 2/12; McCague, 131.

64. Lavender, 130. Judah's expense ledgers show that it had cost the company $7,533.34 to send him east, including his salary and transportation. Judah papers, UCB/B C-B 575, vol. 1, n.p.

65. Wilson and Taylor, 17. See also Crocker papers, UCB/B, C–D 764, 2/29.

66. Lavender, 130.
67. *San Francisco Chronicle,* May 6, 1898, 2.
68. Huntington papers, UCB/B, C–D 773, 2/11; Lavender, 130.
69. Kraus, *High Road,* 54.
70. *Railroad Record,* November 10, 1864, 459.
71. Lavender, 143; *Great Dutch Flat Swindle! The City of San Francisco Demands Justice!* (San Francisco, 1864); Clark, 206; Kraus, *High Road,* 84.
72. Daggett, 31–32.
73. Deed receipt, October 30, 1863, in HL, MS film 368, roll 4; McCague, 57.
74. *Sacramento Union,* August 22, 1862, 3; Kraus, "Central Pacific," 48.
75. Jones, 111.
76. Poor, "Railroad to the Pacific."
77. See *Report of the Chief Engineer on the Preliminary Survey, Cost of Construction, and Estimated Revenue of the Central Pacific Railroad* (Sacramento, October 22, 1862), pamphlet, n.p.
78. Judah notebooks, HL, L17 G3, n.p.
79. McCague, 44.
80. Crocker papers, UCB/B, C–D 764, 2/43.
81. Lavender, 134; Jones, 142–43. E.B. was destined to be the company's largest stockholder, with 103,851 shares in 1876. His brother was next with 94,394. At that point E.B. alone held almost 20 percent of all outstanding shares. See HL, MS film 368, roll 6, for the July 11, 1876, list of stockholders.
82. Lavender, 136.
83. Huntington to his brother Solon, December 8, 1862, HL, HEH 515; McCague, 44.
84. Kraus, *High Road,* 85.
85. Wilson and Taylor, 14; Latta, 34.
86. Hopkins papers, UCB/B, C–D 749, 3/4.
87. Quoted in Clark, 188.
88. See *Messages and Papers of the Presidents* (Washington, D.C., 1910–21) 8:3361.
89. Griswold, 29; McCague, 59.
90. Lavender, 130.
91. McAfee, 65.
92. Griswold, 32.
93. "Old Block," 11; Clark, 202; Griswold, 32, and Harvey Fisk and Alfrederick Hatch, *Railroad Communication with the Pacific, with an Account of the Central Pacific Railroad of California,* (New York, October 1867), 17. Fisk and Hatch were the Boston brokers of Central Pacific stocks and bonds.
94. Daggett, 35–37.
95. Hopkins papers, UCB/B, C–D 749, 5/14.
96. Howard, 144.
97. Lavender, 135.
98. HL, MS film 368, roll 4; Griswold, 36; Jones, 166.
99. Howard, 145. Eventually, he invested most of his personal resources.
100. Galloway, 83–84.
101. Howard, 111; Galloway, 84, Kraus, *High Road,* 298.
102. McCague, 49; Crocker papers, UCB/B, C–D 764, 2/43.
103. Jones, 167; Huntington papers, UCB/B, C–D 773, 2/10.
104. CPRR, *Report of the Chief Engineer, July 1, 1863* (Sacramento), pamphlet, n.p.
105. Crocker papers, UCB/B, C–D 764, 2/49; Clark, 181; McCague, 76–77.
106. Howard, 145; *Great Dutch Flat Swindle!*, p. 14.
107. Lavender, 139.
108. Ibid.
109. Quoted in Jones, 167.
110. Anna Judah papers, UCB/B, C–D 800, 3/10.
111. Jones, 173.

112. Sabin, 59.

113. McCague, 59; Lavender, 139.

114. Anna Judah papers, UCB/B, C–D 800, 3/6. Anna, it is known, did retain *some* shares.

115. Huntington papers, UCB/B, C–D 773, 6/2.

116. Wilson and Taylor, 14; Jones, 174; McCague, 58.

117. Wilson and Taylor, 23–25.

118. Anna Judah papers, UCB/B, C–D 800, 3/16.

119. Quoted in Clark, 190.

120. Ibid., 197.

121. Attorney A. P. Catlin to D. R. Sessions, December 25, 1889, in Anna Judah papers, UCB/B, C–D 800, 3/11.

5: SCHEMING IN THE WILD EAST

1. Sabin, 80; Brown, 53.

2. Howard, 163. See George L. Anderson, *Kansas West,* San Marino, Calif., 1963, 11–15.

3. Train, 286; Griswold, 55; NSHS, MS 3761, SG 1, series 3, box 1.

4. Train, 292.

5. Galloway, 206.

6. Robert G. Athearn, *Union Pacific Country* (Chicago, 1971), 30.

7. Ames, 38–42.

8. Ibid., 19–21.

9. Athearn, 31.

10. Chandler, 4.

11. Griswold, 56–57; McCague, 71–72.

12. List of directors and other officers compiled by the staff of the NSHS.

13. Perkins, 104; Griswold, 54; Dodge, 9.

14. HL, MS film 721 (Dodge), 437; Perkins, 104, 133.

15. HL, MS film 721 (Dodge), 602. It has long been assumed that Lincoln did choose Council Bluffs and that he communicated this in writing to Durant. The Doctor, it is said, hid the communication and later influenced the president (through Interior Secretary Usher?) to issue another directive naming Omaha. See Perkins, 288–89.

16. Perkins, 288–89; Johnson, 110–11.

17. Quoted in *Railroad Record,* December 9, 1863, 497.

18. Ames, 47.

19. John Carson, *The Union Pacific: Hell on Wheels!* (Santa Fe, 1968), 10.

20. Quoted in Nichols, 51–58.

21. Galloway, 196.

22. Sabin, 86; McCague, 75.

23. Nichols, 79.

24. UPRR, *Report of the Chief Engineer, with Accompanying Reports of Division Engineers for 1866* (Washington, D.C., 1868), 54–56, pamphlet. See also Johnson, 103–4.

25. Quoted in Sabin, 39.

26. Leonard and Johnson, 109; Lavender, 141.

27. Ibid.; Lavender, 146–50.

28. O'Connor, 39.

29. Howard, 165.

30. Ibid., 174–75.

31. Griswold, 100.

32. Howard, 164–65.

33. Ibid.

34. Recorded in Hopkins papers, UCB/B, C–D 749, 2/79.

35. Ibid., 2/80.

36. Ibid., 2/79.

37. Ibid., 2/70; Howard, 166; O'Connor, 42–44.

38. See *Collections of the Kansas State Historical Society,* vol. 12 (1911–12), 383n.

39. Ames, 27–28; Brown, 58.

40. Hopkins papers, UCB/B, C–D 749, 2/72.

41. Lavender, 150.

42. Poor, *The Pacific Railroad: The Relations Existing Between It and the Government of the United States* (New York, 1871), 42, 49; Griswold, 66–74.

43. Poor, *The Pacific Railroad,* 42, 49.

44. Ames, 30–33.

45. Howard, 170.

46. Daggett, 25–26.

47. Train, 284. How Durant kept coming up with cash in this epoch is a wonder never explained.

48. Ibid., 284–85.

49. *Crédit Mobilier of America* (New York, 1866), pamphlet, n.p.

50. *The Pennsylvania Fiscal Agency* (New York, 1863?), pamphlet, n.p.

51. Oliver Barnes and Charles Hall agreement with George F. Train, n.d., NSHS, MS 3761, SG 23, series 1, box 1.

52. Oliver Barnes to George F. Train, March 22, 1864, ibid.

53. Charles Hall telegram to George F. Train, March 28, 1864, ibid., and Oliver Barnes receipt, May 28, 1864, "Received of Geo. Francis Train five hundred dollars . . . ," ibid.

54. Train, 285–86.

55. Ibid.

56. Frederick, 164. Savvy indeed. Holladay sold his stage lines in 1866 (to Wells, Fargo), less than three years before they were rendered redundant by the railroad. See Bancroft, *History of Utah,* 753; Moody, 302.

57. Ames, 112.

58. McCague, 73.

59. NSHS, MS 3761, SG 23, box 1. The entire box deals with the Crédit Mobilier.

60. Ames, 48; McCague, 90.

61. Nelson Trottman, *History of the Union Pacific* (New York, 1923), 21.

62. NSHS, MS 3761, SG 14, series 1, "Engineering." See vol. 2, "Estimates."

63. Ibid.

64. Ames, 44.

65. HL, MS film 721 (Dodge), 606–7.

66. Galloway, 249.

67. Brown, 119.

68. NSHS, MS 3761, SG 23, series 1, box 1. Receipt dated September 23, 1864.

69. McCague, 91.

70. Ames, 48.

71. McCague, 91.

72. Train, 286.

73. Quoted in Brown, 119.

74. UPRR, *Report of Jas. A. Evans,* 2; Ames, 98–99.

75. HL, MS film 721 (Dodge), 620; Peter Dey to John Dix, December 7, 1864. See also Johnson, 123, 128.

76. Ibid., 124, 130, 131–34; UPRR, *Report of the Hon. Springer Harbaugh, Government Director of the Union Pacific R.R. Co., to the Secretary of the Interior, July 20, 1865,* and UPRR, *Letter of J. L. Williams on the Location Between Omaha City and Platte Valley, January 2, 1865,* pamphlets, n.p. In retirement, Dey found an outlet for his moral energies, serving the Iowa Railroad Commission for years, regulating the state's railroads. In 1908 history caught up with Seymour, when, after extensive new surveys, his Mud Creek oxbow was abandoned and the line rebuilt along Dey's original route, regaining the lost nine miles.

77. Leonard and Johnson, 187; Ames, 48.
78. Griswold, 68.
79. Bancroft, *Chronicles,* 5:605.
80. Arthur M. Johnson and Barry E. Supple, *Boston Capitalists and Western Railroads: A Study in the Nineteenth-Century Railroad Investment Process* (Cambridge, Mass., 1967), 205.
81. HL, MS film 721 (Dodge), 518; Ames, 70–77; Hofsommer, 73.
82. Train, 286; Ames, 112.
83. Ames, 76; NSHS, MS 3761, SG 23, series 1, box 1.
84. Lavender, 164.
85. Ames, 49.
86. HL, MS film 721 (Dodge), 1204; Johnson and Supple, 204; Perkins, 277; Trottman, 94.
87. Anna Judah papers, UCB/B, C–D 800, 3/11; Ames, 91.
88. McCague, 50.
89. Van Gelder and Schlatter, 433, 285.
90. Ibid., 79.
91. The full report is in *Railroad Record,* October 10, 1864, 457.
92. Griswold, 84.
93. Kraus, *High Road,* 114.
94. Haymund, 166.
95. Griswold, 93.
96. Kraus, *High Road,* 102.
97. Quoted in Clark, 210.
98. Crocker papers, UCB/B, C–D 764, 3/11. This is the Robinson letter to the Nevada legislature, February 3, 1865.
99. Kraus, *High Road,* 86.
100. Wilson and Taylor, 104–5.
101. O'Connor, 71–72; Griswold, 76–77.
102. McCague, 78; O'Connor, 73.
103. Ibid.
104. Griswold, 84.
105. CPRR, *Annual Report, 1864,* pamphlet, n.p.
106. Griswold, 85.
107. Wilson and Taylor, 19–20; Kraus, *High Road,* 87.
108. Galloway, 103.
109. Ibid., 157; Kraus, *High Road,* 70.
110. McCague, 101.
111. Griswold, 93.
112. Reprinted in *Railroad Record,* October 10, 1864, 458.
113. CPRR, *Report of the Chief Engineer, October,* [sic; *December*] *8, 1864,* pamphlet, n.p.
114. CPRR, *Annual Report, 1864,* pamphlet, n.p.
115. Bancroft, *Chronicles,* 6:52; Crocker papers, UCB/B, C–D 764, 13/26.
116. Crocker papers, UCB/B, C–D 764, 1/30, 58.
117. Quoted in Griswold, 150.

6: THE CHINESE FACTOR AND THE INDIAN THREAT

1. Kraus, *High Road,* 87, 100.
2. Lavender, 188; CPRR, *Annual Report, 1865,* pamphlet, n.p.
3. Lynne Rhodes Mayer and Kenneth E. Vose, *Makin' Tracks* (New York, 1975), 26.
4. Kraus, *High Road,* 298; Griswold, 91; Galloway, 85.

5. Griswold, 91.

6. Kraus, *High Road,* 134.

7. As printed in *Railroad Record,* May 25, 1865, 165–66.

8. Davis, 140.

9. See documents and censuses relating to the Chinese in California, UCB/B, C–B 761, box 1.

10. Thomas W. Chinn, ed., *A History of the Chinese in California: A Syllabus* (San Francisco, 1969), introduction, n.p.

11. Documents and censuses relating to the Chinese in California, UCB/B, C–B 761, box 1.

12. Howard, 226–27.

13. See *California History* (Spring 1978), passim.

14. Arthur B. Stout, M.D., *Chinese Immigration and the Physiological Causes of the Decay of a Nation* (San Francisco, 1862), pamphlet, n.p.

15. Chinn, 11–13.

16. Ibid., 14–15.

17. Ibid., 4.

18. B. S. Brooks, *The Chinese in California* (San Francisco, 1876?), pamphlet, n.p. Mark Twain, *Roughing It* (New York, 1882), 2:110; Chinn, 65.

19. Chinn, 67.

20. Ibid., 65.

21. Twain, 2:107.

22. *Oriental,* January 4, 1855, 2.

23. Ping Chiu, *Chinese Labor in California: An Economic Study* (Madison, Wis., 1963), 41.

24. Chinn, 44.

25. Griswold, 110; Mayer and Vose, 27.

26. Documents and censuses relating to the Chinese in California, UCB/B, C–B 761, box 1 (November 25, 1876).

27. See letter book of Oliphant and Company, Shanghai, 1867–69, UCB/B, C–E 76/1442. Noted here are wages of coolies in China, ranging from ten dollars monthly (in Mexican silver) for common labor to twenty dollars for "head coolies."

28. Chiu, 46; McCague, 104; O'Connor, 74.

29. CPRR, *Report of the Chief Engineer, December 30, 1865,* pamphlet, n.p.

30. Griswold, 112.

31. Ibid., 145; Chiu, 45–46.

32. Lavender, 180, and letter in HL, HM 4257–66.

33. Chinn, 44.

34. Sabin, 184; McCague, 105.

35. Twain, 2:110.

36. In Mayer and Vose, 32.

37. See letter book of Oliphant and Company, Shanghai, 1867–69, UCB/B, C–E 76/1442.

38. Mayer and Vose, 32.

39. Chiu, 49; Howard, 228.

40. See NSHS, MS 3761, SG 20, series 4, "General Supplies." The Casements themselves owned a store, operated by a G. S. Judd.

41. Brooks, 7.

42. Howard, 228.

43. Twain, 2:110.

44. *The Gamblers* (Time-Life Books, The Old West Series, Alexandria, Va., 1978), 89–90; McCague, 105; and *Railroad Record,* November 30, 1865, 494.

45. E.g., UCB/B, C–G53, folder 1, "Invoice slips for merchandise, chiefly opium, tobacco, cigarrettes, etc.," Wo On Chung Company, Dutch Flat, December 1866.

46. Brooks, 5.

47. Howard, 231, 235.

48. Greeley, 289.

49. Augustus Ward Loomis MS on Chinese in California, UCB/B, C–E 158, folder 1, n.p.

50. Documents and censuses relating to the Chinese in California, UCB/B, C–B 761, box 1. Apparently *no* women came at all in 1865, only 1 in 1866, 27 in 1867, and 14 in the first half of 1868; 13,605 Chinese males arrived during that period.

51. Aaron A. Sargent, *Speech of the Hon. A. A. Sargent to the Senate of the United States, March 7, 1878* (San Francisco [?], 1878), pamphlet, n.p.

52. Carlos U. López, *Chilenos en California* (San Francisco, 1973), n.p.

53. *Railroad Record,* November 30, 1865, 494.

54. Griswold, 112; Lavender, 143–45.

55. Bancroft, *Chronicles,* 6:151; McCague, 110.

56. Lavender, 186.

57. Kraus, *High Road,* 107.

58. Ibid., 114.

59. Bancroft, *Chronicles,* 6:62.

60. Crocker papers, UCB/B, C–D 764, 1/61.

61. Kraus, *High Road,* 114.

62. CPRR, *Report of George E. Gray, July 31, 1865* (Sacramento, 1865) pamphlet, n.p.

63. Howard, 180–81.

64. Sabin, 105; Griswold, 123; *Railroad Record,* September 28, 1865, 386.

65. Griswold, 141.

66. CPRR, *Report of George E. Gray;* McCague, 109.

67. *Railroad Record,* September 28, 1865, 386.

68. Griswold, 141.

69. CPRR, *Report of Chief Engineer,* 1865, n.p.; Griswold, 122.

70. Griswold, 121.

71. Van Gelder and Schlatter, 290–96.

72. HL, MS film 428 (Bissell), 64, 39.

73. Arthur N. Fergusen, diary, n.p., NSHS, MS 3761, SG 14, series 1, vol. 6.

74. Ames, 21.

75. HL, MS film 428 (Bissell), 61.

76. Fergusen diary (1865), NSHS.

77. Frederick, 211.

78. Ibid., 202–3.

79. Ralph K. Andrist, *The Long Death: The Last Days of the Plains Indians* (New York, 1964), 83.

80. Ibid., 82.

81. HL, MS film 721 (Dodge), 465–66.

82. *Omaha Weekly Herald,* November 21, 1865, 1.

83. Frederick, 201; Andrist, 91.

84. Frederick, 208.

85. Stanley, *Autobiography,* 226.

86. Bakeless, 90.

87. HL Library, MS film 428 (Bissell), 43.

88. Ibid., 42–44; Bakeless, 92.

89. Howard, 177. Indian raids all but crippled the UPED that year.

90. American Railway Engineering Association, "Construction of the Pacific Railroad," *American Railway Engineering Association Bulletin* 23, no. 237 (1922), 41.

91. UPRR, *Report of the Chief Engineer, 1866,* pamphlet, n.p. L. L. Hills took Ainsworth's place.

92. Howard, 183; Leonard and Johnson, 138.

93. Dodge, 12.

94. Perkins, 157, 176.

95. HL, MS film 721 (Dodge), 600.

96. Ibid., 484.

97. Howard, 185.

98. HL, MS film 721 (Dodge), 600.

99. UPRR, *Report of Jas. A. Evans,* 14.

100. Dodge, 16; Galloway, 243.

101. Dodge, 16–18; Perkins, 182; HL, MS film 721 (Dodge), 689–93.

102. HL, MS film 428 (Bissell), 51–53.

103. Sabin, 133.

104. Galloway, 253.

105. Augustus A. Belden, "Daily Journal," NSHS, MS 3761, SG 14, series 1, vol. 1, n.p.

106. Fisk and Hatch, 1; *Our Pacific Railroads,* 13–14. The map in Copley (1867) is even more accurate.

107. Johnson and Supple, 203; Ames, 104–5.

108. Ames, 111.

109. *Railroad Record,* June 15, 1865, 206; Galloway, 271.

110. Ibid.; Ames, 137; McCague, 96.

111. Howard, 195.

112. Quoted in Leonard and Johnson, 90.

113. See *Railroad Record,* June 15, 1865, 205, for an excellent description of the new gadget; Trottman, 21; Griswold, 136.

114. *Railroad Record,* June 15, 1865, 205.

115. American Railway Engineering Association, "Construction of the Pacific Railroad," 32–33.

116. Fisk and Hatch, 14.

117. Howard, 196.

118. Ibid.

119. Athearn, 44.

120. Sabin, 143; Brown, 53. The latter claims that Seymour's kickbacks might have caused the outlandish prices.

121. *Railroad Record,* June 15, 1865, 206.

122. Griswold, 137.

123. *Railroad Record,* November 10, 1864, 456.

124. Ibid., October 5, 1865, 394; E. H. Derby, *The Overland Route to the Pacific: A Report on the Condition, Capacity, and Resources of the Union Pacific and Central Pacific Railways* (Boston, 1869), 23. This author, an engineer, found sand still used as ballast in the Platte Valley in 1869.

125. Derby, 23.

126. John Simpson Ross, *Crossing the Continent by Rail in 1869* (Mendocino County Historical Society, Fort Bragg, Calif., 1969), 6, pamphlet.

127. Leonard and Johnson, 143; Griswold, 137; Fergusen diary (1865), NSHS; HL, MS film 721 (Dodge), 982.

128. Ames, 111, 113.

129. Ibid., 113.

130. Reported somewhat confusingly in *Omaha Weekly Herald,* December 22, 1865, 4.

131. Ames, 113. The Glidden and Williams letters are but an early warning sign of unrest in the Crédit Mobilier.

132. Griswold, 138; McCague, 96–97.

133. Reported in *Railroad Record,* December 28, 1865, 511.

134. *Omaha Weekly Herald,* December 11, 1865, 4. This letter was addressed to a W. H. Bailmachine (?). One never knew when to trust G. F. Train.

135. Athearn, 38.

136. *Omaha Weekly Herald,* November 10, 1865, 1.

137. *Omaha Daily Herald,* August 23, 1867, 1.

138. Fisk and Hatch, 17.

139. McCague, 110.

140. Chinn, 45; McCague, 18.

141. Sabin, 110–13.

142. Ibid., 119; Griswold, 146.

143. Quoted in Kraus, *High Road,* 135; "Old Block," 6.

144. "Old Block," 18.

145. Charles Godfrey Leland, *The Union Pacific Railway, Eastern Division; or, Three Thousand Miles in a Railway Car* (Philadelphia, 1867), 41.

146. Galloway, 187.

147. Mayer and Vose, 40; Kraus, *High Road,* 141; testimony of Lewis Clement, in *CP vs. U.S., Summary of Facts* (New York, 1887), pamphlet, n.p.

148. *Railroad Record,* October 4, 1866, 396. One order that year was for 150 tons, a full 300,000 pounds of special steel!

149. Ibid.

150. See Clement testimony in *CP vs. U.S.;* Sabin, 120–24.

151. Kraus, *High Road,* 135.

152. *Railroad Record,* October 4, 1866, 396.

153. Sabin, 115; Arthur Brown testimony in *CP vs. U.S.*

154. Kraus, *High Road,* 149–53, for an excellent description of tunneling; Galloway, 146; Clement testimony in *CP vs. U.S.*

155. Kraus, *High Road,* 123. The first snow fell on September 24 above thirty-five hundred feet.

156. *Railroad Record,* November 23, 1865, 483.

157. Mayer and Vose, 40.

158. Loomis MS on Chinese in California, UCB/B, C–E 158, folder 1. There was a negative flow of Chinese in only five of the eighteen years for which Loomis collected figures.

159. In HL, HM 4257–4266, n.d.

160. Kraus, *High Road,* 123.

161. See correspondence between Huntington and Hopkins, 1865–66, HL, MS film 368, reel 1; Howard, 193.

162. Galloway, 152–54; Arthur Brown testimony in *CP vs. U.S.*

163. *Railroad Record,* November 30, 1865, 494.

164. See CPRR, *Annual Report, 1865,* and *Report of the President upon Receipts and Expenses and Estimated Revenue of the CPRR of California, December 1, 1865,* pamphlets, n.p.

7: THE UP GETS AN ARMY; THE CP GETS A RACE

1. Howard, 195.

2. Ames, 76.

3. Poor, "The Proposed Pacific Railroad."

4. Russell F. Weighley, *The American Way of War: A History of the United States Military Strategy and Policy* (Bloomington, Ind., 1973), 155.

5. Stanley, *Autobiography,* 129.

6. Fergusen diary, September 9, 1866, NSHS.

7. HL, MS film 721 (Dodge), 476.

8. Quoted in Fisk and Hatch, 17.

9. *Omaha Weekly Herald,* April 12, 1867, 1.

10. Ibid.

11. Perkins, 174–75.

12. *Railroad Record,* January 25, 1866, 598.

13. Sabin, 94–95.

14. Griswold, 169.

15. Bross, *Address of the Hon. William Bross* (New York, 1866), 13–20.

16. Poor, *The Pacific Railroad* (New York, 1866), 14.

17. HL, MS film 721 (Dodge), 721.

18. Ibid., FAC 714 (Casement papers), 5/223.

19. Lavender, 98.

20. HL, FAC 714 (Casement papers), 4/3.

21. Ibid.

22. Ibid., 7/262, 263.

23. HL, MS film 721 (Dodge), 701.

24. Ibid.

25. Quoted in Perkins, 281.

26. Ibid., 265.

27. Dodge to B. F. Kilbourn, July 16, 1869, in HL, HB box 16, 14. See also McCague, 114.

28. HL, MS film 721 (Dodge), 702.

29. McCague, 118–19.

30. HL, MS 428 (Bissell), 62.

31. Davis, 140; Perkins, 200.

32. UPRR, *Report of the Chief Engineer, with Accompanying Reports of Division Engineers for 1866* (Washington, D.C., 1868), pamphlet, n.p.

33. Dodge, 31.

34. HL, MS film 721 (Dodge), 716.

35. Ibid., MS film 428 (Bissell), 65–66.

36. Henry Morton Stanley, *My Early Travels and Adventures in America and Asia* (2 vols, New York, 1905), 1:104–5.

37. George A. Crofutt, *Great Trans-Continental Railroad Guide* (Chicago, 1869), 33. Crofutt's title helped publicize the word (and concept) *transcontinental,* which soon superseded *Pacific* as a description of this railroad.

38. Ibid., 30–39; McCague, 127.

39. *Omaha Weekly Herald,* September 14, 1866, 5.

40. McCague, 128.

41. Fergusen diary, July 26, 1866, NSHS.

42. C. Exera Brown, *Brown's Gazeteer of the Chicago and Northwestern Railway, and Branches of the Union Pacific Rail Road* (Chicago, 1869), 288–95.

43. Athearn, 60.

44. Stanley, *My Early Travels,* 1:105.

45. O'Connor, 48.

46. McCague, 166.

47. O'Connor, 49.

48. HL, MS film 428 (Bissell), 67.

49. O'Connor, 49.

50. Martin, 79.

51. HL, MS film 721 (Dodge), 829; McCague, 237; *Frontier Index,* 1867–68, passim.

52. Quoted in Leonard and Johnson, 170.

53. Crofutt, 40.

54. *Omaha Weekly Herald,* June 29, 1866, 3; Huntington to Hopkins, July 4, 1866, in HL, MS film 368, reel 1.

55. Lavender, 183.

56. Huntington to Hopkins, April 4, 1866, in HL, MS film 368, reel 1.

57. Ibid., September 22, 1866.

58. Huntington papers, UCB/B, C–D 773, 3/31.

59. McAfee, 79; Lavender, 404n.

60. David D. Colton, *The Colton Letters: The Inside Story of an Infamous Procedure* (San Francisco, 1889?), pamphlet, 7.

61. Crocker papers, UCB/B, C–D 764, 1/42.

62. Both before and after completion of the road; see testimony reprinted in the *San Francisco Chronicle,* May 14 and 15, 1898, about his role in "explaining" things to Congress and the press.

63. Leland, 14.
64. Huntington papers, UCB/B, C–D 773, 2/79.
65. Kraus, *High Road,* 300.
66. Crocker papers, UCB/B, C–D 764, 1/49.
67. Ibid., 1/51.
68. McCague, 150; see photo there.
69. Strobridge testimony in *CP vs. U.S.;* Wilson and Taylor, 19, 21.
70. McCague, 146.
71. Kraus, *High Road,* 153.
72. Ibid., 152.
73. L. E. Hoyt, "From the Golden Spike to the Space Age in Railroading," in Miller, ed., *The Golden Spike* 31.
74. *Railroad Record,* August 2, 1866, 421.
75. Ibid.
76. Van Gelder and Schlatter, 406–8; Sabin., 146.
77. *Omaha Weekly Herald,* August 23, 1867, 1.
78. Kraus, *High Road,* 151.
79. McCague, 159.
80. Gillis testimony in *CP vs. U.S.;* Kraus, *High Road,* 152.
81. *San Francisco Union,* April 19, 1867; McCague, 160.
82. Van Gelder and Schlatter, 391, 408.
83. Ibid., 391.
84. *San Francisco Union,* March 27, 1867, 3.
85. Griswold, 158.
86. Sabin, 124.
87. "Old Block," 22.
88. *Our Pacific Railroads,* 7.
89. Bakeless, 386.
90. Odie B. Faulk, *The Crimson Desert: Indian Wars of the American Southwest* (New York, 1974), 123–25.
91. Bancroft, *Chronicles,* 6:229.
92. Haymund, 32–33.
93. Crofutt, 163.
94. Mayer and Vose, 93.
95. Huntington papers, UCB/B, C–D 773, 2/66.
96. Crofutt, 199.
97. Sabin, 115; Kraus, *High Road,* 141; McCague, 149.
98. *Railroad Record,* October 4, 1866, 395.
99. *Omaha Weekly Herald,* May 10, 1867, 1. See also Carson, 10.
100. Griswold, 179.
101. Silas Seymour, *Incidents of a Trip Through the Great Platte Valley, to the Rocky Mountains and Laramie Plains, in the Fall of 1866* (New York, 1867), 94–97.
102. Griswold, 184.
103. McCague, 134.
104. Seymour, 76. This is the way the dishes are presented on the menu.
105. Ibid.
106. HL, MS film 721 (Dodge), 738–39.
107. Seymour, 100–1.
108. Ibid., 102–3.
109. Ibid., 106–7; HL, MS film 721 (Dodge), 739; McCague, 132–33.
110. Athearn, 53.
111. Griswold, 173.
112. Seymour, 126–27.
113. HL, MS film 721 (Dodge), 737.
114. Griswold, 186.

115. McCague, 138.

116. HL, MS film 721 (Dodge), 720–21.

117. Ibid., 719–20; UPRR, *Report of the Chief Engineer, with Accompanying Reports,* 112–13.

118. Galloway, 269.

119. Seymour, 125; Fishlow, 262–300.

120. Galloway, 255.

121. Copley, 91.

122. Ames, 151–52.

123. Ibid., 152–53.

124. HL, MS film 721 (Dodge), 709; O'Connor, 52.

125. Fergusen diary, August 15, 1866, NSHS.

126. Ibid. See October 22 for one such fatal brawl.

127. HL, MS film 428 (Bissell), 67.

128. Andrist, 135.

129. Weighley, 157–58.

130. Andrist, 113; Griswold, 179.

131. Andrist, 113, Robert M. Utley and Wilcomb E. Washburn, *The American Heritage History of the Indian Wars* (New York, 1977), 241.

132. Fergusen diary, November 12 and 14, 1866, NSHS.

133. Griswold, 187–88.

134. Nichols, 124.

135. *Railroad Record,* August 23, 1866, 313; Griswold, 187; *Omaha Weekly Herald,* December 28, 1866, 1.

136. Crofutt, 43.

137. Griswold, 156.

138. Lavender, 137.

139. Ibid., 176.

140. Kraus, *High Road,* 141.

141. Jones, 184–85.

142. CPRR, *Annual Report, 1866,* pamphlet.

143. CPRR, *Lands of the Central Pacific Railroad* (San Francisco, 1871); n.p. Fisk and Hatch, 21.

144. Haymund, 129–30.

145. John R. Robinson, *The Octopus: A History of the Construction, Conspiracies, Extortions, Robberies, and Villainous Acts of the Central Pacific . . . , Union Pacific, and other Subsidized Railroads* (San Francisco, 1894), 59.

146. Crocker papers, UCB/B, C–D 764, 13/19; CPRR, *Lands of the Central Pacific Railroad.*

147. Clement testimony, *CP vs. U.S.*

148. Sabin, 124.

149. Griswold, 158.

150. Mayer and Vose, 53; Griswold, 158.

151. McCague, 158; Griswold, 159.

152. Wilson and Taylor, 23.

153. Griswold, 160.

154. Wilson and Taylor, 23–24; Gerald M. Best, *Snowplow: Clearing Mountain Rails* (Berkeley, Calif., 1966), 13.

155. Kraus, *High Road,* 148.

156. Chinn, 45.

157. Kraus, *High Road,* 149.

158. Galloway, 149; McCague, 161; Mayer and Vose, 40.

159. McCague, 161; Chinn, 45; Mayer and Vose, 48.

160. Quoted in Kraus, *High Road,* 136.

161. Mayer and Vose, 49.

162. Wilson and Taylor, 22; Kraus, *High Road,* 148.

163. Quoted in Kraus, *High Road,* 136.

164. Galloway, 149.

165. *Our Pacific Railroads,* 17; Brown testimony in *CP vs. U.S.,* n.p.

166. Crofutt, 202; Galloway, 90; Kraus, *High Road,* 300.

167. Kraus, *High Road,* 159.

168. William A. Bell, *New Tracks in North America: A Journal of Travel and Adventure Whilst Engaged in the Survey for a Southern Railroad to the Pacific Ocean During 1867–8* (London, 1870), 488. See also CPRR, *Annual Report, 1866;* Sabin, 117.

169. Fisk and Hatch, 21; CPRR, *Annual Report, 1866.*

8: WAR WHOOPS ON THE PLAINS AND THE OCTOPUS IS BORN

1. See Casement daily reports, NSHS, MS 3761, SG 20, series 3. For example, on May 27 they had on hand 84,092 hardwood and 136,195 "soft" ties at North Platte.

2. See Ibid., series 1, box 5.

3. HL, FAC 714 (Casement), Jack Casement to wife, April 13, 1867.

4. Ibid., MS film 721 (Dodge), 788.

5. Fergusen diary, April 17, 1867, NSHS.

6. Printed in *Omaha Weekly Herald,* April 12, 1867, 2.

7. Sabin, 155.

8. L. B. Boomer files, NSHS, MS 3761, SG 23, box 1, folder 5. For example, see June 11, 1867.

9. Ibid.

10. Fergusen diary, May 2, 1867, NSHS.

11. Ibid., May 21, 1867.

12. Ibid., May 5.

13. HL, MS film 721 (Dodge), 788–89.

14. *Railroad Record,* May 16, 1867, 141.

15. Ibid., 142.

16. HL, MS film 721 (Dodge), 783.

17. Ibid., 788, 791.

18. UPRR, *The Union Pacific Railroad Company, Chartered by the United States: Progress of Their Road West from Omaha, Nebraska, Across the Continent* (New York; 1867), 13.

19. Leonard and Johnson, 188. Exactly who bought the bonds is difficult to determine, but the names Durant, Bushnell, McComb, et al., certainly figure prominently.

20. *Omaha Weekly Herald,* January 11, 1867, 1.

21. HL, MS film 721 (Dodge), 778.

22. Ibid., 778–79.

23. *Omaha Weekly Herald,* May 3, 1867, 1.

24. Bancroft, *Chronicles,* 5:312.

25. HL, MS film 428 (Bissell), 73.

26. Fergusen diary, May 18, 1867, NSHS.

27. HL, MS film 721 (Dodge), 792–94.

28. Mayer and Vose, 90.

29. HL, MS film 721 (Dodge), 799.

30. O'Connor, 56.

31. HL, MS film 721 (Dodge), 802.

32. Carson, 19.

33. Fergusen diary, June 2, 1867, NSHS.

34. Carson, 21.

35. HL, MS film 428 (Bissell), 70.

36. Ibid. (Dodge), 814; Griswold, 217.

37. Fergusen diary, January 1867, NSHS.
38. See "Employees List," NSHS, MS 3761, SG 14; and HL, MS film 721 (Dodge), 823.
39. Fergusen diary, July 27, 1867, NSHS.
40. Quoted in Griswold, 216.
41. HL, MS film 721 (Dodge), 867.
42. Fergusen diary, August 8, 1867, NSHS.
43. *Omaha Daily Herald,* August 14, 1867, 1.
44. Fergusen diary, August 11, 1867, NSHS.
45. *Omaha Weekly Herald,* August 8, 1867, 2.
46. Ames, 221.
47. Stanley, *Autobiography,* 155–56.
48. Ibid., 158.
49. Quoted in Davis, 141.
50. Stanley, *Autobiography,* 154–55; Ames, 221–22.
51. Quoted in Mayer and Vose, 95.
52. *Omaha Daily Herald,* August 20, 1867, 4; Fergusen diary, September 27 and June 4, 1867, NSHS.
53. Nichols, 125.
54. O'Connor, 65.
55. HL, MS film 721 (Dodge), 910.
56. Edward Vernon, *Travelers' Official Railway Guide, for the United States and Canada* (New York, 1868), passim.
57. Twain, 1:41.
58. McCague, 186–87.
59. HL, MS film 721 (Dodge), 828.
60. McCague, 186; O'Connor, 61.
61. Stanley, *Autobiography,* 166.
62. Ibid., 166, 167.
63. *Frontier Index,* July 25, 1867, 1, 3.
64. Stanley, *Autobiography,* 166.
65. HL, FAC 714 (Casement), 5/226, Casement to wife, April 13, 1867.
66. Ibid., MS film 721 (Dodge), 828.
67. Ibid.
68. Ibid., 829.
69. Ibid.
70. McCague, 188.
71. HL, MS film 721 (Dodge), 829.
72. Crofutt, 44.
73. *American Railroad Journal,* June 22, 1867, 1.
74. UPRR, *The Union Pacific Railroad Across the Continent,* 6.
75. Quoted in Ames, 164.
76. Ibid., 166.
77. Ibid., 167.
78. Ibid., 169.
79. Ibid., 169, 171.
80. Ibid.
81. HL, MS film 721 (Dodge), 799; a letter from Oliver Ames to Dodge, n.d.
82. Ames, 171.
83. Wilson Committee, *Affairs of the Union Pacific Railroad Company,* House Report no. 78, 3rd session (Washington, D.C., 1873), pamphlet, 40–41.
84. HL, MS film 721 (Dodge), 811.
85. *Railroad Record,* May 16, 1867, 141.
86. HL, MS film 721 (Dodge), 825.
87. Griswold, 189–90; Kraus, *High Road,* 145; CPRR, *CP vs. U.S.,* for the engineers' appreciation of work that winter.

88. Griswold, 200.

89. *Railroad Record,* April 18, 1867, 97.

90. Samuel Bowles, *Our New West* (Hartford, Conn., 1869), 67.

91. Quoted in Kraus, *High Road,* 145–46.

92. *Railroad Record,* April 18, 1867, 97.

93. Mayer and Vose, 44; Martin, 47.

94. Kraus, *High Road,* 187.

95. Quoted in Chinn, 46.

96. *Railroad Record,* October 31, 1867, 401.

97. Twain, 2:105.

98. Kraus, "Central Pacific," 51.

99. Crocker testimony, November 25, 1876, UCB/B, C–B 761, documents and censuses relating to the Chinese in California.

100. McCague, 160.

101. Mayer and Vose, 63.

102. "Old Block," 18–19.

103. McCague, 157.

104. Wilson and Taylor, 131; Chiu, 45.

105. Augustus Ward Loomis MS, and census of California Chinese and their occupations, UCB/B, C–B 761, box 1.

106. Ibid.; UCB/B, C–E 158, folder 1. The Loomis census covers the years 1848 to July 1, 1868, while the other documents take the figures through 1870.

107. *Railroad Record,* October 4, 1867, 396.

108. Anonymously written document in UCB/B, C–B 761, box 1, documents and censuses relating to the Chinese in California.

109. Testimony before the Chinese Congressional Committee, November 25, 1876, ibid.; O'Connor, 77.

110. Quoted in Kraus, "Central Pacific," 52.

111. McCague, 196.

112. Ibid., 197; *Railroad Record,* March 28, 1867, 60.

113. Kraus, *High Road,* 160.

114. Sabin, 145; Van Gelder and Schlatter, 285; "Old Block," 13.

115. Crocker papers, UCB/B, C–D 764, 1/19.

116. Crocker testimony before the Chinese Congressional Committee, November 25, 1876, in documents and censuses relating to the Chinese in California, UCB/B, C–B 761, box 1.

117. Kraus, *High Road,* 141, 160.

118. Griswold, 200.

119. McAfee, 79.

120. Wallace D. Farnham, "Shadows from the Gilded Age; Pacific Railwaymen and the Race to Promontory—or Ogden," in Miller, ed., *The Golden Spike,* 10.

121. Ibid., 8.

122. *San Francisco Chronicle,* May 12, 1898, 3.

123. Ibid.

124. Ibid., May 14, 1898, 7; Huntington papers, UCB/B, C–D 773, 2/19; CPRR, *Answer of the Central Pacific Railroad Company, Submitted by Leland Stanford, President, at San Francisco, Calif., July 28 and 29, 1887* (San Francisco, 1887), 54–63, pamphlet, n.p.

125. Farnham, 10.

126. *San Francisco Chronicle,* May 14, 1898, 3.

127. John R. Robinson and Frank Norris, *The Octopus* (New York, 1901).

128. Clark, 237.

129. Hopkins to Huntington, April 10, 1867, HL, MS film 368, reel 4.

130. Clark, 237, 242; Haymund, 83.

131. Ibid.

132. Articles of Agreement, October 12, 1867, in HL, MS film 368, reel 6.

133. Other, undated documents referent to railroad acquisitions, ibid. See also Kraus, *High Road,* 168; Poor, *Poor's Manual,* 68.

134. Poor, *Poor's Manual,* 50 (advertisement).

135. Wilson and Taylor, 47; McAfee, 91; Clark, 228.

136. Lavender, 186.

137. Hopkins papers, UCB/B, C–D 749, 1/6.

138. Huntington papers, UCB/B, C–D 773, 2/11.

139. Julius Grodinsky, *Transcontinental Railroad Strategy, 1869–1893: A Study of Businessmen* (Philadelphia, 1962), 7.

140. Huntington papers, UCB/B, C–D 773, 2/9.

141. *San Francisco Chronicle,* May 12, 1898, 9.

142. Crocker papers, UCB/B, C–D 764, 7/4.

143. *Railroad Record,* March 28, 1867, 60.

9: INTO DARKEST WYOMING AND THE SIERRAS SURRENDER

1. HL, MS film 721 (Dodge), 817.

2. Howard, 247.

3. Ibid., 259.

4. HL, MS film 721 (Dodge), 865.

5. Ibid., MS film 428 (Bissell), 85.

6. *Railroad Record,* September 7, 1868, 401.

7. Bancroft, *History of Utah,* 755.

8. Howard, 263–64.

9. HL, MS film 721 (Dodge), 887; Griswold, 225.

10. UPRR, *Report of G. M. Dodge, Chief Engineer, to the Board of Directors on a Branch Railroad Line from the Union Pacific Railroad to Idaho, Montana, Oregon, and Puget's Sound, (Dec. 1, 1867)* (Washington, D.C., 1868), 11, pamphlet, n.p.

11. *Our Pacific Railroad,* 14, 26.

12. Howard, 264.

13. Sabin, 150, Griswold, 225.

14. McCague, 205–6; Carson, 17.

15. Ibid.

16. Brown, *Brown's Gazeteer,* 298.

17. Carson, 24; Crofutt, 46.

18. HL, MS film 721 (Dodge), 911.

19. Beebe and Clegg, 11.

20. HL, MS film 721 (Dodge), 913; Ames, 182–83. Actually, these figures were not to be in round, hundred-mile segments: the forty-five-thousand-dollar-per-mile stretch would be from mile 347 to 514, or, 167 miles. See Ames, 184.

21. Ames, 184–185.

22. Quoted ibid., 185.

23. Ibid.; Wilson and Taylor, 167.

24. Ames, 187–88.

25. Ibid., 189–90.

26. HL, MS film 721 (Dodge), 920.

27. Leonard and Johnson, 194.

28. Ames, 192; NSHS, MS 3761, unit 1, SG 2 (Office of the President, UPRR), series 1, passim.

29. HL, MS film 721 (Dodge), 1143.

30. Ibid., 1069.
31. Ames, 196.
32. Ibid.; NSHS, MS 3761, unit 1, SG 23 ("Crédit Mobiler of America and Ames-Davis Contract"), box 1, folders 3, 4.
33. Ames, 198–99.
34. Ibid., 207–9.
35. HL, MS film 721 (Dodge), 1090.
36. Fergusen diary, June 19, 1867, NSHS.
37. *Railroad Record,* October 15, 1868, 896.
38. Dodge, 22.
39. HL, MS film 428 (Bissell), 79.
40. Ibid., 61; Wilson Committee report, 568.
41. Fergusen diary, September 3, 1867, NSHS.
42. *Omaha Daily Herald,* September 23, 1867, 1.
43. Fergusen Diary, September 13, 1867, NSHS.
44. Ibid., October 2, 3.
45. Ibid., October 3.
46. Brown, 301–4.
47. McCague, 205–6.
48. HL, MS film 721 (Dodge), 890.
49. Ibid., 925.
50. Ibid., 895.
51. Trottman, 69. This was later rectified.
52. Crofutt, 27–29.
53. Galloway, 285; *American Railroad Journal,* June 22, 1867.
54. HL, MS film 721 (Dodge), 890.
55. According to the official schedule. Vernon, 176.
56. UPRR, *The Union Pacific Railroad from Omaha, Nebraska, Across the Continent . . . Its Construction, Resources, Earnings, and Prospects* (New York, 1867), 3–4, 10–11, 14, 16, pamphlet; Griswold, 230.
57. Chiu, 47.
58. Ibid.; Chinn, 45–46; McAfee, 77.
59. Crocker papers, UCB/B, C–D 764, 1/53; McAfee, 77.
60. Davis, 150.
61. *Our Pacific Railroads,* 27.
62. Huntington papers, UCB/B, C–D 773, 2/66. Crocker told Huntington the story, and years later the latter related it to an interviewer.
63. Haymund, 45–46.
64. McCague, 199.
65. Kraus, *High Road,* 162.
66. McCague, 199.
67. Haymund, 143.
68. Ibid., 191.
69. Kraus, *High Road,* 168.
70. Griswold, 235.
71. Kraus, "Central Pacific," 55.
72. Galloway, 149–51; *Railroad Record,* August 29, 1867, 324.
73. Ross, 21; McCague, 256.
74. Brown testimony in *CP vs. U.S.;* McCague, 256; NSHS, MS 3761, unit 1, SG 23, series 1, box 1, folder 5 ("L. B. Boomer, estimates, contracts, letters, etc.").
75. Crocker papers, UCB/B, C–D 764, 1/49.
76. Ibid., 1/61; also, CPRR, *Lands of the Central Pacific Railroad* (San Francisco, 1871), n.p.
77. McCague, 162–63; Kraus, "Central Pacific," 55; Mayer and Vose, 41.
78. McCague, 202.
79. "Old Block," 13–14.

80. Griswold, 204.

81. McCague, 202; Sabin, 127.

82. Griswold, 202; McCague, 201.

83. Mayer and Vose, 44.

84. Quoted in Kraus, *High Road,* 182.

85. Ibid.

86. McCague, 232.

87. *Railroad Record,* April 14, 1867, 97. This observation, while perhaps true in December, was a bit premature in April.

88. HL, MS film 368, reel 6; various undated documents concerning the railroads' purchases; Kraus, *High Road,* 168. Kraus errs in asserting that the California & Oregon was acquired in 1867.

89. CPRR, *Statement of the Central Pacific Railroad Company of California to the Committee of the Senate of the United States on the Pacific Railroad* (Washington, D.C., 1869), 3, pamphlet, n.p.

90. Sabin, 128.

91. Hopkins report, n.d., in HL, MS film 368, reel 4.

92. Kraus, "Central Pacific," 55.

93. CPRR, *Annual Report, 1867,* n.p.

94. CPRR, *Lands of the Central Pacific Railroad.*

95. Crocker to Stanford, April 15, 1869, in HL, HEH, HM 47835.

10: BACKSTABBING ACROSS THE PLAINS AND BLESSEDLY FLAT NEVADA

1. McCague, 238.

2. Fergusen diary, January 1868 (dates illegible), NSHS. He waxed almost Shakespearian about Hills's corpse, and at great length.

3. Ames, 67.

4. HL, MS film 721 (Dodge), 921–23.

5. Ibid., 920.

6. Ibid., 920–21.

7. Quoted in Ames, 212.

8. HL, MS film 721 (Dodge), 920.

9. The texts of all three letters appear in Ames, 210–12.

10. Ibid., 213.

11. Ibid., 242–44; see NSHS MS 3761, SG 5, series 3, vol. 3.

12. Quoted in Weighley, 158.

13. Both letters are in HL, MS film 721 (Dodge), 926.

14. Ames, 238.

15. Ibid., 239.

16. Poor, *Poor's Manual,* 43.

17. Sabin, 164.

18. Boomer records, NSHS, MS 3761, SG 14, series 1, vol. 2, various bridge estimates, with notes on wages. See 1868. Also, his February 7 bid, with Union Pacific Secretary H. C. Crane's scrawled acceptance.

19. Ibid. Boomer estimated on March 6, 1869 that the timbers alone for Dale Creek Bridge cost $14,469.75, and his contract with the company called for it to pay the wages of his men when they were idle due to transportation delays. One such February 1868 delay led to his billing the Union Pacific for $2,268.91 in labor charges.

20. *Brown's Gazetteer,* 313.

21. HL, MS film 721 (Dodge), 954.

22. Ibid., MS film 428 (Bissell), 66–67, 77.

23. *Railroad Record,* January 2, 1868, 541.

24. Ibid., October 15, 1868, 896.

25. Quoted in Ames, 274.

26. Ibid., 272.

27. Boomer records in NSHS, MS 3761, SG 14, series 1, vol. 2.

28. Ibid., vol. 4, October 23, 1868.

29. Ames, 275–76.

30. NSHS, MS 3761, SG 14, series 1, folder 1. He resigned June 12.

31. Ames, 276, 280.

32. *Our Pacific Railroad,* 27.

33. Athearn, 83.

34. Bancroft, *History of Utah,* 770–72. There were actually a series of contracts; Sabin, 180; Athearn, 90; Ames, 279. The contract was officially approved June 10.

35. Bancroft, *History of Utah,* 755.

36. Quoted in Athearn, 79.

37. HL, MS film 428 (Bissell), 96.

38. Ames, 277.

39. Ibid., 280.

40. Sabin, 171.

41. James L. Ehrenberger and Francis G. Gschwind, *Sherman Hill* (Cheyenne, 1973), 17.

42. Barry B. Combs, *Westward to Promontory* (Palo Alto, Calif., 1969), 24.

43. Boomer records, NSHS, MS 3761, SG 14, series 1, vol. 2; Combs, 24; Ames, 273; McCague, 239.

44. HL, MS film 428 (Bissell), 91; Ames, 273.

45. Fergusen diary, various May 1868 entries, NSHS.

46. McCague, 239–40.

47. Ehrenberger and Gschwind, *Sherman Hill,* 30.

48. Brown, *Brown's Gazetteer,* 313; McCague, 240.

49. *Frontier Index,* March 24, 1868, 4; Bowles, *Our New West,* 53.

50. *Omaha Daily Herald,* November 9, 1867, 3.

51. *Omaha Weekly Herald,* May 3, 1867, 4. *Omaha Daily Herald,* August 21, 1867, 4.

52. HL, FAC 714 (Casement), 6/229 (April 19), and 6/238 (April 28).

53. Griswold, 265.

54. HL, MS film 721 (Dodge), 965.

55. Fergusen diary, April 30, 1868, NSHS.

56. Leonard and Johnson, 168.

57. Ames, 265.

58. HL, MS film 721 (Dodge), 965. See also p. 828.

59. *Report of Jas. A. Evans,* 5.

60. Ames, 224–28.

61. For earlier route changes, see Augustus A. Belden journal, NSHS, MS 3761, SG 14, series 1, vol. 1. Eng., August 27, 1867: "Worked in Black Hills till September 4th changing previous surveys."

62. *Report of Jas. A. Evans,* 5; Griswold, 267; McCague, 241.

63. Ames, 266–67.

64. NSHS, MS 3761, SG 13, series 1 "Land Department," boxes 1, 2; Howard, 288–89.

65. Belden journal, NSHS. See August 1868. See also Ames, 266–68.

66. Howard, 289–93.

67. HL, FAC 714 (Casement), 6/42 (May 2, 1868).

68. Trottman, 59; Samuel Bowles, *The Pacific Railroad—Open: How to Go, What to See. Guide for Travel to and Through Western America* (Boston, 1869), 45; J. Debin to Jason Evans, September 29, 1868, about the water trains, NSHS, MS 3761, SG 14, series 1, vol. 1.

69. Crofutt, 84.

70. Kraus, *High Road,* 184.

71. Howard, 301; Galloway, 275.
72. Ibid.; also, McCague, 271.
73. Van Gelder and Schlatter, 285–86.
74. Howard, 310; Ames, 241; UPRR, *The Union Pacific Railroad Across the Continent West from Omaha, Nebraska* (New York, 1868), pamphlet n.p.
75. Ames, 275.
76. Ibid., 246–47.
77. HL, MS film 721 (Dodge), 975–76.
78. Farnam, 11.
79. Ames, 261.
80. Griswold, 268, 276.
81. Quoted in Ames, 249.
82. Griswold, 268.
83. Telegram printed in *Railroad Record,* January 14, 1869, 554.
84. Daily track records, NSHS, MS 3761, SG 20, series 3, passim.
85. Wilson and Taylor, 93.
86. Griswold, 268.
87. UPRR, *Annual Report, June 30, 1868,* pamphlet, n.p.; McCague, 164.
88. That is their value on paper. With discounts and other adjustments, the real cash value was closer to $140,000—still a numbing figure.
89. *The Nation,* February 13, 1868, 47.
90. Lavender, 200; Wilson and Taylor, 17.
91. Lavender, 203.
92. HL, MS film 368, reel 6, for the February agreement.
93. Lavender, 404n.
94. HL, MS film 368, reel 1, March 14, 1868.
95. Van Gelder and Schlatter, 128.
96. Quoted in Clark, 246.
97. Quoted in Griswold, 248.
98. In Lavender, 200.
99. *Our Pacific Railroads,* 13.
100. *Railroad Record,* July 16, 1868, 239; Lavender, 229.
101. Huntington papers, UCB/B, C–D 773, 2/16, for his relation of the story.
102. Griswold, 234; Wilson and Taylor, 16; Lavender, 204.
103. *Railroad Record,* July 16, 1868, 239–40.
104. Sabin, 183.
105. Kraus, *High Road,* 194.
106. McCague, 220; Griswold, 238–39.
107. Griswold, 238.
108. Ibid.
109. Beebe and Clegg, 27–28.
110. Crocker papers, UCB/B, C–D 764, 10/7.
111. Bowles, *Our New West,* 65.
112. Crofutt, passim, for elevations.
113. Haymund, 142.
114. Ibid.; Sabin, 185.
115. Jones, 188.
116. Sabin., 187; Crocker papers, UCB/B, C–D 764, 2/17.
117. Griswold, 248.
118. *Railroad Record,* July 16, 1868, 239.
119. Ibid., January 2, 1868, 541.
120. Poor, *Poor's Manual,* 48.
121. McCague, 256.
122. *The Transcontinental,* no. 6 (May 31, 1870), 3.
123. Haymund, 148; Wilson and Taylor, 24.

124. Kraus, *High Road,* p. 191.
125. Brown testimony, in *CP vs. U.S.;* Wilson and Taylor, 24.
126. Beebe and Clegg, passim.
127. Howard, 303. Loomis notes on California Chinese, in documents and censuses relating to the Chinese in California, UCB/B, C–B 761, box 1.
128. Ibid. Elsewhere, he claims one hundred were murdered.
129. Stout, 18.
130. Bowles, *Our New West,* 114.
131. Griswold, 245; Kraus, *High Road,* 201.
132. Quoted in Mayer and Vose, 124.
133. Crocker papers, UCB/B, C–D 764, 1/35.
134. Lavender, 246.
135. Crocker papers, UCB/B, C–D 764, 1/36–37.
136. Ibid.
137. Bowles, *Our New West,* 59.
138. Sabin, 184.
139. McCague, 260.
140. Howard, 301.
141. Kraus, *High Road,* 200.
142. Sermon reprinted in *Railroad Record,* July 9, 1868, 229.
143. McCague, 214; Jones, 188.
144. Jones, 188–89.
145. McCague, 214–15.
146. Jones, 188.
147. Ibid., 192.

11: THE UNION PACIFIC DOES NOT BEAR SCRUTINY WELL

1. Howard, 279.
2. Bowles, *Our New West,* 57.
3. Quoted in Davis, 146.
4. Bowles, *Our New West,* 56–57.
5. Crofutt, 94.
6. U.S. Department of Commerce, *Historical Statistics,* 2:1101.
7. Fergusen diary, July 1, 1868, NSHS.
8. Leonard and Johnson, 167.
9. HL, MS film 721 (Dodge), 1013–14.
10. Weighley, 158; McCague, 245–46; Utley and Washburn, 265–66.
11. Howard, 294.
12. Ames, 283; Howard, 294.
13. Ames, 283.
14. HL, MS film 721 (Dodge), 1017–18.
15. Ames, 283.
16. Leonard and Johnson, 174–75.
17. HL, MS film 721 (Dodge), 1022–23.
18. American Railway Engineering Association, 44–46.
19. Dodge, 24. The duplicate cuts and grades can still be seen, and, in fact, driven on as part of a self-guided automobile tour.
20. Ames, 267.
21. HL, MS film 721 (Dodge), 1035.
22. Dodge, 29.

23. Ibid.

24. Perkins, 230.

25. Ames, 249.

26. Griswold, 276.

27. Ames, 251.

28. Ibid., 250.

29. Durant to Ames, October 20, 1868, NSHS, MS 3761, SG 2, series 1, box 3, folder 169.

30. Durant to a Mr. Bent, October 24, 1868, ibid.

31. Ames, 252.

32. HL, MS film 721 (Dodge), 1060.

33. Belden journal, NSHS, MS 3761, SG 14, series 1, vol. 1, n.p.

34. Wilson and Taylor, 90.

35. HL, MS film 721 (Dodge), 1063–66.

36. Ibid., 1070.

37. Ibid., 1072.

38. Ibid.; Farnam, 12.

39. Report in HL, MS film 721 (Dodge), 1084–87, and well summarized in *Railroad Record,* December 24, 1868, 518.

40. Ames, 253.

41. Ibid., 250.

42. *Railroad Record,* December 24, 1868, 518.

43. Ames, 254; HL, MS film 721 (Dodge), 1088–89.

44. Jason Evans, records of work done, NSHS, MS 3761, SG 14, series 1, box 2. Casement brothers, records of work done, ibid., box 1, folders 31–44; Griswold, 277.

45. Ames, 269.

46. HL, MS film 721 (Dodge), 1099–1100; Ames, 269.

47. Ames, 270.

48. Ibid. See also HL, MS film 721 (Dodge), 1103.

49. Ibid., 1101.

50. Ames, 254.

51. *Railroad Record,* December 24, 1868, 518.

52. McCague, 282; HL, MS film 721 (Dodge), 1088.

53. Quoted in Kraus, *High Road,* 208; Crocker papers, UCB/B, C–D 764, 5/19.

54. HL, MS film 721 (Dodge), 1113.

55. Jason Evans records of work done, NSHS, MS 3761, SG 14, series 1, box 2, various telegrams between Evans and Snyder, Reed and McGugan.

56. HL, MS film 721 (Dodge), 1114.

57. Ibid.; McCague, 249.

58. Quoted in Mayer and Vose, 147.

59. Ames, 256.

60. *Railroad Record,* July 9, 1868, 228.

61. Ames, 323.

62. HL, MS film 721 (Dodge), 1021.

63. McCague, 298; Ames, 259.

64. Ames, 254.

65. Ibid., 255.

66. HL, MS film 721 (Dodge), 1123.

67. Sabin, 173.

68. *Railroad Record,* December 24, 1868, 518; Derby, 23–24, 57.

69. Sabin, 177; Casement brothers records of work done, NSHS, MS 3761, SG 20, series 1, box 1, folders 61–69.

70. Howard, 304.

71. HL, MS film 721 (Dodge), 1056.

72. McCague, 273–75.

73. Jason Evans to E. B. Pike, October 9, 1868, NSHS, MS 3761, SG 14, series 1, box 2.

74. HL, MS film 721 (Dodge), 1056; Sabin, 180; Jack Casement to wife, August 17, 1868, HL, FAC 714, 6/249.
75. *The Transcontinental,* no. 9, June 28, 1870, 3.
76. Jack Casement to wife, October 31, 1868, HL, FAC 714, 6/255. And Fergusen diary, September 19, 1868, and September 25, NSHS.
77. Jack Casement to wife, August 17, 1868, HL, FAC 714, 6/249.
78. Bowles, *Our New West,* 41; HL, MS film 721 (Dodge), 1093.
79. See NSHS, film record, MS 3761, "Inventory Sheet" 21A.
80. Quoted in Ames, 351.
81. HL, MS film 721 (Dodge), 1040, 1028.
82. Bancroft, *History of Utah,* 756; Athearn, 86.
83. Casement brothers, records of work done, NSHS, MS 3761, SG 20, series 1, box 2, folder 89. See Casement to Snyder, October 6, 1868.
84. Quoted in McCague, 259.
85. Quoted in Howard, 316; Mayer and Vose, 120.
86. Mayer and Vose, 120.
87. McCague, 259; Carson, 14; Howard, 316–17.
88. Brown, *Brown's Gazetteer,* 320. A report in the *Salt Lake City Daily Telegraph* (November 20, 1868) claimed 25 killed, 60 wounded.
89. Mayer and Vose, 120.
90. Fergusen diary, July 24 and July 14, 1868, NSHS.
91. Ibid., July 8, 1868.
92. In *Omaha Daily Herald,* September 10, 1868, 5.
93. Fergusen diary, September 25, 1868, NSHS.
94. Ibid., September 29, 1868.
95. Brown, 117.
96. McCague, 253; Sabin, 176.
97. Ross, 25; Helen Hunt Jackson, *Bits of Travel at Home* (New York, 1880), pamphlet, 7.
98. Jack Casement to wife, September 14, 1868, HL, FAC 714, 6/253.
99. *Railroad Record,* October 15, 1868, 897.
100. Kraus, *High Road,* 222; Jack Casement to wife, November 6, 1868, HL, FAC 714, 6/258.
101. Sabin, 181; McCague, 263.
102. Derby, 57; Dee Brown, 117–18; Jason Evans records of work done, NSHS, MS 3761, SG 14, series 1, box 2, for numerous mention of steam pile drivers and steamshovels; HL, MS film 721 (Dodge), 1117.

12: CARVING THROUGH NEVADA

1. Griswold, 240.
2. Ibid., 247.
3. Howard, 301.
4. Sabin, 183; Crofutt, p. 180.
5. Galloway, 162.
6. McCague, 256.
7. Wilson and Taylor, 228; Kraus, *High Road,* 203.
8. Griswold, 238.
9. Howard, 317.
10. Ibid., 313.
11. Ibid., 318.
12. Bancroft, *Chronicles,* 6:237, 240; *District Court of the 15th Judicial District, CAL., 1870,* pamphlet, n.p. Hopkins was named attorney and agent for the Wells, Fargo Company, and the

appointment was witnessed by Leland Stanford; see document, n.d., HL, MS film 368, reel 6. Also, Lavender, 196, 215, 217.

13. Howard, 311.
14. Lavender, 216–18.
15. Ibid., 218.
16. Ibid., 288.
17. Ibid., 215–23.
18. Galloway, 117; CPRR, *Lands of the Central Pacific Railroad;* Fisk and Hatch, n.p. The government in this century has had the same problem with its Nevada lands, which helps explain the vast acreage in that state used for military purposes.
19. *Railroad Record,* September 3, 1868, 327.
20. Farnam, 10.
21. Lavender, 208.
22. HL, MS film 721 (Dodge), 1081.
23. Lavender, 230.
24. Ibid., 229.
25. Howard, 288; Farnam, 14.
26. In *San Francisco Chronicle,* quoted in Kraus, *High Road,* 210.
27. Crofutt, 173.
28. Ross, 19.
29. HL, MS film 721 (Dodge), 1139, 1124. Snyder had informants in the Central Pacific camp.
30. Quoted in Mayer and Vose, 125.
31. McCague, 261.
32. HL, MS film 721 (Dodge), 1139, 1153.
33. David F. Myrick, "Refinancing and Rebuilding the Central Pacific, 1899–1910," in Miller, ed., *The Golden Spike* 86.
34. Sabin, 182, 188, 190; Griswold, 242.
35. CPRR, *Annual Report, 1868,* pamphlet, n.p.; Griswold, 296.
36. Ibid.
37. Beebe and Clegg, 12, 14–15.
38. *Railroad Record,* January 2, 1868, 541.
39. Crofutt, passim; Bowles, *The Pacific Railroad,* passim.
40. Derby, 35.

13: CROCKER'S WAGER AND THE GOLDEN SPIKE

1. Ross, 4.
2. Charles Francis Adams, "Railroad Inflation," *North American Review,* 108 (January 1869), 130–64. Seen in the light of posterity, this article, while critical of the company, was quite moderate in its tone. Another of his articles in the same magazine, was more harsh: "The Government and the Railroad Corporations," 112 (January 1871), 31–61.
3. Ames, 300.
4. HL, MS film 721 (Dodge), 1131; Ames, 300; Johnson and Supple, 212.
5. HL, MS film 721 (Dodge), 1136 (Ames to Dodge, January 8, 1869).
6. Dodge, 23.
7. Quoted in Mayer and Vose, 156.
8. HL, MS film 721 (Dodge), 1148.
9. Trottman, 43; Ames, 248; Derby, 20.
10. In NSHS, MS 3761, SG 2, series 1, box 3, folder 174., n.d.
11. Kraus, *High Road,* 223.

12. Ibid., 229; Lavender, 237.
13. HL, MS film 721 (Dodge), 1107; Lavender, 235.
14. Grodinsky, 1.
15. Ames, 301.
16. Ibid., 301–2.
17. Jack Casement to wife, February 8, 1869, HL, FAC 714, 7/260.
18. HL, MS film 428 (Bissell), 81, 84.
19. Evans work records, NSHS, MS 3761, SG 14, series 1, box 2 (C. L. Frost to W. P. Kennedy, October 20, 1868).
20. HL, MS film 721 (Dodge), 1092–99.
21. Ibid., 1100–2.
22. Haymund, 21.
23. Derby, 20; Johnson and Supple, 212.
24. Ames, 347.
25. Lavender, 407n.
26. Galloway, 283.
27. Griswold, 296, 300–1.
28. Casement work records, NSHS, MS 3761, SG 20, series 4 ("General Supplies"), January 28, February 6, 1869
29. Evans work records ibid., SG 14, series 1, box 2, passim; Griswold, 302.
30. Lavender, 237.
31. HL, MS film 721 (Dodge), 1149.
32. Ibid., 1158.
33. Quoted in Perkins, 238.
34. HL, MS film 721 (Dodge), 1163, 1168.
35. Dodge, 37.
36. Jack Casement to wife, March 8, 1869, HL, FAC 714, 7/275.
37. Kraus, *High Road,* 233, 236; Griswold, 297–99.
38. HL, MS film 721 (Dodge), 1152–53.
39. John C. Fall to Governor Henry G. Blasdell, January 10, 1869, HL, HM 31538.
40. Account in *San Francisco Evening Bulletin,* May 8, 1869, quoted in Kraus, *High Road,* 257.
41. A. A. Sargent, *Speech,* n.p.
42. *San Francisco Herald,* January 22, 1869, 2.
43. Reprinted in *Railroad Record,* February 18, 1869, 613.
44. Griswold, 282.
45. Huntington papers, UCB/B, C–D 773, 2/53–54.
46. Farnam, 18.
47. Ames, 302.
48. Brown, 119.
49. Griswold, 287.
50. HL, MS film 721 (Dodge), 1108–9.
51. Huntington papers, UCB/B, C–D 773, 2/54; Lavender, 238
52. HL, MS film 721 (Dodge), 1171.
53. Farnam, 17.
54. Dee Brown, 122.
55. Lavender, 239.
56. Farnam, 19.
57. Lavender, 241.
58. Farnam, 20.
59. Huntington papers, UCB/B, C–D 773, 2/24.
60. Ibid.
61. HL, MS film 721 (Dodge), 1244.
62. Johnson and Supple, 214.
63. Ames, 324–25.

64. Ibid., 345.

65. Ames, 325–26.

66. Trottman, 49; Ames, 325–27.

67. Trottman, 49; McCague, 298; Griswold, 289–90; Jim Fisk, Jr., *James Fisk Jr. vs. Union Pacific 1869: Opinion of the Court* (New York, 1869), pamphlet, n.p.

68. Griswold, 294–96.

69. Ibid., 300; Ames, 326.

70. Huntington papers, UCB/B, C–D 773, 2/17.

71. Jack Casement to wife, April 6, 1869, HL, FAC 714, 7/262.

72. HL, MS film 721 (Dodge), 1238.

73. L. L. Boomer to Sam Reed, March 19, 1869, NSHS, MS 3761, SG 23, series 1, box 1, folder 5.

74. Ames, 322; McCague, 309; Mayer and Vose, 180.

75. Ames, 321–23.

76. Ibid.

77. Quoted ibid., 331.

78. Brown, *Brown's Gazetteer,* 332.

79. Bancroft, *History of Utah,* 755.

80. Ibid.

81. Ames, 332.

82. Crofutt, 129; Athearn, 98; Ames, 334.

83. Quoted in Kraus, *High Road,* 237.

84. *American Railroad Journal,* June 22, 1867, 98.

85. Howard, 322–23.

86. Kraus, *High Road,* 245.

87. HL, MS film 368, reel 6; Derby, 41.

88. HL, MS film 368, reel 4.

89. Sabin, 204. The Union Pacific had laid 550 miles, with 180 miles of sidetracks and a full 676 miles of grade—all the way to Humboldt Wells—during the same period.

90. Leland, 11. It is worth noting that while everyone asserts that the CPRR would not permit Pullman cars on its road, engineer Augustus Belden, who worked on both roads, recorded riding in a very fancy "Pullman Hotel Train" in Nevada in 1869. See Belden journal, NSHS, MS 3761, SG 14, series 1, box 1 (November 10, 1869).

91. Howard, 326.

92. McCague, 304–6.

93. Kraus, *High Road,* 249.

94. Crocker papers, UCB/B, C–D 764, 1/57–58. Crocker's own description of the work that day is the best.

95. Wilson and Taylor, 99, 156.

96. McCague, 306.

97. Ibid.

98. Crocker papers, UCB/B, C–D 764, 1/57.

99. Griswold, 311; McCague, 307.

100. Mayer and Vose, 177.

101. Crocker papers, UCB/B, C–D 764, 1/57.

102. Ibid., 1/14.

103. Ames, 337.

104. Kraus, *High Road,* 264.

105. HL, MS film 721 (Dodge), 1167.

106. Crocker papers, UCB/B, C–D 764, 11/60. This folder contains an anonymous MS, "Biog. Sketch of Charles Crocker."

107. Athearn, 101.

108. HL, MS film 428 (Bissell), 91.

109. Ames, 339.

110. Athearn, 100; McCague, 317, 325–33.

111. HL, MS film 721 (Dodge), 1256.
112. Griswold, 326.
113. Ibid.; Ames, 340; Kraus, *High Road,* 263.
114. Griswold, 326; McCague, 325.
115. Wilson and Taylor, 177.
116. Kraus, *High Road,* 263; Ames, 342.
117. Kraus, *High Road,* 264; Ames 340.
118. Mayer and Vose, 119.
119. There are many accounts of the ceremony and most of them are in general agreement.
The best are in Kraus, *High Road,* 263–72; Griswold, 323–27; Ames, 339–41.
120. HL, MS film 428 (Bissell), 92.
121. Ibid.
122. Quoted in Ames, 341.
123. Various telegrams, UCB/B, C–D 321, folder 2.
124. HL, MS film 721 (Dodge), 1256.
125. Ames, 343.
126. Dodge, 25.
127. O'Connor, 86–87; McCague, 332.
128. Crocker papers, UCB/B, C–D 764, 1/58.
129. Anna Judah papers, UCB/B, C–D 800, 3/14.
130. *The Times* (London), May 11, 1869, 12.
131. McCague, 333.
132. Derby, 22.
133. Bowles, *The Pacific Railroad,* 8.

14: JUDGMENT DAY

1. HL, MS film 721 (Dodge), 1091–93; Ames, 347.
2. Quoted in Perkins, 239.
3. Martin, passim.
4. Ames, 345.
5. Ibid., 346.
6. Ibid., 346–47, 357.
7. Ibid., 357.
8. Ibid.
9. Ibid.
10. UPRR, *Guide to the Union Pacific Lands* (New York, 1871), pamphlet, 16–24.
11. Some $100,000, according to Ames, 351.
12. HL, MS film 721 (Dodge), 1215.
13. Reed to Oliver Ames, May 29, 1869, NSHS, MS 3761, SG 2, series 1, box 3, folder 169.
14. Reed to Oliver Ames, June 10, 1869, ibid.
15. Jack Casement to Cornelius Bushnell, August 31, 1869, ibid., SG 20, series 1, box 2, folder 96.
16. John Pondir to Oliver Ames, June 16, 1869, ibid., SG 2, series 1, box 3, folder 169.
17. HL, MS film 721 (Dodge), 1229.
18. Ames, 348–49.
19. HL, MS film 721 (Dodge), 1244; Ames, 352.
20. Ibid.
21. L. B. Boomer records, NSHS, MS 3761, SG 23, series 1, folder 5.
22. Ames, 363.
23. Ibid., 356.
24. Athearn, 103.

25. Ibid., 104–11; Ames, 360.

26. E. H. Rollins to Oliver Ames, August 2, 1869, NSHS, MS 3761, SG 2, series 1, box 3, folder 174.

27. Davis, 157; Ames, 367.

28. Trottman, 119; Ames, 363.

29. Trottman, 72–76. He calls these "the carelessly written letters of a careless man."

30. Ames, 346.

31. Bowles, *The Pacific Railroad,* 23.

32. Quoted in Ames, 375.

33. Hopkins papers, UCB/B, C–D 749, 5/11.

34. Crocker papers, UCB/B, C–D 764, introduction, n.p: see also 18/5.

35. Wilson and Taylor, 51.

36. Hopkins papers, UCB/B, C–D 749, 5/8.

37. Huntington papers, UCB/B, C–D 773, 5/3.

38. Crocker papers, UCB/B, C–D 764, 5/16, and unpaginated introduction.

39. Ibid.

40. List of Central Pacific stockholders, July 11, 1876, HL, MS film 368, reel 6.

41. See David Lee, "Chinese Construction Workers on the Canadian Pacific," in *Railroad History,* Bulletin no. 148 (Spring 1983), 43, 50.

42. Chiu, 48.

43. Ross, 17.

44. E. H. Rollins to Oliver Ames, August 2, 1869, NSHS, MS 3761, SG 2, series 1, box 3, folder 174.

45. Ames, 364; Brown, *Brown's Gazetteer,* 98.

46. Articles of Agreement with A. A. Cohen, August 25, 1869, HL, MS film 368, reel 6.

47. SPRR, *Annual Report, December 31, 1869* (Sacramento), pamphlet, n.p.

48. *Congressional Globe,* March 1, 1870.

49. National Geographic Society, *Railroads: The Great American Adventure* (Washington, D.C., 1973), 48.

50. Lavender, 260.

51. CPRR, *District Court of the 15th Judicial District, California: Samuel Brannan vs. Central Pacific Directors* (San Francisco, n.d.), pamphlet.

52. Report of January 1, 1873, HL, MS film 368, reel 4.

53. Lavender, 277–80.

54. Ibid., 44.

55. Robinson, 39.

56. Ibid.

57. Crocker papers, UCB/B, C–D 764, 1/48.

58. Wilson and Taylor, 43.

59. Robinson, 18.

60. April 3, 1871, HL, HM 47837, EG box 29.

61. S. Crittenden to Huntington, January 10, 1871, ibid., MS film 368, reel 1.

62. Johnson and Supple, 217–18.

63. O'Connor, 89.

64. HL, MS film 368, reel 2, for report no. 86, 3rd session, 42nd Congress.

65. Lavender, 210n.; HL, MS film 368, reel 2, for report no. 86, 3rd session, 42nd Congress.

66. Huntington to Hopkins, April 23, 1873, ibid.

67. Wilson and Taylor, 51.

68. Contract signed by the Big Four, minus Stanford, who perhaps wished to retain his interest, n.d., HL, MS film 368, reel 6.

69. Huntington to Hopkins, May 27, 1873, ibid.

70. Quoted by Huntington in a letter to Hopkins, February 27, 1873, ibid. The former was proud of Franchot's performance.

71. Quoted in Johnson, 149; see also 151–53.

72. *Congressional Globe,* February 20, 1873.

73. Quoted in Perkins, 265.
74. *Congressional Globe,* February 20, 1873.
75. J. B. Crawford, *The Crédit Mobilier of America* (Boston, 1880), 71–74.
76. Galloway, 215–22. The *lowest* estimate of Crédit Mobilier profits was $8,141,903.70.
77. Wilson and Taylor, chapter 12, passim.
78. Trottman, 81; *Congressional Globe,* February 11, 1873.
79. *Congressional Globe,* February 27, 1873.
80. Ibid., February 25, 1873.
81. Ibid., February 27, 1873.
82. Dodge, 32.
83. Trottman, 82–83.
84. *Congressional Globe,* February 24, 1873.
85. Trottman, 79–80.
86. List of Central Pacific stockholders, July 11, 1876, HL, MS film 368, reel 6.
87. Newspaper clipping (no heading), ibid.
88. Hopkins papers, UCB/B, C–D 749, 5/23.
89. Crocker papers, UCB/B, C–D 764, 1/38.
90. Colton, 2–3.
91. Crocker papers, UCB/B, C–D 764, 1/38.
92. Galloway, 271–72.
93. Haymund, 214; CPRR, *CP vs. U.S.,* passim.
94. U.S. Department of Commerce, *Historical Statistics,* 2:1104, 1114, 1141–42.
95. Myrick, 101.
96. Haymund, 44–47.
97. Ibid., 33.
98. CPRR, *CP vs. U.S.,* n.p.
99. Haymund, 54.
100. Crocker papers, UCB/B, C–D 764, 1/43–44.
101. Various newspaper clippings, most without headings, ibid., folder 18.
102. Greeley, 272–73.
103. Davis, 173; Senate Executive Document no. 51, 1st session, 50th Congress (1888), pamphlet, passim.
104. Robinson, 57–59.
105. Galloway, 228–29; CPRR, *Answer,* passim.
106. CPRR, *Central Pacific Railroad: Its Relation to the Government. Oral Argument of Creed Haymund, Its General Solicitor, Before the Select Committee of the U.S. Senate March 17 and 26 and April 7, 1888* (San Francisco, 1888), pamphlet, n.p.
107. Ibid.
108. *San Francisco Chronicle,* May 11, 1898, 3.

BIBLIOGRAPHY

DOCUMENTARY material for this book was drawn from several major research collections and repositories, chief among which were the Huntington Library, San Marino, California; the Bancroft Library, University of California at Berkeley; the Nebraska State Historical Society at Lincoln; and the Lilly Library at Indiana University, in Bloomington.

Beyond documents in general, the above repositories have individual collections of great value to the study of the first transcontinental. The most important of these I found to be the Jack Casement, Grenville Dodge, and Hezekiah Bissell papers at the Huntington Library; the Arthur N. Fergusen, Augustus A. Belden, Casement brothers, L. B. Boomer, Jason A. Evans, and Samuel B. Reed papers and/or diaries in the Nebraska State Historical Society; the Stanford, Huntington, Hopkins, and Crocker files, and the Augustus W. Loomis papers at the Bancroft Library, at the University of California, Berkeley; and the Ellison collection of pamphlets at the Lilly Library, Indiana University.

KEY TO ABBREVIATIONS

CPRR   Central Pacific Railroad
HL   Huntington Library, San Marino, California

LL   Lilly Library, Indiana University, Bloomington
NHHS   New Hampshire Historical Society, Concord
NSHS   Nebraska State Historical Society, Lincoln
UCB/B   Bancroft Library, University of California at Berkeley
UPRR   Union Pacific Railroad

PAMPHLETS

Where possible, I have noted the repository in which I found the individual pamphlet.

Brooks, B. S. *The Chinese in California.* San Francisco, 1876(?) (UCB/B).

Bross, William. *Address of The Hon. William Bross.* New York, 1866 (HL).

CPRR. Annual Reports, 1862–70 (UCB/B).

———. *Answer of the Central Pacific Railroad Company, Submitted by Leland Stanford, President, at San Francisco, Calif., July 28 and 29, 1887.* San Francisco, 1887 (UCB/B).

———. *Central Pacific—Articles of Association,* 1861 (UCB/B). *Central Pacific Railroad Company of California.* San Francisco, 1860 (UCB/B).

———. *Central Pacific Railroad: Its Relation to the Government. Oral Argument of Creed Haymund, Its General Solicitor, Before the Select Committee of the U.S. Senate, March 17 and 26 and April 7, 1888.* San Francisco, 1888 (UCB/B).

———. *CP vs. US. Summary of Facts.* New York, 1887 (HL).

———. *District Court of the 15th Judicial District, California: Samuel Brannan vs. Central Pacific Directors.* San Francisco, n.d. (UCB/B).

———. *Lands of the Central Pacific Railroad.* San Francisco, 1871 (UCB/B).

———. *Report of George E. Gray, July 31, 1865.* Sacramento, 1865 (UCB).

———. Reports of the Chief Engineer. 1862–69 (UCB/B).

———. *Statement of the Central Pacific Railroad Company of California to the Committee of the Senate of the United States on the Pacific Railroad.* Washington, D.C., 1869 (UCB/B).

Colton, David D. *The Colton Letters: The Inside History of an Infamous Procedure.* San Francisco, 1889 (UCB/B).

Harvey Fisk and Alfredrick Hatch. *Railroad Communication with the Pacific, with an Account of the Central Pacific Railroad of California.* New York (October 1867) (LL).

Great Dutch Flat Swindle! The City of San Francisco Demands Justice! San Francisco, 1864 (UCB/B).

Harbaugh, Springer. *Report of the Honorable Springer Harbaugh, Government Director of the Union Pacific RR Co., to the Secretary of the Interior.* Washington, D.C., 1865 (LL).

Haymund, Creed. *The Central Pacific Railroad Co.: Its Relations to the Government. It Has Performed Every Obligation.* San Francisco, 1888 (UCB/B).

Jackson, Helen Hunt. *Bits of Travel at Home.* New York, 1880 (LL).

Judah, Theodore Dehone. *A Practical Plan for Building the Pacific Railroad.* New York, 1857 (UCB/B).

Our Pacific Railroads: The Union and Central Pacific and Northern Routes; Their Character and Relative Merits. New York, 1868 (LL).

Poor, Henry V. *The Pacific Railroad: The Relations Existing Between It and the Government of the United States.* New York, 1871 (LL).

Sargent, Aaron A. *Speech of the Hon. A. A. Sargent to the Senate of the United States, March 7, 1878.* San Francisco(?), 1878 (UCB/B).

SPRR. *Annual Report. December 31, 1869.* Sacramento, 1870 (UCB/B).

Stout, Arthur B., M.D. *Chinese Immigration and the Physiological Causes of the Decay of a Nation.* San Francisco, 1862 (UCB/B).

UPRR. *A Description of the Western Resorts for Health and Pleasure Reached via Union Pacific Railway.* Chicago, 1888 (LL).
————. *Guide to the Union Pacific Lands.* New York, 1871 (LL).
————. *James Fisk Jr. vs. Union Pacific 1869: Opinion of the Court.* U.S. Circuit Court, 2d Circuit, New York, 1869 (UCB/B).
Letter from the Secretary of the Interior. New York, 1868 (LL).
————. *Report of Gen. G. M. Dodge, Chief Engineer, on Lines Crossing the Rocky Mountains.* New York, 1867 (LL).
————. *Report of G. M. Dodge, Chief Engineer, to the Board of Directors on a Branch Railroad Line from the Union Pacific Railroad to Idaho, Montana, Oregon, and Puget's Sound (Dec. 1, 1867).* Washington, D.C., 1868 (LL).
Report of Jas. A. Evans of Exploration from Camp Walbach to Green River, dated Jan. 3, 1865. New York, 1865 (NSHS).
Report of the Chief Engineer, with Accompanying Reports of Division Engineers for 1866. Washington, D.C., 1868 (LL).
————. *The Union Pacific Railroad Across the Continent West from Omaha.* New York, 1868 (LL).
————. *The Union Pacific Railroad Company, Chartered by the United States: Progress of Their Road West from Omaha, Nebraska, Across the Continent.* New York, 1867 (LL).
————. *The Union Pacific Railroad from Omaha, Nebraska, Across the Continent . . . Its Construction, Resources, Earnings, and Prospects.* New York, 1867 (NSHS).
Williams, Jesse L. *Letter of J. L. Williams on the Location Between Omaha City and Platte Valley.* Washington, D.C., 1865 (LL).

CONTEMPORARY WORKS

This section contains citations for works originally published as books, or at least as book-length accounts, including guidebooks, memoirs, and autobiographies. The category is sometimes referred to as "Printed Primary Sources," and includes contemporary articles.

Adams, Charles Francis, Jr. "Railroad Inflation." *North American Review* 108 (January 1869): 130–64.
————. "The Government and the Railroad Corporations." *North American Review,* 112 (January 1871): 31–61.
American Railway Engineering Association. "Construction of the Pacific Railroad." *American Railway Engineering Association. Bulletin.* 23, no. 237 (1922): 7–47. A compilation of reports from eminent engineers in 1865, recommending standards for the Pacific Railroad.
Bell, William A. *New Tracks in North America: A Journal of Travel and Adventure Whilst Engaged in the Survey for a Southern Railroad to the Pacific Ocean During 1867–8.* London, 1870.
Bigelow, John. *Memoir of the Life and Public Services of John Charles Frémont.* New York, 1856.
Bowles, Samuel. *Our New West.* Hartford, Conn., 1869.
————. *The Pacific Railroad—Open: How to Go, What to See. Guide for Travel to and Through Western America.* Boston, 1869.
Brown, C. Exera. *Brown's Gazetteer of the Chicago and Northwestern Railway, and Branches of the Union Pacific Rail Road.* Chicago, 1869.
Copley, Josiah. *Kansas and the Country Beyond on the Line of the Union Pacific Railway, Eastern Division, from the Missouri to the Pacific Ocean.* Philadelphia, 1867.
Crofutt, George A. *Great Trans-Continental Railroad Guide.* Chicago, 1869.
Derby, E. H. *The Overland Route to the Pacific: A Report on the Condition, Capacity, and Resources of the Union Pacific and Central Pacific Railways.* Boston, 1869.

Dodge, Grenville M. *How We Built the Union Pacific Railway.* Washington, D.C. 1910.

Farnam, Henry W. *Memoir of Henry Farnam.* New Haven, Conn., 1889.

Frémont, John Charles. *Narratives of Exploration and Adventure.* Allan Nevins edition. New York, 1956.

————. *Report of the Exploring Expedition to the Rocky Mountains in the Year 1842, and to Oregon and North California in the Years 1843–44.* Washington, D.C., 1845 ("Printed by order of the Senate of the United States").

Greeley, Horace. *An Overland Journey, from New York to San Francisco, in the Summer of 1859.* New York, 1860.

Hastings, Lansford. *Emigrant's Guide to Oregon and California.* Cincinnati, 1845.

Leland, Charles Godfrey. *The Union Pacific Railway, Eastern Division; or, Three Thousand Miles in a Railway Car.* Philadelphia, 1867.

Messages and Papers of the Presidents. 23 vols. Washington, D.C. 1910–21. Vol. 8 (Lincoln).

"Old Block." *The Central Pacific Railroad; or, '49 and '69.* San Francisco, 1868.

Parker, Samuel (Rev.). *The Tour Beyond the Rocky Mountains.* New York, 1838.

Poor, Henry V. *Poor's Manual of the Railroads of the United States, for 1868–1869, Showing Their Mileage, Stocks, Bonds, Cost, Earnings, Expenses, and Organizations; with a Sketch of Their Rise, Progress, Influence, etc.* New York, 1868.

————. "The Proposed Pacific Railroad." Printed version of a speech by Poor to the American Geographical Society of New York City, June 1863.

————. "Railroad to the Pacific." Printed edition of a paper presented to the American Geographical Society of New York City, 1854.

Robinson, John R. *The Octopus: A History of the Construction, Conspiracies, Extortions, Robberies, and Villainous Acts of the Central Pacific . . . , Union Pacific, and other Subsidized Railroads.* San Francisco, 1894.

Ross, John Simpson. *Crossing the Continent by Rail in 1869.* Mendocino County Historical Society, Fort Bragg, California, 1969. Typescript edition of 1869 document.

Seymour, Silas. *Incidents of a Trip Through the Great Platte Valley, to the Rocky Mountains and Laramie Plains, in the Fall of 1866.* New York, 1867.

Stanley, Henry Morton. *The Autobiography of Sir Henry Morton Stanley, G.C.B.* Boston, 1909.

————. *My Early Travels and Adventures in America and Asia.* 2 vols. New York, 1905.

Talbot, Theodore. *Soldier in the West: Letters of Theodore Talbot During His Services in California, Mexico, and Oregon, 1845–53.* New York, 1978.

Train, George Francis. *My Life in Many States and in Foreign Lands.* New York, 1902.

Twain, Mark. *Roughing It.* 2 vols. New York, 1882.

Vernon, Edward. *Travelers' Official Railway Guide, for the United States and Canada.* New York, 1868.

White, John H., Jr. "How the Pacific Railroad is Built." *American Railroad Journal* (June 22, 1867).

CONTEMPORARY NEWSPAPERS, MAGAZINES

American Railroad Journal (New York)

Congressional Globe (Washington, D.C.; after 1873, *Congressional Record*)

Frontier Index (Julesburg, Nebraska, and points west)

The Nation (New York)

North American Review (New York)

Omaha Daily Herald

Omaha Weekly Herald

Oriental (Sacramento)

Panama Star (Panama City, Panama)

Railroad Record (Cincinnati)

Sacramento Union
Salt Lake City Daily Telegraph
San Francisco Chronicle
San Francisco Herald
The Times (London)
The Transcontinental (published aboard an 1870 excursion train)
Western Sun (Vincennes, Ind.)

BOOKS

I found the following books, while uneven in quality, the most useful for this study, though I consulted many more. Those marked with an asterisk are, in my opinion, particularly rewarding.

*Ames, Charles Edgar. *Pioneering the Union Pacific: A Reappraisal of the Builders of the Railroad.* New York, 1969.
Anderson, George L. *Kansas West.* San Marino, Calif., 1963.
Andrist, Ralph K. *The Long Death: The Last Days of the Plains Indian.* New York, 1964.
Athearn, Robert G. *Union Pacific Country.* Chicago, 1971.
Bakeless, John. *The Eyes of Discovery: America As Seen by the First Explorers.* New York, 1961.
*Bancroft, Hubert Howe. *Chronicles of the Builders of the Commonwealth.* 8 vols. San Francisco, 1890–98.
———. *History of Utah.* San Francisco, 1890.
Beebe, Lucius. *The Central Pacific and the Southern Pacific Railroads.* Berkeley, Calif., 1963.
Beebe, Lucius, and Charles Clegg. *Virginia and Truckee: A Story of Virginia City and Comstock Times.* Berkeley, Calif., 1963.
Best, Gerald M. *Snowplow: Clearing Mountain Rails.* Berkeley, Calif., 1966.
Brown, Dee. *Hear That Lonesome Whistle Blow.* New York, 1977.
Bryant, Keith L., Jr. *History of the Atchison, Topeka and Santa Fe Railway.* New York, 1974.
Carson, John. *The Union Pacific: Hell on Wheels!* Santa Fe, 1968.
*Chinn, Thomas W., ed. *A History of the Chinese in California: A Syllabus.* San Francisco, 1969.
Chiu, Ping. *Chinese Labor in California: An Economic Study.* Madison, Wis., 1963.
Clark, George T. *Leland Stanford: War Governor of California, Railroad Builder, and Founder of Stanford University.* Palo Alto, Calif., 1931.
Clarke, Thomas Curtis, et al. *The American Railway.* New York, 1889.
Cleveland, Frederick A., and Fred Wilbur Powell. *Railroad Promotion and Capitalization in the United States.* New York, 1909.
Combs, Barry. B. *Westward to Promontory.* Palo Alto, Calif., 1969.
Crawford, J. B. *The Crédit Mobilier of America.* Boston, 1880.
Daggett, Stuart. *Chapters on the History of the Southern Pacific.* New York, 1922.
Davis, John Patterson. *The Union Pacific Railway: A Study in Railway Politics, History, and Economics.* Chicago, 1894.
Egan, Ferol. *Frémont: Explorer for a Restless Nation.* Reno, Nev., 1977.
Ehrenberger, James L., and Francis G. Gschwind. *Sherman Hill.* Cheyenne, 1973.
———. *Smoke Across the Prairie.* 2d ed. Cheyenne, 1975.
Faulk, Odie B. *The Crimson Desert: Indian Wars of the American Southwest.* New York, 1974.
Fishlow, Albert. *American Railroads and the Transformation of the Ante-Bellum Economy.* Cambridge, Mass., 1965.
Frederick, James V., *Ben Holladay, the Stagecoach King: A Chapter in the Development of Transcontinental Transportation.* Glendale, Calif., 1940.
Galloway, John Debo. *The First Transcontinental Railroad: Central Pacific, Union Pacific.* New York, 1950.

Goetzmann, William H. *Army Exploration in the American West, 1803–1863.* New Haven, Conn., 1959.

———. *New Lands, New Men: America and the Second Great Age of Discovery.* New York, 1986.

*Griswold, Wesley S. *A Work of Giants.* New York, 1962.

Grodinsky, Julius. *Transcontinental Railroad Strategy, 1869–1893: A Study of Businessmen.* Philadelphia, 1962.

Howard, Robert West. *The Great Iron Trail: The Story of the First Transcontinental Railroad.* New York, 1962.

Johnson, Arthur M., and Barry E. Supple. *Boston Capitalists and Western Railroads: A Study in the Nineteenth-Century Railroad Investment Process.* Cambridge, Mass., 1967.

Johnson, Jack T. *Peter Anthony Dey: Integrity in Public Service.* Iowa City, Iowa, 1939.

Jones, Helen Hinckley. *Rails from the West: A Biography of Theodore D. Judah.* San Marino, Calif., 1969.

Kemble, John Haskell. *The Panama Route: 1848–1869.* Berkeley, Calif., 1943.

Kennedy, William. *O Albany! Improbable City of Political Wizards, Fearless Ethnics, Spectacular Aristocrats, Splendid Nobodies, and Underrated Scoundrels.* New York, 1983.

Kirkland, Edward C. *Charles Francis Adams, Jr., 1835–1915: The Patrician at Bay.* Cambridge, Mass., 1965.

*Kraus, George. *High Road to Promontory.* Palo Alto, Calif., 1969.

Latta, Estelle. *Controversial Mark Hopkins.* Greenberg, N.Y., 1953.

*Lavender, David. *The Great Persuader.* New York, 1970.

Leonard, Levi O., and Jack T. Johnson. *A Railroad to the Sea.* Iowa City, Iowa, 1939.

López, Carlos U. *Chilenos en California.* San Francisco, 1973.

MacLeod, Murdo J. *Spanish Central America.* Berkeley, Calif., 1973.

Martin, Edgar W. *The Standard of Living in 1860.* Chicago, 1942.

*Mayer, Lynne Rhodes, and Kenneth E. Vose. *Makin' Tracks.* New York, 1975.

McAfee, Ward. *California's Railroad Era: 1850–1911.* San Marino, Calif., 1973.

*McCague, James. *Moguls and Iron Men: The Story of the First Transcontinental Railroad.* New York, 1964.

Miller, David E., ed. *The Golden Spike (Symposium).* Salt Lake City, 1973.

Moody, Ralph. *The Old Trails West.* Salt Lake City, 1963.

Mountfield, David. *The Railway Barons.* New York, 1979.

Myrick, David F. *Railroads of Nevada and Eastern California.* Vol. 1, *The Northern Roads.* San Diego, 1962.

National Geographic Society. *Railroads: The Great American Adventure.* Washington, D.C., 1973.

Nichols, Joseph. *Condensed History of the Construction of the Union Pacific Railway.* Omaha, 1892.

Nock, O. S. *The Golden Age of Steam.* New York, 1974.

Norris, Frank. *The Octopus.* New York, 1901.

O'Connor, Richard. *Iron Wheels and Broken Men.* New York, 1973.

*Perkins, Jacob R. *Trails, Rails, and War: The Life of General G. M. Dodge.* Indianapolis, 1929.

Sabin, Edwin L. *Building the Pacific Railway.* Philadelphia, 1919.

Stover, John F. *Iron Road to the West: American Railroads in the 1850s.* New York, 1978.

Time-Life Books. *The Gamblers.* The Old West Series. Alexandria, Va., 1978.

Trottman, Nelson. *History of the Union Pacific.* New York, 1923.

Tyler, Alice Felt. *Freedom's Ferment.* New York, 1944.

U.S. Department of Commerce. Bureau of the Census. *Historical Statistics of the United States: Colonial Times to 1970.* 2 vols. Washington, D.C., 1975.

Utley, Robert M., and Wilcomb E. Washburn. *The American Heritage History of the Indian Wars.* New York, 1977.

Van Gelder, Arthur Pine, and Hugo Schlatter. *History of the Explosives Industry in North America.* New York, 1927.

Weighley, Russell F. *The American Way of War: A History of the United States Military Strategy and Policy.* Bloomington, Ind., 1973.
Wilson, Neill C., and Frank J. Taylor. *Southern Pacific: The Roaring Story of a Fighting Railroad.* New York, 1952.

ARTICLES

Best, Gerald M. "Richard Norris Locomotives in California." *Railroad History.* Bulletin no. 127 (October 1972): 45–55.
———. "Pullman's Board of Trade Special: The Train That Came Down Market Street." *Railroad History.* Bulletin no. 135 (August 1978): 79–94.
California History (Spring 1978). Special issue on the Chinese in California.
Chandler, Alfred D., Jr.. "Henry Varnum Poor, the American Geographical Society, and the Pacific Railroad." In *The Golden Spike: A Centennial Remembrance,* edited by Wilfred Webster. American Geographical Society, Occasional Publication no. 3 (New York, 1969).
Collections of the Kansas State Historical Society 12 (1911–12): 383.
Cronon, William, and Richard White. "Indians in the Land." *American Heritage* (August–September 1986): 18–25.
Farnham, Wallace D. "Shadows from the Gilded Age: Pacific Railwaymen and the Race to Promontory—or Ogden." In *The Golden Spike,* edited by David E. Miller, 1–22. Salt Lake City, 1973.
Hofsommer, Donovan L. "A Chronology of Iowa Railroads." *Railroad History.* Bulletin no. 132 (Spring 1975): 70–83.
Hoyt, L. E. "From the Golden Spike to the Space Age in Railroading." In *The Golden Spike,* edited by David E. Miller, 29–36. Salt Lake City, 1973.
Kraus, George. "Central Pacific Construction Vignettes." In *The Golden Spike,* edited by David E. Miller, 45–61. Salt Lake City, 1973.
Lee, David. "Chinese Construction Workers on the Canadian Pacific." *Railroad History.* Bulletin no. 148 (Spring 1983): 42–56.
Myrick, David F. "Refinancing and Rebuilding the Central Pacific, 1899–1910." In *The Golden Spike,* edited by David E. Miller, 85–117. Salt Lake City, 1973.
Nash, Gerald D. "Government and Railroads: A Case Study in Cooperative Capitalism." In *The Golden Spike,* edited by David E. Miller, 119–26. Salt Lake City, 1973.
Post, Robert C. "Manuscript Sources for Railroad History." *Railroad History.* Bulletin no. 137 (1977): 38–63.
Shaw, Robert B. "The Profitability of Early American Railroads." *Railroad History.* Bulletin no. 132 (Spring 1975): 56–69.

INDEX

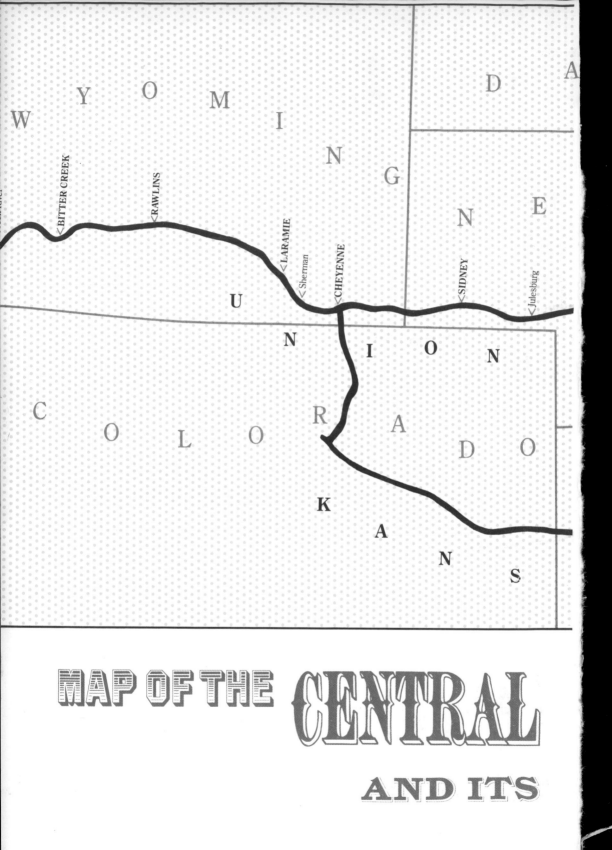

W

WYOMING

D

A

G

N

E

BITTER CREEK

RAWLINS

LARAMIE

Sherman

CHEYENNE

SIDNEY

Julesburg

U

N

I

O

N

C

O

L

O

R

A

D

O

K

A

N

S

S

MAP OF THE CENTRAL

AND ITS